Rhetorical Thought
in John Henry Newman

Rhetorical Thought
in John Henry Newman

Walter Jost

University of South Carolina Press

BX
4705
.N5
J67
1989

Copyright © University of South Carolina 1989

Published in Columbia, South Carolina, by the
University of South Carolina Press

First Edition

Manufactured in the United States of America

Library of Congress Cataloging-in-Publication Data

Jost, Walter, 1951–
    Rhetorical thought in John Henry Newman / Walter Jost. — 1st ed.
    p. cm.
    Revision of the author's doctoral thesis (University of Chicago).
    Bibliography: p.
    Includes index.
    ISBN 0-87249-620-1
    1. Newman, John Henry, 1801–1890—Style. I. Title.
BX4705.N5J67   1989
282'.092—dc20   89-33521
                                                          CIP

CONTENTS

Preface ix

List of Abbreviations xvii

Chronology xix

One   Between Theory and Fact   1

Two   Toward a Philosophic Rhetoric   28

Three   Rhetorical Reason   63

Four   Method in Theology   108

Five   Thought, Word, and Thing   139

Six   "A Comprehensive View"   170

Seven   Philosophic Rhetoric   209

Notes to Chapters   236

Select Bibliography   296

Index   319

To Marcella, Alex, and Alison

PREFACE

In the present study I consider the works of John Henry Newman (1801–1890) in a way that is difficult to categorize. In Newman studies intellectual division of labor has tended to bifurcate what Newman liked to call the whole man: on one side of the fence are students of his theology or philosophy, on the other students of his literary art, and though the two groups can see each other, and though each occasionally shouts something not wholly unintelligible to the other side, both seem to think, no doubt correctly enough, that each of them has plenty to do in its own field. Newman himself was sympathetic to the requirements of this sort of specialism and accepted the increasing division of labor in the pursuit of knowledge. As rector of the Catholic University of Ireland, he made substantial provisions for the medical school and founded or planned departments for all of the sciences. But Newman also shrewdly assessed the risk involved in our specializing, and his ideal of liberal learning—a broadly synthetic "view" of the whole of knowledge, which was neither a specialist's expertise nor a dilettante's "smattering of a hundred things" (*Idea,* 109)—continues to challenge prevailing theory and practice.

It is in this spirit of liberal knowledge or "philosophy," the activity of gaining a comprehensive view of a complex whole, that I attempt to bridge the standing division in the study of Newman's thought. Detailed, focused, technical analyses of Newman clearly require no defense (there are, for example, the excellent works by Lash, Ferreira, Fey, Culler). And certainly the present work seeks to be detailed, focused, and technical, though in its own way. For what has been lacking in the study of Newman (by virtue of that "trained incapacity" that is the strength of other approaches) is a "real apprehension" and a "view," to use Newman's language, of the complex, concrete whole of Newman's thought. It is difficult to say up front, clearly, and in a sentence, what such a view entails. But Newmanian views in general call for comprehending an object from a particular angle, in all of its relevant practical aspects—not from the

Olympian heights of abstract theory, but at the level of effects and consequences. In the present case, this translates into a concern with *what* Newman thought in light of *how* he went about doing his thinking, with his characteristic ways of conceptualizing problems and solutions. I am interested, in other words, in explicating Newman's method of thought, and some of his techniques of elaboration and expression, in most of the many fields in which he worked. Throughout, I have tried to stay centered on Newman and to disregard domestic disciplinary fences. My hope is that the intellectual portrait of Newman that emerges here will stimulate the general reader to turn to the original writings and encourage specialists in theology, philosophy, and literary studies (as well as in Newman's works) to consider his views, and their own, in a new way.

The central insight of the view offered here is that Newman's intellectual stance is thoroughly and persistently rhetorical, and my basic concern is to articulate the implications of this fact. "It is obvious," wrote George Levine in his study of Newman in *The Boundaries of Fiction* (Princeton, 1968, p. 195), "that everything [Newman] wrote was aimed at producing an effect, or, to use Mill's terms, at working, 'upon the feeling, or upon the belief, or the will of another.' " For various reasons the full import and scope of this claim have never been pursued. My own conviction is that whatever topic Newman touched—the development of Christian doctrine, the character of the British constitution, the function of literature, the "idea" of a liberal education, the nature of inference and assent—he systematically operated with rhetorical principles and methods of inquiry, argument, interpretation, and judgment. He aimed, in fact, at a rhetorical ideal of mind, which combined, in ways that I explain and qualify, philosophy and rhetoric, thought and word, and theory and practice.

To be sure, to call Newman a rhetorician is tantamount for some to calling him at best an equivocator, at worst a calculating liar. "Like the sophists of old," Charles Kingsley said of Newman in 1864, "he has used reason to destroy reason." But Aristotle, for one, had a high regard for rhetoric, not as sophistry but as an art of informed argument on contingent matters. Rhetoric provides an illuminating set of terms and distinctions for both theory and criticism, and it is in the willingness to be interdisciplinary in this further way—combining Newman studies with rhetorical studies—that we are able to grasp what Newman is doing. By exploring along the way, without trying to be exhaustive, selected matters important to the rhetorical tradition, I hope to render Newman's thought intelligible or consistent when it seems not to be, to apply to it new and more appropriate criteria of evaluation, and to locate Newman's place in the rhetorical tradition and his contributions to rhetorical theory.

To some, the extension of the study of rhetoric into Newman's practice of theology and philosophy may at first seem peculiar. But simply to link Newman with rhetorical skill as such is not new and can hardly be surprising. What distinguishes this work from that of Holloway, Gates, or Houghton, however, is the respect I accord rhetoric as an intellectual discipline. Readers familiar with contemporary advances in rhetorical studies and literary theory are aware of the wide range of meanings of rhetoric and the sometimes contradictory ends to which the term is enlisted. Marxist critics such as Terry Eagleton or Frank Lentricchia assimilate rhetoric to politics and power; deconstructionists such as Barthes or Derrida, or a Renaissance scholar such as Richard Lanham, refer rhetoric not to politics but to "pleasure" or "freeplay." And the alchemical Kenneth Burke mixes power and pleasure with guilt, suffering, and redemption, exalting rhetoric to a position of dominance in human life bearing the titles of symbolic action and Logology. However much these theorists differ, all agree in the need to take rhetoric seriously. Yet it is just this sense of the omnipresence and importance of rhetoric that has been absent from Newman studies. With few exceptions rhetoric has been understood to be synonymous with composition and style, at best with a persuasion divorced from the full depth and range of Newman's thought. At worst it has been feared, by N. D. O'Donoghue, Harold Weatherby, Jay Newman, and others, as the herald of skepticism, subjectivism, relativism, and sophistry. On the other hand, recent theorists who have accepted some more radical version of rhetoric are likely to find Newman infected either with the deadly "metaphysics of presence," or with the allegedly fatal liberal-humanist elitism associated with Arnold, Leavis, and Eliot.

But what we are being offered is a false alternative. Newman is neither skeptically subversive nor dogmatic. On the contrary, he embodies the best in the modernist turn to indeterminacy without sacrificing the intellect and the traditional search for truth. He is at once "suspicious" in his work of "restoration." Such a combination of opposites is possible because the kind of rhetoric Newman theorized about and practiced recognizes the limits of probabilistic reasoning while it nevertheless aims at truth. To be sure, there is no guarantee in rhetoric that truth will out (any more than in political revolution, scientific experiment, or metaphysics), but rhetoric as it is conceived of here offers at least a means to informed judgment and assent.

It is just this sense of rhetoric that John Holloway sometimes fails to appreciate in his study of Newman in *The Victorian Sage*. Holloway's analysis is unquestionably important, but it may be questioned whether his overall assessment of Newman is accurate. Because he abstracts from Newman's thought and practice, providing only a partial portrait, he leaves the unmistakable impression that Newman was, after all, very shifty, someone who skirted controversial points and who could fill the reader's mind with his vision, but only "for a while," that is, until the critical intellect returned to expose the sham. In short, Holloway deprecates Newman's rhetorical techniques, but only, I think, because he failed to consider them within Newman's larger rhetorical purposes and practice.

Unlike Holloway and others, I am not concerned in this work to trace the verbal techniques Newman employed—matters of style and tone, kinds of argument, and the like. Instead, I am intent on showing how pervasive are the intellectual principles and methods of rhetoric for Newman's thought and habits of mind. It is this larger methodological context that has not yet been understood or sufficiently appreciated, that can supplement the strictly literary study of Newman and correct mistaken estimates of Newman's purposes and results.

In a recent essay entitled "The Conversable World: Eighteenth Century Transformations of the Relation of Rhetoric and Truth,"[1] Nancy S. Struever provocatively suggests that Hume, who is often considered to have presided over the demise of rhetoric, in fact effectively rearticulated the classical rhetorical program into the "conversable worlds" of moral truth and literary taste. This importation of rhetoric from the public to the private-but-not-subjective realm was aided and abetted, Struever shows, by the novelist Jane Austen, the conversable worlds of whose novels rhetorically resituate aesthetic and social judgment: "[C]onversation [in Austen] is not simply an idle, leisurely occupation but the purposeful construction of life and attitude and value . . . ."[2] Now, this reappearance of rhetoric as "conversation" at the end of the eighteenth century may help us to appreciate the transformation Newman himself wrought in the fortunes of rhetoric in the nineteenth. In his major works, particularly in *The Idea of a University* and the *Grammar of Assent*, Newman reappropriated rhetorical "judgment" from aesthetics and morals and generalized it *back* into the public domain of reason and knowledge—most notably, religious faith. Once again rhetoric offers a rationale for a much wider range of truths, because it is anchored (as it was for Aristotle) in "judgment": " 'Judgment does not stand here for a certain homely, useful quality of intellect, that guards a person from committing mistakes to the injury of his fortunes or common reputation; but for that master-principle of business, literature, and talent, which gives him strength in any subject he chooses to grapple with, and enables him to seize the strongpoint in it'" (*Idea*, 151–52). Newman in fact is the first modern thinker to articulate what rhetoricians these days call "epistemic" rhetoric—the view that rhetoric has an epistemological or truth function—and in so doing shows himself to be a rhetorical theorist of vastly greater interest than his Oxford tutor, the influential Richard Whately. In this way it can be seen not only that rhetoric illuminates Newman, but that Newman sophisticates our knowledge of rhetorical theory and our critical appreciation of rhetorical practice.

Struever's remarks also help us to recognize that rhetoric is more than a literary affair. Under Newman's hands philosophy and theology themselves are inseparable from interpersonal persuasion. The question for us then is what it means to be a philosopher or theologian who thinks and talks like a rhetorician. A recent study of the *Grammar of Assent* proposes a series of misreadings of Newman's theory of belief for lack of appreciation of how integral rhetoric is to Newman's version of philosophy. *The Idea of a University* itself often falls flat even for highly educated readers, for lack of knowledge of rhetorical culture and ideals sufficient to enable the reader to discern their presence in the text. Among current theologians, only Nicholas Lash and John Coulson seem to appreciate the overwhelming importance for Newman studies of the recent work in hermeneutics and rhetoric. The present effort is meant to aid in opening these new lines of thought about Newman's theology and philosophy.

It remains for me to clarify several points about my own method. It may objected by those familiar with Newman's thought that rhetoric is too rule- and language-oriented to handle cognitive processes that, as described by Newman, virtually defy codification as "arts" and "methods." As Newman writes in the *Grammar of Assent*, "This is the mode in which we ordinarily reason, dealing with things directly, and as they stand, one by one, in the concrete, with an intrinsic and personal power, not a conscious adoption of an artificial instrument or expedient" (*G.A.*, 214). If the artifice we normally associate with rhetoric seems far removed from such an attitude, however, we might note that it is not so far removed as it might be—as far off, for example, as traditional conceptions of "logic" and "science" are—and that the affective and imaginative habits of mind and language of the rhetorician might well be the closest we can get to the subtle mental processes Newman describes. Rhetoric, moreover, allows us to shift easily from the psycho-epistemological theory of the

Grammar to the textual practice (and reflection on practice) of his works, and in so doing enables us to exhibit the fundamental unity of theory and practice, as well as the unity of the individual works taken together. In sum, in the interest of showing the nature, unity, and legitimacy of his theory and practice of persuasion, I use rhetoric to move freely between Newman's first-order uses of rhetorical principles and methods and his second-order reflections on those principles and methods.

A second point. The various life-stage Newman passed through, and the corresponding changes and developments of his mind and thought, have been well-documented and assimilated by Newman's readers and commentators. What is now needed, it seems to me, is that ahistorical view—in its own way limited of course, but still comprehensive within those limits—that I mentioned above. A large part of my thesis is that what Newman thinks about any question needs to be read in the light of how his formulation of problem and solution deploys important terms, values, beliefs, feelings, arguments. Newman himself never tired of tying theory to practice, and in different ways scholars have also grounded their studies in the "practical" in one sense or another—in biographical, historical, or social-cultural contexts. A study of Newman's method as rhetoric might similarly be expected to stabilize itself in the "particular" and "concrete" in these senses, and to analyze the historical audience, the occasions, and the effects of Newman's rhetoric, the cultural contexts of his controversies, the social milieu in which he moved, and so on. The present study is a necessary precursor even to this traditional approach, however, since it locates the starting point for the appreciation of Newman's more specific rhetorical responses.

Indeed, a more traditional study, as interesting and important as it might be, would be in danger of failing to be fully "philosophical" in Newman's sense of the word. One of Newman's most important epistemological insights is that "facts" or "things" in the world (under which he included even highly complex, "living" ideas) must be viewed in terms of the cumulative circumstances and converging probabilities that constitute them. It may be thought something of a paradox that a rhetorical study could for the most part ignore such coordinates as effects on historical audiences (although in fact responsible rhetorical criticism is fully possible without considering such matters). Actually the paradox lies deeper. Scholarly attention to the cultural and historical details, as indispensable as they are for answering other questions, ultimately forestalls a just appreciation of the nature and scope of Newman's rhetorical theory and practice—its supreme flexibility in new conditions and situations, its openness and creativity. One-sided focus on history risks losing us amidst particulars and missing the more philosophical, comprehensive "view" that Newman insisted was the mark of method and the aim of philosophy. The present study seeks to cut in between pure theory (what Newman said) and pure fact (where, when, and to whom) in an attempt to show how the action of Newman's texts themselves is an appropriate (and corrective) practical context for viewing Newman as a whole. Thus, at some risk of distortion, I side-step worrying about the chronological development of Newman's thought and its various biographical and other contexts, not because I think them unimportant, but because, first, for my purposes Newman's thought is virtually of a piece; second, these matters are amply treated elsewhere; and third, these matters would ultimately obscure the study of Newman's intellectual praxis.

Finally, it should be clear that I am attempting to address several disparate audiences, primarily students of rhetorical criticism and theory as well as of Newman, and after these, students of Victorian literature, literary theory, philosophy, and theology—as well as the general reader. I have no illusions that this pan-rhetoricism is without difficulties. The least of these difficulties is that not all readers will find all of the chapters relevant to their interests; more seriously, not all will accept my theoretical grounding or interpretations. I can only say that I have tried to show what a broad and open-ended conception of rhetoric looks like and can do, and that this has necessitated talking across fences and fields in a way that may appear, or be, interloping.

Chapter One introduces the reader to a set of questions about Newman that are largely unexplored and that I frame with respect to the enterprise of rhetoric. Chapters Two and Three lay out the case for Newman's account of reasoning and arguing and trace selected links between his and other accounts in the rhetorical tradition. Chapters Four, Five, and Six apply Newman's theoretical-methodological remarks about reason to the fields of theology, history, literature, science, and education; this last field in particular affords its own comprehensive view of the whole of Newman's thought from the perspective of "philosophy" itself. Finally, Chapter Seven seeks to show some of the ways in which Newman contributes to contemporary investigations in rhetoric.

I am grateful to my parents, and to my late grandmother Edith C. Odell ("Deed" to her grandchildren), who made it possible for me to attend graduate school at an important time in my life. Everyone who knew her recognized her great generosity and deep love for her family. With pleasure I acknowledge my debt of appreciation to Professors David

Smigelskis, Wayne Booth, and David Tracy, who read an earlier version of this book as a doctoral dissertation at the University of Chicago. Each lives the life of the mind with abiding vitality, freshness, and humor. I am grateful to the University of Virginia for a grant that enabled me to purchase needed books and xeroxing. I thank my colleagues Hugh M. Davidson of the French Department and Jamie Ferreira in Religious Studies for many stimulating conversations and helpful criticisms; William Lee Miller and John Sullivan in the Department of Rhetoric and Communication Studies for their ongoing support; and my graduate assistant, Mary Renstrom, for her careful reading of text and notes. Professor Eugene Garver at St. John's University (Collegeville) made several helpful comments; Professors John Angus Campbell at the University of Washington and Ray McKerrow at the University of Maine read the entire manuscript and made many important suggestions; and my good friend Neil Pritz saved me from numerous stylistic and substantive misjudgments. None of the above (nor all together) could save me from all of my errors of vision and execution, for which I take responsibility. Above all I thank my wife, Marcella, who saves me from errors far more serious, and who continues to teach me in innumerable silent ways the meaning of *cor ad cor loquitur*.

LIST OF ABBREVIATIONS

Citations refer to editions of Newman's works by Longmans, Green and Company unless otherwise noted.

Apo.	*Apologia Pro Vita Sua.* Oxford, 1967.
Ari.	*The Arians of the Fourth Century.* 1891.
A.W.	*Autobiographical Writings.* Sheed and Ward, 1957.
Corr.	*Cardinal Newman and William Froude, FRS: A Correspondence.* Johns Hopkins, 1933.
D.A.	*Discussions and Arguments.* 1891.
Dev.	*An Essay on the Development of Christian Doctrine.* Christian Classics, Maryland, 1968.
Diff.	*Difficulties of Anglicans.* 2 vols., 1918.
DMC	*Discourses to Mixed Congregations.* 1921.
ECH	*Essays Critical and Historical.* 2 vols., 1919.
G.A.	*An Essay in Aid of a Grammar of Assent.* Oxford, 1985.
H.S.	*Historical Sketches.* 3 vols., 1908.
Idea	*The Idea of a University.* Oxford, 1976.
L.C.	*The Letters and Correspondence of John Henry Newman.* 2 vols., 1890.
L.D.	*The Letters and Diaries of John Henry Newman.* 31 vols., Thomas Nelson and Sons, 1961.

Abbreviations

Letter	*Letter to His Grace the Duke of Norfolk.* University of Notre Dame, 1962.
OUS	*Newman's University Sermons: Fifteen Sermons Preached before the University of Oxford, 1826–1843.* S.P.C.K., 1970.
On Con	*On Consulting the Faithful in Matters of Doctrine.* Sheed & Ward, 1961.
P.N.	*The Philosophical Notebook of John Henry Newman.* 2 vols. Nauwelaerts, 1969.
PPS	*Parochial and Plain Sermons.* 8 vols., 1891.
Prepos.	*Present Position of Catholics in England.* 1893.
SSD	*Sermons Bearing on Subjects of the Day.* 1918.
SVO	*Sermons Preached on Various Occasions.* 1919.
T.P.	*The Theological Papers of John Henry Newman on Faith and Certainty.* Oxford, 1976.
V.M.	*The Via Media of the Anglican Church.* 2 vols., 1885.
Ward	*The Life of John Henry Cardinal Newman.* 2 vols., 1913.

CHRONOLOGY

1801	"I was born in London—my father was a Banker. . . . my mother was of a Huguenot Family."
1808	"I went to school at 7 years old at Ealing near London. . . . I remained there till the age of 15."
1810	Edward Copleston publishes *A Reply to the Calumnies of the Edinburgh Review Against Oxford*.
1816	"I was entered a commoner at Trinity College Oxford."
1817	Coleridge begins publication of the *Encyclopaedia Metropolitana*.
1818	"When 17, I gained the Trinity Scholarship."
1820	"When 19 I passed my examination and took my degree, failing in obtaining high honors."
1822	"I have this morning been elected Fellow of Oriel"; ". . . the turning point in [my] life, and of all days most memorable. It raised [me] from obscurity and need to competency and reputation."
1824	Publishes "Personal and Literary Character of Cicero" in *Encyclopedia Metropolitana*.
1825	"After being first noticed by [Whately] in 1822, I became very intimate with him in 1825, when I was his Vice-Principal at Alban Hall." May 19: "I have this day been ordained a priest."

1826   "I gave up [Alban Hall] in 1826, when I became Tutor of my College." Whately publishes *The Elements of Logic*.

1828   Whately publishes *The Elements of Rhetoric*.

1832   "At this time I was disengaged from College duties, and my health had suffered from the labour involved in the composition of my volume [*The Arians of the Fourth Century*]. It was ready for the press in July, 1832, though not published till the end of 1833. I was easily persuaded to join Hurrel Froude and his Father, who were going to the south of Europe for the health of the former."

1833   Illness in Sicily; Keble preaches the Assize sermon on "National Apostasy"; start of the Oxford Movement.

1837   Publishes *Lectures on the Prophetical Office of the Church*.

1838   *Lectures on Justification*.

1841   Tract 90. "From the end of 1841, I was on my death-bed, as regards my membership with the Anglican Church."

1843   Publishes *Sermons Preached before the University of Oxford (Oxford University Sermons)*.

1845   Publishes *An Essay on the Development of Christian Doctrine*. Received into the Catholic Church on October 8.

1847   Finishes preparatory studies in Rome and is ordained Catholic priest on Trinity Sunday, June 1.

1848   Establishes Oratory in Birmingham.

1850   Publishes *Difficulties of Anglicans*.

1851   Delivers *Lectures on the Present Position of Catholics in England to Brothers of the Oratory*. Assumes rectorship of the Catholic University of Ireland.

1852   Delivers *Discourses on the Scope and Nature of University Education* (revised edition, *The Idea of a University*, appears in 1870).

1858   Resigns as rector of the Catholic University.

1864   In six weeks writes *Apologia Pro Vita Sua*.

1870   *An Essay in Aid of a Grammar of Assent.*

1875   *A Letter Addressed to His Grace the Duke of Norfolk.*

1879   Pope Leo XIII raises Newman to the cardinalate.

1890   Dies on August 11.

Rhetorical Thought
in John Henry Newman

1

BETWEEN THEORY AND FACT

> *In trying to decide what a great man meant by his original formulations, it is always good to find out what he was talking against at the time, or what previous overstatement he was trying to correct. . . .*
>
> Erik Erikson,
> *Young Man Luther*
>
> *[T]hough truth is one, . . . arguments are many, and there are always two sides in every dispute. . . .*
>
> (*Prepos.,* 5)

EYES AND NO EYES

In a little-known essay entitled "The Theology of St. Ignatius" (1839), commenting on the hermeneutical difficulty of discriminating a "sophistical from a genuine interpretation" of patristic texts, Newman relates:

> There is a popular story called "Eyes and No Eyes," which we need hardly do more than recall to the reader's recollection:—two boys take a walk together, and return the one full and the other empty of intelligence gained in the course of it. Thus students rise from the Fathers, some profited by them, others disappointed, complaining that there is nothing or little in them, or much that is very fanciful; and all because they do not know what to look for, or are possessed with one or more ideas which they in vain seek to find in them. Their notion of the matter of divinity is so different from what prevailed in primitive times, that the surface of their minds does not come into contact with what they read; the points on which they themselves would insist slip on one side, or pass between those of the Fathers. . . . Thus they are ever at cross-purposes with the author they are studying; they do not discern his drift . . . (*ECH,* I, 226–27).

There is much that is suggestive in this commentary of Newman's on "Eyes and No Eyes." In the first place, similar language has been levelled by some of Newman's defenders against some of his critics, who impose (it is claimed) foreign meanings on whatever he is saying or more or less straitjacket him with impossible criteria of success. Such complaints are not in themselves unusual, though they raise the interesting question whether a viewpoint and vocabulary are discoverable (or have been discovered) that discern Newman's drift—not only his thought, but his method of thought. More fundamentally, the quotation above bristles with a profusion of issues that were of central importance to Newman and his contemporaries and are even more vital today: the question of historical relativity, the relations between knower and known, the nature and role of theory in the human sciences, the difficulty of distinguishing erroneous from valid textual interpretations. In certain matters, Newman argues in the *Grammar of Assent* (1870) and elsewhere, pure theory blinds us; it allows the "facts" of new cases to go unrecognized in their novelty:

> What is the meaning of the distrust, which is ordinarily felt, of speculators and theorists but this, that they are dead to the necessity of personal prudence and judgment to qualify and complete their logic? Science, working by itself, reaches truth in the abstract, and probability in the concrete; but what we aim at is truth in the concrete (*G.A.*, 181).

It was not just any sort of theory that Newman distrusted, but pure theory that forced unique cases into precast molds. Unlike many of his contemporaries, Newman operated on the premise that "seeing" is never reducible to scientific theory, much less to having (or not having) eyes, to somehow possessing unmediated fact (in this he is un-empirical and post-Kantian). Seeing is rather an affair of adjusting our ideas and scaling our perception to the very problem we are attempting to interpret. Exactly how one does this outside of abstract theoretical construction is not made clear in the essay just quoted, although Newman hints that enabling ideas of some sort—"knowing what to look for," attaining what he often called a "view" situated between theory and fact—are indispensable. We will need to ask what the difference is between "theory" and "enabling ideas," and between both of these and "facts." But, on starting, it is enough to note that Newman expressed throughout his writings and career an unmistakable concern for fact over theory, for the personal over the abstract, and for the popular and practically effective over the "theoretical and unreal."

This lifelong orientation of Newman's to the individual and concrete, to facts and "particulars," is perhaps best summed up in his cardinalatial motto, *Cor ad cor loquitur*, heart speaks to heart, though it can also be met with in the convenient gathering of quotable quotes toward the end of "The Tamworth Reading Room" (1841): "Life is for action,"[1] we are told there. "If we insist on proofs for everything, we shall never come to action" (*D.A.*, 295). "Logic makes but a sorry rhetoric with the multitude" (*D.A.*, 294); "deductions have no power of persuasion" (*D.A.*, 293)—remarks resembling Newman's quotation of Ambrose in the *Grammar of Assent* to the effect that God did not employ dialectic as the means of saving His people. "The heart is commonly reached, not through the reason, but through the imagination, . . . by the testimony of facts and events . . ." (*D.A.*, 293). In the *Apologia* (1864) he reports, "I had a great dislike of paper logic. For myself, it was not logic that carried me on;" "It is the concrete being that reasons" (*Apo.*, 155). And from the *Grammar*: "Words, which denote things, have innumerable implications; but in inferential [syllogistic] exercises it is the very triumph . . . to have stripped them of all these connatural senses, to have drained them of that depth and breadth of association which constitute their poetry, their rhetoric, and their historical life, to have starved each term down . . . so that it may stand for just one unreal aspect of the concrete thing . . ." (*G.A.*, 174).

For all of his emphasis on the personal and practical, Newman did not ignore what he took to be the proper use of the theoretical and abstract. Jouett Lynn Powell is correct to argue that Newman's thought cannot simply be reduced to apologetics and that "reason" for Newman is not coextensive with persuasion.[2] Powell shows that Newman recognized limits to the contributions that concrete or informal thinking made in the acquisition of knowledge, and Powell's "grammar of Christian discourse" seeks to explain shifting relations of faith and reason in Newman in terms of the mental activities most prominent in each kind of discourse he adopted. Thus, discourse concerned with "coming to faith" features implicit persuasive reasoning, that with "exercising the faith" reliance on mental imagery, and that with "explicating the faith" dependence on abstract argument. In short, facile reduction of Newman's writings to persuasion, imagery, or logic is simplistic and misleading.

But again, once we acknowledge some such typology, it is as correct as it is commonplace to assert that Newman's theory and practice are geared to the practical broadly conceived—that is, to facts, people, action, the popular and timely, and effects. Though many of Newman's works do not serve the cause of Christian apologetics, they do serve the larger purpose of defending the idea of belief itself, of arguing for its reasonableness. As Henry Tristram observed, "If they are viewed in perspective, it becomes at once apparent that his many volumes fall into place as parts of a magnificent *Summa Apologetica*" (*A.W.*, 18). Although for several years, as an avid protegé of Richard Whately and the "Noetics" at Oriel College, Newman inhaled the intellectual atmosphere of a reading room which "stank of logic" (*Apo.*, 156), he soon awoke to the dangers rationalism posed to the religious spirit and realized how little, after all, "reason" working alone could do in such matters. As he stated at various times,[3] from that period onward he opposed the antidogmatic principles of philosophical rationalism and the religious "liberalism" it underwrote. With the Reformation and its elevation of private judgment, and with the Enlightenment rejection of authority and tradition, the Church came under severe attack by objectivist rationalism. Newman stood firm against this "usurpatory" (*OUS,* 54) reason, which outlawed claims for the rationality of faith (religious or otherwise) on the ground that science and logic were alone the tests of propositions. He equally resisted the uncritical turn, whether romantic or evangelical, to the feeling heart.[4] Seeking to counter such "unreal" positions, Newman appealed to the "facts": "We must take the constitution of the human mind as we find it, and not as we may judge it ought to be" (*G.A.,* 142); "we must take things as they are, if we take them at all" (*Idea,* 255).

More specifically, Newman is intent in all of his writings to remind us of the severe limitations of the logical and scientific, to use and defend "extra-theoretic criteria"[5] in the judgment of truth in concrete cases and disciplines, and to generate theory that is sensitive to opportunities for invention and change. His method is one in which personal experience, the interpretation of facts and truths by "antecedent considerations," and the personal and interpersonal evaluation of evidence and "converging probabilities" were the tests of any theory. Behind Newman's reflections on faith and reason, and grounding all of his intellectual inquiries, lay the conviction that theory must be controlled and tested by persuasive insight and argument; in this way, theory is informed and qualified by action without simply collapsing into it or ceasing to be able to affect it.[6] As early as 1820 he could write: "A priori [purely theoretical] arguments seem to me the most fallacious of the fallacious" (*A.W.,* 164–65). And fifty years later, in 1870: "Real apprehension" of what is "concrete" "has the precedence, as being the scope and end and the test of notional" (*G.A.,* 30). In such a view, science and logic are severely restricted in their functions and purposes and are not allowed to usurp other functions and purposes.[7] Indeed, science and logic themselves are shown to depend on principles not themselves scientifically or logically justified. And ultimately "reason" requires, in order to be adjusted properly to the individual case, what Newman calls a "supplement" (*G.A.,* 205) to formal logic.

The line of critics who have seen in this approach the shadow of the sophist, equivocator, skeptic, subjectivist, "mere" rhetorician, and outright liar is by now a long enough one to warrant the attempt to confront directly those things in Newman's writings that are slippery, unstable, shifting, equivocal—or should we say mercurial, dynamic, comprehensive, and adaptive?[8] What Newman believed on most issues, his "drift" in the substantive sense, is increasingly understood and assimilated; but how he generated and supported those views is not. Without a sense of Newman's own intellectual "action" we cannot, I suggest, fully appreciate what he did believe, and the method by which he found and sustained it—his "drift" in a more subtle sense. Whether we have eyes to see may finally entail placing aside certain abstract theories and expectations in favor of more flexible ideas that better enable us to discern the action of Newman's texts themselves.

ENABLING IDEAS

It is, to repeat, a commonplace that Newman was drawn to the personal, practical, and concrete. In fact it may be just because Newman's orientation to fact and action is so obvious, and so pervasive, that no one has troubled to examine it for its underlying rationale. To fix on this issue is really to raise the fundamental question of what it meant to Newman to inquire, to do philosophy as he conceived it in *The Idea of a University* (1853) and the *Grammar of Assent*[9]—that is, it is to ask what the principles were according to which he thought systematic inquiries of any sort were to be conducted and what the intellectual and verbal strategies were that he derived from those principles. It is a question, in other words, of method.[10]

One way to go about answering this question of method is to view Newman, first, as a rhetorical theorist who articulated the essential features of an art of persuasion; and second, as a thinker for whom the principles and techniques of classical rhetoric, renovated and expanded, were uniformly his means of conception and proof. Newman offers us, in other words, a theory and practice of persuasion, or more broadly of persuasive "realization," having historical antecedents and the hope, at least, of philosophical justification. This approach will have, I think, a dual effect.

First, it should help free some of the commentary on Newman from the empirical and analytical fetters that sometimes bind it, and suggest new vocabularies and attitudes better able to disclose the nontechnical and humanistic cast of Newman's theology and philosophy.[11] Without disparagement to the illuminating studies, for example by Fey and Cameron, of Newman's philosophical relationships to Locke and Hume, the Newman reader can still heed Nicholas Lash's call for a greater "appreciation of the extent to which . . . *literary* patterns of argument and exposition have an indispensable role to play, a role often better suited to the subject-matter of Christian theology than are more formal, or theoretical, modes of reflection and explanation."[12]

In the second place, this approach should help to shift the issues and emphases of the discussion of rhetoric itself, specifically of rhetorical theory and practice in the eighteenth and nineteenth centuries. Martin Svaglic has noted that all of the major Victorians are rhetoricians (in practice if not theory), regardless of their frequent rejections of the blandishments of rhetoric. Yet rhetoric as a practice and concept remains uncharted through the nineteenth century; with one or two exceptions, Newman specifically has not been considered a rhetorical theorist at all.[13] These are surprising oversights until we recall just how recently rhetoric as an intellectual discipline has emerged from its ignominious past. The intention here is to show how one of the most acute intellects of the age was thoroughly imbued with rhetorical ideals and how his principles and methods transform immediate predecessors such as Hume, Campbell, and Whately, as well as classical sources such as Cicero and Aristotle.

One advantage to this approach is that it avoids reifying the practical and persuasive as fixed and determinate positions or doctrines.[14] Critics in the past who have discussed Newman's method have often done so, understandably, to illuminate larger contexts of religion, theology, philosophy, or literature.[15] In so doing, however, they have tended to harden fluid concepts and artificially isolate them from the dynamic flow of Newman's thought.[16] To study method as such makes possible a more nuanced understanding and introduces new channels for investigation. It provides us with an ensemble of rhetorical questions that should illuminate not only Newman but other literary figures (Carlyle, Macaulay, Arnold, Pater), theologians (W. G. Ward, Matthew Arnold, F. D. Maurice), philosophers (Bentham, Mill), and scientists (Huxley, Darwin, Spencer). What are the starting points of such method, its strategies of invention and argument, its means of finding and managing data? How much stress is placed on feeling, values, contingency, conscience, experience, imagination, and probability? What kind of argument is metaphor, image, symbol, or narrative? How does persuasion relate to faith? to emotions and values? to intellect and character? How does thought direct speech, and language embody thought?[17] In practice, of course, method is quite inseparable from subject matter; but Newman also reflects on method and thus invites the close "philosophical" scrutiny his theory and practice in any case deserve. The task, then, is not to separate method from subject matter, but to grasp how Newman's method, and his ideas on method, condition his understanding of subject matter.

6

Perhaps most importantly, to view Newman rhetorically is to substitute a set of suggestive concepts and informal criteria of adequacy for those "formal or theoretical" approaches that have been applied in the past. The question has recently been raised (again) whether Newman is a "'real' philosopher like Aristotle and Spinoza and Kant."[18] The answer is no, if by "real philosopher" we expect to find in Newman exact definitions, systematic unfolding of concepts, and proofs fashioned *sub specie aeternitatis*. As Cameron has noted,

> The strict definition of terms is not a part of Newman's method. He inherits a number of terms from the eighteenth-century writers— "reason," "feeling," "the passions," "the moral sense," "moral perceptions," "nature," "the heart"—and employs them in the then received sense, a sense not very strictly determined, and perhaps incapable of being strictly determined, if these terms are to be adequate to the many uses to which they are put.[19]

Language of the type Newman employed thus often appears to the trained philosopher or theologian as ill-formed, ill-bred, and ill-used. But rather than cite once more, as Jay Newman has done, Newman's failure to meet one standard, what happens when we invoke another? What purpose might language as indeterminate as Newman's have? Is his thought confused, or is it rather thought adapting to new circumstances? Is it inconsistent thinking, or thinking that must change to be consistent in a deeper way? Instead of determinate theories and strict criteria of argument, it may have been Newman's achievement to see that the indeterminacy of concepts suitable to a rhetorician was necessary in general if one were to hope to stay close to shifting facts without losing the reach of a larger "view." For the same reason, the study of Newman's thought may require advertence to indeterminate concepts—terms like knowing and acting, theory and practice, reason and faith, persuasion, argument, character, feeling—purposely kept open and ambiguous in order to adapt to the circumstances of Newman's practice.

Without, then, insisting on direct literary dependence, we might learn a good deal by recalling that Newman assimilated rhetorical habits of mind and rhetorical ideas from Aristotle, Cicero, Augustine and other Church Fathers, Bacon, Bishop Butler, and Richard Whately—all of them in some sense and measure rhetoricians.

THE RANGE OF RHETORIC

It is known that Newman had a "deep fondness"[20] for Cicero and a lifelong "special affection"[21] for Aristotle's *Rhetoric,* but it is generally

7

forgoten in what high esteem rhetoric, as a study and practice in ideas and expression, was held in the Oxford of Newman's day. Edward Copleston, Fellow and later Provost (1814–1828) of Oriel, in a defense of classical learning occasioned by an attack in the *Edinburgh Review,* claimed for rhetoric a virtual preeminence in the curriculum[22] that would have appeared perfectly normal to Gibbon, Johnson, or Burke, but which now, even more than in the past, was being called into question outside Oxford as belletristic and useless.[23] At seventeen, as a Trinity undergraduate in 1818–19, preparing for examinations in which he failed to achieve even second honors but which did not prevent his own election as Fellow of Oriel in 1822, Newman attended lectures on rhetoric by W. Morgan Kinsey, diligently pored over Cicero's *De Oratore* and made an "elaborate analysis"[24] of Aristotle's *Rhetoric.* As a tutor Newman enthusiastically recommended not only Aristotle's treatise but Richard Whately's *Elements of Rhetoric* (1828),[25] which in 1826 he possessed only in manuscript.[26] Whately, later Archbishop of Dublin, was, of course, Newman's mentor, the man who had handpicked him for the fellowship at Oriel, and more importantly the one who "opened my mind, and taught me to think and use my reason" (*Apo.,* 23). Later Whately was to say that, if he were given three wishes, they would all be for a mind like Newman's.[27]
. As a new Fellow Newman had been the "anvil" on which Whately had hammered out his ideas for his successful *Elements of Logic* (1826),[28] and almost certainly, in these years of close collaboration, Newman performed a similar service in the drafting of the equally influential *Elements of Rhetoric* (1828).[29] In the *Apologia* Newman makes clear that he was deeply influenced by Bishop Butler's maxim that "Probability is the guide of life" (*Apo.,* 23),[30] and it was Whately (like Copleston a "keen controversialist"[31]) who afforded Newman a stimulating elaboration of this truth.[32] To be sure, neither of Whately's textbooks could wholly have pleased the young Newman, and for much the same reason: the *Logic* because it totally ignored the personal dimension in coming to belief, and the *Rhetoric* because it similarly divorced knowledge from action, "conviction" from "persuasion." Thus "probability" for Whately (as for Butler) meant something different than it came to mean for Newman. These and related matters will be treated in some detail in the following chapter. Here I simply wish to indicate that Whately's preoccupation with logic and rhetoric helped to frame Newman's approach to epistemological questions. The empiricist tradition of Hume and Locke is unquestionably important for locating many of the problems Newman faced, but the *manner* in which Newman was to conduct his own inquiries

8

was unmitigatedly rhetorical. Indeed, in an article on Cicero written at this time (whose publication in Coleridge's *Encyclopedia Metropolitana* was arranged by Whately), Newman provides an account of Cicero's rhetorical treatises that has been called "the most qualified and complex response to [Cicero's] rhetorical theories"[33] of the age. Newman was twenty-three.

Beyond this early period of considerable literary-rhetorical study of the ancients, reinforced by prolonged involvement in logic and rhetoric, a further rhetorical influence on Newman's developing thought was his intense study of the Church Fathers, from 1828 until 1832 and intermittently from then on. "The broad philosophy of Clement and Origen carried me away; the philosophy, not the theological doctrine" (*Apo.*, 36).[34] This is not the place to examine that philosophy, but all of the Fathers were steeped in, even when they sometimes rebelled against, the rhetorical culture of Greece and Rome. To cite only the most notable example, Augustine himself was a professor of rhetoric for many years, and though his *De Doctrina Christiana* was understood thenceforward to relegate rhetoric proper to matters of style exclusively, the first three books, on the interpretation of Scripture, exhibit on every page his appropriation of Cicero's rhetorical mode of inquiry.[35]

Scattered remarks throughout Newman's *Arians of the Fourth Century* (the first product of Newman's patristic labors) reveal an easy familiarity with the rhetorical tradition from the time of Gorgias to the Second Sophistic.[36] More importantly, Newman learned from the Fathers to view nature as a "sacrament:" nature was but a "manifestation to our senses of realities greater than itself" (*Apo*, 36). This principle accorded well with his early belief that "life might be a dream, and I an Angel, and all this world a deception" (*Apo.*, 16), but it was also connected with the parallel doctrine of the Economy. In the *Arians* Newman explains the Economy as "setting [truth] out to advantage" (*Ari*, 65), and in the *Apologia* he writes: "The principle of the Economy is this; that out of various courses, in religious conduct or statment, all and each *allowable antecedently and in themselves,* that ought to be taken which is most expedient and most suitable at the time for the object in hand" (*Apo*, 299). Hence, even in substantive matters ostensibly far removed from rhetorical doctrine, it is relatively easy to detect Newman's essential identification with the need to adapt to audiences, times, places, and occasions. In his note on the Economy in the *Apologia*, Newman wryly observes: "When we would persuade others, we do not begin by treading on their toes" (*Apo*, 301).[37] Understood as a function of communication, the sacramental principle itself might be called a divine rhetoric of nature, and the Economy a rhetoric of revelation.[38]

In a small way, I have been suggesting that classical rhetoric in one form or another was a live option at Oxford. Yet there is no denying that the battle of the books waged by figures like Copleston and Whately was a failing rearguard action. De Quincey, who had also attended Oxford, in a review essay of Whately's *Elements of Rhetoric* the year it was published, was uttering a truism when he wrote:

> No art cultivated by man has suffered more in the revolutions of taste and opinion than the Art of Rhetoric. There was a time when, by an undue extension of this term, it designated the whole cycle of acomplishments which prepared a man for public affairs. From that height it has descended to a level with the arts of alchemy and astrology. . . . If we look into the prevailing theory of Rhetoric, under which it meets with so degrading an estimate, we shall find that it fluctuates between two different conceptions, according to one of which it is an art of ostentatious ornamentation, and according to the other an art of sophistry.[39]

These conceptions were, of course, long-standing. In the *Gorgias*, Plato had patiently dismantled an imperialistic account of rhetoric advanced by the well-intentioned but confused sophist Gorgias, showing it to be wholly unable to provide a coherent explanation of his art, much less of that justice and injustice Gorgias had claimed as its purview. In Socrates' not always ingenuous arguments, rhetoric is portrayed as trafficking in merely what appears to be, whereas philosophy seeks what is; the rhetorician knows only images or opinions, whereas the philosopher, who practices dialectic, can articulate parts and wholes, and aspires to those eternal forms or patterns that the world of becoming only approximates. Even if well-intentioned, therefore, the rhetorician deceives, since he mistakes belief for knowledge. Similarly, we find in Book IV of Augustine's *De Doctrina Christiana* at least the de jure reduction of rhetoric to ornamental style.

Like De Quincey, then, Whately, in his preface to the *Elements of Rhetoric*, complains of these two mistaken notions of rhetoric among the "vulgar." It did not, however, escape De Quincey's notice that, in defining rhetoric as it did, Whately's treatise (in great measure a practical handbook for schoolboys on the composition of themes) was itself an example of that "descent from the heights" De Quincey was bemoaning. In explicit opposition to Aristotle and Cicero, and in a move at least analogous to those of Plato and Augustine, Whately denied that rhetoric had anything

10

to do with the substance of argument, removing from the realm of rhetoric altogether and consigning to logic or an appropriate antecedent science all responsibility for discovering or establishing truth. Henceforth rhetoric was simply to "manage" the premises supporting a claim by selecting suitable logical forms of arguments (e.g., cause, sign, analogy, etc.). Though not totally reduced to style as it had been in the Renaissance doctrine of Peter Ramus, rhetoric for Whately was nothing more than a "gofer" for logic and science.[40]

Of course, Whately's reduction of the role of rhetoric to formal matters of argument and style was itself hardly new. On a more speculative level in the preceding century, George Campbell's *The Philosophy of Rhetoric* (1776) had already implicitly substituted associationist doctrine and the experimental method for the Ciceronian *inventio* of earlier theorists, just as Lord Kames's *Elements of Criticism* (1762) and Hugh Blair's *Lectures on Rhetoric and Belles-Lettres* (1783) had deflected rhetoric from its function as an art of persuasion to a science of criticism.[41]

In short, there was a range of meanings for rhetoric familiar to Newman and his contemporaries: rhetoric as expression or style, or as sophistic deception, or as criticism, or as the transmission of truth found by other means. But I have hinted that Newman (like De Quincey) knew and appropriated another, more classical sense of the term: "What . . . is the art of rhetoric but the reduction of reasonings, in themselves sound, into the *calculus* of the tastes, opinions, passions, and aims of a particular audience?" (*ECH*, I, 288–89)[42] This definition is too imprecise for our purposes; we will ultimately need a fuller explanation of the kind of rhetoric Newman learned and practised. It should be borne in mind, however, that our purpose is not, at least in the first instance, to track one theory of rhetoric from its classical source to its appearance in Newman's writings, nor to urge that rhetoric was the only or even the most important influence on Newman's thought. In his more than forty volumes, Newman never proposed a unified theory of rhetoric, and the variety of influences on Newman is too well established to be questioned here. The primary purpose rather is to locate that sense of rhetoric that Newman seems to have been influenced by and used, and which, more importantly, we can use to illuminate his method, irrespective finally of the question of influence.

Because literary critics and even an occasional philosopher and theologian have wrestled with this question of rhetoric in Newman (usually some part of the style-deception-transmission triad), it will be useful first to sort out the major strengths and weaknesses of their views. Given their purposes, these views are immensely helpful; nevertheless, as the argument will indicate, they sometimes miss the larger methodological context that alone can render Newman's practice philosophically intelligible and convincing.

DISABLING OPPOSITIONS

To view Newman as rhetorician is in fact rather common. Countless allusions are made in the literature, usually in passing, to his mode of argument as apologetical, polemical, controversial, jurisprudential, persuasive. Occasionally Newman himself speaks in this way to characterize his reliance on informal inference in concrete matters.[43] He never formally designated his method as rhetorical, primarily, I suspect, for rhetorical reasons. Typically he took up words with reference to their popular uses and was quite sensible of the fact that "rhetoric" was generally taken to signify a "realm separable from theory and philosophy":[44] hence, with reference now to his role as propagandist for the Oxford Movement, he wrote to Hurrell Froude in 1836, "You and Keble are the philosophers, and I am the rhetorician" (L.D., 225). Further, Newman could hardly have failed to consider the near-contempt in which rhetoric was held by many of his contemporaries. In "Characteristics" (1831), for example, Carlyle rates the "Debater and Demonstrator . . . as the lowest of true thinkers." The reason for this is that they worked in circles far removed from the deeper "region of meditation" Carlyle subscribed to, preoccupied with a logic that was mechanical and overly scientific.[45] For a Huxley, Clifford, Spencer, or Comte, on the other hand, these circles were simply not scientific enough. This widespread (though usually only nominal) revilement of rhetoric as an intellectual discipline (what Valesio calls the "rhetoric of anti-rhetoric") in the nineteenth century, and its subsequent slide into obscurity in the twentieth, partly explains the failure of many otherwise perceptive critics of Newman's philosophy and theology to exploit their insights into his rhetorical mode of thought.

And yet if rhetoric was not philosophically respectable, it nevertheless survived, in a more or less truncated form, as the study and practice of composition, or was absorbed into literary study *toto coelo,* matters quite distinct in either case from those of philosophy or science. Literary studies of Newman frequently focus their interest on style generally, or on the occasions, contexts, motives, and strategies of argument in particular; not surprisingly the *Apologia* has attracted the most attention.[46] The best of this criticism, it should be said, does evince a larger awareness of the philosophical issues at stake. In "Newman as a Prose Writer," for instance, Lewis E. Gates clearly appreciates the importance to Newman's practice in the *Apologia* of his theory of reasoning in the *Oxford University Sermons* (1843).[47] David J. DeLaura has yet a deeper understanding that a work like the *Apologia* "sought nothing less than an entrance into the buried springs of morality, perception, and feeling in the reader. The implicit object is a transference of values, and a transformation of the reader. . . ."[48] On the other side of the fence philosophically, John Holloway provocatively casts suspicion on Newman's theory and practice, raising once more the question that has plagued the rhetorician since antiquity, namely whether or not his methods are responsible ones:

> All in all, this is a kind of thinking which at present seems steadily to be gaining interest and prestige, . . . so much so, in fact, that modern admirers tend at times to exalt it indiscriminately, without considering whether (as with the narrower thinking of logic) there may be an invalid form of it as well as a valid. "The whole man moves" is Newman's well-known phrase; and he himself did not fail to notice that a whole man might sometimes move awry, though he gives this very little attention . . . to my mind, revealingly little.[49]

In fact Newman gave far more attention to the problems of truth than Holloway and others have suggested. Nevertheless, Holloway's criticism of the modern infatuation with rhetorical modes of reasoning is astute. J.-H. Walgrave has written:

> Holloway's account of Newman's literary and dialectical genius is wonderfully clear. . . . To deal with it thoroughly would require a whole book. The main question concerns his qualification of Newman as a "sage," with all that the word connotes—his opposition of the sage and the poet to the philosopher and scientist, as if the object of these latter were the truth, whereas with the sage and poet, it is open to question "whether the sense of 'true' and 'false' relevant in this field of thought is something we fully understand" (297 [London: Macmillan, 1953]).[50]

Walgrave seems to me to be correct about the "main question." Holloway's positivistic assumptions tend to insinuate a disabling opposition between philosophy and rhetoric that cripples judgment. We might state the matter this way: if rhetoric comprehends more than style, if it performs a constitutive role not only in the realm of action but in the acquisition of knowledge, then we can no longer oppose Newman as literary artist (sage) to Newman as philosopher and theologian. Yet how can rhetoric and philosophy, special pleading and epistemology, peace-fully lie down together? In what sense could a rhetorical sage be a theologian?

Readers familiar with pragmatist, existentialist, or hermeneutical thought should have little trouble entertaining the question posed here. What I am suggesting is that the flawed conception of rhetoric as "decep-tion," or the oversimplified conception of it as style apart from substance, or style and argument in the service of substance found elsewhere, or finally as persuasion only in the realm of overt action, must inevitably give us a one-sided version of Newman. In this, Holloway is by no means alone. George Levine is virtually "possessed of ideas he in vain seeks to find" in Newman. Intent on uncovering Newman's "irrationalism," he is forced to admit that he is "curiously rational." Determined to measure Newman against an a priori theory of fictional technique, he naturally finds him wanting.[51] Walter Houghton reads the *Apologia* with great sensitivity, but consistently opposes feeling and argument in violation of everything Newman says about informal inference.[52] A. Dwight Culler and Harold L. Weatherby implicitly oppose rhetoric to reponsible thought,[53] and John Beer, in an otherwise astute account of the romantic impulse in Newman, tends to stress feeling as something opposed to reason.[54] Among philosophers, Jay Newman, in his recent analysis of the *Grammar of Assent,* "using only the tools of the analytical philosopher," at least confesses a concern for comprehensiveness by promising to move continually "back from the logic of the intellect to the logic of the heart." What he does not make clear is how Newman's rhetoric will be ade-quately treated using only "logical" tools; more importantly, it is simply assumed again that intellect is something distinct from and opposed to the heart.[55]

It has not always been thus. It was Newman's own biographer, Wilfrid Ward, who was the first to appreciate that Newman's method was a coherent whole: "From first to last the method is the same. It is that of an artist, who is likewise poet, historian, thinker and theologian. . . ."[56] In a passage summing up many of his own previous remarks on Newman as a rhetorician, Charles Frederick Harrold writes:

> [Newman] broke down the common antithesis between the special
> pleader (which critics like Leslie Stephen thought him to be) who
> had his eye constantly on effects, and the genuine seeker after truth.
> Newman was in fact both. In the *Grammar of Assent,* he is more: he
> is at once the artist, the rhetorician, the theologian and the logician
> . . . and none of it is merely special pleading or *mere* rhetoric. . . .[57]

Whether or not Harrold is correct in asserting that Newman's approach is not "merely special pleading or *mere* rhetoric" is of course a further question. A close student not only of Newman but of the fiercely rhetorical Carlyle, hence one familiar with the vulnerability of rhetoric to philosophic critique, Harrold was fully aware that for others Newman's method appeared to be a "subtle and delicately lubricated illative rhetoric by which you are led downward on an exquisitely elaborated inclined plane, from a truism to a probability, from a strong probability to a fair probability, and from a fair probability to a pious but most improbable belief."[58] And whether or not this last claim really opposes Harrold's is yet a further question, for it may be that, though Newman's uses of the method may have been sometimes faulty, the method itself can be justified. Walgrave, for one, thinks that it can.[59] In the spirit of such contemporary literary critics as David DeLaura and Martin Svaglic, it is suggested here that Newman's practice as well as theory is a coherent and defensible yoking together of thought and speech for the purpose of persuading to authentic religious insight and intellectual knowledge.[60]

To investigate that claim we require a context in which to place the notion that Newman's method unites special pleading and philosophy, that it is what can be called a philosophic rhetoric. Coulson and Prickett have begun to work out literary contexts for such a view, but it has not been made clear how to unite the literary and philosophic study of Newman. To that end, a brief overview of the classical conception of rhetoric can provide a useful point of departure.

FROM PURE THEORY TO RHETORICAL TOPICS:

"The understanding of commonplaces leads us to a sober, but at the same [time] deep and broad, comprehension of the nature of man." (Valesio, Novantiqua, p. 36)

According to Aristotle, rhetoric is the counterpart (*antistrophos*) of dialectic. This latter is conceived as a universal art of testing opinions on general questions, in the attempt to effect the transition from propositions about what is intelligible to an audience of experts (e.g., of philosophers), to what is unqualifiedly intelligible in the order of being.[61] Opinions that withstand this critical sifting might then function as *arche* or first principles of the sciences. Rhetoric, like dialectic, is conceived by Aristotle as a universal art and not a principled inquiry, but unlike dialectic, rhetoric deals with particular and not general questions, and requires, in addition to proofs of a logical sort, an appeal to character and feeling. Aristotle defines it as "the faculty of discovering all of the available means of persuasion" (*Rhetoric*, 1355b) in matters about which men deliberate. Its primary vehicle of argument is the rhetorical syllogism or enthymeme and its end is "judgment" (*Rhetoric*, 1377b).[62]

Cicero and Quintilian later cultivate a stronger and more explicit orientation to the true and the just. Cicero, it is true, sometimes speaks as if appeal to the emotions (and thus, by implication, winning at all costs) were the sum and substance of rhetoric,[63] but on the whole his works clearly establish that it is the union of wisdom and eloquence, thought and word, at which the ideal orator aims. Thus rhetoric is not confined, as in Aristotle,[64] to *particular* "causae" or "hypotheses," but is applied architectonically to *all* thought, much as it had been earlier in Isocrates.[65] Quintilian too finds the essence of the art in argument, in "making a case;"[66] defines rhetoric as "the science of speaking well," where "well" means both artistically and morally; and like Cicero before him extends the range of rhetoric to all subjects.[67]

As a *techne* rhetoric is resolutely antitechnological in this sense, that it deals with contingent, not fixed and determinate questions, in a way that makes them common and accessible to all. Indeed, even the technological expert (as Polanyi has shown us) must rely on rhetorical intuitions and even proofs not calculable in terms of his expertise alone. Rhetoric moreover is anti-expert in that it lies beyond the expert's competence. It is neither scientific rule, nor poetic license, nor luck, but a kind of *esprit de finesse* directed toward the sensitive and resourceful adaptation to change of problems, persons, and purposes.

In antiquity rhetoric was understood to comprise five "offices"—invention, arrangement, style, memory, and delivery—but only the first three are relevant here. Invention refers to the discovery and formulation of the data, arguments, and other appeals thought likely to be acceptable to an audience. It entails finding arguments pertaining to the substance *(pragmata* or *logos)* of the case, the character of the speaker *(ethos)*, and the emotions *(pathe)* of the hearers. These three *pisteis* or persuasives are each indispensable, since the kinds of contingent questions designated as appropriate for rhetorical discourse involve the beliefs, values, feelings, and so on of those involved.[68] Thus, whereas dialectic might scrutinize abstract definitions of "the state," rhetoric would treat the particular—say, "the state of the union"—which implies a specific time, place, and people. The persuasives are also interpenetrating: an argument about what is true or beneficial in a situation might possess a high emotional and ethical charge and thus suggest simultaneously (if only implicitly) a line of reasoning about the speaker's character and about facts or events that arouse feeling. By the same token, emotion itself is construed as a cognitive and rational judgment.[69]

The second and third rhetorical offices, arrangement and style, refer respectively to the disposition of the arguments and parts of speech and to the manner of expression that best communicate meaning and thought. As such, they are analytically independent of, but ultimately subordinate to, invention. Because invention is an elusive doctrine, yet is central not only to rhetoric but to our grasp of Newman, it may be helpful if we consider it at somewhat greater length.

In the activity of inventing his "speech," a central resource the rhetor employs is the topics (*topos* = place, hence *loci,* commonplaces, special or proper places).[70] Strictly speaking these appear to have meant, for Aristotle, *propositions,* particularly value propositions used as inference warrants,[71] but Cicero and Quintilian define the topic as any "general heading" or "source" or "region" or "seat" *(sedes)* from which to draw out possible arguments for a case, and Bacon calls the topic a "place for inquiry and invention" where a thing may be looked for.[72] Bacon additionally notes that topics are "of use not only in argumentations, where we are disputing with one another, but also in meditations, where we are considering or resolving anything with ourselves."[73] Historically, then, a topic was construed as any category or proposition with more or less undetermined content useful for searching out the relevant aspects or circumstances of a case.[74] To borrow a phrase Newman applied to notional assents, we can say that topics comprise part of the "furniture of the mind" (*G.A.,* 41), that is, they are enabling ideas and dispositions by which we live and in which we move and have our being, providing what the hermeneutic tradition calls our "horizon of understanding,"[75] and what Newman calls a "view."

Aristotle discusses three types of topics: common topics *(koinoi)* applicable to any matter (for example, "more and less," "possible and impossible"); special topics *(eide),* which technically belong not to rhetoric but to the specific subject matter from which they are drawn, but which constitute the primary sources for rhetorical arguments[76] (for example, the concepts, distinctions, values, and the like that we would need to discuss any political problem); and formal topics *(koinoi topoi)* or "elements,"[77] the inferential patterns that govern major premises of enthymemes (for example, definition, genus, species, cause, sign, circumstance, consequence, etc.). Cicero and Quintilian seem to designate any device of inquiry or questioning a topic, as does Bacon, whose *Novum Organum* impresses rhetorical *topoi* even into the service of scientific investigation.[78] Historically, lists of *topoi* fluctuate considerably from theorist to theorist and periodically degenerate from devices of inquiry to things-to-be-memorized—what Bacon called "promptuary" devices[79]— as in Renaissance "commonplace" books.

Hence, family disputes about the number and types of topics are unending. The transformation of topics into truisms, however, is a warping of their function.[80] The very rationale of a topic is its *relative indeterminacy;*[81] that is, applicability to a broad band of matters, or to evolving exemplifications of a single matter, and freedom from predetermining what its user will discover, render it the analogue or counterpart in the human sciences of the exact concept, algorithm, or mathematical proof in sciences more exact. Rhetorical situations are novel and changing, and a device like the topic is indispensable for coping with the ambiguity and novelty they present, since only the topic can be *adjusted* to its object. Thus the rhetorical thinker aspires to a fluidity of thought that the scientific thinker seeks ultimately to arrest in a formula, and this is quite as it should be if they are to function within their respective spheres at all.

An example may help here. The concept of the state has meant many things, but in Plato's *Republic* it represents a fixed and absolute order of relations and an ideal standard and test for practical activity. As a pattern or idea, the state is immutable, and though we may articulate or embody it differently at different times, it is not subject to negotiation or compromise. By contrast, for the rhetorician or rhetorical thinker the state is always an "essentially contested concept,"[82] a "place" the rhetor consults or explores for its persuasive possibilities in a given case. Thus John Dewey, in *The Public and Its Problems,* objects to the Platonic attempt to ground the theory of the state in such a "metaphysical nisus" as the "essence" of man: "It is not the business of political philosophy or science to determine what the state in general should or must be."[83] Rather, "The only statement which can be made is a purely formal one: the state is the organization of the public effected through officials for the protection of the interests shared by its members."[84] Regardless of what we may think of such a definition, its formal nature precludes any fixed and determinate way of establishing what a state will specifically look like, how it will function, or where we will find one. Dewey is working topically in the sense that his definition is little more than a device to explore. It is not meaningless or simply equivocal, since its component terms call forth meanings out of the beliefs, values, traditions, feelings, and interests of those who use it; their "conjoint" life enables them to search for meanings, applications, and transformations: "The formation of states must be an experimental process."[85]

In Newman, common and special topics are omnipresent, usually appearing as paired terms that structure his inquiries.[86] In "Who's to Blame?" (1855), for example, a series of letters to *The Catholic Standard* protesting British involvement in the Crimea, Newman constitutes the British Constitution as the attempt to negotiate two mutually significant but antithetical values. He variously designates these as power and liberty, war and peace, martial law and constitutional freedom, a Rule and a Constitution: "The two principles are in antagonism from their very nature; so far forth as you have rule, you have not liberty; so far forth as you have liberty, you have not rule" (*D.A.*, 325). Later Newman similarly contrasts the State and the Nation, "rule" or "centralization" against "the people." His complaint is that John Bull had grown conceitedly theoretical in believing that Power can do all things, that British superiority is an immutable law transcending time and place, whereas in truth British institutions are poor instruments for war. What is lacking, in other words, is national sensitivity to practical circumstances and facts: ". . . and in every case the problem to be decided is, what is the most advisable compromise, what point is the *maximum* of at once protection and independence" (*D.A.*, 325)?

Thus Newman is not seeking, here or elsewhere, a dialectical transcendence to a third term that will reconcile these paired oppositions. On the contrary, he allows each term or topic to exfoliate, so to speak, into diverging illustrations and examples, probabilities and signs, further facts and topics, to allow one to discern the powers and limits of each side, and (in this particular case) to exhibit the preponderance of evidence in favor of the pacific nature of the British constitution. Newman focuses on the concrete and contingent, the realm of rhetoric: "To arrive at the fact of any matter, we must eschew generalities, and take things as they stand, with all their circumstances" (*G.A.*, 199); ". . . nor do I speak as grumbling at things as they are;—I merely want to look facts in the face" (*D.A.*, 360); "We must take things as we find them" (*Letter*, 79). A sure way to miss facts is to impose on concrete problems preconceived theories as their sole determinants, since such theories either arbitrarily fix what is indeterminate (thus begging the question) or run the risk of treating one-sidedly what is unique, multiform, and contingent.[87]

19

Newman, by contrast, cuts under the abstractness and inutility of pure theory, yet holds himself above the level of discontinuous fact and circumstance, by means of open-ended ideas that enable him to organize experience without dictating to it. These ideas, or topics, are relatively abstract "notions" and thus partake in that pure theory that Newman tried to avoid; but because they are *forms seeking specific content* they are really much closer to the realm of "fact" he embraced: "We are in a world of facts, and we use them; for there is nothing else to use" (*G.A.*, 223). Again and again we can see Newman generate the opposite side of a received position (usually the more personal, popular, and practical side, though not always, since one can err in that direction as well) in an attempt to locate the full range of possibilities that a given contingency involves. As Valesio notes, *topoi* locate "places of dramatic tension between opposite extremes."[88] One need but reflect on any of Newman's formulations of a problem to perceive his use of dialectically arranged terms:

> inference is *implicit* or *explicit, informal* or *formal*
> conscience involves the *moral sense* but also *duty*
> religion is *knowledge* but also *action*
> the Church is *visible* and *invisible*
> the Church is a "conspiratio" of *hierarchy* and *laity*
> changes in doctrine are *corruptions* or *developments*
> gifts of the Spirit are *miraculous* or *moral*
> dogma involes *Scripture* and *interpretation* of Scripture

These *topoi* are personal or received judgments grounded in what is believed to be antecedently probable, or true, or somehow relevant to what is at stake in the case. They function as places to locate the circumstances and probabilities that will resolve the case without predetermining it. And the assent or adherence one seeks is thus "created in the mind, not so much by facts, as by probabilities; and since probabilities have no definite ascertained value, and are reducible to no scientific standard, what are such to each individual, depend on his moral temperament" (*OUS*, 191). Critics who think of rhetoric as sophistic relativism are likely to find in this statement support for the view of Newman as subjectivist and irrationalist; rhetoric would then seem to provide a handsome fit indeed. But the idea of an intellectually defensible rhetoric must be correspondingly troublesome, suggesting that Newman himself might have a defensible program for assent. The question will require, in fact, much of the remainder of this book to answer. In the meanwhile, we need to pursue one other aspect of rhetoric, that of its scope.

ARCHITECTONIC RHETORIC IN NEWMAN:

"Judgment then in all concrete matter is the architectonic faculty" (G.A., 221).

Newman made it clear that the *Grammar* sought to articulate a *novum organum investigandi* that would more accurately represent the way in which the ordinary man comes to know or believe propositions that are not demonstratively certain. Newman aimed chiefly, of course, to defend the reasonableness of religious faith against that "rationalistic infidelity"[89] which held that a claim was properly established only when it could be proved scientifically or logically, and that religion, accordingly, was a matter of opinion, not truth. Newman tried to discern the kinds of reasons we use in coming to assent to religious and indeed to all beliefs. The *Grammar*, like the Oxford sermons forty years before, intended to clarify and defend the method responsible for the "popular, practical, personal evidence for the truth of Revelation" (*T.P.*, 81) or of any concrete issue.

The crux of the matter as Newman saw it was "informal inference," an exercise of personal interpretation and induction from particulars consisting of "The cumulation of probabilities, independent of each other, arising out of the nature and circumstances of the particular case which is under review; probabilities too fine to avail separately, too subtle and circuitous to be convertible into syllogisms, too numerous and various for conversion, even were they convertible (*G.A.*, 187)."

As Newman suggests in chapter III of the *Grammar,* the apprehension of reality is in some measure indeterminate, since the real requires ongoing interpretation from the perceiving subject (*G.A.*, 23, 30). More or less removed from these initial apprehensions, the complementary methods of experimental science and formal inference treat of relative fixities in thoughts, words, and things, in the interest of formulating general truths or laws abstracted from particulars of sense data, and of deducing equally abstract truths from them. The data of a given science and, in Newman's terms, the "notional" concepts and propositions one fashions are more or less fixed and determinate entities. As such, they are amenable to precise methods of inquiry, argument, and evaluation.

For Newman the method of reasoning in the concrete, in matters of human conduct and choice, is at once more living, "delicate," and "effective" (*G.A.*, 189) than those of science or logic, and more ambiguous, dynamic, and difficult to assess. In those cases where even what is at stake is a matter of conscious or unconscious selection on the part of the

21

inquirer, we cannot, Newman declares, rely exclusively or even primarily on the rules of abstract science or logic. If we are to take up individual cases as complex particulars and facts to be known as such, and not merely as members of a general class or instances of an abstract law, we must possess means that will enable us to determine the contingent and unique. In fact we rely on a wide range of such resources for resolving problems: various sorts of "first principles," and the general and specific propositions they engender; our values and beliefs, our estimates of the likely and unlikely, and the opinions we find around us; common sense; the testimony of those we know or trust; authority and tradition; feelings and intuitions; our "prejudices" and "presumptions" and "views of life" (*OUS*, 228). In Newman's thought these resources function as *topoi*, as guidelines to explore and determine what is otherwise more or less incoherent or disputable. To be sure, science and logic are profitably employed to examine concrete realities, but not *in* their uniqueness, for "Science in all its departments has too much simplicity and exactness, from the nature of the case, to be the measure of fact. In its very perfection lies its incompetency to settle particulars and details" (*G.A.*, 185).

It follows that informal inference is not a "mere method or calculus" (*G.A.*, 205), a fixed set of concepts and rules. Indeed it is often unconscious or partly so, though this is not the same as saying, as Carlyle, or critics stressing the romantic aspect in Newman have done, that such reasoning cannot be identified and described.[90] We have indicated that it was just the purpose of the *Grammar* to do so. And though never entirely "brought under a logical rule" (*G.A.*, 195), informal inference is nevertheless not illogical; it is rather "one and the same with [logic], only it is no longer an abstraction, but carried out into the realities of life, its premises being instinct with the substance and momentum of that mass of probabilities, which . . . carry it home to the individual case" (*G.A.*, 189–90).

To be sure, Newman never set out to compose a full-dress *rhetorica docens*. He had no specific overriding interest in the speaker or writer as such. Yet the *Grammar* is justly called "a significant rhetoric text"[91] since, in exploring how we do come to be persuaded, Newman offers perhaps the first truly modern psychology of persuasion. Unlike Aristotle's *Rhetoric*, it does not so much delineate *topoi* and the kinds, parts, and functions of arguments, as locate an art of reasoning and argument relative to other arts and methods, and describe its essential features. Profoundly aware of the difficulty of articulating inferential processes, Newman nevertheless offers a "grammar" of rhetorical persuasion, or at least "an essay in aid of" such a grammar. As a general propaedeutic and heuristic, therefore, Newman's rhetoric is not a rhetoric in the usual sense. Yet this is ultimately beside the point if his works illuminate the ground we wish to explore.

In addition to serving the purpose just noted, Newman's theory and practice depart from Aristotelian rhetoric in a more significant way. For Aristotle, rhetoric featured the realm of practical action; for Newman the method of "informal inference," guided and governed by the illative sense, provides *the* perspective or "view" from which Newman regarded all claims to truth. In this sense, rhetoric in Newman's thought is architectonic, not because it alone arbitrates claims to truth, but because rhetoric reveals the otherwise hidden personal aspect of all inquiries into, and tests of, truth. Newman fully allowed other means of argument and proof. In spite of his antipathy to logic, he never set out to compromise the principles and procedures of the sciences. What he does assert, however, is that formal inference and scientific methods are themselves ultimately inseparable from the personal and persuasive. The most accurate way to state the relationship is to say that Newman sought to combine theory and practice in such a way as to adjust to the exigencies of varying subject matters (what Richard McKeon has called a "problematic" method). Without question, the most frequent charge Newman brought against an array of opponents in a long life of controversy and discussion was that they were "one-sided," "abstract," "unreal"—precisely because they attempted to dictate answers to concrete questions out of theories abstracted from particular cases. In Newman's view, theory must be bonded to practice, each keeping the other from just this one-sidedness, with the "practical" as the ultimate court of appeal.

If practice controls theory, moreover, the *Grammar of Assent* itself must be understood as rhetorical, in the sense not only that it articulates a rhetoric of persuasion, but that it exemplifies one as well. Thomas J. Norris is quite correct to say that chapters five and ten of the *Grammar* are examples of how Newman uses the method of informal inference. But this is to see only half the story, and to overlook implications for a new understanding of Newman's modus operandi. For the whole *Grammar* is an example of arguing by antecedent and converging probabilities: it is the discovery and discussion of modes of apprehension, inference, and assent by means of *topoi* that locate a broad spectrum of persuasive appeals, aimed at a particular sort of audience. In Aristotle's formulation, Newman uses all available means of persuasion to gain assent—*not*, as one critic insists, an assent primarily to religion or Christianity,[92] but rather to Newman's formulation of the problem of reason generally, and

23

to his solution of it in particular. Whether the solution is ultimately skeptical and relativistic, as some critics also insist, will deserve our attention; but it may be that rhetoric itself can help to legitimize Newman's account.

PHILOSOPHIC RHETORIC

As a means of integrating the leading themes of this chapter, in particular the nature and scope of rhetoric in Newman, it may be helpful to outline the philosophic rhetorics of two contemporary theorists, Kenneth Burke and Richard McKeon. No attempt is made here to do justice to these two thinkers nor to account for the considerable differences between them; we are seeking only rough coordinates that will be helpful in plotting Newman's position.

In the first place, as the common ground for both of these philosophies, "rhetoric" cannot be restricted to classical (or modern) definitions of the term as a "verbal art" of expression, or argument, or communication generally. It includes these certainly; but rhetoric has come to assume (in the way that hermeneutics has) a far richer meaning and an almost indefinitely expanded scope. In Kenneth Burke's "motivorum" project, for example, where we encounter a grammar of motives for action centered upon the concept of "substance" and given methodological effectiveness in the dramatistic pentad of terms for analysing (and deconstructing) attributions of substance (motives), we learn that all such attributions, because linguistic, are inescapably rhetorical: "Paper need not *know the meaning* of fire in order to burn. But in the 'idea' of fire there is a persuasive ingredient. By this route something of the rhetorical motive comes to lurk in every 'meaning,' however purely scientific its pretensions. Wherever there is persuasion, there is rhetoric. And wherever there is meaning, there is 'persuasion.' "[93]

This is actually putting it mildly, since for Burke the "rhetorical motive" does not simply "lurk" in those attributions of substance that really count for us—our "non-scientific" uses of language in daily life, art, religion, philosophy, politics. Grounded as these are for Burke in our *attitudes*, such language uses are inescapably bound up with the drive to "induce cooperation in beings that by nature respond to symbols[94]—that is, with rhetoric.

Here rhetoric has taken on dimensions not present, or at best only lurking, in Aristotle, and only partly present, for example, in Cicero. Rhetoric is, first of all, an inevitable characteristic of all language; in fact it is the *primary* feature about language for Burke, since the use of symbols generally—what Burke calls symbolic action—is first and foremost a matter of attitudes, interests, and values that shape our perceptions of and claims about the world. His "grammar" is thus, like Newman's, equally a "rhetoric."

Second, rhetoric remains an art or method of expression, argument, and "persuasion." But Burke expands this art so that it becomes a method not only of persuasion but of "identification," including all unconscious as well as conscious attribution and analysis of motives.[95] Hence it contains a *critique* of unconscious motives—of "ideology," political or otherwise—that went unthematized in the ancients.

Finally, as constitutive of Burke's system, symbolic action as rhetoric is the organizing principle of everything that comes to be known by man. Indeed, man's own "dialectical substance" is just this ability to act symbolically in language in "naming" the world—or, as one critic has it—in *seizing political power* by seizing the means by which *anyone* names the world (or calls the shots).[96]

In McKeon we witness a similar elevation of rhetoric as an architectonic philosophic principle capable of coordinating all of our knowing, doing, and making.[97] Where previous philosophic approaches had grounded truth in things, thoughts, or actions, McKeon argues that words and communication—rhetoric—provide a more useful and plausible approach for technological man. McKeon is perfectly aware of the history of rhetoric in its more narrow sense as a verbal art, but his focus is not language as such, nor the use of such an art to communicate truths or beliefs whose sources lie outside rhetoric. He is concerned rather with the renovation and invention of intellectual devices to function as means of invention—or more fully, of invention, interpretation, relation, and systematization. And here too rhetoric is not in the first instance "persuasion" in the civic realm (though it includes this), but the persuasive determination of the indeterminate in any problem. As Mark Backman has recently put it, "Invention refers not only to words but to facts, data, methods, and systems. Rhetoric is more than an expressive art; it is an organizational principle that provides the framework within which we can reveal and arrange the significant parts of any human undertaking."[98]

What is the end of this rhetoric? Whereas for Burke it is arguable at least that the aim of rhetoric is the critique of ideology and the seizure of the language of politics *"ad bellum purificandum,"* for McKeon rhetoric aims at truth-through-communication. What is known or knowable must survive the crucible of argument and persuasion; intersubjective agreement over time by qualified inquirers who have accepted the evidence and arguments is the test of truth. Mark Backman has suggested that McKeon's is an "edifying" philosophy of the sort that Richard Rorty extols,[99] but it is more plausible I think to place Burke among the "edifiers" and to open up a middle category (between "edifying" and "systematic" philosophers) where the likes of McKeon (or Perelman, Toulmin, and Booth) embrace neither the epistemological absolutism Rorty and Burke so successfully explode, nor the urbane ("neo-stoic") resignation to "social practices" or will-to-power they appear to prefer. Perhaps it is not so implausible to think, as McKeon does, that there is truth, and that we can know it, and that both truth and knowledge are "rhetorical" in a more stable sense.

But what, then, of Newman, who never called his philosophy "rhetoric," but for whom nevertheless rhetoric is recognizably its informing principle? We might end by making four points. First, "rhetoric" for Newman must again be understood in that expansive sense we find in Burke and McKeon. In Newman, "informal inference" is a mode of rhetorical argument; but we also find an architectonic principle of "judgment" that looks to indeterminacy as the locus of theory and to action as the test of truth.

Second, for Newman language (that is, concrete language) is also ineluctably perspectival, "sermonic" or attitudinal, and vested with interests. It provides, moreover, what Heidegger calls the "house of being," in that "things" ("facts," "the concrete") come to full existence only linguistically—hence rhetorically.

Third, while Newman's distinctions between "real" and "notional," "informal" and "formal" roughly parallel Aristotle's distinction between rhetoric and dialectic, Newman collapses the rhetoric-dialectic dichotomy in just the way that most contemporary rhetoricians do. Newman is ever at pains to explore the rhetorical dimensions to all thought. And while he would have agreed with rhetorician Michael C. Leff that uncritical elevation of rhetoric risks blurring generic differences in modes of argumentation,[100] or with theologian David Tracy that uncritical conflation of rhetoric and dialectic risks unfairly denying extra-rhetorical factors in argumentation,[101] nevertheless rhetoric is the lens through which Newman considers all problems.

Lastly, it is perhaps growing clear by now that, unlike Rorty and Burke, and like McKeon, Newman belongs in that middle category of rhetorical philosophers for whom truth is grounded in rhetorical speech

26

without being simply reducible to verbal practices. Rhetoric as it has been sketched here is not the only element in knowing, but it is foundational, and foundational without succumbing to absolutism or unqualified relativism. What this means, and how Newman contributes to an answer, are the subjects we need to explore.

2

TOWARD A
PHILOSOPHIC RHETORIC

*Truth, in the great practical concerns of life, is so
much a question of the reconciling and combining of
opposites that very few have minds sufficiently
capacious and impartial to make the adjustment with
an approach to correctness. . . .*
John Stuart Mill,
On Liberty

The rhetorician as conceived of here has a characteristic way of
looking at and thinking about the world, one that features three related
notions in particular: the specific concrete case governs all previous theorizing, which theorizing can never be more than one source of determination among several; the specific case is more or less unique, never the
same in all respects as past cases; and what is required to deal sensitively
with that uniqueness and novelty are resources or devices that enable the
rhetor to handle "both sides"—actually the full range of possibilities—of a
given contingent problem.

Perhaps the lawyer or statesman best exemplifies the consummately
rhetorical thinker. Cicero at least thought so. Yet the popular estimate of
the lawyer as a technician for the cunning reminds us of the conventional
estimate of the rhetorician, namely that he is or is given to be a crafty
opportunist who twists and turns facts to a preordained (and self-serving)
end. This temptation is probably a permanent occupational hazard of
rhetoric (and law). Newman in any case was very sensitive to the fact that
for most of his life he seemed almost to invite the charge that he sought
persuasive effects at the expense of honesty and truth.[1] This had been, of
course, the accusation brought against him in 1864 by Charles Kingsley,
to whom Newman's motives were those of all dogmatic and unscrupulous
Catholics.[2] Whately thought he discerned some more personal motive to
power in Newman (*Apo.*, 27), and Samuel Wilberforce thought Newman
had an "ambitious temper."[3] In an early journal entry Newman faulted
his own "self esteem," confessing "I am not straight forward in speech, I
exaggerate, misrepresent" (*A.W.*, 210). Isaac Williams years afterward
remembered that, as a tractarian, Newman was "in the habit of looking
for effect, and for what was sensibly effective."[4] This is a habit that entails
just that opportunistic adaptation to circumstances so characteristic of the
rhetorician.

To Newman it was an objective characteristic of life itself: "In a
higher world it is otherwise, but here below to live is to change, and to be

28

perfect is to have changed often" (*Dev.*, 40). In this regard, despite certain affinities, the Coleridgean and Carlylean pursuit of a realm of transcendent ideas could not provide a sharper contrast to Newman's characteristic attitude. Newman too embraced the eternal, but always by way of human change and innovation (witness, for example, his choice of the Incarnation as the leading idea of Christianity).

A REALISTIC PLIANCY

In the previous chapter I intimated that intellectually Newman *was* an opportunist, in the sense that he thought that questions should be raised and answered, and problems located and solved, by consulting the circumstances, facts, and particulars, all of the opportunities for inquiry and resolution, of each individual and unique case. "[To] reconcile theory and fact is almost an instinct of the mind" (*Apo.*, 233). Logically such a stance need be neither anti-intellectual nor unscrupulous, since concrete contingencies may require, if they are to be adequately addressed, wide experience and learning, cultivated feelings and imagination, and a finely tuned moral sense. It takes a rhetorician to observe that, "Technically, everyone should be an opportunist, in the sense that he should change his policies in response to changes of situation. But this pliancy is realistic, rather than demoralizing, only insofar as one's verbalizations become correspondingly mature."[5] The mature rhetorician, we might say, is not one who has no principles, but one whose principles do not have him. Perhaps Newman had something like this in mind when he wrote to Henry Wilberforce in 1848: "Ought not conscience to be the child of such a pair as heart and rhetoric" (*L.D.*, XII, 157).

Of course Newman was not the only nineteenth-century intellectual whose approach was systematically opportunistic in assimilating theory to practice, though he may have been the most discriminating and thorough, qualities which tend to make his stance at least *look* sophistical. Macaulay, for example, evinces throughout his writings and career not just that impatience with abstract theorizing characteristic of a Hume or Locke enamored with matters of fact, but the specifically rhetorical infatuation with effects, experience, expediency, and the adjustment of principle to circumstance. One need only consult his defenses of those arch-opportunists Bacon and Machiavelli, or his admiration for Edmund Burke's keen practical sense, or his own pragmatism as a public figure, to catch his sympathies.[6] The difference is that while Newman pushed forcibly against the age, striving to expand its vision of what the "prac-

tical" might involve, Macaulay was a thinker and writer "not of exploration but of statement. His thinking was unoriginal and his sensibility
limited. . . . His role, as he himself fully recognized, was not critical or
innovatory but didactic and expository. . . ."[7]

In a similar way, as literary or social critic, or as theologian, Matthew
Arnold, notwithstanding his ostensible rejections of rhetoric, habitually
geared principle to practice and studiously avoided the studious and
technical. In spite of his own pseudo-Platonic rhetoric, in *Culture and
Anarchy,* his lofty talk of "disinterestedness" and "the intelligible law of
things," the fact remains that his attempt to counter Hebraism with
Hellenism (or later Hellenism with Hebraism, in *Literature and Dogma*)
was itself the response of the rhetorician to current audience needs and
problems, just as his conception of culture was thoroughly imbued with
the adjustment of thought to practical circumstance:[8] "For if, casting
aside the impediments of stock notions and mechanical action, we try to
find the intelligible law of things respecting a great land-owning class such
as we have in this country, does not our consciousness readily tell us that
whether the perpetuation of such a class is for its own real good and for
the real good of the community, depends on the actual circumstances of
this class and of the community?"[9]

In the same way that Macaulay had been accused of being belletristic
in his writing of history,[10] moreover, Arnold was accused of ama-
teurishness and lack of rigor in his literary criticism.[11] In *Culture and
Anarchy* his own self-deprecating irony actually highlights his self-satisfaction at being a "mere dabbler"[12] in philosophy. With considerably less
self-satisfaction and more realism, Newman late in life expressed the cost
of this rhetorical expansiveness across subjects and disciplines:

> It has been my misfortune through life to have dabbled in many
> things, and to have mastered nothing. I am not speaking as if I could
> not have done something if I had confined myself to one line, but I
> have in fact taken up nothing in particular, not history as Milman,
> not theology as Robert Wilberforce and many a Catholic Priest, not
> Christian Evidence as Butler and Davison. I have lived from hand to
> mouth, doing nothing but what I was forced to do. . . . (*L.D.,*
> XXIV, 225–26)

By contrast, for other nineteenth-century figures (the later Carlyle,
for example), the subordination of theory to practice, and more particularly the rhetorical ability to consider both sides of a question, hard-
ens into one-sidedness, the balance of "Signs of the Times" degenerating
into the hysteria of "The Nigger Question." This one-sidedness we find

again in Huxley's and Whewell's rejection of literature in favor of science. This inability to hold in tension opposed practical principles has led Walter Houghton to identify it as a mark of the age,[13] but surely this is not applicable to the major thinkers: Mill struggled to combine Bentham and Coleridge, Arnold "sweetness" and "light," Pater typically thought in dialectical terms,[14] and Willey has observed of George Eliot that "From the very outset . . . she showed the instinct—which was deeply imbedded in the consciousness of the century as a whole—to see both sides of any question: to tolerate the ordinary while admiring the ideal, to cling to the old while accepting the new, to retain the core of traditions while mentally criticizing their forms."[15] Perhaps more than any other Victorian thinker Newman embodied this rhetorical ideal of arguing *in utramque partem,* on both sides of any problem, and of adjusting theory to practice.

If Newman's was a Victorian attitude and task, however, to say as much may be to risk unfairly tipping the balance of another of those antithetical pairs, the permanent and the transitory. As a rhetorician, Newman was emphatically *in* the world—he speaks of his "habit, or even nature, of not writing and publishing without a *call* . . . or invitation, or necessity, or emergency" (*A.W.,* 272)—but in one sense not *of* the world. The major works at least are signally free of mere topicality: "What concerns him is not the local and the transient, but the perennial plight of fallen man . . . If Newman was unmoved by the specific challenges of his own century, it was because he saw in them merely the reincarnation of early heresies, over which the Catholic Church had triumphed centuries ago."[16]

But it is no good to attempt to pronounce categorically that Newman's chief preoccupation was either permanence or change. It was *both,* now with the emphasis on one value, now on the other, *as the particular case required.* As he says in *The Idea of a University,* "It is no principle with sensible men, of whatever cast of opinion, to do always what is abstractedly best" (*Idea,* 25). This capacity to adjust and change, however, was disciplined by permanent principles, and much of the later chapters of the present work attempts to demonstrate that the same principles, under changing guises, underlie all of Newman's thought, providing a consistency, integrity, and balance that we can fairly call philosophical. Indeed, Newman often says as much. In the *Apologia* he observes that his spiritual journey from Anglicanism to Catholicism was the slow unfolding of uniform principles of thought and action (*Apo.,* 214, 252). In *The Idea of a University* he states that his views on liberal education "have known no variation or vacillation of opinion" (*Idea,* 3). Even in the *Essay on the*

31

Development of Doctrine, change is the means by which ideas or principles stabilize, develop, and become "perfect:" "Principles require a very various application according as persons and circumstances vary, and must be thrown into new shapes according to the form of society which they are to influence" (*Dev.,* 58). This continuity amidst change in Newman's thought is perhaps most evident in the subject of this chapter and the next, his "fascination with argument"[17] and epistemological matters. For the war he waged against religious and epistemological "liberalism" was, excepting some change of players, much the same in 1870 as in 1830, and his later campaign in the *Grammar* is but an extension and deepening of earlier intimations.

It is for this reason that we will be able to move easily in this chapter and the next between Newman's two major works on belief—the *Oxford University Sermons,* written between 1826 and 1843, and the *Grammar of Assent,* completed and published in 1870.[18] The question is what these two works in particular can tell us about the way Newman handled such mutually important principles as permanence and change, principles and circumstances, reason and faith, theory and practice, each of these pairs among others providing crucial "aspects," as he would say, of the whole of Newman's intellectual life.

By thus bringing the vocabulary, attitudes, and strategies of rhetoric to bear on Newman's theory of belief, we can elicit its intrinsically rational character in a way that will enable us to make sense of his practice of persuasion. The analysis begins with Newman's views on faith and reason in the *Oxford University Sermons,* since these views present in some ways the clearest theoretical formulation of his method. In principle this formulation should apply to all of Newman's own inquiries and should suggest what he is likely to emphasize in any given area of study. As we will see, these sermons are not sufficient for my purpose, so I turn in Chapter Three to the *Grammar* to complete important lines of thought.

Although the Oxford sermons are a somewhat heterogeneous group, eight of the fifteen are explicitly concerned with one complex theme, that of the "relation of faith to reason" (*OUS,* x).

Religion considered in itself, whether natural or revealed, Newman conceived as the knowledge of God and our duties towards Him. It is a *revelatio revelata,* comprising, first, a more or less clear and exalted system of doctrines and creeds expressing divine realities, and comprising, second, "a rule of duty" (*OUS,* 21). In keeping with this dual conception, Newman described religion considered in relation to the believer (in other words, religious faith),[19] as "an instrument of knowledge and action" (*OUS*, 179). For Newman, the mutual values of "knowing" and "acting" are as complex as they are pervasive (another formulation is "theory" and "practice"), requiring any adequate discussion of faith to account for divine objects as knowable, and for practical duties to be fulfilled in attitude and act. The principle of dogma (*Apo.*, 54) partly accounts for the first value, and faith as a "principle of action" (*OUS*, 177, 188)[20] for the second.

Religious faith can never be reduced to one value alone:[21] "Newman . . . found it impossible to accept either [the] evidential approach or the Evangelical alternative to the link between faith and reason."[22] To confine faith to knowledge gained by secular reason, for example, would be "too mechanical in presuming to convince all men of good will and open mind,"[23] and would lose faith as a principle of action. As mere sentiment or will, faith either sacrifices its claim to knowledge of the divine, or lacks rigor of thought and its normative force; as mere human virtue, it loses its divine sanction.[24]

Although Newman resists both types of reductionism in these sermons, he primarily opposes the so-called evidential school of Christian apologetic represented primarily by William Paley (1743–1805),[25] for whom allegedly scientific and logical criteria were the standard of truth, not only in the sciences but in religion. What precisely "scientific" and "logical" meant for Newman, and how the meanings of these terms changed, we will see. For now we can say that Newman's main target was those who were enamored with popular notions of scientific induction (*OUS*, 229) and with the syllogism in logic (*OUS*, 230, 258). In Newman's eyes it was just this reduction of faith to "secular" principles and impersonal procedures of reasoning that precipitated the religious crisis of his times and that bore the bad fruit of liberalism, whose "fundamental dogma is, that nothing can be known for certain about the unseen world" (*Idea*, 319).[26]

Though he included under the term liberalism the notion that "no theological doctrine is anything more but an opinion which happens to be held by bodies of men" (*Apo.*, 260), he chiefly employed it to indict the misuse of reason: "Now by Liberalism I mean false liberty of thought, or the exercise of thought upon matters, in which, from the constitution of the human mind, thought cannot be brought to any successful issue, and therefore is out of place. Among such matters are first principles of any kind. . . . Liberalism then is the mistake of subjecting to human judgment those . . . doctrines which are in their nature beyond and independent of it" (*Apo.*, 255–56).

It is well known that one of the chief stumbling blocks in reading Newman is what he meant on a given occasion by "thought" and "first principles," and especially "faith" and "reason." With regard to these last two in particular, if we are to grasp the relations between them it will make most sense to take up the terms as Newman himself does in these sermons and watch how he uses them, even at the cost of moving somewhat slowly at first. But we must also keep in mind our ultimate purpose: although we are interested in seeing how Newman formulated the reasonableness of religious faith specifically, religious faith is but one example, it is an application upon religious principles, of a mode of reasoning employed upon a great variety of subject matters and questions, and it is that method finally that we are after.

INDETERMINACY IN THE OXFORD UNIVERSITY SERMONS

As he proceeds in these sermons Newman gets more precise in his language, but on starting he characteristically makes use of the "popular sense" of the terms faith and reason. "Faith is the judging on weak grounds. . . . by Faith is meant a feeling or sentiment, by Reason an exercise in common sense; Faith is conversant with conjectures or presumptions, Reason with proofs" (*OUS*, x–xi). Later he specifies that reason strictly speaking is simply "a faculty of proceeding from things that are perceived to things which are not. . . . of gaining knowledge upon grounds given" (*OUS*, 206–7). Understood as an inference from grounds to a conclusion, faith too may be seen as an exercise of reason. But insofar as its grounds are insufficient or weak, faith is something contrasted to reason: ". . . [the] popular view is this—that Reason requires strong . . . and Faith is content with weaker evidence" (*OUS*, 185).

For religion, of course, the implications of this skepticism were devastating: since religion had little argumentatively to stand on, it could not, by holding fast to its presumptions and sentiments, make good its claims to truth. For this reason, such figures as Paley, Butler, Copleston, and Whately attempted to save religion, to "secure it from running . . . to seed, and becoming superstition or fanaticism" (*OUS*, 233), by grounding it in "processes of a logical or explicit character" (*OUS*, 233, n. 2) and in evidences of Christianity—"exercises of Reason in proof of its divinity, *explicit* and *a posteriori*" (*OUS*, 65, n. 2).[27]

The objections Newman brings in these sermons against this enlightenment account of the rationality of belief are chiefly these: it does not fit the facts of religious faith, or supply what religion requires in a believer; it does not square with Scripture; and it does not accord with how we come to what we call knowledge in daily life or in various disciplines, being a faulty theory raised upon unproved presumptions of its own, and abstractly imposed on matters to which it is not suited.[28] These objections are found mostly in sermons IV, X, XI and XIII, juxtaposed with a corresponding variety of arguments in favor of his own view of the matter. But to the objections we turn first.

Ultimately the farthest reaching of these objections is that the so-called proofs of religion are not as compelling as alleged: "There is no act on God's part, no truth of religion, to which a captious Reason may not find objections" (OUS, 55). More often the evidences are not actual proofs of Christianity but merely useful rebuttals to critics (OUS, 65). The reason for this inadequacy lies in the varying estimates men frequently give of the same facts: "From the sight of the same sky one may augur fine weather, another bad; from the signs of the times one the coming in of good, another evil . . ." (OUS, 209). Newman was familiar with the view that such variance in belief results from failures on the part of reasoners to reason well (OUS, 210); on this view it followed that what was needed was not the abandonment of evidences and logic but rather the increased intellectual sophistication of inquirers; this was, in fact, Whately's position in the Elements of Rhetoric.[29] But it was a position Newman regarded as simply mistaken: "In practical matters, when their minds are really roused . . . when their interest is concerned . . . men commonly are not bad reasoners." "[E]xperience of life contains abundant evidence" (OUS, 211) that this is so.

Newman's explanation of the varying estimates of the facts, and often of what the facts *are*, is rather that men approach them with "the constraining influence of their several principles" (OUS, 212); "so much lies in the character of the mind itself, in its general view of things, its estimate of the probable and the improbable, . . . its anticipation derived from its own inbred wishes . . ." (OUS, 218).

Not only do evidence and argument fail to demonstrate, they do not persuade in religious matters to the self-committing profession of faith, or to the dutiful acts and sacrifices one is required to make as a believer. Newman argues that (rhetorically) the evidences "have no warmth" (OUS, 200), are "useless for any practical purpose" (OUS, 197–98), and "do not answer to the needs of daily life" (OUS, 188). . . ."[30] Nor do they square with Scriptural accounts of faith: "What is here said [in the Gospels] about exercises of reason, in order to believing?" (OUS, 235).[31]

Such are Newman's objections to the popular view that faith depends for its truth on reason in its ratiocinated and evidentialist senses. As to his own view of the matter, I alluded above to the paired values of "knowing" and "acting," which constitute faith, and turn now to the foundation on which Newman establishes them, namely his conception of conscience.

With regard first to natural religion—viewed not theoretically but "in fact," in the "actual state of religious belief of pious men in the heathen world" (*OUS*, 18)—Newman postulates the following: "Now, in the first place, it is obvious that Conscience is the essential principle and sanction of Religion in the mind. Conscience implies a relation between the soul and a something exterior, . . . a difference in the nature of actions . . . and an obligation of acting in one particular way in preference to all others" (*OUS*, 18–19).[32]

Conscience brings no proof of its truth, it acts on its own authority, and adherence to it is of the nature of faith. Conscience is not only the sanction of moral truth in the mind, but the informant regarding divine realities and the basis of natural religion. In both respects, however, that of conduct and that of knowledge of God—natural religion is deficient. Although it provides for our deepest religious feelings, it does not fulfil the very desires it awakens; it does not present an "object" of veneration, a "personality," which would urge and illustrate virtue (*OUS*, 22), and would adjust and complete the many inconsistent pictures of God that the conscience engenders in different times and places (*OUS*, 24).

This deficiency, Newman argues, is remedied by revealed religion. Knowledge of God communicated by conscience is clarified and completed by Christ, the facts and actions of Whose life rhetorically "move the heart" (*OUS*, 27, 23). And it is conscience that is the chief means by which the multitude of men come to belief, for it puts them on the "look out," it predisposes them to expect, the revelation that will be its fulfillment: "One of the most important effects of Natural Religion on the mind, in preparation for Revealed, is the anticipation which it creates, that a Revelation will be given . . ." (*G.A.*, 272).

With the idea of conscience providing an "antecedent probability" for revelation we draw close to the core of Newman's thought, not only on the reasonableness of faith, but on the nature of reason generally, now reconstituted from common practice and accepted notions. We know that Newman rejected at least two senses of reason in reference to religion, explicit logical argument and factual "scientific" evidence. One sense of reason, however, he applied to faith, "the faculty of gaining knowledge upon grounds given." In support of his view that faith is a right exercise of reason, Newman offers various arguments, all of which are erected on the assumption that each division of thought has its own proper first principles (*OUS*, 54, n. 1). Although he nowhere specifies what he means by "principles," Sermon IV, "The Usurpations of Reason" (1831), offers sufficient clues to his meaning. There he combats that "aggressive reason" (*OUS*, 59, n. 7), whose principles he associates with objective and certifiable sense data, and the criteria of formal and explicit argument. Reason so conceived is thus "opposed as such to the moral qualities" (*OUS*, 58) and to the "spiritual discernment" (*OUS*, 55, n. 3) of the conscience. But religion too relies on its own principles, and on the evidences and arguments such principles help to generate—what Newman loosely terms the "moral feelings" (*OUS*, 195). Again, the most important of these is the conscience, which is responsible in turn for producing more specific propositions and views (antecedent probabilities and considerations), which may function also as first principles. In short, just as one may turn to conscience to establish the existence of God, so the proposition that there is a God, or the concomitant feelings of love and fear of Him, or the probable claim of a more determinate revelation, are among the first principles of revealed religion that the conscience can be said to reveal.[33]

Throughout the Oxford sermons, the most important argument supporting this view is that the use of antecedent considerations is in fact a widespread means of securing what we call knowledge in daily life and throughout the range of contingent matters: "This is the way in which judgments are commonly formed concerning facts alleged or reported in political and social matters, and for the same reason, because it cannot be helped" (*OUS*, 228).

It cannot be helped in the first place because the multitude has neither the time nor the talent for sifting and weighing conflicting facts and reports.[34] It cannot be helped in the second place because the nature of the subject matter of religion (and much else besides) is indeterminate, in the sense that purely theoretical investigation and logical deduction cannot force one to view matters of faith in a certain way.[35] This is far from saying that religion is indeterminable; we can arrive at truth. But the evaluation of what is at stake in such a question arises from principles not demonstratively or empirically certain, but which rest on persuasives, or which are simply used on their own authority and validated (or invalidated) in that use. Faith, then, is an intellectual act, but "Most men must and do decide by the principles of thought and conduct which are habitual to them; that is, the antecedent judgment, with which a man approaches the subject of religion, not only acts as a bearing this way or that . . . it practically colours the evidence, even in a case in which he has recourse to evidence, and interprets it for him" (*OUS,* 227). In religion, in daily life, in all subjects to a lesser or greater degree, "[M]en judge of [evidence] this way or that, according as they are credulous or not, or wish it to be true or not, or are influenced by such or such views of life, or have more or less knowledge on the subject . . ." (*OUS,* 228).

In short, most of what is called knowledge is grounded in personal and interpersonal choices or construals of what is the case, and justified by a wide range of appeals—feelings, values, shared facts and opinions, probabilities, presumptions, interpretations—what we may call "all available means of persuasion."

The strength of Newman's account of the reasonableness of faith lies in several directions. It accounts first of all for the popular conception of faith as a test of a man's "heart" (*OUS,* 226) and a measure of his Christian ethos. It accounts for the fact that children, and the busy, and the uneducated have what is called faith, for they often rely on grounds that they themselves cannot articulate and that cannot be proved according to more rigorous standards of truth but that nevertheless must be used (for there is nothing else), and that in any case often secure what is probable or true. Again, this account provides for the practical, actional dimension of religion, since the arguments it mobilizes are persuasives that move men to attitude, belief, and act: "A mutilated and defective evidence"—enspirited by antecedent probabilities and presumptions—"suffices for persuasion where the heart is alive" (*OUS,* 200).[36] Finally, this account parallels Scripture, where it is shown that "a certain moral state, and not evidence, is made the means of gaining the truth, and the beginning of spiritual perfection" (*OUS,* 237).

Faith, then, is and is not reasonable (*OUS,* 195, 223)—not reasonable if we mean in conformity with allegedly objective and strict proof, reasonable if we allow the fact that in much of our rational investigation we employ presumption and antecedent considerations admitting of no scientific standard. To be sure, Newman recognizes that such antecedent considerations are not necessarily true, but for now it is enough to note that genuine faith for Newman, influenced by antecedent judgments, is nevertheless "the presumption of a serious, sober, thoughtful, pure, affectionate and devout mind," safeguarded from error in part by "love" (*OUS,* 250), in part by Christian "wisdom" (Sermon XIV).

Newman does not deny that "external" evidence is normally necessary to the process of coming to faith, or to explicating it.[37] In our coming to faith, antecedent probabilities combine with evidence in an illuminating and not distortive way, as when, for example, our expectation of meeting a friend at the corner enables us a block away to make him out from signs that might seem vague to another. In explicating the faith, it is the task of theology to explicate the objective grounds of faith. Theology as a science is conducted by means of what Newman calls "explicit" reasoning, as distinct from that initial "implicit" thought that brings a believer to belief. Implicit reasoning is simply another term, then, for that reasoning upon presumption and antecedent probability that Newman feels is so common to all men in a wide variety of matters and that proceeds more or less unconsciously, "not by a rule, but by an inward faculty." The mind in its natural state "passes on from point to point, gaining one by some indication, another on a probability; then availing itself of an association; then falling back on some received law; next seizing on testimony; then committing itself to some popular impression, or some inward instinct . . ." (*OUS, 257*).[38]

By this means the mind arrives at judgment. Implicit reason is thus often hidden, subtle, complex, personal. Explicit reason is the reflection on and analysis of our implicit process with the aim of getting clearer about what we know and why. But here a problem arises. In implicit reasoning to faith, one uses grounds that are "vague and abstruse." In the explicit reason of theology, however, one is faced with trying to objectify and systematize to the satisfaction of "all rational minds" what is actually recondite, personal, and more or less particular to the believer. As a result, when theology reflects on faith, it rarely reaches the real grounds of religious belief: "The science of divinity is very imperfect and inaccurate" (*OUS, 266*). For this reason, Newman implicitly refuses to restrict at least this branch of theology (apologetics) in the way others have done, to those proofs erroneously forwarded as the means to faith and its justification. Rather, theology must concern itself with the *full* matter and evidence for faith: "By the Evidences of Religion I mean the systematic analysis of all the grounds on which we believe Christianity to be true. I say 'all,' because the word Evidence is often restricted . . ." (*OUS, 264*). Like "reason," theology is here also implicitly reconstituted, denied its status as an exact science in light of a more rhetorical account.[39]

In terms of persuasion, then, religion and theology can be said to be rhetorical in two interrelated ways: first, their content consists in the various kinds of persuasive appeals and arguments that the multitude of men implicitly use in coming to faith and that the theologian uses in articulating faith's rational grounds; second, the very possibility of coming to *any* view of what religion is depends for Newman on "something

assumed which is ultimately incapable of [rigorous] proof" (*OUS*, 213).[40]
For Newman that assumption is conscience and the related principles it
generates.

It may be objected here that Newman's discussion of religion and
theology in Sermon XIII ends with the view that any account of the
grounds for faith is virtually impossible. Far from being rhetorical, it
would seem, theology is portrayed as virtually tongue-tied or autistic. But
we must not forget Newman's own rhetorical purpose in this sermon. His
chief goal is to stress the complexity, variety, and subtlety of the true
grounds of faith, in order to counter the prevalent view that evidences are
exclusively a posteriori and logically valid. Thus he observes that no
"analysis is subtle and delicate enough to represent adequately the state of
mind under which we believe . . ." (*OUS*, 267). But this is not to say that
an analysis is impossible, or that it should be handed over to the evidentialist school by default. On the contrary, this is at least an implicit
argument in favor of rhetoric. A "painting" of the real reasons for faith
may never be more than a "very rude description of the living mind"
(*OUS*, 268); still it can "create an impression" (*OUS*, 276) by giving
"hints towards, and samples of, the true reasoning, and demand an active,
ready, candid, and docile mine, which can throw itself into what is said,
neglect verbal difficulties, and pursue and carry out principles. This is the
true office of a writer, to excite and direct trains of thought . . ." (*OUS*,
275).

If the true office of a writer is not to "compel" but to "move," and to
do so not mainly by means of objective evidence and strict logic but by
suggestion, probability, appeals to feelings, values, and beliefs, then we
have an indication at least of the argumentative method to be employed
upon those subject matters able to be viewed in the same light as religion
and theology.

It remains to be seen exactly what those subject matters are, although
we have had indications that they span the range of contingent affairs. In
this and other respects, the sermons are (for my purposes, not for Newman's) deficient: one cannot infer with any real assurance how far or into
what areas the method of reasoning and arguing by antecedent probabilities extends; one learns little, other than that antecedent considerations locate and interpret evidence, about what these considerations and
probabilities are and how they are to be found and used; and—what is
altogether slighted—one learns nothing about how inquiries get initiated
and problems get solved. In order to better approach these questions, we

need to know more about the nature and provenance of antecedent probability.

"THE IMPORTANCE OF ANTECEDENT PROBABILITY IN CONVICTION"

In general an antecedent probability for Newman is anything we conjecture likely to be—based upon experience, analogy, testimony, commonly accepted opinions, and the like.[41] Strictly speaking, the term applies to a "method of thought" (*OUS*, 258), that is, a *form of argument*. But this exact sense should not deflect us from the fact that Newman's use of the term is often loose and that it sometimes overlaps with, stands proxy for, and in general blends in with *all* of those "antecedent considerations" (*OUS*, 187) that influence an individual's assessment of a concrete case or claim. Thus Newman will refer to "those views, theories, principles, or whatever they are to be called" (*Prepos.*, 276–77), "previous notices, prepossessions, and (in a good sense of the word) prejudices" (*OUS*, 187), "that large outfit of existing thoughts, principles, likings, desires, and hopes, which make me what I am" (*G.A.*, 273), "antecedent views, presumptions, implications, associations and the like, many of which it is very difficult to detect and analyze" (*OUS*, 273). These more comprehensive antecedent considerations sometimes function as enabling dispositions or "states of mind" (*OUS*, 258), more or less complex and unconscious propositions of value, belief and the like, brought forth to illuminate a problem—similar to what Kenneth Burke calls an "orientation," "a bundle of judgments as to how things were, how they are, and how they may be," and what Thomas Kuhn calls a "paradigm;" and sometimes as more focused, consciously discursive "hypotheses" (*V.M.*, I, xx) or "views" employed to map out and organize a case, quite in the way that topics are used by the rhetor to open up possibilities.

In fact Newman explicitly adverts to the rhetorical provenance of antecedent probability in Sermon X (1839). There he compares it to the *eikos*, one of the central terms of Aristotle's *Rhetoric*, meaning the "probable," "that which is generally the case" (*Rhetoric* 1357a15). Newman writes: "Faith, then, as being a principle for the multitude and for conduct, is influenced more by what (in language familiar to us of this place [Oxford] are called εἰκότα [*eikota*] than by σήμεια [*semeia*],—less by evidence, more by previously entertained principles, views, and wishes" (*OUS*, 188).[42]

Elsewhere Aristotle calls the *eikos* a "generally accepted proposition

41

[*endoxon*[43]], something known to happen, or to be, for the most part thus and thus; e.g. 'the envious hate,' 'loved ones show affection' " (*Prior Analytics* 70a3). It refers to what is understood by a particular audience to be objectively (or intersubjectively) probable, in the *qualitative* sense that it depends upon their common sense and experience.[44] Aristotle's lists of special topics in Book I of the *Rhetoric*—propositions regarding happiness, undisputed and disputed goods, virtues and vices, criminal motivation, and so on—are *eikota* that can function as major premises of enthymemes. They are generated by or at least referable to topics understood in another sense, as larger subject-matter areas, ideas, or categories—what Newman called "views"—often structured as pairs of terms ("war/peace," "more/less," "imports/exports," "accusation/defence") to cover both sides of a contingent case.

In his "First Tetralogy" (fifth century B.C.), for example, the rhetorician Antiphon observed that, in detecting and exposing crafty criminals, "you must place implicit confidence in any and every indication from probability *(eikos)* presented to you,"[45] and he proceeds to argue a legal case from antecedent probabilities in this way:

> Malefactors are not likely to have murdered him [the victim], as nobody who was exposing his life to a very grave risk would forego the prize when it was securely within his grasp; and the victims were found still wearing their cloaks. Nor again did anyone in liquor kill him: the murderer's identity would be known to his boon-companions. Nor again was his death the result of a quarrel; they would not have been quarrelling at the dead of night or in a deserted spot. Nor did the criminal strike the dead man when intending to strike someone else; he would not in that case have killed master and slave together.[46]

In the second speech against Catiline, Cicero impugns the defendant's character thus: "[T]here is no one in the gladiatorial school a little too eager for crime who does not claim Catiline for his intimate friend; there is no one on the stage rather trivial or a bit inclined to vice who does not claim that he was almost his boon companion."[47]

Perhaps the best known of Newman's arguments from antecedent probability, alluded to in many of his works, is the antecedent probability that a revelation has been or will be given by God.[48] As a faculty of mind, conscience generates the nexus of values, feelings, anticipations, fears, and the like that locate, select, and "colour" (*OUS*, 227) evidence; evidence that otherwise "to the world [would seem] like nothing . . . were it not for [this] bias of the mind" (*OUS*, 191):

42

One of the most important effects of Natural Religion on the mind, in preparation for Revealed, is the anticipation which it creates, that a Revelation will be given. That earnest desire of it, which religious minds cherish, leads the way to the expectation of it. Those who know nothing of the wounds of the soul, are not led to deal with the question, or to consider its circumstances; but when our attention is roused, then the more steadily we dwell upon it, the more probable does it seem that a revelation has been or will be given to us. This presentiment is founded on our sense, on the one hand, of the infinite goodness of God, and, on the other, of our own extreme misery and need—two doctrines which are the primary constituents of Natural Religion. It is difficult to put a limit to the legitimate force of this antecedent probability. Some minds will feel it to be so powerful, as to recognize in it almost a proof . . . (G.A., 272).

At times arguments from antecedent probability can be so strong that "very little positive evidence seems to be necessary when the mind is penetrated by the strong anticipation which I am supposing" (G.A., 272); "We do not call for evidence until antecedent probabilities fail" (OUS, 189). In this particular case the antecedent probability that a revelation is likely would combine with, for example, miracles, Scripture prophecy, and tradition to constitute further arguments.

Newman never specified the logical status of the argument that combines antecedent probability with evidence; perhaps it is most plausible to construe it as an induction to a particular.[49] More interesting for our purposes here is its irreducibility to scientific measurement. This can be seen clearly when we inquire how such an antecedent probability is itself derived. The argument would seem to be as follows. Major premise: A loving, hidden God is likely to answer a natural desire to know Him. (We are reminded here of Aristotle's common topic in the Rhetoric, "Things which we love or desire naturally are possible" [1392a].) Minor premise: we have such a desire. Ergo, a (further) revelation is likely.[50] The force of this argument obviously turns on the degree of probability we are willing to award the major premise: the more probable it is, the more probable the conclusion; and the more probable the conclusion, the more probable the ultimate claim that a revelation indeed has been given. As is the case with topoi, the antecedent probability is not quantifiable. The belief it produces is rather "created in the mind, not so much by facts, as by probabilities; and since probabilities have no definite ascertained value, and are reducible to no scientific standard, what are such to each individual, depends on his moral temperament" (OUS, 191).[51]

At least implicitly, then, Newman seems to have in mind in these sermons topics not only as *eikota* (probable propositions within an enthymeme), but as general dialectical categories ("principles," "prejudices," "antecedent views"), postulated as likely areas of concern to stimulate inquiry and interpretation. As dialectical pairs[52] these views function as did the *dissoi logoi* of Protagoras—two *logoi* (categories or propositions), each true in the abstract, placed in opposition in order (as one critic has phrased it) to "kindle the intelligence of the speaker and then of the audience." [K]indling intelligence," it is added, "is different from discovering a way of persuading an audience,"[53] an important observation that will help us later to distinguish Newman's indirect rhetoric from more direct forms of persuasion. These companion notions of antecedent probabilities and of views as *dissoi logoi,* are simply fundamental to Newman: "If I have brought out one truth in any thing I have written, I consider it to be the *importance of antecedent probability* in conviction. It is how you convert factory girls as well as philosophers" (*L.D.,* XV, 381). Or again, said otherwise: "It is difficult for me to take a step without what I should call *a view*" (*L.D.,* XIX, 26).[54]

Others have noted that the immediate source for Newman's conception of antecedent probability is Whately's *Elements of Rhetoric.*[55] Like Newman, Whately traces this type of argument to the *eikos* in Aristotle.[56] For Whately there were two types of argument, "cause" (also known as "a priori" and "antecedent" probability) and "sign." The latter is described as an "argument from an *Effect* to a *Condition;*" the former as an argument employed "to account for [a] fact or principle, supposing its truth granted." Whately gives this example: a murder is imputed to a man on the basis of his having a hatred for and interest in the death of the deceased. Although here the minor premise is the "cause" or antecedent probability, elsewhere Whately specifies the major as the *eikos.*[57] In order to grasp how Newman understood the concept, it is useful to draw two distinctions, the first aligning Newman with Whately against Aristotle, the second (and more important) showing how Newman draws on Aristotle to counter Whately's rationalism.

Whately and Newman share, first of all, a considerably more individualistic and subjective sense of probability than Aristotle possessed. Ray McKerrow has shown that for Whately a concept such as "contingency" referred, not to events (as it did for Aristotle), but to an individual's knowledge of the event.[58] "Probability is not an objective quality of things but a subjective assessment by agents, quite as it is in Hume.[59]

For Newman, similarly, although probability is often used to refer to the modal status of propositions, it is otherwise employed to designate an individual's personal estimate of a belief. "It is commonly and truly said, that Faith is a test of a man's heart. Now, what does this really mean, but that it shows what he thinks likely to be?—and what he thinks likely, depends surely on nothing else than the general state of mind, the state of his convictions, feelings, tastes, and wishes" (*OUS*, 226). Not so in Aristotle: "Rhetoric will not consider what seems probable in each individual case, for instance to Socrates or Hippias, but that which seems probable to this or that class of persons" (*Rhetoric*, 1357a).[60]

On the matter specifically of the *truth* of probable claims, secondly, Whately is a committed empiricist for whom observation and experiment (so far as these can be systematized) are the basis of belief.[61] In many of his writings, Whately is at pains to expose the dangers of "party feeling" and "party-spirit," of prejudice and "passion,"[62] which, however acceptable as goads to action, distort the purer search for knowledge. For truth one requires "an unbiassed state of mind,"[63] "impartially weighing the evidence,"[64] "accuracy in the logical processes."[65]

Whately's position in this regard is perhaps more understandable when we recall that he considered himself obliged to fight those "who deprecate the christian-evidences altogether,"[66] that is, those who saw no possibility of grounding religion in *any* sense of reason; he wished to supply the deficiency of such reasons against enlightenment attacks on the faith. Although religiously opposed to a David Hume or John Toland (1670–1772), Whately nevertheless stands squarely in the tradition of Locke and Hume and the struggle against innate ideas, "enthusiasm," realist "universals," and rhetorical "topics."[67] Students of rhetoric are well aware that it is this orientation that is responsible for the progressive degeneracy of rhetorical thought in the nineteenth century. Having been robbed by centuries of strip-mining for its wealth of *inventio,* rhetoric here stands empty as an independent intellectual discipline, wholly inferior to logic and "science," an easy target for the condescension and abuse I. A. Richards heaps upon it in *The Philosophy of Rhetoric.*[68]

Yet students of rhetoric may finally see too much in this swerve from classical rhetorical thought.[69] In a limited way, at least, Whately recognized the importance and pervasiveness—if only fitfully the complexity— of antecedent probability as an interpretive device, when he admitted the influence of our moral sense on the evaluation of evidence for religion.[70] For this reason, and almost in spite of himself, Whately recalled the Aristotelian sense of the *eikos* and dimly anticipated the epistemic function of rhetorical argument in Newman and others to come.

The preceding sketch of antecedent probabilities and considerations gives rise to questions about their source, their nature and function as instruments of discovery and proof, and particularly their truth-status. On this last point, Newman himself argues in Sermon Twelve: "Antecedent probabilities may be equally available for what is true, and what pretends to be true. . . . They seem to supply no intelligible rule what is to be believed, and what not" (OUS, 232); and later, ". . . the φρόνησις [phronesis] may be easily biassed by our wishes, by our will" (Ward, II, 249). This situation is exacerbated by the fact that no scientific rule exists to adjudicate among competing probabilities, and that "It is almost a proverb, that persons believe what they wish to be true" (OUS, 189).[71] Granting this, what then distinguishes a true antecedent probability from a false one? We cannot retreat to the premises underlying such probabilities, since the question merely recurs: which of these premises are true, and which false? To avoid an infinite regress and in order to enable judgment, some ground must be available, some set of first premises or principles.[72] What are these first principles?

FIRST PRINCIPLES AS TYRANTS OR GUIDES

Part of the difficulty of answering this question lies in the amount of verbal untangling one is forced to do of what Newman said first principles were, and in comparing what he said with how he used them. Newman was neither systematic nor unequivocal in his definitions, having always addressed the question somewhat ad hoc and from different aspects; this is evident in the way his discussion in the Oxford sermons of antecedent probabilities and considerations cuts across and overlaps on his talk a decade later, in *The Present Position of Catholics* (1851), of *two* sorts of "prejudice" and the way they differ from "first principles." In these latter lectures one sort of prejudice, called "presumption," is equivalent to antecedent probability and is distinct from a first principle. In the *Grammar* two decades later, however, a "first principle" is called a "presumption," and makes up one of various types of "notional assent," among which are "credences" that look suspiciously like antecedent probabilities, antecedent considerations, and presumptions-as-prejudices. Others before me have sifted this confusion in order to highlight one aspect or another of this issue of first principles,[73] but there remain, I believe, two aspects that have not been sufficiently appreciated—the historical relativity of some "first principles," and the nonrelativistic ontology that stabilizes and controls them. A word is in order to indicate what is at stake here.

Newman considered some first principles "beyond proof," as John

Holloway has observed,[74] but without further explanation and qualification than this, such a "truth" implies either arbitrariness or dogmatism. A fuller grasp of rhetoric, and what Newman says and does, suggests that this is a one-sided view. By drawing several distinctions here regarding first principles, and by developing the argument in the next chapter, we can make at least a strong prima facie case for Newman's position. We need to consider three different discussions, those of the Oxford sermons, *The Present Position of Catholics,* and the *Grammar of Assent.*

In the Oxford sermons, Newman does no more than point towards the principles that underlie antecedent probabilities, prejudices, presumptions, and prepossessions:

> [H]owever precise our producible grounds may be, however systematic our method, however clear and tangible our evidence, yet when our argument is traced down to its simple elements, there must ever be something assumed ultimately which is incapable of proof, and without which our conclusion will be as illogical as Faith is apt to seem to men of the world (*OUS*, 213).

But in these sermons Newman makes no move to specify what these elements are or how they relate to antecedent probabilities. First principles, we learn in the *Grammar,* are,

> the recondite sources of all knowledge, as to which logic provides no common measure of minds,—which are accepted by some, rejected by others,—in which, and not in the syllogistic exhibitions, lies the whole problem of attaining to truth,—and which are called self-evident by their respective advocates because they are evident in no other way (*G.A.*, 175).[75]

In *The Present Position of Catholics,* a series of polemical lectures attacking Anglican bigotry towards Catholics, Newman *contrasts* "prejudice" with "first principles." The former is properly a "pre-judgment," "a judgment which is formed prior to the particular question submitted to us, yet is made to bear upon it" (*Prepos.*, 227).[76] It is "not more than an opinion or inference" (*Prepos.*, 228) which "[r]ests on argumentative grounds" (*Prepos.*, 277). Actually there are two types of prejudice: those that are held dogmatically, as if they were infallible and as if counterarguments were impossible—prejudice "in its bad and culpable sense, the sense in which the word is commonly used" (*Prepos.*, 228–229); and those that are held critically, open to confirmation or refutation, which Newman calls "presumptions" (*Prepos.*, 277). Presumptions are among those prejudices that Gadamer seeks to rehabilitate when he discusses "prejugés legitimes" as the "condition of understanding" and the substance of "tradition;"[77] what Polanyi says constitute the authority of community;[78] and what Newman had sometimes called antecedent probabilities. They are "just" or fair prejudices because they are probable, and probable because they rest on previously accepted grounds.

First principles, on the other hand, are "opinions and beliefs which do not depend on previous grounds, which are not drawn from facts for which no reasons can be given, or no sufficient reasons, which proceed immediately from the mind . . ." (Prepos., 278). Newman gives several examples: "It is a First Principle that man is a social being; a First Principle that he may defend himself; a First Principle that he is responsible; a First Principle that he is frail and imperfect; a First Principle that reason must rule passion" (Prepos., 280–81). Like antecedent probabilities or prejudices, first principles "are not necessarily true," although there are "ways of unlearning them" (Prepos., 279), and indeed it is our duty to do so when they are false.

In the Grammar of Assent Newman picks up many of his earlier points. Here first principles, now called "presumptions," are one of five types of "notional assent," or assent to abstractions apart from consideration of the facts from which they were drawn: "By first principles I mean the proposition with which we start in reasoning on any given subject-matter" (G.A., 45). Newman proceeds to record several examples—for instance, the universal proposition "that there is an external world" abstracted by induction from "our ever-recurring experiences" of individual sense of phenomena (G.A., 47). Or again, we conclude and assent to the abstract proposition that God exists "by means of that induction from particular experiences of conscience" (G.A., 47). Our knowledge of right and wrong, true and false, the beautiful and the ugly, and causation (G.A., 48–53), all are first principles. Moreover, all are inferences, a fact that confuses matters, inasmuch as Newman had claimed earlier, in The Present Position, that first principles "proceed immediately from the mind," that is, they had no grounds and thus were not inferences. Now we learn that they do have grounds, since they are "in themselves . . . abstractions from facts, not elementary truths prior to reasoning" (G.A., 49). This is made doubly perplexing when we recall that, four pages earlier, Newman had termed first principles propositions "with which we start in reasoning on any given subject-matter" (G.A., 45, emphasis added). If we start with them it is difficult to see how they themselves could have previous grounds.

Recently M. Jamie Ferreira has persuasively argued that for Newman first principles, as inductive inferences, may nevertheless rightly be said to be "ungrounded," in the sense that the premises on which they depend are no better known than the principles themselves.[79] In a strict sense, then, first principles are not "elementary truths prior to reasoning," since it is the phenomena from which they are abstracted that constitute those elementary and irreducible facts. On the other hand, first principles *are* propositions with which we start in reasoning *on any given subject matter*. They are themselves reasoned to from sense data, but they support all higher-level reasoning above this "instinctive" (*G.A.*, 47) level.

From the preceding it is possible to venture four distinctions that will aid us in settling the nature and source of first principles, in showing how antecedent probabilities function as first principles, and in determining the truth-status of both.

Strict and Loose First Principles. First, beyond the obscurity that Newman's unsystematic method engenders, it is possible to distinguish a stricter from a looser sense of first principles. In each of the more systematic discussions cited above, Newman is interested in first principles *strictly speaking*—in that which is *ungrounded* in the sense specified, and behind which it is not possible to locate premises better known than the first principles themselves. Elsewhere, however, and far more frequently, Newman speaks of (or uses) "first principles" in a much looser, more analogical way.[80] In this looser sense even antecedent probabilities and prejudices can function as first principles. This is significant, since it means that antecedent probabilities, though strictly speaking grounded in previous premises, can be used to *constitute* and *explore* a problem, in addition to aiding in the interpretation of evidence and the prosecution of argument. "First principles," in other words, does not necessarily signify metaphysical elements discovered by the noetic faculty, but may include wholly contingent conclusions *selected* by the prudential faculty—what Newman later called the illative sense. In point of fact, Newman often used antecedent probabilities as first principles and designated them as such. In *The Present Position* the prejudice (in the negative sense) of a prejudiced man is called a first principle (*Prepos.*, 237); "prejudice thinks its first principles self-evident" (*Prepos.*, 313–14). In *The Idea of a University* (1852) "memory" and "reason"—both highly indeterminate concepts, not specific propositions—are the "first principles" of a liberal education and of philosophy (*Idea*, 117), just as "liberal" and "useful," "secular" and "sacred," and numerous other pairs function as the first principles of Newman's own inquiry. In the Oxford sermons, the antecedent probability of a revelation is a first principle of religion (*OUS*, 55, n. 3), and "benevolence" a first principle of God's governance (*OUS*, 105). In the *Apologia* "dogma," "tradition," and "anti-Romanism" are the first principles of Newman's religion. In the *Grammar*, the concepts of "real" and "notional," "informal" and "formal" are among Newman's first principles of apprehending, inferring, and assenting. These and similar pairs can be thought of as antecedent considerations and probabilities postulated as plausible first principles of thought.

The point here is that we need to recognize that prejudices, antecedent probabilities, antecedent considerations, and so on play fundamental roles in constituting inquiry; that at times antecedent probabilities and considerations are simply postulated, and rest, for all intents and purposes, on nothing other than themselves; and that they are drawn forth out of practical experience to function as grounds of proof as well as means of discovery. This recognition helps us to avoid the erroneous belief that Newman's primary interest is in first principles strictly speaking. It is more accurate to say that, whereas Newman wished at times to trace premises down to their fundamental source, his stronger interest was practical, and thus that "first principles" in its much looser sense is in many ways his greatest concern of all (as it is also in *The Idea of a University*). He wished to find and use what was at hand, particularly the personal, popular, and practical, in order to ground inquiry in truth that made a difference. This last point can be clarified by a further distinction.

Determinate and Indeterminate First Principles. Newman is usually ready to acknowledge, sincerely if without much enthusiasm, that "all sciences, except the science of religion, have their certainty in themselves; as far as they are sciences, they consist of necessary conclusions from undeniable premises, or of phenomena manipulated into general truths by an irresistible induction" (*Letter,* 132).[81]

Now in fact Newman's attitude towards science is far more nuanced than this excerpt suggests. Nevertheless, what is significant here is that Newman recognized that some first principles, especially those in the natural sciences, could be not only universal, but fixed and determinate concepts. As he says in the *Grammar,* "Science in all its departments has too much simplicity and exactness, from the nature of the case, to be the measure of fact" (*G.A.,* 185). In its abstraction from fact, science of any type ("logic" is his exemplar) aspires to a one-to-one correspondence between word and thing, and thought and word. Its excellence is that of the symbolic calculus (*G.A.,* 173), and its goal is self-enclosed systematization. This, again, is not Newman's full view of science, but one formulation of *its own* self-understanding in his time. As such, it allows us to recognize the radical indeterminacy and contingency of *his own* first principles. In the *Idea,* for example, "memory" and "reason" are not determinate but ambiguous concepts that open out onto what Newman construes as the actual contingency and indeterminacy of thinking and remembering in specific inquiries. Because those instances change as purposes and subject matters change, no fixed and dogmatic account of these principles can adequately serve the range of such contingencies. What are required are concepts and propositions that will change as the facts change, without collapsing into sheer equivocalness.

Universal and Particular First Principles. A related, equally powerful distinction is that between universal and particular first principles. While some principles, such as causality or right and wrong, are received by all, the rest, by far the majority, are "local" in some sense. They may be strictly personal, in which case they may possess little or no authority, or be specific to a locality, class, society, or culture, at one time and not another. Many of the notional assents that Newman calls "credences" in the *Grammar* could function as such relative first principles. Credences are those myriad opinions, views, values, beliefs, and the like by which the rhetor (or hermeneut) is "always already" possessed. Family, schooling, friends and associates, our large social and cultural institutions, all are bearers of these fundamental commitments, commitments that we take on as our various horizons of understanding: "[E]very one must use such opinions as he has; there is nothing else to be done" (*Prepos.,* 289). One of the clearest examples of these particular, relative first principles is Newman's thought on the development of Christian doctrine, and of ideas generally, that we can use to help summarize this line of thought.

In the Fifteenth Oxford sermon, and again two years later in the *Essay on the Development of Christian Doctrine,* Newman ventures the hypothesis (itself constructed upon two relative first principles, "corruption" and "development"[82]) that the history of Christian doctrine and indeed of all concrete ideas was one of mediation and interpretation, of seeing the real out of "not-innocent" eyes:

> [A]n idea not only modifies, but is modified, or at least influenced, by the state of things in which it is carried out, and is dependent in various ways on the circumstances which surround it. . . . it may be coloured by the received tone of thought into which it comes, or depraved by the intrusion of foreign principles, or at length shattered by the development of some original fault within (*Dev.,* 39).

This view concurs with the notion of rhetorical theology touched upon earlier. Although it would be extreme, Newman concedes, to urge that

51

Christian doctrine admits of no scientific treatment and systematization at all (*OUS*, 327–29), nevertheless the progress towards dogmatic definition starts with objects that "have a character of their own" (*OUS*, 329), distinct from those of the sciences—objects that "force on us a persuasion:" "One proposition necessarily leads to another, and a second to a third; then some limitation is required; and the combination of these opposites occasions some fresh evolutions from the original idea, which indeed can never be said to be entirely exhausted" (*OUS*, 329). In what does this dialectical-rhetorical movement consist?

As Newman describes it in the *Essay* on development, men bring to bear on the *depositum* of faith the range of their antecedent considerations. Since doctrine is historical, moreover, the historical attempt to articulate that history is itself interpretive. Both history itself, and historical inquiry, are thus *perspectival* processes of persuasive inquiry and argument. As Newman says, we always see an idea from a certain "aspect." As Philip Wheelwright has put it, "To think or speak about reality is always to do so through one perspective rather than another, and to compare one perspective with another must involve the adoption of a third perspective which will be only partly pervious to them both. Thus reality as a whole cannot be typed, for to type it is to limit it to an arbitrarily chosen perspective."[83]

Such perspectivism has many implications, among which two are pertinent. First, all knowing or understanding is at the same time a disclosure and a concealment. When Newman himself speaks of employing "all available means of arriving at a right judgment on the matter in question" (*Letter*, 136), the "all" refers to the selections one's perspective allows or encourages. But this is as it should be: a perspective or "aspect" ("view") does not exhaust its object, and one can only try to be comprehensive within it by running (in Vico's words) "through the complete set of the *loci* which schematize the evidence."[84] Newman explores the matter of the articulation of doctrine by the Church in terms of a "*conspiratio*" between hierarchy and laity: "[T]he two, the Church teaching and the Church taught, are put together, as one two fold testimony, illustrating each other, and never to be divided" (*On Con*, 71).

Disclosure/concealment and particular/universal are themselves useful dialectical principles for constituting perspectives on Newman. With regard to this latter pair, various combinations have been suggested: that Newman was "torn" between the two sides; or, on the contrary, that he embraced a dogmatic absolutism of permanent universal principles; or again that he was a relativist. A fourth view, generally overlooked, is that it is precisely Newman's achievement to have exploited such tensions as mutual correctives and controls: truth is neither fixed nor determinate *simpliciter,* but emerges from conflict "with how many swayings to the right and to the left" (*OUS,* 317).

We might now tentatively summarize our findings. "First principles" is an analogical concept ranging from irreducible ungroundable inferences to any concept or proposition that is logically first in an inquiry. First principles may be universal, but are more often relative to people, times, and places. As such they are more or less indeterminate, because employed to be adequate to a historical and changing reality.

True and False First Principles. We must now ask: can first principles be true or false, or are they the result of blind will to power, or an arbitrary imposition of preference? Perhaps they are the prize of conscience, that "privileged access to truth" wielded by Newman (some allege) as an *obscuram per obscurius.* My intention is not to clinch the matter here, but merely to suggest that Newman neither absolutized nor relativized first principles.

In *The Present Position of Catholics* Newman designates first principles as "guides and standards," in full recognition of the fact that they might lead astray:

> They are the means of proof, and not themselves proved; they rule and are not ruled; they are sovereign on the one hand, irresponsible on the other: they are absolute monarchs, and if they are true, they act like the best and wisest of fathers to us: but, if they are false, they are the most cruel and baneful of tyrants. . . . They are our guides and standards in speculating, reasoning, judging, deliberating, deciding, and acting (*Prepos.,* 283).

Several things should strike us here: first, first principles, as guides and standards, are not strict rules or scientific concepts; second, the *use* of such guides and standards is not a matter of strict rule; and third, if first principles can be true or false there must be some way of recognizing this fact. Here it will suffice to say that in every major discussion Newman undertook he had one eye on the *criteria of adequacy*—the "clues," marks, and signs—by which one arrives at truth in the concrete.

At the very least there is a strong prima facie case that Newman worked out a central role in his thinking for the truth-status of first principles and the system of thought to which they give rise. In spite of verbal confusions and changes of expression, and in spite of the lack of systematic or unified expression, Newman suggested a coherent, and perhaps defensible, account of the basis, methods, and discipline of inquiry, argument and interpretation.

THEORY/PRACTICE

It should be evident that Newman's epistemology is thoroughly interpretive, predicated on the indeterminacy of the concrete and the mediatorial role of mind and language. As such it was a scandal, more or less, for those not yet habituated by romanticism to the importance of "imagination" and "self," which in the decade of the thirties was virtually everybody. At the same time it should be growing clearer that, for all of the affinities that Newman himself remarked between himself and Coleridge, for example, his own position is quite distinct from the intellectual methods of the romanticists. When Carlyle writes, "To *know;* to get into the truth of anything, is ever a mystic act—of which the best Logics can but babble on the surface"—we may be tempted to identify his attitude with that of Newman. But the "mystic act" that Carlyle intended meant not only a subtle and rapid activity with which logic was unable to keep up—Newman too saw the mind as incalculably rapid, subtle, mysterious—Carlyle meant not only this, but an intuitive, *non-inferential* act, an insight into immutable, eternal verities beyond all sense and all empirical reality. In short, Carlyle had in mind what Newman expressly rejected—a faculty of mind sui generis, distinct from the mundane inferential activities that only the lowest of thinkers, the logicians and rhetoricians, practiced, for lack of ability equal to those greater, the poets and the "orators." This Platonizing simply cannot be found in Newman. Intellect is not a mystical faculty, "Reason" opposed to "Understanding," but an integrated ability to infer universal truths, among other truths, much in the way that we infer that it's raining—by attending to a shifting, historical, concrete reality from the perspective that we happen to inhabit.

To be sure, we have not yet seen on what basis Newman constructs this epistemology, nor how he ultimately justifies his conceptions of explicit and implicit (later formal and informal) inference. We have, however, laid the foundation for understanding that in Newman's view "knowing" is a function at least in part of "acting" or "doing." The chief message of the sermons we have considered, after all, is that any theory of "reasoning" or "believing" (or any other theory for that matter) will be adequate to the "facts" it purports to describe only if it is grounded in those facts, is faithful to the practice of (in this case) men and women as they go about reasoning and believing.

Taking our cue from Newman, whose stress on interpretation and praxis is widely shared in modern philosophy and rhetoric, we need to see how he puts theory into practice by testing this theory against his actual practice of reasoning in the Oxford sermons: how does Newman himself reason, and how does this relate to what he *said* about reasoning, and in particular about arguing by antecedent probability? Does Newman argue in this way, and if so, what does it allow him to do? How does he engage his own audience in what he is doing? These are not arbitrary questions, but spring from the very heart of Newman's theory. When applied to Newman himself, they require that we seek his meaning in his *activity*, in his practice of meaning and knowing, for only here are we fully in touch with the "concrete fact." How, then, does Newman acquit himself? Is his claim to reasonableness reasonable, or is it rather a disguised religious dogmatism and sleight-of-hand persuasion?

We can begin to answer these questions by considering briefly three different discussions from the sermons—Newman's reasoning about "reason," his reasoning about religion, specifically the question of Divine Justice in Sermon Six, and his reasoning about antecedent probabilities and their control by "love." These topics provide us with a comprehensiveness—a range from secular to sacred—but more importantly they allow us to ask whether or not the kinds of attitudes and claims Newman defends regarding reason are carried over into his discussion about the substance of religion. Is Newman's an open and intellectual vision of reason, or a dark and dogmatic one? Is he arbitrary, mystical, subjective? Is he equal to the "unreal" theorizing of the evidentialists whom he wishes to challenge? How can he dislodge them without being equally "unreal?"

MODES OF REASONING

We saw that Newman attempted to supplement in several ways the view as to the nature of reasoning held by men such as Paley and Whately, and later Mill, Spencer, Clifford, Comte, and others. Newman had attributed to the evidentialist school the characterization of reason as (1) explicit, (2) a posteriori, and (3) based on secular assumptions (*OUS*, 88, n. 7), a view generated by the Enlightenment stress on universal reason and the Baconian strain of British empiricism, and promulgated as the ideal of rationality by those enamored of its seeming certainty. But it was Newman's argument that such a characterization flounders on at least two insurmountable difficulties. First, it was vulnerable to the reductio ad absurdum: much of what men call knowledge, and are unwilling to call anything else, would in fact be as unreasonable as faith is alleged to be were it measured against more rigorous criteria. The method of reasoning by antecedent probabilities and considerations "is the way in which judgments are commonly formed concerning facts alleged or reported in political and social matters . . ." (*OUS*, 228). Second, the demand for explicit and demonstrative proof at every stage of inquiry is not fulfilled even in those sciences set forth as paradigms of rationality. The notion, for example, that "there are things existing external to ourselves" (*G.A.*, 46), which of course Newman has no wish to deny, is nevertheless only assumed and not proved in the sciences (*OUS*, 213), as is the principle of causality or the trustworthiness of our memories. Farther-reaching in its effects is the assumption of the existence of efficient but not final causes. Admittedly, "in theory" the sciences must be said not to deny but only to suspend the issue of final causes; "in practice," however, "reasoning" is widely assumed to involve *only* "secularist" assumptions, namely those based on an efficient and not a final cause. Hume's argument against miracles, or Gibbon's attack on Christianity, are cases in point. This was, of course, precisely Newman's objection to the evidentialists, who were thus tolerant in theory, dogmatic in fact. Assumptions there must be; but to tilt against religion for failing to provide "proof" is to prove too much, and inadvertently to run through the scientific model as well.

It is interesting that Newman's key term in this discussion is "reason" and not "faith," for it gives a hint as to his method. Using the position of his opponents as argumentative reference points from which he is driven to account for "all" of the facts and "circumstances" of the case, Newman can be seen to construct four related "ranges," as it were, of facts and reasons, that need to be included in any concrete account of reason. For Newman, "reason" is

(1) *explicit,* but also *implicit;*
(2) built on *"external"* and *a posteriori,* but also on *internal* and *a priori,* facts and reason;
(3) based on *secular,* but also on *sacred,* assumptions (e.g., God as a final cause); and
(4) concerned with *determinate* system, order, and method, but also with *indeterminate* "genius" and similar personal abilities and dispositions of inquirers.

This is not to say, of course, that every instance of reasoning will include equally, or even include at all, the characteristics of each of the pairs. On the contrary, the characteristics of each pair oppose each other; and Newman clearly allows the legitimacy of what we might call Reason$_1$

in cases suited to it—namely any abstract or determinate problem that admits of explicit logical or "scientific" formulation.

But Newman adds to Reason$_1$ a Reason$_2$, a species of "reason" that itself can make selected use of explicit forms and external evidence, but which *features* the use of antecedent considerations of a nonscientific kind, to be employed on problems not admitting scientific and strictly logical calculation. Schematically, then, Newman reconstitutes "reason" this way:

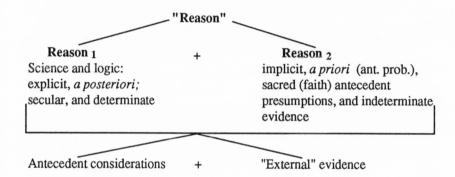

The diagram has the virtue of helping us to see that Newman approached the problem of "reason" (and a fortiori that of "faith") as one that was itself indeterminate and that his two conceptions of reason function for him as antecedent considerations—"first principles" that enable him to structure and explore the issue. If these are his principles, moreover, his "evidence" resides in the various references to and arguments he makes with the facts (as he sees them) of experience: other subjects and problems are resolved in this persuasive way; faith should be expected to be reasonable; introspection reveals that we reason in this way; science itself relies on persuasion regarding fundamental principles; Christian doctrine can be seen to develop according to persuasive appeal over time; the Bible speaks of faith in this way.

In other words, Newman supposes that the question of reason is indeterminate, avails himself of nondemonstrative antecedent principles to structure his inquiry, and appeals to a diverse set of facts and persuasive arguments (for example, that religious truths and facts can count as proofs) to build a cumulative case. But note that his establishment of Reason$_2$ is prima facie at best. We might venture the generalization that, in most of his works, it was the principles themselves Newman wished to focus on, not their argumentative justification or their systematic elaboration beyond a necessary minimum.

DIVINE JUSTICE, AND THE SAFEGUARD OF LOVE

This last point can be made clearer by our adverting to Newman's discussion in Sermon Six, "On Justice, as a Principle of Divine Governance." Here Newman challenges the too-sanguine view that the Bible is simply "a message of peace." "It cannot be denied," Newman concedes, "that . . . the information of Scripture results in a cheerful view of human affairs, and condemns gloom and sadness as a sin, as well as a mistake" (*OUS*, 100). But this is a view, true as far as it goes, that is nevertheless the result of a limited experience of the world, born of "times of political peace and safety, when the world keeps well together, no motions stirring beneath it to disturb the continuity of its surface . . ." (*OUS*, 102). In the context of emerging Victorian optimism and its gospel of material and social progress, Newman points (in good Marxian or Freudian fashion) to this bourgeois picture of heaven and earth as one-sided. It is a picture ultimately coincident, it so happens, with the Scriptural message, but it is one so abstracted from the fullness of that message as to falsify in fact what it conveys only in theory. Indeed, it is itself "but a theory; it gains no influence over others" (*OUS*, 103). It is feeble "in practical matters" (*OUS*, 104). They who hold it "assume they know it, or conceive of it after some work of 'natural theology,' " rather than studying it "as a matter of fact" (*OUS*, 105, 109). Here again, Newman seeks to round out a range of concerns on an indeterminate question by supplying a felt deficiency of principles.

In both of the preceding examples, Newman's method of reasoning and arguing is rhetorical along the indefinite lines laid down in his description of religious belief (a species of Reason$_2$), and a summary account of those methods here will allow us to fill out what his own broad principles of rational persuasion—namely "antecedent probability" and "evidence"—intentionally left unspecified.

For example, in each case Newman seizes on the unreal simplicity of principles or methods or both in his opponents' positions—what he calls their "theoretical and unreal" views. Views are "theoretical" in a benign way when they are systematic and abstract second-order accounts of recurrent stabilities—Newman had no trouble accepting the need for and usefulness of "theory" in this sense. But views are also "theoretical" when they are lifted from previous cases and forcibly imposed on the question at hand, on the supposition that the new case is but another instance of the theory, rather than something new and unique for which the theory would provide but one source of exploration. "Theory" in this latter sense is already "unreal." But views can also be unreal when they are applicable but one-sided, hence inadequate to the contingency at hand. Our two examples exhibit theoretical and unreal views, but they have the additional advantage of being able to show that Newman indicts not only the "logical" and "scientific"—Reason$_1$ in its attempt to dictate the meaning of "reason"—but *also* the "rhetorical" Reason$_2$ in its attempt to dictate the meaning of "Divine Governance." This latter employs just those nondemonstrative antecedent probabilities it is Newman's aim ultimately to justify; but they are used in a predetermining way, a way closed to the possibility that the question might have more than one side. In both cases, then, much the same thing occurs: the evidentialists oversimplify by locking into one sense of "reason," and the (rhetorical) religious fundamentalists into one mode of "governance."

Newman's lesson here is to show us how to discriminate whenever faced with contingent questions, to seek antecedent principles that will enable us to inquire into the whole complexity before us. The problem with those whom he opposes (and here we note again the *range* he takes on—rationalists, but also those who are religious; "scientists," but also rhetoricians)—the problem again is that each group resists turning to experience to establish its views, insists naively on simple answers, and conflates what should be kept separate. By discriminating new principles, Newman exemplifies that sensitivity to the concrete that he also recommends.

Newman does more than this, however, for in so discriminating he does in fact offer us new principles, indeed a new vocabulary, not for religious faith alone, but for reason in all of its manifestations. It is true that his language is sometimes vague or inconsistent, or, even when consistent, is nevertheless multiple, suggestive, associative, and thus confusing. In this regard neither the Oxford sermons nor the *Grammar of Assent* are philosophical in the technical and abstract sense. Newman is ever picking up the "ordinary sense" of words, "popular language," appealing to his audience's feeling for what is probable and what is not. Thus, his very argument on behalf of antecedent probabilities rests on an antecedent probability Newman assumed or hoped his audience shared: "[A] merciful Providence may . . . have so ordered the relation between our minds and His revealed will, that presumption, which is the method of the many, may lead to the same conclusions as examination, which is the method of the few" (*OUS*, 229).

But to concede this multiplicity of views and the instability of his language is from another perspective to urge its richness, flexibility, and complexity. Newman rarely defines *per genus et differentiam*. He is all example, synonym, analogy, comparison and contrast, citation and authority. Consider, for example, how he discusses "love" in Sermon XII. Love is the safeguard of faith against the superstitious, bigoted, and improbable. What is love?

> The safeguard of faith is a right state of heart. This it is that gives it birth; it also disciplines it. This is what protects it from bigotry, credulity, and fanaticism. It is holiness, or dutifulness, or the new creation, or the spiritual mind, however we word it, which is the quickening and illuminating principle of true faith, giving it eyes, hands, and feet. It is love which forms it out of the rude chaos into an image of Christ (*OUS*, 234).

Whatever the drawbacks may be, Newman's language and method are clearly appropriate to just those kinds of indeterminate questions he is at pains to have us recognize, those that are relative to the emotional, moral, spiritual, as well as cognitive capacities of people. In fact such language ultimately precludes any discrimination of such faculties as distinct categories. We are asked both to think about and to feel a "love" that is simply not reducible to sentiment, for it is a love that disciplines thought at the same time that it safeguards faith. It is variously associated with "duty," "spiritual mind," and "holiness," and we are evidently expected to call upon our own experience to give sense to these terms operating together. That this is not simply an arbitrary blending of loaded words for emotional effect (hence an example of what Newman purports to condemn) is not self-evident from this passage. Yet it is difficult to consider Newman's subsequent rhetorical strategies—his quotations from Scripture, his linkages of "love" with "sympathetic feeling" and "newness of spirit," the analogy of a child's trust in a parent, the characterization of Christ as the "Object correlative" of love's affection, the expansion of the term "love" to encompass "a certain moral state" (*OUS*, 237), and finally the linkage of "love" with "reason" (Reason$_2$), that is, with "holy, devout, and enlighted presumptions" (*OUS*, 239)—it is difficult to consider the growth of this term and not recognize the invitation it extends to consult our own experience, and to question our own "enlightened presumptions," as a test of the reasonableness of the passage itself. This is therefore an associative language and method, and a cumulative one, and it is not possible to equate these qualities with "mystification" or "emotionalism." Even if one disagrees with Newman ultimately, Newman requires that we do so, and exemplifies the way in which we can do so, in *argument* that is neither pure abstraction nor sophistic sentiment.

Love, it is fair to say, does not get clearly defined in this passage, its linkages remain unexplored; nor is it quite clear how love has a counterpart in the secular realm of "reason" (although Polanyi's more recent discussion of "conscientiousness" as a controlling factor in scientific inquiry is foreshadowed here).[85] In sum, Newman's discussion and method may finally raise more questions than they solve. And yet, again, for all of its limits, Newman's prose is an exercise in discrimination that enriches the discussion of faith on both of its "sides": against the evidentialists it introduces the undeniable personal and interpersonal factor in thought, and against the romantics and Evangelicals (and sophists) it dares to insinuate a love tempered and disciplined not only by duty and holiness but by antecedent probability and rhetorical definition, discrimination, and argument.

In so doing, moreover, Newman's method is integrative on various levels. Discriminated terms—for example, Reason$_1$ and faith, Reason$_1$ and love, science and rhetoric, rationalist and religious, love and feeling—are integrated into new wholes, in much the same way that Newman's language integrates thought and feeling, knower and known. On reflection it becomes clear, for example, that Newman never rejects his interlocutor's viewpoints as wrong simply; on the contrary, we will see that it is always with those viewpoints that he chooses to initiate his own inquiries into the facts of a given case. Indeed, if the only way to discover what is involved in an indeterminate question is to "face the facts," then one needs to begin *somewhere,* and no better place exists than those *common places* one shares with others. Since indeterminateness of the sort Newman identifies in these sermons is relative to the community of inquirers—their traditions, experiences, history, beliefs, values—then it is but rhetorically prudent to start there; all hope of persuading, which is all that the question allows (or requires), turns in a serious way on addressing those beliefs and values of others. It is precisely this focus on persuasion that gives Newman's prose its tension, its perpetual thrust and counterthrust on either side of the question, and yet also its unity, since Newman integrates opposing sides within comprehensive ranges of principles that enable him to stay open to new contingencies.

It is fitting to close this chapter by noting one other, perhaps the most important, feature of Newman's attitude in these sermons, namely its "aspective" or "perspectival" character. We have seen that reality for Newman can be known only from a perspective, and that to know a concrete case *as a whole* requires multiple exposures, the "saying and re-saying" that only a dialectical-rhetorical method is capable of. Newman himself suggests that, regardless of whether one agrees with a speaker, the true value of an inquiry often resides in the performance itself:

> It often happens that, in pursuing the successive stages of an in-vestigation, the mind continually reverses its judgment to and fro, according as the weight of argument passes over and back again from the one alternative of the question to the other; and in such a case the ultimate utility of the inquiry does not consist in the con-clusion finally adopted, which may be no other than that with which the inquiry was commenced; but in the position in which we have learned to view it, and the circumstances with which we have associated it . . . so that we must never say that an individual is right, merely on the ground of his holding an opinion which happens to be true, unless he holds it in a particular manner; that is, under those conditions, and with that particular association of thought and feeling, which in fact is the interpretation of it (*OUS*, 100–1).

To speak of interpretation under particular conditions and in light of unique "circumstances" (itself a vintage rhetorical concept) is to reiterate the interest of the present chapter in Newman's move toward a phi-losophic rhetoric, that is, toward an ontology and epistemology grounded in contingency and directed at redefining truth, knowledge, persuasion, and belief. I have tried to suggest that Newman's theory of belief combines the strengths of two related but distinct tendencies in the post-Renais-sance development of rhetoric, namely the more theoretical "psycho-epistemological"[86] inquiries of Hume and George Campbell, and the less speculative, more practical and "ratiocinated"[87] rhetoric of Richard Whately. Newman pioneers, in Culler's words, a "judicious admixture"[88] of classical and modern, and theoretical and practical trends; in doing so, he anticipates, and at times even surpasses, contemporary rhetorical the-ory and criticism. We will come to see, I think, that for this reason Newman has much to teach us about communication and truth. In the following chapter we move a step closer by examining the grounds upon which Newman places this philosophic rhetoric.

3

RHETORICAL REASON

Logic is good, but it is not the best.
Thomas Carlyle,
"Characteristics"

From 1859 onward, Newman became increasingly involved in an investigation of the rationality and ethics of belief that culminated eleven years later in the *Grammar of Assent*. Actually he had been preoccupied with this matter all his life, from his early theorizing in the Oxford sermons to the rationalizing of the Anglican theological position in the *Via Media*, the analysis of the development of ideas in the *Development of Christian Doctrine*, the meditation on philosophy in *The Idea of a University*, and the reflection on what constitutes an honest believer in the *Apologia Pro Vita Sua*. Behind the variety of themes in these works lay many of the selfsame questions about belief, questions that prompted a correspondance in the sixties with Newman's good friend, the scientist William Froude: what is a reasonable faith? What is it to be a religious believer? How does faith relate to scientific study? What is belief? Proof? Assent?[1]

Between 1860 and 1866 Newman amassed a pile of papers in his attempts to articulate a defensible view of belief, but it was not until 1866, travelling in Switzerland, that he saw his way clear to the view that the *Grammar* articulates:

As to my Essay on Assent . . . it is on a subject which has teazed [sic] me for these twenty or thirty years. I felt I had something to say upon it, yet, whenever I attempted, the sight I saw vanished, plunged into a thicket, curled itself up like a hedgehog, or changed colours like a chameleon. I have a succession of commencements, perhaps a dozen, each different from the other, and in a different year, which came to nothing. At last, four years ago, when I was up at Glion over the Lake of Geneva, a thought came into my head as the clue, the "Open Sesame," of the whole subject, and I at once wrote it down, and I pursued it about the Lake of Lucerne. Then when I came home I began in earnest, and have slowly got through it (*Ward*, II, 245).[2]

Newman made it clear that the purpose of the *Grammar* was twofold: to show that we can legitimately believe what we cannot entirely comprehend, and that we can legitimately believe what we cannot demonstratively prove. It is correct to say that the book's two sections embodying these respective purposes—Chapters One through Five on apprehension and assent, and Chapters Six through Ten on assent and inference—do not, strictly speaking, entail each other,[3] although in this chapter I stress the continuity between them. Nevertheless, the main concern here is to continue the investigation of the knowing subject begun in the previous chapter. We need to ask how antecedent probabilities and first principles structure perception, how they are themselves a function of the "whole man," and how the reasoning (and arguing) we called rhetorical in the Oxford sermons, which Newman calls "informal" in the *Grammar*, is a coherent and defensible model for attaining certain kinds of truths, and how it is of a piece with his previous theorizing. In the first section of this chapter, therefore, I examine Newman's doctrine of real apprehension as fundamentally interpretive; in the second section I use Aristotle's ethical and rhetorical theory to help us understand this interpretive apprehension and to suggest how perception, interpretation, and rhetorical persuasion are all implicated in the concept of the "whole man;" and in the third section I pursue this triad of perception-interpretation-persuasion as it applies to reasoning and arguing with "really" and "notionally" apprehended terms and propositions. By continuing to advert as we go, to select issues and figures in the rhetorical tradition, we should be able to further our appreciation of Newman's great capacity for innovation as a means, paradoxical as it may be, of establishing continuity with the past.

MODES OF APPREHENSION

The full effect of Newman's thought on belief does not register until the section titled "Informal Inference" in Chapter Eight of the *Grammar*, at once the basis of that real assent Newman most valued and the means by which real apprehension is put to effective use. In order to understand, in a "real" or contextual and not merely "notional" or theoretical way, what Newman meant in this crucial section, it is necessary first to grasp just that fundamental distinction between "real" and "notional." As one critic has observed, this distinction "is based on [Newman's] understanding of the constitution of reality."[4] As such it supports his further distinctions between informal (or "real;" *T.P.*, 138) inference and formal (notional) inference, and real and notional assent. Although other distinctions operate throughout the *Grammar*, especially that between conditional inference and unconditional assent, Newman's major rhetorical innovation and achievement (already anticipated in the stress he placed on the importance of antecedent probability) is to have grounded his thought in the "real" as he defines it.[5]

In Chapters One through Four of the *Grammar*, Newman variously defines apprehension as the "imposition of a sense" (*G.A.*, 12) on the terms of a proposition, or again as the "intelligent acceptance of the idea, or of the fact which a proposition enunciates" (*G.A.*, 20). Although one is said to apprehend words, specifically propositions, these propositions are taken as signifying ideas or things, which are the proper objects of the apprehension. But to "apprehend" such objects is not necessarily to "understand" them: "I may take a just view of a man's conduct, and therefore apprehend it, and yet may profess that I cannot understand it. . . . I have not the key to it, and do not see its consistency in detail: I have no just conception of it" (*G.A.*, 20). More specifically, apprehending (at least in its minimal instance) is imposing a sense on the *predicate only* of a proposition; understanding is having a comprehensive grasp of both subject and predicate, perceiving "the upshot of the whole" (*G.A.*, 20).[6] There are two ways of apprehending, which we can examine in turn.

In the first place, for Newman "all things that are, are units" (*G.A.*, 22); "experience tells us only of individual things" (*G.A.*, 27), what we can call, after Hume, matters of fact and existence, but without the Humean doctrine of simple impressions and ideas, and their aggregation (by the "imagination") into wholes: "In knowledge, we *begin* with wholes, not with parts. We see the landscape, or the mountain, or the sky. We perceive men, each individually being a whole. Then we take to pieces, or take aspects of, this general and vague object, which is before us" (*P.N.* II, 8; emphasis added). When an individual, then, "imposes a sense on" or apprehends the predicate of a proposition in such a way as to grasp it as signifying particular and individual *things* and not general *concepts,* he can be said to have "really" apprehended.[7]

When two people meet, each begins at once to draw on his useable past to select, arrange, and interpret experience. To the extent that he relies on personal familiarity with "facts," with the lived experience of the person before him as it intersects his own previous lived experience, beliefs, values—to that extent apprehension of the other person will be "real." It follows that real apprehension is the more basic mode of encountering reality, at once more engaging of who we are as *people,* as well as more powerful emotionally, because dealing with "things," not abstractions:

> As notions come of abstractions, so images come of experiences; the more fully the mind is occupied by an experience, the keener will be its assent to it, if it assents, and on the other hand, the duller will be its assent and the less operative, the more it is engaged with an abstraction; and thus a scale of assents is conceivable . . varying

from an assent which looks like mere inference up to a belief both intense and practical . . . (*G.A.*, 30).

Notions, on the other hand, are those abstractions and generalizations from the particular and concrete. They are common terms, examples of what Philip Wheelwright has called steno-language, "meanings that can be shared in exactly the same way by a very large number of persons,"[8] made for the purpose of "grouping and discriminating, . . . framing cross classes and cross divisions, and thereby rising from particulars to generals" (*G.A.*, 27). As common terms, notions apply only to that "aspect" of the concrete things from which they are originally induced (*G.A.*, 26ff.). Real apprehension is aspectual or perspectival also, but in a different way: real apprehension need not but may at least grasp the "whole" of an idea or thing from its own angle (not thereby exhausting its contents, but affording a sense of the integral whole); whereas the perspective of a "notion" is always by definition an abstraction from the whole, that is, it is both partial and removed from the concrete thing. Notional apprehension is thus the apprehension of a particular strictly with respect to what it shares with similar particulars. I read about someone in the papers, I see her on the news, my neighbor is acquainted with her, perhaps I meet her myself. But I encounter, not an individual, but a type: she is a Republican, a mechanic, a stockbroker, an academic bourgeois humanist, a Buddhist—anything but this particular individual before me. " 'Man' [or 'woman'!] is no longer what he really is, an individual presented to us by our senses, but as we read him in the light of those comparisons and contrasts we have made him suggest to us" (*G.A.*, 27). Real apprehension, it is true, also suggests comparisons and contrasts; but it does so with a view to understanding the particular *as such*. The notional always looks beyond. In notional apprehension, "man" is "attenuated into an aspect, or relegated to his place in a classification" (*G.A.*, 27).

The same concrete datum can be apprehended really or notionally, or really and notionally in turn, depending upon one's experience and purpose. A child can be expected to have only the most rudimentary or notional sense of "the United States" or "justice" or "social worker," yet the most real or lively sense of "family," "friend," "school," "work," "happiness."

Newman offers in the *Grammar* several examples of "concrete" matters or questions, that is, those that involve real apprehension more than notional, and at one point he even identifies "experimental science [in its observational phase or dimension], historical research, [and] theology" (*G.A.*, 231) as activities that take as their inferentia the mass of interpreted facts that make up the component parts of some richer, more complex whole.[9] Again, the question—shall I one day die?—is treated *notionally* when one merely refers it to the general law that all men die. To this Newman asks what power the case of others has over his own (*G.A.*, 191). This is Hume's point about the *logical* unpredictability of the future. Actually, Newman continues, this question is treated properly only when it is treated concretely or "really": what "logic cannot do, my own living personal reasoning, my good sense . . . does for me" (*G.A.*, 195). Again, Newman cites the deliberations of jurors over the arguments in a case of law, the divining of the authorship of a text, the reflections on immortality of a "poor dying factory-girl." Although these examples are given in the section on informal inference, we need but recall that such inferences involve for the most part (or result in) real apprehensions.

The real or concrete is not restricted to physical phenomena. While it includes the data of our bodily senses (*G.A.*, 22), it includes also a great diversity of our mental sensations—"mental acts of any kind, of hope, inquiry, effort, triumph" and "a hundred others" (*G.A.*, 24).[10] In the opening chapters of the *Essay on the Development of Christian Doctrine* (1845), Newman denominates a species of ideas as "living" (*Dev.*, 36), meaning that they are not *in the first instance* abstractions, but concrete complex wholes that "attract and influence" (*Dev.*, 36) the whole person. In other words, although such complex ideas may eventually undergo theoretical systematization, they begin as dimly felt possibilities of life, of thought and action, interpreted by historical subjects in light of their own horizons of understanding. This ongoing mediation is an idea's "development." In the *Essay* on development, Newman gives examples of such concrete ideas, citing Platonic philosophy as an "intellectual fact" (*Dev.*, 35) and Christianity as a "fact in the world's history" (*Dev.*, 3).[11] Newman thus recognized the material basis of ideas, and, had he known it, would have appreciated at least Marx's fundamental premise regarding the economic basis of thought.

What should be growing clearer is that Newman does not favor the real at the expense of the notional. That he gives precedence to the real is not in question, since he is himself explicit on this point: the real is both the basis of the notional, and itself the unique means of coming into contact with some of the fullness and unpredictability, with the indeterminateness, of the concrete (*G.A.*, 29–30). But it does not follow from this that Newman wished to do away with notions and thereby to reduce discussion and argument to overpowering "imagery," or (as is sometimes maintained) that he perversely preferred the imprecision connected with real apprehension, inference, and assent to the greater precision possible to abstract ideas.[12]

No doubt Newman himself is partly responsible for such misconceptions. In particular his distinction between real and notional is overdrawn. Bastable, Ferreira, Price, and Jay Newman among others believe that Newman expresses this distinction as a *stark contrast*.[13] Real apprehension, after all, is said to deal with "things simply external to us," notional with "ideas existing in our own minds" (*G.A.*, 12). Real employs "singular nouns, . . . unit and individual," notional "common nouns . . . as standing for what is abstract" (*G.A.*, 13). Real "excites and stimulates the affections and passions," notional does not (*G.A.*, 14). In turn, what this contrast *seems* to imply is: first, that real apprehension is superior, since it is in closer contact with reality; second, that concrete imagery, albeit more ambiguous than notions and less easy to rationalize, is nevertheless better for the same reason; third, that real apprehension, contrasted as it is with concepts, must itself be nonconceptual; and fourth, that, when it is "real," religious or any other belief is therefore beyond the reach of intellectual criticism.

These charges are formidable, covering not only the *Grammar*, but numerous fugitive observations about the "concrete" and "practical" throughout Newman's works. These charges turn, however, on a few basic misconceptions, understandable in the light of Newman's frequently unsystematic and unclear approach, but no less profoundly misleading as to his intentions and meaning.

In the first place, with respect to Newman's formulation of the distinction between real and notional, we may note that his language suggests a *graduated* scale of difference. Newman speaks of "*rising* from particulars to generals" (*G.A.*, 27; emphasis added); the concrete may be "attenuated" (*G.A.*, 27) into notions. Individual propositions about the concrete "*almost* cease to be" when treated scientifically (*G.A.*, 28; emphasis added). In Chapter Eight, in speaking of notional or formal inference, Newman asserts that concrete terms in logic and science are "stripped" and "drained" and "starved" of "their poetry, their rhetoric, and their historical life" (*G.A.*, 174). Nicholas Lash has rightly pointed out in this regard a truth that too many of Newman's severer critics have missed:

> In Newman's prose, meaning and style, meaning and method of argument, are so closely interwoven that any attempt to separate them is a hazardous undertaking. His lack of any systematic and

68

technical terminology, in most of his writing, is irritating to a certain temper of mind, which cannot appreciate the possibility that, even for a thinker of Newman's delicacy and precision, *the unit of meaning may be the paragraph, or the page, rather than the individual term.* Literary and scientific precision are not necessarily the same thing.[14]

In the second place, and along the lines Lash is suggesting, to abstract the *Grammar* from the concrete whole of Newman's thought is to succumb to just that notional or theoretical treatment of the concrete that Newman warned against. Instead, we need to avail ourselves here of what we learned of Newman's views of reason in the Oxford sermons, for really the "unit of meaning" for Newman is, ultimately, the *whole* of a person's thought.

Real and notional, for example, are clearly opposites when seen from one angle, but from another Newman is clear that they supplement each other: "Each use of propositions has its own excellence and serviceableness, and each has its own imperfection. To apprehend notionally is to have breadth of mind, but to be shallow; to apprehend really is to be deep, but to be narrow-minded. The latter is the conservative principle of knowledge, and the former the principle of its advancement" (*G.A.*, 29). It has been objected, it is true, that while he may have conceded benefits to the notional and admitted limits to the real, Newman's habit was clearly to attack theory, logic, system, abstract language, notions, formal inference. Such attacks are undeniable, but what they signify is less clear; for it does not follow of necessity that the "real" is anti-intellectual, nonconceptual, irrational, that notional theorizing is unimportant, or that such theorizing exhausts the category "theory."

In point of fact, as reflection on Newman's own theorizing in the Oxford sermons makes clear, apprehending the concrete question of religious faith, for instance, is consummately a conceptual and "reasonable" matter, notwithstanding Newman's surface contrast of "faith" and "reason." Antecedent probabilities and considerations, what we have called topics, are clearly concepts, "notions" at least to some extent, and Newman makes no attempt whatsoever to assert otherwise: to do so would land him squarely in that romantic-Evangelical emotionalism he wished to avoid. Real apprehension and inference about the concrete are rather made possible by these notional topics that enable reflection on, indeed that partly constitute, experience—"facts" in Newman's extended sense of the term.[15] Another way to say this is to answer H. H. Price's question—can real apprehension and assent be wholly un-notional?—in the way that Price does, with a firm "no:" "I would suggest that there is something incurably notional about the entertaining of propositions."[16] But this means that the real is *from the first* an intellectual concern, in principle at least susceptible to some degree of critical scrutiny, that is, to criticism and reflection. This is, of course, perfectly in keeping with traditional conceptions of rhetoric, which use *topoi* to explore and argue a case: such topics and arguments may be wrong, or inappropriate, but there is nothing about them intrinsically that necessitates that they be so, or that shields them from criticism.

Granting this, why did Newman cast his distinction so starkly? And why his interminable attacks on "theorists and speculators?" Our analogy with real/notional and faith/reason may help us to appreciate that Newman's distinctions, and his consistent downplaying of the notional, is an important rhetorical move, in part a deliberate attempt to dislodge what had come to be recognized even in his own time as an ingrained overestimation of the power of scientific "reason" and "notions" as they were usually defined. Newman's point, in the *Grammar* as in the Oxford sermons, is decisively not to abandon reason for unreason, but to invite his readers to recognize that, among the other types of belief they embrace, faith is itself a mode of reasoning, one exercised on a concrete indeterminacy and as such not amenable (if one is to focus on the concrete) to that theoretical "reason" to which faith had been compared in the past. By the same token, Newman's slighting of "theory" and "notions" is not the abandonment of thought or concepts for quasi-mystical glorying in "things" and images,[17] but is rather part of his argument that purely notional theorizing has limited powers, and that the concrete, treated as such, requires a particular mode of apprehension, inference, and assent. Indeed, on his own theory, only such rhetorical sensitivity to his audience will satisfy Newman's own attempt to consider his subject—belief—concretely or "really," for the subject is not simply a theoretical concern knowable outside of one's experience, but a question of how real people do in fact experience *and* justify belief.

Just as antecedent considerations and first principles enable one to come to a belief, moreover, so "real" and "notional" are themselves comparatively notional topics that Newman employs to explore his subject concretely. This sensitivity to the concrete explains why Newman so stressed the real over the notional; why he never gives (for example) a precise definition of "apprehension," or attempts to measure how much apprehension of a predicate is necessary to apprehend a proposition; and why the notions of "real" and "notional" themselves are not given a more scientific (notional) treatment.[18] In all of these cases, no greater determinacy is necessary or desirable, even were it possible. Newman's purpose here is to enable his readers to recognize, to "really" apprehend, that their own thinking is *fundamentally interpretive,* at least in that great range of matters he calls the concrete. For this reason he argues by example, not by scientific induction and formulation, as a means of evoking particular experiences *as indeterminacies.* Thus, it is more or less academic (notional or theoretical) to object that his typology of notional assents, for example, is not scientifically compelling.[19] Newman's point is not to nail down a single right typology, any more than his purpose in the *Essay* on development is to furnish a "theory" of development.[20] His purpose is rather to engage and enlarge the views of an audience. At least in his major works, and in many of his lesser ones, Newman seeks to *open up a place,* to invite an audience to consider, where before a one-sidedness had occluded its vision. And he does this by persuasive argument, not abstract science or logic. For this reason it is simply unreal to complain that Newman's method is polemical, personal or persuasive.[21] Given his theory it could not be otherwise. Moreover it is recognizably the same method as that used in the Oxford sermons, one that employs publicly available arguments. We shall see again what was argued in the previous chapter, that Newman's theory calls for such arguments, and that in this way he encourages (and cultivates) critical scrutiny and judgment.

A previous question, however, remains unanswered: whence derives the concept of real apprehension? Price has suggested Hume's *Treatise on Human Nature* as a possible source.[22] It has been argued more strongly that:

> Newman seems to have accepted uncritically the view of his British empiricist teachers that perception is the paradigm of knowing (and the related view that the perceptible object is the paradigm of a real object); starting with such an assumption, he was naturally led to the conclusion that all other modes of knowing [i.e., notional] are *based on* perception and therefore must fall short of it in terms of quality and influence.[23]

A brief examination of Newman's stance in relation to Hume's, and of the rhetorical theory of George Campbell, will help to show Newman's originality and locate him further with respect to the rhetorical tradition. As a point of departure, it may be useful to consider how real-notional relates to the doctrine of his teacher, Richard Whately.

THE LIVELY IDEA

What is at once clear about Newman's emphasis on real apprehension, inference, and assent is the way it reaches back behind Whately's *Rhetoric* and *Logic*, reappropriating the psycho-epistemological concerns of Reid, Campbell, Kames, Priestly, and Hume.[24] We know that Newman never intended to offer a practical manual of argument to convince or persuade—a "rhetoric" in its conventional sense—as Whately did. Of course the *Grammar* is resolutely practical (*G.A.*, 222) and a manual of sorts, but not for the rhetor as such. What Newman sought was something more akin to Campbell's "philosophy of rhetoric," a pursuit of those "radical principles"[25] of human nature underlying belief and expression. In other words, whereas Whately's *Rhetoric* is simply an extension on the practical level of the more speculative theory Campbell had mapped out before him (in good measure using the coordinates of Humean epistemology), Newman departs in crucial ways from both, by showing what each overlooks.

First of all, in spite of having worked closely on, indeed having written parts of, the *Elements of Logic* (1826),[26] Newman rejected Whately's religious liberalism and philosophical rationalism. Whately, committed as he was to the defense of the faith, had subscribed to a "reason" that was neither Cartesian rationalism nor the inductive empiricism of Bacon, Locke, and Hume. In his *Elements of Logic* "reasoning" was, instead, coextensive with the syllogism. To Whately, much of the difficulty in religion and many other areas of inquiry was simply that men were faulty reasoners.[27] To be sure, Whately was not suggesting that logic could do everything. Much of the reason for its low reputation was its longstanding association with the scholastic logic-chopping of the Middle Ages, when (according to Whately) logic was erroneously thought to furnish "the sole instrument for the discovery of truth."[28] For Whately logic had in fact no such imperial power; it was strictly the science and art of the syllogism. As such its rules ensured correct, and controlled against erroneous, deductions, while possessing no responsibility for premises as such. These were the affair of the sciences, specifically of "induction," which for Whately, as for Copleston before him, meant only the observation of particulars.[29] It is noteworthy that, while the *Logic* mentions the "simple apprehension" of objects, it does nothing more than this, and even analogizes such apprehension to "the perception of the senses."[30] Neither logic nor rhetoric as such had anything to do with apprehension, and Whately, moreover, implicitly relies on empiricist presuppositions to explain perception and apprehension.[31] Thus Whately did not so much

72

spur Newman on in his own thinking about apprehension as raise (or maintain) considerable roadblocks in his way.[32]

As for rhetoric, Whately's combination of empiricism and syllogistic was decisive. For one thing, it perpetuated the venerated division between "conviction of the understanding" and "persuasion of the will."[33] The former was taken to be exclusively a rational and cognitive act; the latter, an addition of emotional excitation onto otherwise rational thought and argument.[34] How one *feels* about an object is thus separate from and posterior to one's cognition of it. This cognition is "notional," moreover, at least in this sense: apprehension of the concrete, even of the concrete *as* concrete, is nevertheless in principle an impersonal and objective act. Thus the exemplar of rational thought is sense perception. Persuasion, it follows, is merely the subjectivization of thought necessary to mobilize the will, and Whately, in Part II of the *Elements of Rhetoric,* elaborates the notion of "energy" so crucial to this mobilization. "Energy" is a vintage rhetorical concept, but its most recent manifestation had been Campbell's notion of "vivacity," itself derived from Hume's doctrines of the "lively idea" and "belief."

In his *Treatise* (1740) Hume distinguishes between sense impressions and ideas, the latter being less lively or vivid or forceful images of the original impressions. Ideas can be simple, composed of a single impression, or can be made complex by an "imagination" that combines simple ideas into more complicated wholes. These complex ideas may be entirely fanciful or may represent real things, events, people, states of affairs— "matters of fact and existence." Our experience of the world is thus the mediation by the senses of impressions arrived we know not from where,[35] combined into wholes and sequences. These are then stored in memory according to the order and form of their occurrence. Ultimately, then, all ideas are for the empiricist "cashable" by sense data.

Just as ideas are distinguished from impressions, memory may be distinguished from imagination by the "liveliness" or "vivacity" of its ideas—by the "belief" that attends on them. In memory reside those experiences that have (or that we think have) happened; these are attended by a feeling of actuality that is simply absent from ideas of imagination (whether fictional or true). This idea of vivacity is so central to Hume's understanding of belief (this latter one of the central concepts of rhetorical theory), and both belief and vivacity so greatly overlap on Newman's concepts of real apprehension and assent, that we need to consider them more closely.

Hume's task in the *Treatise* is to identify and explain the nature of our knowledge of matters of fact, a knowledge he termed "belief" and contrasted to the analytic knowledge of the relations of ideas. By belief Hume refers, not to our experience of present sense impressions, but to propositions about the world beyond present impressions of sense and feeling. He first denies the possibility that what we do when we believe is to attribute existence to the object believed, on the ground that the idea of existence adds nothing to the idea of the object itself; he suggests rather that belief differs from disbelief by the *manner in which we conceive a proposition*. An idea in which we believe "*feels* different from a fictitious idea, that the fancy alone presents to us: and this different feeling I endeavour to explain by calling it a superior *force*, or *vivacity*, or *solidity*, or *firmness*, or *steadiness*."[36]

"Vivacity" here is not the equivalent of vivid mental imagery. Being able to vividly imagine a golden mountain does not thereby commit one to believing in its existence, and Hume—in spite of Campbell's accusation to the contrary—does not assert that it does.[37] As Newman himself was later to state, "A proposition, be it ever so keenly apprehended, may be true or may be false" (*G.A.*, 58). As Hume intends it, belief is a holding-fast, an adherence, to a proposition as true, a recognition of and confidence in its claim, *explainable in terms of the association of ideas*—that is, in terms of the repeated experience of ideas belonging together, whether from their resemblance, contiguity, or repeated conjunction (cause and effect). To have seen several times a billiard ball hit another and send it rolling is to come to a lively belief that a causal relation exists between the two, that the next time we see one ball headed toward another it will again send the second careening. "Vivacity" in Hume thus refers either to the vivid mental imagery we have of impressions, or to the beliefs we come to through experience. These two are not equivalent concepts, though they do overlap.

George Campbell, Scottish minister, admirer of Hume, and, with Reid, member of the Aberdeen Philosophical Society, largely took over this epistemology. In Book I of his *Philosophy of Rhetoric*, for example, the association of ideas is a crucial explanatory concept for the way all discourse functions; and in Books II and III, "vivacity" is put forward as a primary goal of communication, particularly persuasive communication. In these latter books, Campbell introduces this problem: how does the rhetor give abstract ideas of imagination force or vivacity, both in the sense that they will be concrete and engaging, affective and effective, and in the sense that they will be found to be plausible beliefs?

Campbell's answer to this question lies in the transfer of vivacity through the rhetor's language according to the principle of association. Concrete and particular words evoke relatively clear and forceful images of people or events, and the energy or vivacity inherent therein can be transferred to ideas with which the rhetor associates those images. By the same token, concrete imagery will more easily trigger associations of conjunction or resemblance or contiguity than would abstract terms. If a rhetor, through "pure and perspicuous language,"[38] successfully casts on one's mental vision the concrete image of a child skipping thoughtlessly into the street after a ball, my own knowledge of recurrent events—e.g., cars coming along—will lead me to associate the child with the possible danger; I am therefore more likely to listen to, and to accept, an otherwise abstract argument for driver safety associated with the image.

In the rhetorics of both Campbell and Whately, then, as in the philosophy of Hume, the conviction of the understanding is strictly a cognitive process—not that one does not have feelings about objects perceived, or that such feelings may not be involved in conviction, but that they are properly ancillary to conceptualization and cognition. The vivid impression of a present experience, or the vivacity felt from concrete language, is always in principle reducible to "meanings that can be shared in exactly the same way by a very large number of persons. . . ."[39] This explains the Lockean account of language as a kind of calculus in a one-to-one relationship with reality.[40] Ideally, both cognition and language are impersonal. As a result, both vivacity and belief are for Campbell strictly *psychological* and *epistemological* terms, on loan, as it were, to explain rhetorical behavior. Can the same be said of real apprehension?

First of all, real apprehension is akin to Humean vivacity in its feeling of strength and force: "Of the two modes of apprehending propositions, notional and real, real is the stronger" (*G.A.*, 31); "It is in human nature to be more affected by the concrete than by the abstract" (*G.A.*, 31). But real apprehension does not repeat the sort of "energetics" that underwrites vivacity and the association of ideas. On the contrary, in addition to being a psychological-epistemological concept, "real apprehension" is first and foremost a rhetorical one, combining feeling and value with the idea of the *object as such*. In fact there is no "idea of the concrete thing as such" without this personal dimension: the idea *is* the personal interpretation of the object.

Second, it is now possible to see that Newman's reaction on the one hand to Whately, on the other to the empiricism of a Hume or Campbell, is much the same as the response he gave to his interlocutors in the Oxford sermons. In each case, Newman identified a position that he proceeded to argue was one-sided and narrow—not simply false in itself, but inadequate to the richness of our experience and to the language we require to express it. Thus Whately's ratiocinated rhetoric and logic, correct as far as they go, simply do not go far enough, and fail to wrestle with the complexity of apprehension and inductive method. By the same token, Hume's and Campbell's focus on "moral reasoning," on matters of fact, which provided Newman with the sort of supplement he required to balance and complete Whately, nevertheless in turn also suffered from an inadequate model of perception and apprehension. The "mirror of nature" is less innocent an eye than had been supposed, and Newman again attempts to extend his audience's sense of the range of the possible.

In sum, "real apprehension" can be seen to be a central concept for Newman in the way it presupposes first principles and antecedent probabilities and considerations to structure our interpretations of reality. This heralds a decisive break from Newman's empiricist predecessors since it steps beyond (without simply rejecting) mechanical associationism by showing how one's own experience and tradition transform brute impressions into interpreted realities. This step is grounded in a concept of the self as a unified whole and points to the importance of the whole person for communicating truth; it is to this concept, therefore, that we now turn.

"THE WHOLE MAN MOVES":

> ". . . so that his whole self, his bones, limbs . . . life, reason, moral feeling, immortality, and all that he is besides, is his real differentia" (G.A., 183).

The concept of the whole man can rightly be said to provide the foundation of Newman's rhetorical philosophy, meaning both his theory of belief and the application of that theory to the substance and method of his thought in various fields. It underwrites real apprehension, informal inference, and real assent by explaining, first, how "the imposition of a sense on" an experience or proposition arises in real apprehension from the unity of an individual's emotional, cognitive, moral, and imaginative nature; second, how that same unity also mandates a persuasive or "informal" inference; and third, how real assent is a judgment and not an algorithmic calculation or arbitrary decision. Although the concept is explanatory, however, Newman nowhere explains the concept. What is worse, he often formulates his thought in potentially catastrophic ways: "Man is *not* a reasoning animal, he is a seeing, feeling, contemplating, acting animal" (D.A., 294). Lifted out of context and abstracted from the whole of Newman's thought and practice, such a claim can easily be made to support the case that Newman denied "reason" and "logic" altogether. One critic, for example, admitting that emotions play a role in man's mental life, nevertheless strenuously objects to the suggestion that "man's feelings, etc., should flow into his reasoning, should condition his reason intrinsically, so as to have real weight and function in the estimation of what is true and false."[41]

The question here is the epistemological status, for inquiry, argument, interpretation, and judgment, of powers of the mind not normally associated with cognition. Without being able to do justice to the question, reflection on the ethics and rhetoric of Aristotle will help to explain Newman's thought and to exhibit its rational-rhetorical character, and, in so doing, remove a standing bias against it. I wish to focus in this section on two aspects of the "whole man:" the "enabling" or epistemological role that the concept plays in reasoning and arguing, and the influence of the "whole person" as a source and recipient of persuasion.

The "whole man" as an enabling concept. In the *Apologia* occurs perhaps the best-known of Newman's appeals to the whole man:

And then I felt altogether the force of the maxim of St. Ambrose, 'Non in dialecticâ complacuit Deo salvum facere populum suum' [the motto of the *Grammar of Assent*];-I had a great dislike of paper logic. For myself, it was not logic that carried me on; as well might one say that the quicksilver in the barometer changes the weather. It is the concrete being that reasons; pass a number of years, and I find myself in a new place; how? the whole man moves; paper logic is but the record of it (*Apo.*, 155).

Here Newman is focused on reasoning and arguing; in the *Grammar* the same sentiments are expressed regarding real apprehension (and informal inference and real assent). The entire range of emotional, moral, spiritual, and imaginative experiences is drawn upon to provide the individual with all of the "powers and resources" (*G.A.*, 199) necessary to locate and evaluate the concrete: "Shall we say that there is no such thing as truth and error, but that anything is truth to a man which he troweth? and not rather, as the solution of a great mystery, that truth there is, and attainable it is, but that its rays stream in upon us through the medium of our moral as well as our intellectual being . . ." (*G.A.*, 202)?[42]

This unity of one's being is a theme that suffuses Newman's thought on informal inference in Chapter Eight: "And our preparation for understanding . . . will be the general state of our mental discipline and cultivation, our own experiences, or appreciation of religious ideas, the perspicacity and steadiness of our intellectual vision" (*G.A.*, 198). This theme in fact is echoed so often throughout Newman's writings that it would be tedious to rehearse more than a sample. We have seen, for example, how Newman appealed to the whole man in the Oxford sermons. In the *Essay on Development of Doctrine*, similarly, Newman speaks of ideas as relative to the full life of historically placed individuals; in *The Idea of a University* knowledge is intended to be "realized" by the whole person, brought home to his or her experience, its "aspects" thereby developed. In an early letter of 1828 to Blanco White, Newman anticipates his later views, though here they are colored by his distrust of the rationalist sense of "intellect:" "For *words* are not *"feelings*—nor is intellect ἠθος—Intellect seems to be but the attendant and servant of right moral feeling in this own [sic] weak and dark state of being . . ." (*L.D.*, II, 60).[43]

The question again is just how singular Newman is, and how wrong or right he might be, in urging that "the personality (so to speak) of the parties reasoning is an important element in proving propositions in concrete matter" (*G.A.*, 207). Students of Newman are aware that his concept of the illative sense extended Aristotle's ethical notion of *phronesis* into epistemological matters; and it is increasingly understood among rhetoricians that ethics and rhetoric share a much closer relationship than previously thought.[44] A brief consideration of Aristotle's thought may help us to place Newman's program in a more tenable light.

The notion that the virtuous man, the man of practical wisdom, bears any resemblance to the rhetor is foreign, to say the least, to the conventional view of the orator as merely sophistic or bombastic. Yet the Roman ideal of the good man skilled in speaking deeply influenced the Renaissance, and it reappears in a new guise in Newman, who as we know was conversant with the ancient authors. In Quintilian we read: "My aim, then, is the education of the perfect orator. The first essential for such an one is that he should be a good man, and consequently we demand of him not merely the possession of exceptional gifts of speech, but of all the excellences of character as well." These values, which are present of course in Cicero also,[45] are considerably less pronounced in Aristotle's *Rhetoric*, and more than one theorist denies them a place in Aristotle's rhetorical theory altogether;[46] but recent scholarship paints a different picture.[47]

For Aristotle rhetoric aims not at persuasion at all costs but at a judgment (*Rhetoric* 1355b 14) regarding means and (proximate) ends in matters primarily of public good, virtue, and justice. For Aristotle the primary vehicle to affect judgment is the rhetorical syllogism or enthymeme, which is capable of combining reason and emotion in premises that address the concrete affairs of daily life. The rhetor is defined in terms of his ability to discover and advance persuasives drawn from the substance (*pragma*) of a case, as this is related to and conditioned by his own character and emotions and the emotions (and character) of the audience. In what relation does the rhetor stand to the *phronimos*, the man of practical wisdom, and how do both involve the "whole" man?

In Book VI of the *Nicomachean Ethics*,[48] Aristotle contrasts theoretical or scientific knowledge (*episteme*) with art (*techne*) on the one hand and practical wisdom (*phronesis*) on the other. Science treats what exists necessarily, that which is fixed and eternal, hence is a matter of insight (*nous*) and demonstration, not debate (1139b 15–35); whereas both art, which concerns production, and practical wisdom or prudence, which concerns action (*praxis*), treat "things which admit of being other than they are" (1140a), particulars as well as universals (1141b 14) and matters about which men deliberate (1141b 7). Aristotle further contrasts art, which is a "characteristic of producing under the guidance of true reason" (1140a 20), with moral action, which produces nothing but rather is complete in itself. Moral action, furthermore, is rationally guided by *phronesis,* which cannot be a science because it is concerned with particulars as well as universals and contingencies rather than fixities, nor an art, because it results in no product, nor an action, because it guides action. Aristotle calls it a "characteristic of action" (1140b) and defines it as the "capacity of deliberating well about what is good and advantageous for oneself" (1140a 25).

More specifically, for Aristotle moral virtue or conduct is intimately tied to this intellectual virtue of *phronesis,* which leads to informed judgment and reasoned choice about the good. The man of practical wisdom is the one who can deliberate discerningly about genuine goods for man, and for himself in particular, and one whose choices reflect this deliberation. He intuits the standard or norm of judgment, and his desire and choice follow suit. The ethical realm, furthermore, is that of the contingent and relative, and the end of ethics is action and not knowledge; choice accordingly can never be a matter of deductively imposing universals on a particular case. Ethics is not the algorithmic application of a calculus of pleasures and pains, as in Bentham, or of laws and rules, as often in historical jurisprudence, but rather involves an individual's *judgment* about particulars in light of a general standard, the embodiment or instantiation of the abstract, conditioned by the give-and-take of specific existential problems. Newman himself illuminates this point in the *Grammar,* showing that he stands squarely in a tradition running from Aristotle and Cicero to Vico and to Gadamer: "An ethical system may supply laws, general rules, guiding principles, a number of examples, suggestions, landmarks, limitations, cautions, distinctions, solutions of critical or anxious difficulties; but who is to apply them to a particular case? whither can we go, except to the living intellect, our own, or another's" (*G.A.*, 228)?

Action, then, is virtuous when reason directs desire to that choice of particular goods which, *in the circumstances,* appropriately embodies universal moral ends. Deliberation enables the discovery of particular means and (proximate, not ultimate) ends, provided that one is already morally virtuous and sees and desires ultimate goods. This is not circular because the man of practical wisdom is one whom both virtuous upbringing and education (within a stable framework of laws), as well as his own past choices and actions consequent upon good deliberation and right desire, have habituated to aiming at genuinely good ends for himself as a particular human being.

At all stages of Aristotle's analysis, one can discern the combination of reason and desire. In specific cases of moral choice, for example, one's choices as to how to instantiate what is abstractly good involves enlisting one's passions or desires in the service of what reason determines concretely to be correct—for thought alone cannot move to action (1139a 35). But such capacity to deliberate well, to *discern* the good, itself presupposes the synthesis of desire and reason embodied in moral virtue (1102b 30). That is, an individual is able personally to *see* what reason dictates, both in the abstract and in the concrete, only if his desires have not corrupted his reason.[49] And this ability to see is, in the particular case, precisely that of prudence or good deliberation.

For Aristotle, then, rhetoric as a *techne* provides the intellectual and deliberative tools for practical wisdom, whether one speaks to the many or only deliberates within himself (*Rhetoric* 1391b 18).[50] For the rhetorician's art resides in just his ability to deliberate well, that is, to discover viable reasons for action and judgement within the realm of the contingent and particular.[51] Moreover, in the act of discovery (*inventio*) as well as in the thing discovered or invented (*pisteis*, premises and enthymemes), reason and emotion are combined. It is true that Aristotle warned against emotion warping judgment (*Rhetoric* 1354a 6), but he also made clear that emotion as such must play a role in our perception and judgment of concrete affairs: "the judgments we deliver are not the same when we are influenced by joy or sorrow, love or hate" (*Rhetoric* 1356a).[52] As to the reasons discovered and shaped into enthymemes, by virtue of their origin in concrete particulars about which the rhetorician cares deeply and regarding which he seeks to effect action or attitude, these too combine thought and feeling. Grimaldi writes: "The enthymeme as the main instrument of rhetorical argument incorporates the interplay of reason and emotion in discourse."[53]

Clearly, no division of the faculties of the mind is operating here, as it does in Campbell's and Whately's distinction between rational conviction and emotional persuasion. Though he had no concern for the orator as such, Newman is far closer to Aristotle than to Campbell or Whately regarding this fundamental tenet.[54] The difference between Newman and Aristotle is that Newman extended the principle that knowledge was a product of the whole man from the moral sphere to the intellectual generally. Knowing of all kinds is rooted in real apprehension of concrete particulars, and the knowing subject, like the good rhetor, is one who uses not only his conscience but all of his "antecedent probabilities" to apprehend the real; and this is always a matter, more or less, of character and feeling as well as thought. More accurately, thought is itself both cognitive and emotional.

Newman's privileging of real apprehension, therefore, and his interpretation of it as involving the whole man, is thoroughly rhetorical in the sense that it features probability and persuasion and explains the importance of character or "personal influence" in perception.

The whole man as a source (and recipient) of persuasion: "Persons influence us, voices melt us, looks subdue us . . ." (D.A., 293). Given the complexity of conditions and factors in arriving at truth in the concrete, Newman was skeptical about the possibility of communicating such truth in argument or controversy. In part, of course, this is a problem that arises from men's divergences over first principles, a problem for which there is little direct remedy: "Half the controversies in the world are verbal ones; and could they be brought to a plain issue, they would be brought to a prompt termination. Parties engaged in them would then perceive, either that in substance they agreed together, or that their difference was one of first principles" (OUS, 200).

Even when it is not a matter of first principles, however, communication is hardpressed to replicate the nuances of the concrete, a problem that gets exacerbated in controversy and polemic: "I declare I think it is a rare thing, candour in controversy, as to be a Saint" (L.C., II, 324). Unlike Aristotle, who holds in the *Rhetoric* that the true is intrinsically more persuasive than the false (1355a 12), Newman considers that argument and controversy favor error because they lack the detail and subtlety

81

necessary to evoke complex truth: "[T]he warfare between Error and Truth is necessarily advantageous to the former, from its very nature, as being conducted by set speech or treatise; and this, not only for a reason assigned, the deficiency of Truth in the power of eloquence, and even of words, but moreover from the very neatness and definiteness of method required in a written or spoken argument" (*OUS*, 89–90).[55]

Still, controversy can perform an important negative function. While it may be the case (Newman perhaps overstates it) that, in establishing truth, "we need not dispute, we need not prove,—we need but define" (*OUS*, 200), nevertheless in resisting error, in preventing the triumph of one-sided or mistaken views, controversy is crucial.[56] Even here, however, and all the more when one wishes not to fight but to communicate truth (the *Apologia* is a case in point), the more subtle and complex the processes of thought and feeling, the more we naturally tend to rely on the credibility of the speaker: "According as objects are great, the mode of attaining them is extraordinary" (*OUS*, 219).[57] Newman knew well Aristotle's doctrine from the *Rhetoric* that character could be the most effective source of persuasion,[58] and in the *Grammar* he places ethos at the center of communication in the concrete realm: ". . . our criterion of truth is not so much the manipulation of propositions, as the intellectual and moral character of the person maintaining them" (*G.A.*, 196). Even as early as 1832, in the fifth of the Oxford sermons titled "Personal Influence, the Means of Propagating the Truth," Newman located much of the persuasiveness of Scripture in its human witnesses:

> We shall find it difficult to estimate the moral power which a single individual, trained to practise what he teaches, may acquire in his own circle, in the course of years. While the Scriptures are thrown upon the world, as if the common property of any who choose to appropriate them, he is, in fact, the legitimate interpreter of them, and none other; the Inspired Word being but a dead letter (ordinarily considered), except as transmitted from one mind to another. While he is unknown to the world, yet, within the range of those who see him, he will become the object of feelings different in kind from those which mere intellectual excellence excites (*OUS*, 94–5).[59]

Thus, in the *Apologia,* to give a further example, Newman quotes a letter of his regarding the importance of individual witness in the "Tracts for the Times:" "They were not intended as symbols *ê cathedrâ*, but as the expression of individual minds. . . . No great work was done by a system; whereas systems rise out of individual exertions. Luther was an individual. The very faults of an individual excite attention . . ." (*Apo.*, 48).[60] Or again, Newman conceived of the Church as a personal "system," as an "ethos" known by its fruits.

If the discovery and communication of truth implicate the whole man, no less does the *reception* of truth: even discussion leavened with the ethos of the speaker avails nothing *unless one is fitted to hear*. For this reason, Newman repeatedly contrasts those who listen in a spirit of sympathetic, or at least receptive, identification—"inquirers"—with those "disputants" and "controversialists" whose purposes are merely polemical and "rhetorical:" "I wish to deal, not with controversialists, but with inquirers . . . as preferring inquiry to disputation in a question about truth" (*G.A.*, 273, 275). In the matter of religion, Newman contrasts those who are open to religious first principles and those who are not— religious persons versus rationalists—but the distinction is generalizable:

> Such is the temper . . . of a philosopher. He may hold principles to be false and dangerous, but he will try to enter into them, to enter into the minds of those who hold them; he will consider in what their strength lies, and what can be said for them; he will do his best to analyze and dissect them; he will compare them with others; and he will apply himself to the task of exposing and disproving them (*Prepos*, 297).[61]

Only a sympathy born of a fundamental identity of quest can mitigate the opacity and intractability of language, and it is with this in mind that Newman begins his own philosophic work, the *Grammar of Assent,* with what amounts to a miniature "rhetoric" for reading philosophers in general and himself in particular:

> [I]n a philosopher it is a merit even to be not utterly vague, inchoate and obscure in his teaching, and if he fails even of this low standard of language, we remind ourselves this his obscurity perhaps is owing to his depth. No power of words in a lecturer would be sufficient to make psychology easy to his hearers; if they are to profit by him, they must throw their minds into the matters in discussion, must accompany his treatment of them with an active, personal concurrence, and interpret for themselves, as he proceeds, the dim suggestions and adumbrations of objects, which he has a right to presuppose, while he uses them, as images existing in their apprehension as well as in his own (*G.A.*, 21).

The question that remains, then, is what Newman's conceptions of real apprehension and the whole man signify for reasoning and arguing: how does reasoning deal with the concrete? can any arguments convey the subtlety of real apprehensions and the complexity of the "whole man?" what role does "rhetoric" play for Newman?

MODES OF INFERENCE: FORMAL:

> *"Logic makes but a sorry rhetoric with the multitude;" "Logicians are more set upon concluding rightly, than on right conclusions."*
> (D.A., 294).

Newman's skeptical attitude toward controversy is of a piece with his even greater skepticism toward what he understood as "logic." His antipathy dates back to his collaboration on Whately's *Logic* when he was a young tutor at Oxford and persists throughout all of his works, particularly in the *Grammar of Assent*. Skepticism and distrust, however, do not necessarily lead to rejection, although rejection of logic is precisely what critics such as Leslie Stephen claim to have found: "Because logic [for Newman] cannot supply us with a decisive test, applicable at once, its use as an organizing and unifying principle is virtually denied."[62] On the rejection hypothesis, however, it is difficult to account for the sophisticated and pervasive use of logical argument throughout Newman's works, for it is hardly credible that Newman would miss such an obvious contradiction between his theory and practice. If we try to save the hypothesis by supposing that Newman meant that logic was irrelevant only to informal (not formal) inference, we must assume that such informal inference is distinct from the (logical) method Newman practiced—an assumption that clearly contradicts his repeated identification of his mode of inquiry and argument as that of antecedent and converging probabilities, that is, of informal inference. The only escape is the unlikely possibility that Newman simply missed or ignored this glaring inconsistency.

An alternative hypothesis, one that was suggested earlier regarding Newman's apparently sharp distinction between real and notional apprehension, is that Newman's charges against logic are part of a larger rhetorical argument about logic *at its limits,* and about the limits of this "logic." On this reading formal and informal inference, quite like notional and real apprehension, or reason and faith, are different in degree, not kind, and constitute a continuum of "reasoning" that ranges from the limit-conditions of natural inference at one end, to the limit-conditions of formal inference at the other: natural is difficult if not quite impossible to verbalize, formalize, manipulate, and control; formal is the opposite.

Informal partakes of both. The real question here, I propose, is not so much the alleged inutility of logic as it is the nature of an essentially inductive method that nevertheless partakes of some of the devices (including the syllogism) of formal inference. Otherwise said, Newman's problem is not the syllogism per se, but the syllogism as a structure of purely notional terms incapable alone of leading to real assent. That Newman spoke unclearly and in an exaggerated way about the syllogism, and logic generally, is commonly admitted (if not clearly understood). But it can be seen, I think, that his mistakes do not really deny what is now accepted as "logic," as critics such as Stephen have suggested. Like Mill, whose *System of Logic* (1843) Newman seems to have known well, but without the former's empiricist presuppositions, Newman breaks free of (without abandoning) Whately's undue confidence in the syllogism in favor of a far more sophisticated and nuanced version of reasoning and arguing. In this section I wish primarily to explore Newman's errors as a way of clarifying his real achievement.

It is known that Newman shared with William Hamilton and others a psychological conception of logic according to which it represented and regulated the laws of thought.[63] This view of logic has since been discredited, and a new conception, that logic deals with valid and invalid forms of argument, has taken its place. As a result we need to pay careful attention to how the word is used; when someone says "Newman rejected logic," we need to ask what is meant. According to Newman there were actually two rather distinct processes of mental reasoning: natural and informal inference, similar complex and subtle forms of reasoning ultimately beyond the capacity of words to represent adequately; and formal inference, a verbal process of thought that attempted to bring to expression the original process of informal (or natural) inference, which the science of logic was thought to regulate by providing unequivocal terms and propositions and casting them in correct deductive forms. The emphasis in such a view of logic is not on validity but on "pure"—i.e., unequivocal—language.[64]

This distinction of Newman's between formal and informal inference repeats that of the Oxford sermons between implicit and explicit reasoning: informal is (more or less) implicit, concrete, and unconscious; formal is the explicit verbalization of the implicit, largely unverbalized mental reasoning. But what are the reasons behind this distinction? One is that, in our attempt to interpret the world, we require devices beyond individual genius for investigation (*G.A.,* 169–70); a similar one is that we require common devices and a common standard for proof:

The conclusions of one man are not the conclusions of another; those of the same man do not always agree together; those of ever so many who agree together may differ from the facts themselves, which those conclusions are intended to ascertain. In consequence, it becomes a necessity, if it be possible, to analyze the process of reasoning, and to invent a method which may act as a common measure between mind and mind, as a means of joint investigation, and as a recognized intellectual standard . . . to secure us against hopeless mistakes, and to emancipate us from the capricious *ipse dixit* of authority (*G.A.*, 170–71).

Thus logic as Newman understands it—the scientific attempt to provide a common standard of proof by examining our mental reasonings and exhibiting their rules—fashions such a measure or standard by transforming ordinary language into artificial, unequivocal, unambigous terms and propositions:

Let then our symbols be words: let all thought be arrested and embodied in words. Let language have a monopoly of thought; and thought go for only so much as it can show itself to be worth in language. Let every prompting of the intellect be ignored, every *momentum* of argument be disowned, which is unprovided with an equivalent wording, as its ticket for sharing in the *common search after truth*. Let the authority of nature, common-sense, experience, genius, go for nothing. Ratiocination, thus restricted and put into grooves, is what I have called Inference, and the science, which is its regulating principle, is Logic (*G.A.*, 171; emphasis added).

Specifically, how does this transformation occur?

It follows from this, that the more simple and definite are the words of a proposition, and the narrower their meaning, and the more that meaning in each proposition is restricted to the relation which it has to the words of the other propositions compared with it,—in other words, the nearer the propositions concerned in the inference approach to being mental abstractions, and the less they have to do with the concrete reality, and the more closely they are made to express exact, intelligible, comprehensive, communicable notions, and the less they stand for objective things, that is, the more they are the subjects, not of real, but of notional apprehension,—so much the more suitable do they become for the purposes of Inference (*G.A.*, 172).

But note what this conception of logic entails. Rather than say, as any modern logician does (as Whately himself did[65]), that logic ignores the existential content of terms and propositions in its task of formulating valid relations of entailment, Newman held that logical thought *requires the emasculation* of that content. In order more successfully to manipulate categories and sentences (class inclusions and exclusions, for Newman took traditional Aristotelian syllogistic as the paradigm of logic), logic requires clarity and unequivocality of language. The ideal is a notational calculus. Logical formal inference "stints" the import of words by making them "as much as possible . . . the *calculi* of notions, which are in our absolute power, as meaning just what we choose them to mean . . ." (*G.A.*, 173), "starving" each term down "till it has become the ghost of itself . . . so that it may stand for just one unreal aspect of the concrete thing to which it belongs, for a relation, or a generalization, or other abstraction . . ." (*G.A.*, 174).

Now, two errors spoil this conception of logico-formal inference. First, for Newman formal inference is here understood to stand in for or represent informal and natural inference. But it is able to substitute in this way *only by replacing concrete terms with notions.* As Brian Wicker has argued, however,[66] notions (as universals) cannot substitute in this way when they are understood to perform a "naming" function, for universals cannot name individuals ("man" does not name a particular man), and if they are understood as so doing, they result in "an incoherent theory of the distribution of terms."[67]

Secondly, Newman erroneously believes that "logic" needs to attenuate the meanings of ordinary language, to abstract from concrete circumstances and to provide ersatz particulars, namely "notions."[68] In fact, however, although the science of logic requires unequivocal terms and propositions in order to articulate laws of valid inference, the application of logic to concrete cases is perfectly achievable *so long as the terms have a minimum commonly accepted signification.* And clearly terms and even abstractions "really" apprehended, *can,* at least at times, meet this requirement. Thus, for example: All cars illegally parked in this lane will be towed; this rusted Volvo is illegally parked; ergo, it will be towed.

In light of Newman's mistaken view that ordinary language rendered only as pure "notions" is the proper subject matter of "logic," it is hardly any wonder that formal inference is understood by him to be inimical to concrete reason. What Newman has done in effect is to combine what we consider "logic" with the abstraction necessary to "science"—to think that logical structures operate only when terms have been made general and unequivocal (whereas in fact logical entailments obtain even with terms apprehended in a "real" way). According to Newman, formal inference is thus an abstraction from informal, which itself is already at one remove from the concrete "things" it represents. Logic as a verbal science regulates and shapes this abstract formal inference. It follows from this that only those studies that work with abstractions, with unambiguous terms and propositions, laws, theorems, theories, are best suited to "logical" operations. Conversely, the more concrete a study is, the less it responds to formal rules governing language. On these grounds Newman attacks concepts (i.e., "pure" notions) and thus the logical manipulation of them, as mere shadows of the more personal action of thought.

But Newman's account is not meaningful. Since the science of what we now call logic need have nothing to do with ordinary language, it need not "attenuate" it at all. Once this psychologizing is dropped, moreover, Newman's real concern with the rationality of belief remains untouched, since formal inference so understood is then simply irrelevant to concrete matters. To be sure, formal logical validity is relevant, not only to formal but to informal inference, and it is with respect to this point that Newman's conclusions about "logic"—here meaning validity—are still pertinent. For Newman is quite right to note that "As to logic, its chain of conclusions hangs loose at both ends; both the point from which the proof should start, and the points at which it should arrive, are beyond its reach; it comes short both of first principles and concrete issues" (G.A., 185). But then, once this is said, we have merely been reminded of what Aristotle knew quite well, that logic is concerned with validity and not truth,[69] and that the function it performs is the same that it performs for all thought, namely, organizing propositions and insuring their consistency as one control against error.[70] Newman himself says as much. Logical inference "is the great principle of order in our thinking; it reduces a chaos into harmony; it catalogues the accumulations of knowledge; it maps out for us the relations of its separate departments. . . . Our inquiries fall spontaneously into scientific sequence, and we think in logic, as we talk in prose, without aiming at doing so" (G.A., 185–86).

Given his psychologized view of logic as co-extensive with purely notional thought and expression, it is understandable at least that Newman would overstress the dangers of taking notions and "logic" as an ideal, since arguments in concrete matters are weakened by notions and cannot achieve the strict logical certainty of the "analytic paradigm."[71] Once Newman's view is adjusted, however, by jettisoning the requirement that concrete language be attenuated into notions to be made suitable for logical manipulation, it should be clear that logical validity is in no way opposed to or destructive of informal inference. It is limited with regard to informal inference, but then these limits have long been recognized. Logic cannot help us with arguments that are not formally valid but are sound on other (inductive, analogical) grounds, nor does it inform us about the truth or probability of propositions. For probability and truth in the concrete, Newman rightly turns to the "facts" and "circumstances" of the given case, and to the standards of argument relevant to different fields. It is just this "field-dependency"[72] of arguments that is central to Newman's theory of belief, since modal expressions such as "probable" are *judgments*, not calculations or deductions.

MODES OF INFERENCE: INFORMAL:

> *"To say 'I think' is to tease and distress, not to persuade"* (Apo., 203).

The method that Newman advances as the more realistic account of sound reasoning in concrete cases has since been forwarded, in various forms, by Michael Polanyi, Hans-Georg Gadamer, Raphael Demos, Kenneth Burke, Chaim Perelman, and a host of others: "It is the cumulation of probabilities, independent of each other, arising out of the nature and circumstances of the particular case which is under review; probabilities too fine to avail separately, too subtle and circuitous to be convertible into syllogisms, too numerous and various for such conversions, even were they convertible" (*G.A.*, 187).[73]

The "probabilities" of which Newman speaks here are those facts, truths, values, beliefs, and the like that are (or are able to be) "really" apprehended (or that cumulatively result in a real apprehension), not general ideas or propositions whose meaning one recognizes and can manipulate to some extent, but for whom those meanings lack specifics. Vividness of apprehension guarantees no truth, but without it whatever truth one does achieve must lack those particulars that constitute the concrete: "Abstract can only conduct to abstract; but we have need to attain by our reasonings to what is concrete (*G.A.*, 175). "Probability," moreover, points both to the personal factor in judgment, and to the fact that Newman offers us here not simply a psychological analysis, but an epistemological one, since probability is senseless without the correlative concept of evidence (*G.A.*, 210). Although obvious risks attend this method—psychological rationalization, bias of one sort or another, the "systematic distortion" of ideology, personal eccentricity or inadequacy in reasoning, and so on—nevertheless "evidence," and specifically the extension of that concept beyond traditional limits, is Newman's central epistemological concern.

Not only what Newman says, but the many examples of informal inference that he provides, bear witness to his concern with providing a rational basis for assent. "Let us suppose," Newman begins one such example,

> I wish to convert an educated, thoughtful Protestant, and accordingly present for his acceptance a syllogism of the following kind:— "All Protestants are bound to join the Church; you are a Protestant; ergo." He answers, we will say, by denying both premises; and he does so by means of arguments, which branch out into other arguments, and those into others, and all of them severally requiring to be considered by him on their own merits, before the syllogism reaches him, and in consequence mounting up, taken altogether, into an array of inferential exercises large and various beyond calculation (*G.A.*, 187–88).

Now, two souces of confusion and objection require attention if we are to appreciate how informal inference embraces all of our concerns thus far. These two points are (1) the relation of informal inference to language, and (2) the relation of informal inference to logic. In view of Newman's illicit conflation of "logic" with "notions," it is no surprise that Newman considers both language and logic inadequate instruments at best for conveying thought. But it will be seen that, once we adjust for Newman's views on logic, little harm has been done to his real interest in reasoning in the concrete. In order to have a minimum basis here from which to generalize, let us consider another of Newman's examples:

> A learned writer says, "In criminal prosecutions, the circumstantial evidence should be such, as to produce nearly the same degree of certainty as that which arises from direct testimony, and to exclude a rational probability of innocence. . . ." So far is clear; but what is meant by the expression "*rational* probability?" for there can be no probability but what is rational. I consider that the "exclusion of a rational probability" means the "exclusion of any argument in the man's favour which has a rational claim to be called probable," or rather, "the rational exclusion of any supposition that he is innocent"; and "rational" is used in contradistinction to argumentative, and means "resting on implicit reasons," such as we feel, indeed, but which for some cause or other, because they are too subtle or too circuitous, we cannot put into words so as to satisfy logic (*G.A.*, 210).

The relation of informal inference to language. In the first place, Newman nowhere says that informal inference is simply nonverbal, as one critic has suggested.[74] This point is crucial, since, had he said so, he would have opened himself to the charge that he has placed informal inference beyond public scrutiny, rendering it thereby impervious to public criticism. On the contrary, however, he says that informal inference requires premises (G.A., 208), which is to say verbal propositions. On the other hand, it is true that informal inference is somehow opposed to verbal reasoning. Newman claims, for example, that "Verbal reasoning, of whatever kind, as opposed to mental, is what I mean by inference, which differs from logic only inasmuch as logic is its scientific form" (G.A., 172). Here he equates verbal reasoning and (as the context shows) *formal* inference (and these in turn with logic or syllogistic), and seems to suggest that, as a mental activity, *informal* inference must be nonverbal. But this implication will simply not hold up in the light of Newman's other statements, the examples he actually gives in this section of informal inference, and indeed his own exemplification of informal inference in this and other works.

For example, in summing up the method of informal inference he writes: "Such being the character of the mental process in concrete reasoning, I should wish to adduce some good instances of it in illustration . . . but these are difficult to find, from the very circumstance that the process from first to last is carried on as much without words as with them" (G.A., 208–09). Elsewhere Newman says that informal inference is "more or less implicit" (G.A., 190). In these and numerous other statements, he is clearly claiming, not that informal inference is completely nonverbal but that it may be and often is *more difficult to verbally articulate* than the "notional" reasoning of formal inference, and that to some extent this articulation is impossible. If the mental process may be conducted as much with as without conscious employment of words,[75] then in principle it admits to some extent of conscious articulation—Newman's own examples being cases in point.

Formal, informal, and natural inference, then, must be thought of as on a continuum, quite as we saw that notional and real apprehension must be. Our ability to verbalize lags behind the richness of our experience and the complexity of our thought in handling it. But this is far from saying that language is not crucial in our conceptualization: "It will be our wisdom to avail ourselves of language, as far as it will go, but to aim mainly by means of it to stimulate, in those to whom we address ourselves, a mode of thinking and trains of thought similar to our own . . ." (G.A., 200–1). Verbal formal inference is simply the most general and structured expression of our thought, while informal inference may (or may not) find expression in appropriate and adequate language.[76] A glance at Newman's characterizations of informal inference in Chapter Eight supports this view, for he is continually using phrases such as "accumulated premises," "lines of argument," "grounds for thinking." While we may be able to think about such grounds and premises as imaged forth in the mind without verbalization, nevertheless such verbalization is not precluded: "I only mean that we cannot analyze a proof satisfactorily" (*G.A.*, 192). In short, there is nothing in Newman's doctrine here that requires that we suppose he is placing informal inference beyond the reach of critical scrutiny. Rather the opposite, I think, will become apparent.

The relation of informal inference to "logic." This problem is made more troublesome by Newman's own misconception of the nature and scope of that science. He was aware of competing formulations for logic (*T.P.*, 51–62),[77] but throughout the *Grammar* he frequently suggests that logic must be simply irrelevant to informal reasoning. "Here is an informal argument for the immortality of the soul. As to its force, be it great or small, will it make a figure in a logical disputation, carried on *secundum artem*" (*G.A.*, 202)? "Can we ascertain its force by mood and figure" (*G.A.*, 198)? At the same time Newman appears to contradict himself when he urges that informal inference:

> does not supersede the logical form of inference, but is one and the same with it; only it is no longer an abstraction, but carried out into the realities of life, its premises being instinct with the substance and the momentum of that mass of probabilities, which, acting upon each other in correction and confirmation, carry it home definitely to the individual case . . . (*G.A.*, 189–90).

Again, of a particular product of informal inference Newman states that it can be "powerfully stated" and even logically cast—"the logic of its . . . wording" (*G.A.*, 200). In light of this ambivalence, it is necessary to ask whether informal inference is what contemporary logicians (and rhetoricians) would call logical or not.

Logic, he claims, "cannot proceed without general and abstract propositions" (*G.A.*, 197).[78] Newman gives an example: "We shall have a European war, *for* Greece is audaciously defying Turkey" (*G.A.*, 197). The assessment of such an argument resides for Newman in concrete facts—"the [real] argument is from concrete fact to concrete fact . . . and practically syllogism has no part, even verificatory, in the action of my mind" (*G.A.*, 197). Here syllogism is equated with universals *notionally* apprehended, the implied major premise being "All audacious defiances of Turkey on the part of Greece must end in a European war." In fact, however, the terms of such a syllogism are quite capable of being "really" apprehended.[79] It is quite as though Newman equates logical expression and general terms with the communication of such to an audience *for whom the details of the argument are unknown.* Carlyle makes just such an equation in "Signs of the Times" (1829), where logic is "the mere power of arranging and communicating thought."[80] Indeed, the translation of concrete facts and particulars into abstract terms placed in tidy syllogisms for the purpose of communication, will, one can be sure, attenuate the concrete case, and may—*but need not in principle*—encourage an abstract view of the question, since even abstractions can be "really" apprehended by those with sufficient concrete knowledge. Thus, of even a particularly abstract argument by Dr. Samuel Clarke on the characteristics of God, Newman can write: "His words speak to those who understand the speech. To the mere barren intellect they are but the pale ghosts of notions; but the trained imagination sees in them the representations of things" (*G.A.,* 204).

Were logic equivalent to notions, in short, Newman's fears would be well founded. But logic is not equivalent to notions,[81] and once we change the meaning of logic from notional propositions in valid deductive relations to valid deductive relations exclusively, it is quite correct to say (as Newman seems to on occasion) that concrete reasoning can be consummately logical: "We think in logic, as we talk in prose, without aiming at doing so" (*G.A.,* 186). In the modern sense of logic this is to say nothing more than that our reasoning is often consistent or valid and that validity as such has nothing to do with the notions of which Newman speaks. Where he equates "logic" with "notions," the former appears simply irrelevant to informal inference: "How will *mere* logical inferences . . . help us on to the determination of the particular case" (*G.A.,* 197; emphasis added)? This identification lurks behind such a question as "Can we ascertain its force [i.e., the force of a concrete argument] by mood or figure?" The answer to that question is no—force here means material truth, and material truth is never ascertainable by the rules of formal validity. On the other hand, this is altogether a different matter from saying that a concrete argument cannot be cast into mood and figure. Some informal arguments, at least, can be so cast, and Newman's distinction between formal and informal sometimes fails to allow this: "But in truth, I should not betake myself to some one universal proposition to defend my own view of [the concrete] matter; I should determine the case by the particular circumstances . . . (*G.A.*, 197). But why force a choice between the two? One begins with particulars, and in using them one sometimes avails oneself of deductive (or inductive) structures that employ those particulars (or generals interpreted concretely). The two need not clash, and Newman at times says as much.

A useful point of comparison for Newman's position is provided by legal reasoning and its relation to formal logic. Newman was one of the first to draw the now commonplace analogy between legal reasoning and reason and argument in other fields or disciplines, particularly in rhetoric.[82] The point to this analogy is that reasoning in various fields is far less governed by the standards of deductive logic than hitherto believed. In *Legal Systems and Lawyers' Reasonings,* for example, Julius Stone argues at length'that legal reasoning both is and is not "logical," depending upon how extensively one attempts to apply the criteria of logical proof. Like Copi or Quine, Stone defines logic as the stuff of valid implication,[83] and distinguishes between logic kept within its "proper limits" and logic extended beyond those limits. Properly understood, law is often perfectly logical, if by that we mean that logical criteria can and should be the test of valid implication for specific arguments. Lawyers often intend to draw conclusions from premises deductively, and logic is one appropriate criterion of their success. By the same token it is incorrect to assert, as many jurisprudents have done, that a judicial decision is simply the valid logical deduction from a rule of law drawn from a precedent or regulation or statute.[84] In many cases, rules are not fixed entities, and even when they are, " 'the crucial decision is made before the reasoning can be cast into syllogistic form.' "[85]

This "crucial decision" is made through reasoning by analogy or example: "The finding of similarity or difference is the key step in the legal process."[86] Since all cases are to some extent novel and different, and since constitutions, regulations, statutes, and precedents are more or less ambiguous, or can be thematized in conflicting ways, legal reasoning is only sometimes a question of identifying a rule of law as a genus and slotting under it the case at bar as a species. Often legal reasoning is a process of analogizing the instant case to *competing* precedents, and articulating a *new ratio,* one that may depart considerably from the previous rule: "The crucial decision is then as to *relevant* similarities and differences, and this necessarily involves advertance to factors of justice and social policy, transcending any mere syllogistic relation to or among rules of law formally enounced in the available cases."[87]

But observe that this does not require the rejection of logic as "validity" for several reasons. First, formal logic may flourish in spheres of its own, for example, in closed philosophic systems such as those envisioned by Descartes or Spinoza. "There is no need to dethrone the syllogism from its own analytical realm; but . . . we must recognize that judicial creativeness lies largely beyond it."[88] Second, in those legal cases where, once the relevant precedent has been chosen, the rule of law can be seen to be clear, the decision for the instant case can be syllogistically deduced. Third, formal logic is relevant in at least an *ancillary* way to legal or informal reasoning.[89] Like Dewey, at times Newman tended to downplay to the point almost of nullity the suggestion that logic could be helpful at all, but only on the supposition that logic dealt wtih notions.

Thus Newman himself, in asserting that "The end of the Judicature is justice" (*D.A.*, 348), urges the view that justice nevertheless must not be suffered "to flow separate from . . . popular feeling." He cites the instance of a chief justice reversing the precedents of several centuries: "The circumstances explained the act. Those precedents were out of keeping with the present national mind, which must be the perpetual standard and authoritative interpreter of the law . . ." (*D.A.*, 350). Newman summarizes his approval of the legal and political elevation of practical reason over theoretical reasoning: "Such is self-government. Ideal standards, generous motives, pure principles, precise aims, scientific methods, must be excluded, and national utility must be the rule of administration. It is not a high system, but no human system is such" (*D.A.*, 352).

That judicial creativeness lies largely beyond the syllogism is a central point of twentieth-century jurisprudence, just as it was Newman's central point about reasoning in the concrete generally: "Syllogism, then, though of course it has its use, still does only the minutest and easiest part of the work . . ." (*G.A.*, 176). The real work resides in formulating the case, identifying data as relevant and important, summoning past cases as lenses through which to view the present, sifting facts, finding premises, making tentative inferences, and reformulating arguments and conclusions in the light of new evidence. No merely abstract, uncontextualized pronouncement of principle or law suffices to resolve the particular case:

Nor, again, is it by any diagram that we are able to scrutinize, sort, and combine the many premises which must be first run together before we answer duly a given question. It is to the living mind that we must look for the means of using correctly principles of whatever kind, facts or doctrines, experiences or testimonies, true or probable, and of discerning what conclusion from these is necessary, suitable, or expedient, when they are taken for granted . . . (*G.A.*, 232).

If such a process is not deductive, however, it is not strictly inductive either.[90] When Newman speaks of proof by converging probabilities, he seems to have in mind the sort of argument that helps us conclude that our house has been burglarized on the basis of an open door, a chair out of place, the dog whimpering, an open wallet, the mail scattered—all signs that to others may be not signs at all but inert and unconnected facts, but that to us say everything necessary. On analysis these signs do not provide the minor premises for five independent syllogisms; Mill denied that we reasoned that way, and so did Newman (*T.P.*, 110–11).[91] But it is also clear that these facts do not lead to an inductive generalization about a class; we have rather converging proofs leading to a singular.[92] According to Ferreira, Reid likened such convergence to strands of a rope; Newman compared it to a cable or rod, and more recently John Wisdom offered the image of the legs of a chair.[93] Newman writes: ". . . the conclusion in a real or concrete question is foreseen and predicted rather than attained; foreseen in the number and direction of accumulated premises, which all converge to it, and as a result of their combination, approach it more nearly than any assignable difference, yet do not touch it logically" (*G.A.*, 208).

We might, then, summarize our findings thus far about real apprehension, the whole man, and rhetorical reasoning in this way. First, apprehension of meaning (as well as conception of ideas and perception of things[94]) is an *interpretive* act that draws on a wide range of topical resources. Although ultimately beyond the reach of words to express adequately, nevertheless such apprehension (and conception), and the inferential processes they become part of, can to some degree be bodied forth in concrete, or rhetorical, language. Such language is not "non-notional" in the sense of "imagistic" or "non-rational," though it does resist attenuation into pure abstraction.

Second, the sort of inference that best handles *real* apprehension and the concrete generally is not syllogistic (enthymematic)—since syllogism at least tends towards abstraction—but is rather associative, metaphorical and analogical, and inductive. These forms are better able to include within themselves the actual details (facts, their values, the nuances of feeling) that concrete truths comprise, and they are frequently able to condense many lines of argument into one (as in metaphor or irony). According to Newman's doctrine of the "convergence" of probabilities, truth is a matter of discerning patterns within complex sets of interpreted structures, and real *assent* is less a matter of achieving resolution through a demonstration (whether certain or probable) than it is a matter of *transformation* through the evocation of facts and probabilities—what Newman calls "realization."

Third, we must not rush to conclude that the enthymeme, the vehicle of proof that combined thought and feeling for Aristotle, is deemed by Newman to be useless in concrete reasonings. It is true that Newman often did speak of the syllogism (and thus the enthymeme) as an argumentative structure cut off from the concrete. But when we recall that the real and notional are on a continuum; that abstract propositions can be really as well as notionally apprehended at one and the same time; and that Newman's purpose in the *Grammar* is itself rhetorically exaggerated in order to dislodge undue confidence in argumentative structures per se, then it is not difficult to see that the enthymeme—on Newman's own principles—can take on that combination of thought, feeling, and value that Grimaldi (quoting now no other than Newman himself!) argues that it does:

> Aristotle's text [the *Rhetoric*] conveys the strong impression of a theory of discourse which asserts that discourse in all areas, but particularly in the area of the probable and contingent, is never purely logical and notional. It must attend also to the audience and to the confrontation of speaker and audience (*ethos* and *pathos*). The notional exposition of the subject is insufficient in the sense that "demonstrations have no power of persuasion" [*D.A.*, 293].[95]

Thus Newman himself, in spite of his own one-sidedness and in spite of his mistakes about logic, can in principle fully accept the Aristotelian view of the value of the syllogism. But his own point is also true: in those complex and far-reaching questions of value, belief, and faith, the real locus of persuasion is not in the enthymeme *as such,* but in the multitude of details, facts, and vaguely apprehended beliefs that the premises of enthymemes only point to and inadequately represent:

> [W]e grasp the full tale of premisses and the conclusion, *per modum unius,*—by a sort of instinctive perception of the legitimate conclusion in and through the premisses, not by a formal juxta-position of propositions, *though of course* such a juxta-position is useful and natural, both to direct and to verify . . . (*G.A.,* 196; emphasis added).

In short, where rhetoricians speak of persuasion from the perspective of communication, Newman speaks from the perspective of psychological processes that arguments never wholly express. But insofar as they *can* be expressed, Newman clearly looks to rhetorical (rather than to abstract or dialectical) language and arguments.

In an insightful article titled "On Persuasion," the philosopher Raphael Demos arrives at many of Newman's conclusions. For Demos, "proof" arises as it were *behind* the premises of our deductions. That is, not the deductions themselves (save as they act as shorthand), but the facts the premises suggest, the associations they prompt, and above all the frameworks of beliefs they look to, which frameworks provide the interpretation and ranking of those facts—*these* are the real sources of justified assent, or persuasion. We come to believe (if we do come to believe) when we are enabled to enter the "world" of ideas and beliefs of another, to live in and "realize" the total configuration of facts and probabilities: "An idea must not only be thought but experienced and lived with; one must become intimate with it as with a friend, or absorb it, as one absorbs the language and customs of a people by living among them."[96] Like Newman, Demos links such a process of assimilation with real apprehension—vividness or "vivacity:" "Realization is congruent with genuine experience, in the sense of apprehension of a datum, or an idea, or a problem *as real*."[97] But note that, as in Newman, vividness is not merely the presentness of an image of some object or problem, but the felt conviction ("belief") that the claim is true:

> Evocation [of facts, details, etc.] is the only way, but conceived in a wider sense than that of vivid presentation. The mystic or the fundamentalist can be impressed, if at all, by the contemplation of an alternative standpoint in its character as informing a way of life, as a focus of civilization, a motive power of a world. An opponent is led into the milieu in which the idea in question is lived and practiced; he is required to pass judgment upon the whole civilization permeated by the viewpoint in dispute, after he has actively participated in its movement. It is a judgment, through life, of a way of life. . . . After all, vividness proceeds from apprehension of value, of significance, of importance.[98]

To speak of persuasion in the way Newman, Demos, and Grimaldi do is not to reject but to *subsume* the rhetorical syllogism within a more comprehensive account of persuasion. We might say that Newman operates along the range of reason that falls between the emphasis on explicit argumentative structures that we find in Toulmin and Perelman, and the implicit narrative relationships discussed in Burke's "dramatism" and Walter Fisher's "narrative paradigm." Newman usefully serves to remind us that these are not competing *Anschauungen,* but continuous modes of rationality. The final question that remains for us, then, concerns the *justifiability* of this persuasion: when is persuasive argument true? A complete answer is not possible here, but brief consideration of the criteria of adequacy in light of a concrete case may extend the prima facie case for Newman that I have been trying to construct.

A FURTHER EXAMPLE

Let us consider briefly a further example of informal inference, Newman's "factory-girl" argument lifted from Mrs. Gaskell's *North and South* (1855):

> "I think," says the poor dying factory-girl in the tale, "if this should be the end of all, and if all I have been born for is just to work my heart and life away, and to sicken in this dree place, with those mill-stones in my ears for ever, until I could scream out for them to stop and let me have a little piece of quiet, and with the fluff filling my lungs, until I thirst to death for one long deep breath of the clear air, and my mother gone, and I never able to tell her again how I loved her, and of all my troubles,—I think, if this life is the end, and that there is no God to wipe away all tears from all eyes, I could go mad" (*G.A.,* 202)!

About this melancholy plaint Newman says the following:

> Here is an argument for the immortality of the soul. As to its force, be it great or small, will it make a figure in a logical disputation . . .? Can any scientific common measure compel the intellects of Dives and Lazarus to take the same estimate of it? Is there any test of the validity of it better than the *ipse dixit* of private judgment, that is, the judgment of those who have a right to judge, and next, the agreement of many private judgments in one and the same view of it (*G.A.,* 202–03)?

Now it is evident that the factory-girl's lament is not an argument at all—there are no claims and no grounds put forth as such. It is equally clear, however, that we can reconstruct arguments the passage implies,[99] and that some of these, at least, can be formulated so as to be logically valid. Professor Jay Newman suggests the following: " 'Virtue is not always rewarded in this life; goodness must ultimately be rewarded; therefore, virtue is sometimes rewarded in a future life.' "[100] Here is another: God ultimately alleviates suffering; my suffering is not alleviated in this life; therefore, God will alleviate my suffering in Heaven. More plausible still is an inductive argument to a particular: there is a God and an afterlife because (a) otherwise I shall never be able to tell my deceased mother how I loved her or how I suffered; (b) I suffer now; (c) others are similarly afflicted; (d) otherwise this work and all my activities are meaningless; (e) otherwise all life is cruel and hopeless.

However we reconstruct the arguments, it should be plain that our logic and expressions merely scratch the surface of the informal inference at work. To put the factory-girl's thought into inductive and deductive form is, as Newman himself noted, helpful; but logical form is never the same as "force:" "Here then again, as in the other instances, it seems clear, that methodical processes of inference, useful as they are, as far as they go, are only instruments of the mind, and need, in order to their due exercise, that real ratiocination and present imagination which gives them a sense beyond their letter . . ." (*G.A.*, 205).[101] Logical form in isolation is unequal to the *material* weight of the full conditions of the inference, to what Newman calls "the multiform and intricate assemblage of considerations which really lead to judgment and action" (*OUS*, 230). To cast up syllogisms and inductions apart from the situation is to deal in isolated terms and propositions more or less "drained" of their associations, at least for those not privy to the original ideas and their context. Logic, in short, is not rhetoric; and if God did not see fit to save his people by dialectic, perhaps it is because it is through a rhetoric that points beyond isolated terms and propositions to details, data, assumptions, suggestions, and identifications—the "real" apprehensions that carry the probative weight of propositions. And rhetoric does this without sacrificing "logic" (here, valid arguments).

Unless, then, we connect the factory-girl's experience, embodied in the full range of her language, to our own experience, we are simply unable to assess its "force." Logic alone—that is, experience reduced to valid and sound, but also abstract argumentative structures—leaves out these details, and leaves out as well that emotional dimension that Aristotle suggests enables us to see the world (and thus those details) in a certain way—it may be in the proper way. If values such as relevance and importance are necessary to the assessment of a case, and they are, then the reconstruction of argument that fails to capture such values will always be deficient. But this is not an argument against those structures, only a call for more sensitive rhetoric and rhetorical criticism.[102]

Isolated syllogisms miss the details, moreover, because their language is inadequate, being either "notional" or, if "really" apprehended, then not "realizable" enough *in isolation*. In the case at hand, however, the factory-girl's "informal" language may be adequate, for it may be that we can attain by means of it to those concrete circumstances that allow us to assess its force. A real analysis is not possible here, but consider the following:

First, who the speaker is and what her conditions are shape our response to her implied claims, and if we do not *feel* and *see* these conditions, we will not be able to appreciate the evidence. To take but one example: through the language we *feel* the poignancy of her stifled existence in that "one long deep breath" of the clear air. Not only is "breath" here potentially symbolic, but the rhythm of the passage in which it occurs, the anaphora, the spondees, all are signs of both her longing and her exasperation. While it is true, as Aristotle notes, that such signs may stimulate invalid "sign-inferences" (*Rhetoric*, 1408a), nevertheless we can weigh such inferences against the full context of the passage and book and against the context of our own lives, and find the arguments sound (or unsound) for other, nondeductive reasons.

Second, who we are as audience, our familiarity or lack of familiarity with millstones and factories and the rest, is crucial to the epistemological-as-rhetorical success of the implied arguments. If we cannot feel such suffering, we effectively lack some of the evidence for the argument.

Given these conditions for persuasion, it follows that everything depends upon the language: "It will be our wisdom to avail ourselves of language, as far as it will go, but to aim mainly by means of it to stimulate, in those to whom we address ourselves, a mode of thinking and trains of thought similar to our own, leading them on by their independent action, not by any syllogistic compulsion" (*G.A.*, 200–01). But to say this is to suggest that first principles and antecedent probabilities are central to the interpretation of argument of the audience and simply do not exist *sub specie aeternitatis*.

To argue otherwise, to say that "her [the factory-girl's] argument must ultimately be separated from its context if we . . . are to be able to understand and evaluate it"[103] is simply to miss most of what Newman has said. "All of the circumstances of the case," "all of our powers and resources," comprise just those contexts that aid us in interpreting and assessing the argument. To abstract from the context some syllogism, to deny the influence of one's antecedent views, to fail to absorb the emotion and drift of the language, is to preclude judgment, not to enable it. It should be clear by now that an audience totally unfamiliar with rolling-mills or their equivalent will find nothing persuasive about this implied argument, while one who is familiar will (or might); and one for whom such mills and factories are emblems of an oppressive bourgeois hegemony may find this an argument, not for immortality, but for a Marxist account of oppression. In these and like cases, context is three-quarters of the argument.

EVIDENCE AND THE CRITERIA OF TRUTH

The questions of the possibility and identification of criteria to be used in establishing truth in concrete cases of the type we have just seen, questions that no theorist at present in the human or interpretive sciences can avoid, were also not avoided by Newman, although he himself does not distinguish, as many do today, the two levels at which the questions can arise: within any theory, paradigm, or fiduciary framework of belief, social practice, value, and so on, and between paradigms, where the question has mostly been whether two or more such frameworks are "commensurable," that is, "able to be brought under a set of rules which will tell us how rational agreement can be reached on what would settle the issue on every point where statements seem to conflict."[104] This latter question Newman almost never directly addressed (he seems to assume commensurability), though his way of handling the former can be seen to apply to it. We have seen already, of course, that more than one of Newman's critics has argued that Newman worries little about how we determine whether a concrete claim is true or false (Holloway), or that, while he may have professed to care about "truth," his philosophy in practice dismisses or destroys truth (L. Stephen, Jay Newman, Weatherby, O'Donoghue). Needless to say, this is an enormously complex issue that deserves a book in its own right, but, as the means of completing the discussion of the last two chapters, I wish to sketch out, even if only in a programmatic way, some of the strengths and weaknesses in Newman's position.

When we recall, first of all, the subtlety and recondite nature of natural and informal inference and the difficulty of bringing them to expression, and recall also that such inference presupposes first principles that are (often) historically relative, it cannot suprise us that Newman appeared and still appears to many to be susceptible to charges of historicism, fideism, or Sartrean voluntarism. The following, after all, is characteristic:

> Every one who reasons, is his own centre; and no expedient for attaining a common measure of minds can reverse this truth;—but then the question follows, is there any *criterion* of the accuracy of an

inference, such as may be our warrant that certitude is rightly elicited in favour of the proposition inferred, since our warrant cannot, as I have said, be scientific? I have already said that the sole and final judgment on the validity of an inference in concrete matter is committed to the personal action of the ratiocinative faculty, the perfection or virtue of which I have called the Illative Sense . . . and I own I do not see any way to go farther than this in answer to the question (*G.A.*, 235).[105]

Indeed, from his earliest sermons to the late *On Consulting the Faithful in Matters of Doctrine* (1859) and "Letter to His Grace the Duke of Norfolk" (1875), Newman regularly availed himself of a vague and recondite *phronesis* (or "genius" or "taste" or "judgment" or "conscience") as the test of truth in the concrete, and it should not astound us that unsympathetic critics have gone away baffled or unconvinced.

Yet to ignore, as these critics do, that Newman's pronouncements function in part as rhetorical counterweights to an over-scientized age, and to ignore the serious qualifications of such statements that Newman also gives us, naturally results in injustice. In Sermon XIII of the Oxford sermons, for example, we saw Newman appeal to Christian wisdom and love as controls against errors in reasoning—controls, however, that were themselves rooted in the reasons and values of community and tradition, sources Bacon saw as *idola tribus* but which Newman argued were fitting, if not wholly sufficient, tests of truth. In the *Via Media* application of the Vincentian canon in particular cases was said to be controlled by a *collective phronesis*, not by the private judgments of isolated individuals. In *On Consulting the Faithful* we find the appeal to certain general "indicia," "which are the *instrumenta traditionis*, and vary one with another in the evidence which they give in favour of particular doctrines; so that the strength of one makes up in a particular case for the deficiency of another, and the strength of the 'sensus communis fidelium' can make up (*e.g.*) for the silence of the Fathers" (*On Con*, 66).[106]

These indicia or rhetorical signs, which we find again in the second half of the *Essay on the Development of Christian Doctrine*, are attempts to specify, as clearly as the contingent material allows, what are *publicly accessible* sources for rational persuasion. Thus in the *Grammar* Newman cites approvingly Aristotle's dictum from *Nichomachean Ethics* that "we are bound to give heed to the undemonstrated saying and opinions of the experienced and aged . . ." (*G.A.*, 22), and repeatedly appeals to the authority of those who know, to ethos. Progressive Catholics enjoy recalling Newman's remark that "Certainly, if I am obliged to bring religion into after-dinner toasts (which indeed does not seem quite the thing) I shall drink,—to the Pope, if you please,—still, to Conscience first, and to the Pope afterwards (*Letter*, 138); but it is sometimes forgotten that it is not the uninformed individual conscience, or the individual conscience in isolation, but the individual conscience informed and influenced by others that constitutes *one* test for truth: "Is there any test of the validity of [a particular argument for immortality] better than the *ipse dixit* of private judgment, that is, the judgment of those *who have a right to judge*, and next, *the agreement of many private judgments in one and the same view of it*," (*G.A.*, 203; emphasis added)?[107]

Moreover, mere consensus for Newman does not make something true or acceptable (as some literary theorists among others are at present persuaded), but is simply *one* sign of truth among others.[108] In addition to consensus (in fact the explanation of it), arguments must account for the facts, possess scope and coherence, and in general "work" in the way that William James suggests:

> Let me begin by reminding you of the fact that the possession of true thoughts means everywhere the possession of invaluable instruments of action. . . . Agreement [with reality and with others] thus turns out to be essentially an affair of leading—leading that is useful because it is into quarters that contain objects that are important. True ideas lead us into useful verbal and conceptual quarters as well as directly up to sensible termini. They lead to consistency, stability and flowing human intercourse. They lead away from excentricity and isolation, from foiled and barren thinking.[109]

Newman articulates his own version of pragmatism in this way:

> It is by the strength, variety, or multiplicity of premisses, which are only probable, not by invincible syllogisms,—by objections overcome, by adverse theories neutralized, by difficulties gradually clearing up, by exceptions proving the rule, by unlooked-for correlations found with received truths, by suspense and delay in the process issuing in triumphant reactions,—by all these ways, and many others, it is that the practised and experienced mind is able to make a sure divination that a conclusion is inevitable, of which his lines of reasoning do not actually put him in possession (*G.A.*, 208).

We might try to summarize Newman's position by recalling Van A. Harvey's not wholly felicitous phrase "soft perspectivism." For Harvey (as for Newman), perspectivism is simply a given of modern epistemology, historiography, and theological hermeneutics. What Harvey (like Newman) explicitly repudiates is the "hard perspectivist" notion that because facts are theory-laden, are "always already" interpreted artifacts relative to a system, and because any system can verify its truth-claims by showing that it accounts for the very facts that emerge only within its purview, therefore all perspectivism is mere relativism, arbitrary and imposed, the product of hermeneutical strategies of interpreting communities.[110] Against this view Harvey argues what Newman only implies, that while all facts may rightly be said to be theory-laden, still it is possible and necessary to distinguish, for example, certain *events* (facts) from their interpretations. There is, in other words, a *common reality*, interpreted but nonetheless common, which helps to explain why we choose one interpretation over a *really* arbitrary set of codes, meanings, or myths; it is because, in James's language, they "work."[111] Newman would add that there is also a common human nature that, although (again) always interpreted, is nevertheless (like much of sensible reality) part of the *test* of any theory, while in addition it provides material for just those theories.

To talk about orders of reality that are *common* to various paradigms is, of course, a way of locating the grounds for commensurability among paradigms. Referring to an account of Karl Popper's philosophical realism, Gerald Graff observes that ability to account for the "facts" can provide one such criterion: "That we cannot conceive of a fact without *some* interpretive paradigm does not mean that this fact can have no independent status outside *the particular paradigm* [meaning now any theory or hypothesis] *we happen to be testing at the moment"*:

> The assumption . . . is that though all facts are paradigm-bound, any set of individual facts will be "disparate" with respect to certain paradigms. *It is these disparate facts that provide, by a test of falsification, an independent test of these paradigms.* The facts which we have come to regard as "unrefusable" (or as "brute facts") are those which cross-check successfully with so many possible paradigms and conflict with so few of those that we have yet encountered that we feel safe in concluding that they correspond to the way things are.[112]

Now, in *The Present Position of Catholics* (1851) Newman argues that we test the truth of first principles and measure competing first principles (and thus, by implication, the hypotheses, "views," "paradigms" they support) according not only to how well they account for independent, unrefusable facts, but according also to their self-consistency, their scope, their ability to withstand time, their universality, and their extent of reception.[113] In other words, while admitting that facts are theory-laden, we test our theories against common facts by employing diverse rhetorical criteria of adequacy for truth—that is, rhetorical signs: "and I own I do not see any way to go farther than this."

To be sure, I am not suggesting that Newman's position is well defined or without problems. In the first place, it is quite open to the charge that his criteria of truth at whatever level are indefinite and vague; I will return to this objection shortly. In the second place, Newman is also open to the charge that his elevation of the importance of "antecedent probabilities and considerations" in informal inference is intrinsically conservative and even reactionary, as if the problem of coming-to-truth were merely a matter of returning-to-truths-already-established and making further inferences from them. Such a view may be said to enshrine entrenched ideologies (political, psychological, religious). Hans Georg-Gadamer has frequently come under this attack himself:

> But even if we grant Gadamer everything that he wants to say about human finitude rooted in historicity, this does not lessen the burden of answering the question of what is and what ought to be the basis for the critical evaluation of the problems of modernity. . . . It is not *sufficient* to give a justification that directs us to tradition. What is required is a form of argumentation that seeks to warrant what is valid in this tradition.[114]

Habermas makes an even stronger claim when he alleges that "Gadamer's prejudice for the rights of prejudices certified by tradition denies the power of reflection."[115] I have tried to indicate at least that this objection, while an important one, does not do justice to the power of "suspicion," "critique" and "reflection" in Newman's rhetorical philosophy (a philosophy, after all, which has been said to provide a primer of skepticism), although it is also true (as Bernstein says of Gadamer) that Newman is "virtually silent on the complex issues concerning domination and power."[116] The rhetorical use of antecedent considerations derived from one's fiduciary framework, or tradition, or paradigm, or social practice, does not preclude reflection; on the contrary it makes reflection possible since it makes tradition answerable to ongoing testing. To be sure, this does not explain *how* reflection escapes co-option by ideologies.

As for the vagueness with which Newman discusses his so-called illative sense—*phronesis*, judgment—we must certainly admit the fact. Newman attempts to provide none of the analysis (of the sort we get in Habermas, for example) of the conditions that must obtain if *phronesis* is to be effectively practised in a community or society at a given time. And yet we might also ask if Newman's refusal to specify, not conditions but criteria of truth, is not rather a virtue than a vice. If the concrete is as indeterminate as Newman argues, any attempt to lay down determinate criteria of truth would be futile. Again, Richard J. Bernstein seems to me to respect the contingency of the subject matters of rhetoric and hermeneutics when he writes:

> I do not believe it is possible to state once and for all, in a rigorous, determinate, and nonvacuous manner, what are or ought to be the standards, criteria, or rules by which interpretations can be epistemically evaluated. In this respect I categorically reject one of the deepest aspirations of the modern epistemological tradition as a deceptive illusion. But I also do not believe what many have claimed to be a consequence of, or to be entailed by this rejection, namely, that if there is no permanent legitimate and legitimizing matrix of cognitive evaluation, then one must ultimately concede that interpretations are based on assumptions, beliefs, and norms that are epistemically arbitrary.[117]

In sum, Newman's rhetorical philosophy, although consistent and persuasive, is neither complete nor wholly satisfactory. Gaps and questions remain—though we may also note that they remain generally unfilled and unanswered even today. In any case we can admire Newman's ability to discover and map out much of the territory that rhetoric and hermeneutics have explored in our own time. Fortunately, while Newman failed to address many problems that we now see more clearly, his actual practice of inquiry, argument, interpretation and judgment in particular cases indicates concretely (if not as systematic theory) some of those conditions for the procedures of finding truth. As a result, we can proceed in the following three chapters to examine how Newman applied and exemplified his insights in a variety of fields.

4

METHOD IN THEOLOGY

*That if real success is to attend the effort to bring a
man to a definitive position, one must first of all take pains
to find HIM where he is and begin there.*
Kierkegaard,
The Point of View

In the preceding chapters I distinguished the articulation of method
from its practice, attempting to draw out Newman's theory of inquiry and
argument from the Oxford sermons and the *Grammar of Assent*. In this
and the following two chapters I turn to that practice in various subject
matters, making a further distinction, namely that between Newman's
interpretations (*what* he characteristically looks for and at) and his methods of discovery and interpretation (*how* he characteristically does so). In
the first case I am interested in showing how Newman interprets the actual
disciplines of history, theology, literature, and the like, as well as specific
questions, problems, and cases *within* any one of those subject matters.
What sort of knowledge does "history" seek? What does Newman typically consider when he approaches a problem in history, literary criticism, or theology, and on what principles does he do so? What is
historical explanation? What is "science?" What is a theologian? In the
second case, I am interested in correlating the methods of the historian,
theologian, literary critic, and philosopher of education, both as Newman
describes them and as he instances them in his own works.

In both cases I seek to clarify the relationships that hold among
Newman's theory of reasoning and arguing, his interpretations of subject
matters and problems within them, and his actual practice of inquiry,
argument, and judgment in diverse fields. The goal of these chapters,
then, is clearly not to cover in depth each field or discipline that Newman
treated, but rather to identify and explain the how and why of what I am
arguing is a consistent but flexible philosophy and method across intellectual boundaries. Since theology offers the richest store of Newman's own
discussion of method, and best instances it as well, I begin with theological method, and specifically with the *Via Media*.

HISTORICAL METHOD IN THE *VIA MEDIA*

The present focus on what Newman called historical method[1] in the
Via Media and the *Essay* on development applies also to the principles
and methods in Newman's overall approach to history as a discipline and
in his other historical or biographical studies.[2] C. F. Harrold correctly

108

describes Newman's method as "informal, loose, 'journalistic,'" but betrays his own epistemological biases by suggesting that, because Newman does not aim at "objectivity"—that is, because his method is informed by his "ever-present moral sense"[3]—it is not properly historical. We have seen, however, that for Newman the only way to find and order the facts of concrete cases, such as those of history, is to be polemical in at least a general sense of the word: to interpret the real out of the resources or topics of one's experience, the *copia*[4] of thoughts, words, feelings and so on relevant to what is new. Historical cases simply cannot exist outside of the interpretive stance of the historian, and that stance is never exhausted by established facts or laws. This is not to deny that historical investigation includes and relies upon innumerable fixities—"facts which are external to us, present with us, and common to us all" (*Dev.*, 113)—such as make up much of the data of the natural sciences. Nor is it to deny that one can do history in a more exact and scientific way, abstracting general laws to interpret and predict new situations.[5] Nevertheless, one must at least begin with, and ultimately return to, facts to some degree rhetorically interpreted. Thus Harrold is right: "He [Newman] is, after all . . . literary rather than learned, interpretative rather than merely factual in his treatment of history, yet gifted with infallible literary taste." Newman always:

> approaches history with his mind made up and solidly established on principles which, for him, throw light on everything, and are indeed truer and more real than historical facts. Thus he explains the facts in accordance with a philosophy which appears to him much clearer than the facts themselves. . . . For Newman, then, historical writing involved philosophy and psychological insight.[6]

More precisely, just as "philosophy" and "insight" (and the vehicle of them both, topics[7]) allow an inquirer to structure without predetermining his case, so "literary taste" enables him to render that case persuasively to others. Eloquence and *copia* unite with philosophy; the method of the concrete sciences is to some degree, for some purposes, that of rhetoric and literature.

As a way into this study, I mention two other analyses of the method of the *Essay*, those by Thomas J. Norris and Nicholas Lash. Among other things, Norris shows how the method of the *Essay* is an instance of the *organum investigandi* adumbrated in the *Grammar*. That method:

> is a process of investigation which begins from the data relevant to the problem, and moves to a tentative solution of the problem,

which is variously named, as an "antecedent probability," or, more generally, an "hypothesis." This hypothesis is in turn subjected to critical reflection in order to test its soundness and validity, and the result of this "verification" is a certitude of the mind that the hypothesis is the truth.[8]

According to Norris, this "process"—from problem to hypothesis, verification, and certitude—parallels the structure of thought in the *Grammar,* which is understood to describe a movement from experience to apprehension, inference, and certitude. But this way of talking about Newman's method is rough at best, since, among other things, it misses the complex ways one finds or "invents" problems, data, and hypotheses or decides what is and is not relevant.[9] But then Norris is forced to miss these questions, for he merely uses Newman's own grammar, which, as we saw in the second chapter, is incomplete in the sense that it was never intended to be able to talk about invention of cases.[10] Study of Newman's method, however, clearly requires such discussion.

More accurate and interesting is Lash's study, particularly his awareness of the persuasive aspects of the *Essay* (insisted upon by Newman himself) and of the role presumptions and antecedent probabilities play in concrete issues. For now I wish to focus on the second point, and specifically on the attention Lash gives to the importance of "taking a view" in Newman's approach. Lash observes: "Only by employing a synthetic, imaginative, 'historical' method, in which the flair of the interpreter is as important as the data he attempts to interpret and coordinate, can the historian hope to get a 'view' of his subject."[11] By "flair," of course, Lash means to refer (at least in part) to just those antecedent considerations that I previously equated with *topoi,* by means of which an inquirer explores and constitutes a problem: in a word, finds or takes a view. Although Lash is correct, moreover, to say that, in its entirety, or "as an ideal,"[12] a view refers both to the topics that "interpret and coordinate" data, and to the data themselves, nevertheless I wish to discriminate the case or "view" as a whole from the structuring *topoi* or overarching view that makes the location, interpretation, and coordination of the data possible in the first place. Granting the ultimate inseparability of topics from data—for otherwise topics would be not relatively indeterminate but meaningless—still, topics and how they function apart from *determinate* data are the proper methodological focus.

But how does one achieve a view? To note simply, as Norris and Lash do, that one uses "hypotheses" or "flair"—i.e., presumptions, antecedent probabilities, "views of life" (*OUS,* 228), and so on—is correct but incomplete: these tell us the kind of thing that is found and used, but not how it is found, or how it is structured, so that one does indeed achieve a "perspective" rather than something else (for example, simply more facts). I have suggested that a view is an interpretation of a concrete problem, grounded in the experience of the inquirer, and structured so as to comprehend the given case. In this chapter, some examples of this will be analyzed in detail and then correlated with Newman's own explanations as well as with my previous analysis of his philosophic method.

Our road leads ultimately to the *Essay* on development—to its rhetorical components of inquiry and argument and to the main features of Newman's interpretation of doctrinal history. On our way, however, we need to turn briefly to the *Apologia*, and then to venture for some time on Newman's own *via media:* the former provides key facts as to the foundation of Newman's thinking on doctrine and Church, and the latter is both a chief source of the *Essay,* and itself offers an impressive "view" of doctrine deserving close attention as such.

In the introduction to the *Via Media,* Newman explains that he intends "to catalogue, sort, distribute, select, harmonize, and complete" (*V.M.,* I, 24) an Anglican theology that avoids alleged errors of popular Protestantism and "Romanism." But it is in the *Apologia* that Newman explains on what principles he founded and coordinated such a theology and why he sought a path for the Church between Protestantism and Romanism in particular.

The first of his principles is dogma: ". . . dogma has been the fundamental principle of my religion: I know no other religion; I cannot enter into the idea of any other sort of religion; religion, as a mere sentiment, is to me a dream and a mockery" (*Apo.,* 54). As is well known, Newman's battle was, accordingly, with "liberalism," or "the antidogmatic principle and its developments" (*Apo.,* 54), which perforce included much of historical Protestantism and its cult of "private judgment."[13] Dogma "was the fundamental principle of the [Oxford] Movement of 1833" (*Apo.,* 54).

The second of Newman's principles, "based upon this foundation of dogma," was "that there was a visible Church, with sacraments and rites which are the channels of invisible grace. I thought that this was the doctrine of Scripture, of the early Church, and of the Anglican Church" (*Apo.,* 55). To be more complete: in much the same way that the principle of dogma derived in part from an even more fundamental principle of conscience, so the idea of a visible church was involved with Newman's acceptance of other principles—notably, the sacramental principle, tradition, and especially Antiquity as "the true exponent of the doctrines of Christianity and the basis of the Church of England" (*Apo.*, 36). The Fathers are particularly important, for, again, "I thought that the Church of England was substantially founded upon them" (*Apo.*, 60).

A third principle was Newman's anti-Romanism, held "from boyhood" as "a sort of conscience or prejudice," and directed against the Pope as Anti-Christ and against certain "corrupt" doctrines and practices of that church.[14]

These three leading principles—dogma, Church (or, in its essence, Antiquity), and anti-Romanism—provide the grounds, the antecedent considerations, upon which the *Via Media* is raised. They are truths productive of other truths and probabilities, and are themselves the products of persuasive reasoning (however implicit) used to constitute the indeterminate question of religion. In addition, they are the principles with which Newman regards the more specific question of the "doctrinal basis of [Anglican] theology," that is, of *how* the church proceeds in locating and establishing doctrinal truths; this latter is the main question and problem of the *Via Media*.[15] After I review the basic argument, I can more clearly explain several crucial aspects of Newman's method.

Newman initiates his discussion by distinguishing sides taken on the issue of the "sources and rules of faith." He does this quite unobtrusively in his first lecture in two unequal stages, each of which itself has two (unequal) parts. In the first stage Newman begins by noting on what *fact* it is that Anglicans agree with Protestants—namely, "in considering the Bible as the only standard of appeal in doctrinal inquiries" (*V.M.*, I, 26). But he then identifies what *principle* it is that Protestants mistakenly ignore—namely, that the Bible is not a sufficient "informant in divine truths" (*V.M.*, I, 28) and requires some companion principle of interpretation to "strengthen such intimations of doctrine as are but faintly, though really, given in Scripture" (*V.M.*, I, 29). In holding to Scripture exclusively, Protestants are not wrong simply, but one-sided in their view of the case. Newman argues by a reductio ad absurdum: with each sect, indeed with each individual Christian reserving the right to judge the meaning of Scripture, the very idea of revelation, of a something revealed, is overwhelmed by sheer clash of opinion.[16] For lack of an authoritative judge, the Protestant position in effect destroys revealed religion:

> [T]he Bible is not so written as to force its meaning upon the reader; no two Protestant sects can agree together whose interpretation of

the Bible is to be received; and under such circumstances each naturally prefers his own. . . . Accordingly, acute men among them see that the very elementary notion which they have adopted, of the Bible without note or comment being the sole authoritative judge in controversies of faith, is a self-destructive principle . . . (*V.M.*, I, 27).

In the second stage, Newman again postulates opposing positions, now on the question of the interpretive principle itself. He first observes that the conventional Protestant arguments that seek to deny, for example, Rome's stand on tradition as the proper interpreter of Scripture, are in fact destructive of the Protestant's own position, for it is precisely on the basis of Apostolic tradition that *all* Christians accept the very divinity of Scripture. Simply to deny or ignore tradition results again in an absurdity.[17] In opposing Protestantism and Romanism, and in dismissing the former (and for good) when its arguments not only cannot justify but end by destroying its own position, Newman simultaneously removes an antecedent presumption against the latter (their use of tradition), a presumption that many Anglicans shared. More positively, Newman establishes the real contest as that between Romanists and Anglicans, for both parties profess the equally necessary principles of Scripture on the one hand, and an authoritative interpretive tradition on the other.

In the next step of this second stage, Newman engages his real opponent. Having shown that Protestants and Anglicans are in accord on a matter of fact but opposed on principles, he now seeks to argue that Anglicans and Romanists, though in accord on the matter of principles, are opposed on matters of fact (and, as he notes, to argue facts is much more laborious than to argue principles—hence, the lectures following on infallibility, the essentials of the Gospel, and so on). For when it comes to specific doctrines of faith, Rome can be seen to have "corrupted" the original deposit of faith by substituting a "tradition of men, that . . . is not continuous, that . . . stops short of the Apostles" (*V.M.*, I, 37), for the true tradition based on and ultimately found only in (as Rome nominally agrees) Antiquity. In a word, Rome pays "theoretical"[18] lip service to Antiquity while, "in practice," she elevates the authority of the church, of mere men, over truth. Although offering only an hypothesis or "view,"[19] Newman opposes Anglican tradition to Roman pseudo-tradition: ". . . [t]hey supersede the appeal to Scripture and Antiquity by putting forward the infallibility of the Church, thus solving the whole question [of the sources and rules of faith], by a summary and final interpretation both of Antiquity and Scripture" (*V.M.*, I, 48). In so doing, they substitute human words for divine revelations safeguarded in the Fathers.[20]

Now clearly, even the first volume alone of the *Via Media* is considerably more complicated than the preceding sketch discloses, and it may therefore be objected that I have merely provided an outline of only the first section of a long work. I concede the point. But I note that the outline identifies just those key topics from which Newman's discussions in subsequent lectures derive, and from which, when necessary, I can draw forth further relevent points. In effect if not in detail, moreover, the outline duplicates the argument of Lecture Five, which Newman himself calls a "delineation and defence of the *Via Media*" (*V.M.*, I, xviii).[21]

Using this outline as a point of departure, I wish to call attention to several aspects of Newman's approach, whose seeming obviousness actually conceals important implications for method. At the center of the inquiry, for example, are persons and groups—Protestants, "Romanists," Anglicans, the Apostles, the Fathers, the Reformers, those who have transmitted (or corrupted) the *depositum* of faith. Newman is extremely sensitive to their varying historical situations, just as he is to an urgency rising from Anglican history vis-à-vis Roman Catholicism, evident in his very first sentence and never absent subsequently: "at this time," "How we became committed to so ill-advised a course," "the immediate reason for discussing the subject," "What we need at present," and so on. In other words, the problem of faith is construed in terms of people, their actions, events, times, and places, and of one group in particular whose cause is at stake.[22] To make this same point another way, what is at issue regarding faith is not simply *what* is theologically known and asserted, but *how* one knows and asserts, "the sources and rules of faith" as means and method—not the intellectual thing, but the collective, concrete act of knowing and ruling.[23] Moreover, since Newman himself is concretely engaged in such knowing, he implicitly relies on his own principles and sources of religion—dogma, Antiquity, and anti-Romanism—to argumentatively establish and steady his view. In sum, Newman "interprets and coordinates" a more or less indeterminate and multiform religious situation in terms of people in the act of knowing and in terms of a triad of *religious* principles. He does not approach it "abstractly"—on secular principles unsuitable to this case, or in terms of some "truth" apart from the needs of his own time or tradition—but rather concretely, identifying enduring and general religious principles with the positions and actions of relevant groups, who thereby "concretize" them.[24] These principles are simply postulated as givens, as enduring and necessary values for this problem; at the same time they are "general," non-determining "touchstones"[25] that help to locate relevant circumstances and facts (in this case, such things as Scripture, church history, tradition, and the like).

This point can be made clearer by analyzing how Newman works; the method is familiar, for it is the one used in the Oxford sermons. In essence, Newman opportunistically uses what is at hand, by taking up views or positions around him that are relevant to his problem, reducing them to succinct propositions of fact, value, or policy, and then generating opposing positions (also succinctly stated) as equally relevant to the case, but overlooked, forgotten, ignored, or suppressed by his opponent.

Thus Newman picks up a historically if not theologically complex "Protestantism" as something relevant to his problem, insofar as its valuation of Scripture promises to specify concretely the "something said" that his principle of dogma requires. This reduction to *sola scriptura* then functions as a sort of legal brief (and its mnemonic value as such should not be underestimated) for the Protestant side on the sources and rules of faith. But the argument, Newman shows, is simply inadequate to "all of the circumstances" of the case. At this point, he names two: first, the "difficulty" (*V.M.,* I, 27) that Scripture is not a determinate and unambiguous but a relatively indeterminate and contestable "source and rule;" second, the fact that, historically, or in practice if not in theory, Protestant holding to the "surface" of Scripture has precipitated disagreement and schism as to what Scripture means, thus denying the very principle of a "visible Church" (and a fortiori Antiquity).[26] This view of Scripture as indeterminate obviously accords with Newman's earlier thought in the Oxford sermons, and with the later thought of the *Grammar*. But this view also necessitates some way of determining what Scripture means and a visibly authoritative way to conserve the principles of dogma and Church.

At this point Newman alludes to Antiquity; but he does not extrapolate. Rather, as previously indicated, he turns to Roman Catholicism as something also relevant to his problem, insofar as its valuation of "tradition" promises also to maintain the source and rule of dogma in Scripture, and yet also to complete it with the rule and source of an authoritative church interpreting its sense. In other words, Newman uses, in various ways, the Protestant failure to embody the principles of dogma and church in Scripture alone to look about for real or supposed facts to correct and/or complete the case. Protestant failure frees him to consider another—the Roman Catholic—promise; Scripture *sola* he replaces with a tradition that allegedly maintains Scripture *and* interpretation, thus conserving dogma and Church.

In exploring the Romanist side, moreover, Newman uncovers a further fact that cannot be accounted for by the Protestant case (namely, its self-contradiction in its argument against tradition), so that it is now summarily dropped from the discourse as irredeemably incompetent. More important still, Newman alleges to have also located a fact fatal to the Romanist position: while "in theory" Rome's tradition *is* "traditional," tracing its doctrines back through the church to the normative interpretations of Antiquity, "in practice" it can be seen to not genuinely be so, but instead to elevate a church of fallible men over that supposedly normative source.[27] This failure, in turn, will finally permit Newman to submit a via media as the answer to the question. In sum, whereas Protestantism is deficient in principle, a deficiency that causes it to overlook facts, Rome "is far more faulty in the details" (*V.M.*, I, 42) or facts, introducing materials that "corrupt" its principles, in part by taking one of them (interpretation) too far. These inadequacies, again, the *Via Media* is meant to remedy.

With the essential argument of the *Via Media* thus laid out as an interlocking structure of dialectical pairs of terms—either "contradictory" or "correlative" or both, depending upon what one refers them to—I can explain in some detail the rhetorical-philosophical rationale for Newman's method and can apply it to specific examples. Earlier I began with the question of what a "view" is, and turn now to expand upon previous remarks.

THE CONDUCT OF INQUIRY: "VIEW"
AS DIALECTICAL TOPICS OF RHETORIC

In *Loss and Gain* Newman equated a "view" with "perspective," and in the *Idea* he likened it to "rising" above facts "as if mounting some high hill . . . by way of reconoitring [*sic*] [the] neighborhood" (*Idea*, 125), thus "reducing to order and meaning the matter of our acquirement" (*Idea*, 120). The view attained may be farreaching—indeed, at its height, "philosophy" is the taking of a "connected view of old and new, past and present, far and near" (*Idea*, 121)—or the view may be restricted; but "It matters not whether our field of operation be wide or limited; in every case, to command it, is to mount above it" (*Idea*, 125). To get or take a view, then, one somehow "rises above" in order to acquire facts relevant to his problem; orders them according to their "mutual and true relations" (*Idea*, 121); and interprets and judges their meaning and import: "the connexion of fact with fact, truth with truth, the bearing of fact upon truth, and truth upon fact, what leads to what, what are points primary and what secondary. . . ."[28]

On the other hand, one can fail to ascend or achieve a view. As A. Dwight Culler has noted, Newman differentiated a view from two possible degeneracies, from "viewiness" (*Idea,* 12) on the one hand, and narrowness of vision on the other. "Viewiness" is the undisciplined, inconsistent, and often merely "theoretical" attempt to contact the real, "a smattering of a hundred things" (*Idea,* 109). Narrowness of vision is specialism, expertness without comprehensiveness, or merely an acquaintance with facts: "Viewiness, therefore, is the opposite extreme from "mere learning" [specialism]. As mere learning was fact without system, so viewiness is system without fact. The one is reason run mad as the other was memory forgetful of its place. And between these two, with a judicious admixture of reason *and* memory, fact *and* system, the man of philosophic habit is asked to construct a broad but accurate *view.*"[29]

We can thus rationalize a view in this way: because any concrete problem of "fact" will be more or less indeterminate, one requires (in argument and sometimes even in thought) devices of discovery and interpretation, *structured* as opposing terms in order to comprehend the full range of the contingent case and determined so as not to impose but rather to "call forth" all of the phenomena and circumstances of its determination. In contingent matters on which one deliberates, which Newman equated with the concrete and which is the realm of rhetoric par excellence, one needs both reason *and* memory, *system* to ascertain *fact.* In the *Idea,* "method" or "principles" sort out the "things" of a "well-stored mind" (*Idea,* 125–26). I have already mentioned the rhetorical counterparts of these terms: *topics* explore the *copia* of experience. And obviously reason-memory, system-fact, method-things, principles-store, *topoi-copia,* are themselves topics intended to disclose aspects of the contestable material of Newman's view—"views" of what a "view" is.

In the Oxford sermons, and again at every juncture of the *Via Media,* Newman uses terms or propositions as guidelines to explore and build the concrete problem of the sources and rules of faith. For only topics—relatively formal and empty places common to many subjects (theory-practice, principle-fact, external-internal), or places more specialized and determined (Protestant-Romanist, Antiquity-Church, infallibility-Vincentian Canon) allow one to hunt for arguments and data without predetermining or treating one-sidedly the question at hand; rather, the phenomena and arguments called forth will "weight" one side over another (perhaps resulting in a "convergence" of probabilities). How, then, do the topics comprising any "view" function?

First, from out of an inquirer's experience—that *copia* of first principles, "truths and facts," probabilities, imaginations, inferences, "prejudices" and the rest—the inquirer draws forth what promise to be (on the

117

basis of that experience) relevant topics in order to seek arguments on the issue at stake. For example, Newman picks up the Protestant focus on Scripture as relevant to dogma and church, a "place" to hunt for the facts and truths necessary for judgment. The ability to do this effectively is scarcely innate; there are many ways to go wrong. Should memory forget its *own* place, for example, it leads the mind merely to wander among its storehouse of things, unable either to order what it has or to generate *topoi* by which to systematically encounter the new.

Second, Newman frames his questions by opposing terms, or he generates such an opposition when a "place" proves internally inconsistent or inadequate. The main reason for this is that such an opposition provides a comprehensiveness that is necessary when the problem is concrete: Newman can avoid "theoretically" imposing answers on the case, or treating the case one-sidedly. In the Oxford sermons, Newman created such a comprehensiveness by generating the opposite of received definitions of reason; to those who reduced conscience to the moral sense he answered by "completing" it with duty; natural religion he completed with revealed. In the *Via Media* the Protestant reification of "private judgment" and the imposition of it on a question where it is by no means given as the sole answer, simply begs the question of faith. Again, the Romanist appeal to tradition, which provides in theory a dialectical structure (Scripture-interpretation) in response to the Protestants, itself proves inadequate in fact, a "pseudo-tradition" that requires a "genuine" one. In a word, Newman postulates or builds a *range of relevancy,* with his terms as termini within which he expects to find the stuff of judgment. The terms are intended to exhaust the possibilities of the question (for example, nothing falls outside of "theory-practice"), and thus are either correlatives to be combined or contradictions requiring the negation of one or the other.

Third, Newman's own terms range from being wholly empty and formal to relatively informed (for example, "conscience," "development," "informal inference," and so on). In either case, however, his terms are always designed to prevent predetermining a question. A good example that I will return to shortly is Newman's use of the Vincentian Canon: it is a purposeful, general rule that respects the indeterminacy of the Scripture it confronts.

Fourth, a view requires what Culler called a "judicious admixture" of both of its sides (that is, when they function as correlatives and not contradictions—one cannot *combine* "corruption" and "development"): "judicious" because one must judge the individual case, "admixture"

118

because both terms are values necessary to the case. Thus, a "view" abstractly considered requires both topics *and* the facts they disclose. But which topics, and how many facts, and so on, will depend on the individual case. Again, Scripture must combine with interpretation, but how much weight either one will be seen to deserve must clearly depend on the passage, its context, past interpretations of similar passages, and a host of other considerations.

Fifth, each "side" of a dialectical pair can be expected to disclose new meanings and new relationships, or in Newman's terms new "aspects," concrete questions, and even "views" subordinate to the overarching problem. These too can be structured topically, and they in turn will produce further probabilities weighting either side of the opposition. For example, Romanist "tradition" produced Antiquity-Church; the latter term raised the key problem of "infallibility," which in turn was investigated "morally" and "politically"; this pair then called forth new material, and so on.

Finally, one can indeed fail to achieve a view: one may not possess the requisite *copia* of "experience" or may possess it unknowingly or use it wrongly; or one may lack the requisite ability or "flair" to generate appropriate and truly disclosive topics. Topical or rhetorical inquiry—like rhetorical argument—is always attended by the risk of postulating irrelevant terms, or of exploring them blindly or haphazardly, or of not feeling their force. It is always a choice and a risk challenging the "whole man." Said otherwise, practical experience must test and control, by combining with theory, determinacy of doctrine, mere intellect or mere words; and what is intersubjective and "public" must control and combine with the "personal" when the latter would be "unreal" by itself (as in religion, history, ethics, and so on).

Thus, while others have discussed *what* views are constituted of, they have missed *what topics do:* as constitutive and interpretive rules of a more or less enduring and general nature, they disclose phenomena relevant to judgment in contingent cases. But topics—that is, an inquirer using topics—can of course only do so much: as Lash notes of Newman's "range" of data in the *Essay,* it is unrestricted in principle, but in practice it is very much restricted by the ability, interests, and learning of its author (and, one might add, of its intended audience).[30]

With regard to the *Via Media,* similarly, it is now easy to see how Rome is "viewy" and the Protestants "narrow," for the former "pushed principles too far,"[31] while the latter lacked principles sufficient to comprehend the case. Both were thus "theoretical," "unreal," and "abstract" in their own ways, for Rome merely spoke without acting accordingly, and the Protestants imposed a priori a theory of private judgment not suitable to this concrete case.

Newman's use of *topoi,* therefore, is wholly of a piece with his philosophy of reasoning. Since there is no alternative in concrete matters to postulating (consciously or not) the scope and definition of the problem, it is only sensible to begin with those "facts and truths" already located by others, for they provide a way into the problem and a means of exploration. In the *Via Media* Newman explicitly adverts to the fact that he uses Rome in this topical fashion, and that he does so for two reasons: first, Anglicans who feel that the importance of the Church must not be neglected are regularly charged with "Popery," and thus need "to show why they are not Romanists, and how they differ from them" (*V.M.,* I, 5); second, like all Christians, Anglicans have a right to a "positive doctrine," a theology. Whether erroneously or not, Rome offers a coherent view, one that Anglicans must answer if they wish to replace it, since it preoccupies the ground. Thus "Rome" provides at once a port of entry and a point of departure: "But in doing this [stating the Anglican view] we necessarily come across the existing teaching of Rome, and are led to attack it, as the most convenient, or rather only, way of showing what our own views are. It has pre-occupied the ground, and we cannot erect our own structure without partly breaking down, partly using what we find. . . ." (*V.M.,* I, 6).[32]

In the second place, since there is also no alternative in concrete matters to interpreting such questions with respect to "all" of the relevant resources of inquirers, it is simply necessary to address what is valued and believed by others—in a word, it is necessary to attempt to persuade rather than "compel." What is to be known, in other words, is relative to knowers, whose interests broadly speaking thus make up part of the concrete case: if one is to treat that case concretely, one must speak to those interests, to the "whole man." This Newman does in two ways: he freely entertains the possibility of diverging interpretations (or "diverging probabilities"), arguing for the superiority of his own by disclosing the inaccuracy or inadequacy of the other; and he seeks an overall "effect"[33] from many arguments, a "persuasion" (or better, a transformation or conversion) and not merely an intellectual assent. Accordingly, Newman's most frequent line of argument (curiously overlooked by Holloway) is to concede-and-lead: he concedes to his interlocutor as much as he can (or, as he often notes, more than he has to[34]), in order to lead him to what he (the opponent) has overlooked, forgotten, ignored, and the like. Newman's widely lauded sensitivity towards and ability to articulate his opponents' positions is thus not only a personal "flair," but also something methodologically required. Further, the strategy explains how Newman need not "collapse into" the views of his audience or merely play to the crowd: for his topics possess integrity to his own past experience, learning, traditions, and so on, as well as receptivity to the new and divergent. The concrete case is thus bounded on the one hand by relatively enduring principles, and on the other by the facts and circumstances of particular historical situations—a description as much of doctrinal development as of personal appropriation of the concrete. Indeed, when we turn to the *Essay*, we will hear Newman himself describe his method—and the nature of historical development of ideas—in very similar terms. At that time I will have opportunity to specify further "aspects" of inquiry and argument. For now, however, my analysis of the "how" of the *Via Media* requires a corresponding analysis of the substance of Newman's view— the "what" that Newman characteristically looked for and at in all of his works.

THE SUBSTANCE OF ARGUMENT: RHETORICAL PRINCIPLES OF INTERPRETATION

I noted above that Newman looks at method and not doctrine in the *Via Media*. What he has done is to transform the essentialist question, What is our faith? into the existential and actional one, How in fact do we come to know?[35] This is, of course, perfectly in keeping with his thought in the *Grammar* that relative and contingent matters require real as well as notional apprehension and assent. Thus Newman himself is actively engaged in such knowing while he discusses and describes it, seeking the relevant circumstances of the sources and rules of faith. In principle, of course, these include both *what* is known as well as *how*. In practice, however, Newman himself tends to slight the former as either already known and uncontested (in the case of Rome) or as telling results of what is, after all, bad procedure (Protestantism). For example, the question with which he begins is not that Scripture is necessary, but *how* it is to be interpreted. He makes this point again vis-à-vis Rome, when the question is not Scripture and interpretation as necessary abstract principles, but how they operate in practice. Newman is always at pains to get at the doing:[36]

> Romanists would fain confine us in controversy to the consideration of the bare and acknowledged principles of their Church; we consider this to be an unfair restriction; why? because we conceive that

121

Romanism is far more faulty in its details than in its formal principles, and that Councils, to which its adherents would send us, have
more to do with its abstract system than with its practical working
(*V.M.*, I, 42).

On the other hand, it is true that—on the question of the interpretation of Scripture, for example—*what* the doctrines are upon which Anglicans and Romanists differ is indeed important. Thus Rome is accused
of being "neglectful of Antiquity"; and evidence, such as it is, is brought
forth. But even here, the doctrines ultimately referred to *how* they are
created; that is, either according to the Vincentian rule or the "infallibility" of the Church. Similarly, in Lecture Five the problem is not private
judgment, but how and when it applies. And so on.

If Newman's ideas do not collapse into those of his audience, it is also
true that his ideas on the sources and rules of faith are inseparably tied to
the people, arguments, and procedures that made them real. This is what
I mean by Newman's combining theory and practice: between the wholly
abstract idea and the pre-reflective life out of which it rises there exists a
persuasive method, sensitive to both, that is critical to the full enterprise of
philosophy.

Further, one can begin to understand why it is impossible to give
fixed and determinate meaning to Newman's rhetorical principles—the
personal, practical, actional, and so on. Simply, it is the circumstances of
the particular case that will determine them. In one case what is focused
on as the personal and practical may give way to something else in
another; in a given case any number of aspects may be referred to as
"practical": what in one discussion is classified under one rubric ("abstract" or "concrete") may in another be spoken of under its opposite. For
example, by the "practical" nature of the *Via Media*, I refer in one context
to the fact that it has a pastoral purpose; in another context to the fact that
it is geared to method; in a third to the fact that it was a personal
argument for Newman; in a fourth to the fact that it is "historical" and
inductive rather than deductive, and so on. Or again, in the *Grammar*
"judgment" is a personal and practical supplement to logic; but in
dogmatic questions "private judgment" is "mere theory" (*D.A.*, 141)
when it is without external means of judgment to control it; and in yet a
third context, that of theological discussion *within* a dogmatic structure
(e.g., the Catholic Church), judgment in the sense of argument and
discussion is encouraged.[37]

Finally, it is clear that the Oxford Movement itself spoke to and
reflected a more general need to combine theory and practice in religion.

"Both in Oxford and in the country were men whose hearts burned within them for something less speculative and vague"[38] than the "dry" and "dialectical"[39] theories of an Arnold or Whately; men and women, on the other hand, who were intellectually unwilling to settle, like the Evangelicals, for the " 'first beginnings' of Christian teaching."[40] "Thus the time was ripe for great collisions of principles:"[41] "The [Oxford] movement had its spring in the consciences and characters of its leaders. To these men religion really meant the most awful and most seriously personal thing on earth. It had not only a theological basis; it had still more deeply a moral one."[42]

R. W. Church returns to this *topos* repeatedly in his work: "It was, on the one hand, theological; on the other, resolutely practical."[43] Hence what I am calling the rhetorical intent of the *Via Media* refers, as I noted above, to the subject under discussion (the sources and rules as *method*), its own method of argument, and its rhetorical intent. Certainly Newman intended to "catalogue, sort, distribute," and the like. But he also sought an effect, a persuasion "whose main object is not controversy but edification" (*V.M.*, I, 7)—a distinction between kinds of rhetoric to which I shall return. Like the *Essay*, the *Via Media* is the practical extension of what Newman for a long time understood as theology (namely, that it was a "deductive science"). As he later accepted, theology in fact ranged along a continuous band, from formal to informal and pastoral. Newman, needless to say, practiced the latter (He is a master of pastoral theology"[44]) and always tended to think of the former as grounded in and controlled by it.

It follows that, in the *Via Media,* Newman reconstituted not only scattered and opposing positions, but a *people;* the rhetor does not merely persuade, but creates and transforms.[45] We can say here of theology what was said previously of philosophy in the *Grammar,* that it is rhetoric—a rhetorical inquiry and a rhetorical argument and judgment. But it is, at the same time, a rhetoric that recognizes relative and varying determinacy in facts and truths: "dogma" and "church" thus possess a general but crucial meaning; Scripture is indeterminate, but not uniformly so. In other words, here too Newman's principles and methods cannot be understood apart from their concrete application. It is a rhetoric, finally, and as Newman himself notes, that cannot be locked in to controversy, persuasion, deliberation. Using Newman's own method, we might say that the ends of rhetoric extend from a rhetoric of resolution to a rhetoric of conversion and transformation (a distinction that parallels Newman's frequent opposition of "controversialists" and "inquirers").

Perhaps I can best summarize the nature of Newman's rhetoric by turning briefly to the means by which Newman suggested Scripture was to be interpreted. I am not now interested in the richness of his distinctions and arguments or in the correctness or incorrectness of his views that Scripture is relatively indeterminate and that "Antiquity" and not "infallibility" provide the normative basis for faith and church. I wish only to point out the rhetorical nature of the interpretive rule of Vincent of Lerins, which stated that "that is to be received as Apostolic which has been taught 'always, everywhere, and by all'." (*V.M.*, I, 51).

Paradoxically, in upholding the Vincentian Canon, Newman is at his most rhetorical and his least. Least rhetorical because the rule "freezes" in Antiquity the doctrines of the Church and renders tradition a static and immutable fact, essentially unconnected to and in no way constituted by the unique people and events of different historical periods. This curiously un-Newmanian position is, of course, soon overthrown in favor of a dynamic and rhetorical sense of history. On the other hand, Newman is at his most rhetorical since the rule itself functions as a condensed "rhetoric," a statement of three major *topoi* one must use to find arguments to locate doctrine. Newman himself recognizes an almost radical indeterminacy in the rule, so that it almost becomes rhetoric-with-a-vegeance: "For instance: what is meant by being 'taught *always?*' does it mean in every century, or every year . . .? Does '*everywhere*' mean in every country, or in every diocese? And does the *Consent of Fathers* require us to produce the direct testimony of every one of them . . ." (*V.M.*, I, 55–6)?

Now the Catholic Newman calls this rhetoric "unmanageable" (*V.M.*, I, 56, n. 7), while the Anglican Newman recognizes this indeterminacy as a problem in theory but not in practice, appealing to an ongoing, never-quite-specified *phronesis*: ". . . [w]hat degree of application is enough must be decided by the same principles which guide us in the conduct of life, which determine us in politics, or trade, or war, which lead us to accept Revelation at all, for which we have but probability to show at most . . ." (*V.M.*, I, 56).[46] Here more than anywhere else in the *Via Media*, one witnesses the tensions pulling at Newman: the rhetorical impulse urging him to turn to method, history, people, the concreteness of Scripture, the rhetoric of Scriptural interpretation; and a lingering ahistoricism necessitated not only by his anti-Romanism, but by an intellect (and historical period) that had not yet won the insights of developmental historical consciousness.

The *Via Media* was clearly but a step towards the momentous crisis of the *Essay*, so much so that it might be objected that the preceding analysis exaggerates its importance. But that would be to miss the point that method in the *Via Media* is no different from method elsewhere in Newman's work and that the virtue of my analysis lies accordingly in its applicability. It will not be difficult, therefore, to discern in the *Essay* Newman's topical method, his use of persuasives, and so on. For just this reason I intend to concentrate, in my treatment of it, on matters so far only briefly considered.

THE RHETORIC OF HISTORY
IN THE ESSAY ON DEVELOPMENT

It is evident from this work that doctrinal developments are a slow, ethical (*Dev.*, 47, 336), cumulative growth, which elsewhere Newman analogized to the personal appropriation of slowly converging probabilities.[47] If assents can be "grown into," however, they can also be grown out of. A thousand difficulties need not create a doubt—but they might; and when they do, first principles themselves may be proven to have been, all along, "prejudices" (*Apo.*, 53) and even "tyrants" (*Prepos.*, 283).

Of course, this is just what occurred to Newman in the critical years 1839–41, when his theory of the *Via Media* was "absolutely pulverized" (*Apo.*, 99), and part of its foundations—one of his three first principles of religion, Anti-Romanism—was (gradually) knocked away. As early as 1835 (*Apo.*, 94), Newman had divided the issue between England and Rome as he did in the *Via Media* in 1837, namely, Antiquity versus Catholicity (*Apo.*, 101). Each side thus possessed a "special point or plea" (*Apo.*, 101). But this topical opposition is typically more complex than it appears, for, in the first place, it conceals the fact that in 1839 Newman held with the Anglican divines that Rome had "perversely appropriated" (*Apo.*, 102) its note of Catholicity and that it is thus partly by way of concession that Rome comes in Newman's argument to possess it. Second, the more telling objection against Rome is that of "corruption." Finally, Anglicans have troubles of their own: ". . . it is a fact, however we justify ourselves, that we are estranged from the great body of Christians over the world" (*Apo.*, 106–07). Put slightly differently, each side had a special weakness, "the book-theology of Anglicanism on the one hand, and the living system of what I called corruption on the other" (*Apo.*, 101).

In 1839, however, in studying anew the Monophysite controversy[48] as part of his larger effort—mostly historical—to work out a solution to his problem, Newman came to recognize for the first time an untenableness in the *Via Media*. For he saw in the position (vis-à-vis Rome) of the Monophysites in the fifth century, an analogy to that of the

Anglicans in the nineteenth: " 'It was difficult to make out how the Eutychians or Monophysites were heretics, unless Protestants and Anglicans were also . . .' " (*Apo.*, 108).

Matters soon worsened when Newman was brought to reconsider the question of the Donatist controversy, for he now linked Augustine's "Securas judicat orbis terrarum" to the heresy, not of the Donatists, but of the Monophysites:[49] ". . . they were words which went beyond the occasion of the Donatists: they applied to that of the Monophysites. . . . They decided ecclesiastical questions on a simpler rule than that of Antiquity; nay, St. Augustine was one of the prime oracles of Antiquity; here then Antiquity was deciding against itself" (*Apo.*, 110). Newman concludes: "By these great words of the ancient Father, interpreting and summing up the long and varied course of ecclesiastical history, the theory of the *Via Media* was absolutely pulverized" (*Apo.*, 99). In this way the Anglicans were, then, if not wholly cut off from Christ, entirely lacking any positive theology.

This was 1839. Newman converted in 1845, the same year in which he finished the *Essay*, two years after his last Oxford sermon (which prefigured the argument from development[50]), and ten years after he had first formulated the "*status* of the controversy" (*Apo.*, 92) between England and Rome. Augustine's *dictum* had caused a major breakdown, subverting Anglican Antiquity and the Vincentian Canon, while concurrently heightening the antecedent probability of the soundness of the Roman claims.[51] Nevertheless, the charge of corruption still stood against Rome; gradually Newman's question became this: if Anglican "immutability" is not true, can Roman "mutability" be somehow Apostolic?

But we should not cross Newman's bridge to the "development" side of doctrine too quickly, as though all of this were merely a matter of topical juxtapositions and subtle historical interpretations. Indeed, on Newman's own principle argument and assent are not matters of verbal manipulation only, at least not on such profound issues. And in fact the historical and biographical substance and "structure" of Newman's conversion (as found in the *Apologia*) is instructive in its own right. Abstracting from many of the details and generalizing from others, we may note the following:

First, it is clear that, during the years 1839–45, Newman was attempting to clarify in his own mind, and to establish on persuasive grounds, what was initially and for some time only an implicit and imaginative apprehension of a possible truth. Newman's conversion, in other words, was the result (according to the *Apologia*) of slowly accumulating, converging probabilities. Newman writes of the change brought on by Augustine's *securas judicat:*[52] "I became excited at the view thus opened upon me . . . I had to determine its logical value, and its bearing upon my duty" (*Apo.,* 111). "I determined to be guided, not by my imagination, but by my reason" (*Apo.,* 112). These quotations are summational, so to speak, in the following ways. In the first place, Newman elsewhere is the first to defend the idea that most people do and should rely on and rest in what is only credible to their imaginations[53]; indeed, the *Grammar's* defense of natural and informal inference accounts for the truism that most people are quite unable to "weigh and consider" their imaginative assents. Here, on the contrary, imagination is not enough; the case is different and must be taken on its own terms ("God deals with us very differently; conviction comes slowly to some men . . ." *DMC,* 233).[54] In other words, Newman is here documenting a self-reflective use of informal inference, and what might at first blush appear to be an equivocation or contradiction (sufficiency versus insufficiency of "imagination") is diffused by the circumstances of differing concrete cases, since the educated have a duty to inquire (*G.A.,* 144–45).

In the second place, by "logical value" Newman intended pretty much what he meant by "logic" in the *Essay,* namely "a vague but general intellectual coherence,"[55] which might, but very well might not, satisfy a logician (i.e., be logically valid). But Newman is saying little more than that validity alone is not an adequate test of truth: "I had a great dislike of paper logic. . . . It is the concrete being that reasons . . . the whole man moves. . . . All the logic in the world would not have made me move faster towards Rome than I did . . ." (*Apo.,* 155–56). Accordingly, to be guided by "reason" meant to seek probable and persuasive facts and arguments and to look for a convergence from many various inductions, deductions, analogies, metaphors, and the like. "Reason" here thus ranges in meaning from formal validity to inductive soundness, "determinate" to "persuasive" content, thought to feeling, and argument to action ("duty"), with the "whole man" judiciously combining, according to the exigencies of each case, both sides of each opposition.

The second matter of rhetorical concern regarding this conversion is that "all" of the circumstances of his case clearly extend for Newman beyond intellectual doctrinal argument or formulation, though such may be a primary source.[56] That is, ultimately it was the Bishop's rejection of *Tract 90,* and the incident of the Jerusalem Bishopric—the living actions of men in historically unique times and places—that weighted the scales against England. What is at stake for Newman in the *Apologia,* as in the

Via Media, is not a religion and theology in the abstract, but a practice, a polity, a people of God, and a reflection on these alive to *all* of the facts, intellectual and practical. I might generalize here about Newman's thought as a whole and say that the sort of rhetoric that keenly interests Newman is one that necessarily includes but also extends far beyond verbal argument in matters where only the "slow growth" of thought, word, and deed is efficacious. It is not so much a resolutive rhetoric in restricted and relatively superficial questions that engages Newman, but a transformative rhetoric (as far as that is possible in language) of conversion or edification, in the more profound matters of thought and action.[57] The *Apologia*, of course, tells the "story" of such a transformation, but also seeks, like all of Newman's other major works, to *initiate* such a transformation in the reader.[58] In sum, Newman seeks a transvaluation of values[59] not possible if the overall argument is confined to logic proper, to facts common to all, to neat propositions, or to words divorced from actions.[60] "Rhetoric" thus ranges (as we saw in the Oxford sermons, the *Grammar,* and the *Via Media*) from restricted problems requiring resolution to life-choices inviting transformation and *Bildung.* As a result, the Newman critic must always distinguish where within that range Newman "places" a problem of "persuasion," *or* (as in the *Apologia*) in what he seeks to combine the two "kinds."

Topically, then, it should be fairly clear by now how one method and "view"—the immutable tradition of the *Via Media* located in Antiquity by means of the Vincentian Canon—gave way under press of accumulating probabilities to the suggestion that Roman doctrine need not be "corruption" and might be "development".[61] Nor should it appear strange that I call Newman's interpretation of doctrinal development, and of history as an intellectual discipline and a temporal process, rhetorical. As is known, his overall approach was quite different from most of the dominant intellectual currents behind and around him—idealism, empiricism, positivistic science, scholastic apologetics, and so on. It may be true that his method shares something with the historicism of Möhler; certainly with the hermeneutics of Schleiermacher and Dilthey; but, first, Newman had no direct acquaintance with Schleiermacher and none at all with Dilthey, and second, these methods miss crucial elements of Newman's work, so that the whole of it is not uniformly illuminated. More positively, my argument here and throughout is that rhetoric is uniquely suited to explain and justify both theory and practice in Newman. In the present context these refer to (a) his method of interpretation in the *Essay,* (b) his interpretation of the history of doctrine in the Church as a process of persuasion, and (c) his interpretation of the Church as a complex and dynamic rhetorical community. By briefly considering each of these areas, I can bring to light how interconnected yet flexible are the ideas and methods of Newman's theology.

RHETORICAL METHOD

In order to better appreciate Newman's topical philosophy (and a fortiori his theology),[62] it is helpful to contrast it with several competing approaches. With regard to history and doctrinal development as processes, for example, Chadwick shows how Newman departs from scholastic apologetic:

> The "logical sequence" of Newman is not the "logical implication" of the scholastics, though the latter might be a part or aspect of the former. It means rather a subsequent perception of a harmony or congruity or "naturalness" in the way in which ideas have developed.[63]

Now, two points should be stressed: first, "logic" as implication or valid deduction is more or less a part or aspect, but is simply not the whole of "development"; depending on the case, an argument or development might be perfectly syllogistic (as many arguments in the *Essay* are). Second, development and history are "concrete": doctrine grows in the minds, hearts, and actions of all of the members of the Church; it is communicated slowly, over time, and often unconsciously, in rational-pathetic language, as well as in conduct and ritual. As such, historical development is "rhetorical" in that it is persuasive and *relative to* the powers and limits of unique people, times, and circumstances. It is rhetorical connectedness to the concrete that places Newman at one remove from the scholastics and two from an apologist like Bossuet, for whom doctrine did not develop and at most was only "a translation into clearer language."[64] For Newman, a development of Christian doctrine—indeed, in principle the development of any idea, *including the idea of development*—is, in form and content, relative to and known only within the horizon of a specific *Sitz-im-Leben:* hence Newman's own postulation in the *Essay* of a "horizon"—"corruption-development," "doctrine-'life' "—and his stress on persuasion as means and end.

It is just as certain, though perhaps less patent, that Newman shared little with the idealist program of Hegel, for whom material concrete history was an embarrassment only inadequately addressed by means of dialectic. Whatever it is, Newman's method is not a dialectical unfolding

129

of *Geist*, nor, for that matter, a dialectical ascent to a Platonic (Patristic or otherwise) realm of Ideas. While it is not unreasonable to point out, as Lash does, that "development" theologically presupposes the "ontological pre-existence"[65] of the "idea" that develops, nevertheless Newman's philosophical concern is to argue that an "idea" is known only *in time* (*Dev.*, Int. 21), wholly mediated by the probable and changing.

Finally, Cameron convincingly argues in what ways Newman partakes of the empiricist temper, notably Hume's. On the other hand, the low tradition of empiricism, as embodied for example in the positivistic outlook of a scientist like William Froude, is directly opposed by Newmanian rhetoric; as Ong argues, positivism actually makes the same error as idealism: where the latter (one-sidedly) abstracts from the *material* constitutents of being, the former overidentifies thought with scientific induction, and being with only a (one-sided) selection of the facts. Ong writes:

> Froude had made the typical mistake here. He had mistaken *a* use of facts for *the* use of facts; he had the knack of using them as the physicist does. And because it was a knack, because this knack, nothing else than a way of making an induction, was so basic a process, so elemental an item in the life of the intellect, that it could not very well be described in terms more elemental than itself, he took it for granted that it went with the facts themselves and that his particular method must always accompany the use of facts. In doing this, he, consciously or not, discards whole worlds of reality which do not fit in with his method. When he saw Newman employing another method, he took it for granted that Newman was denying to facts the kind of primacy which they should enjoy.[66]

In the *Essay* Newman himself employs a positivistic sense of "experimental science" (i.e., Baconian physics; *Dev.*, 110, 112) as the topical contradictory to method in "Moral" subjects (e.g., history, ethics, political science, religion, theology; *Dev.*, 110, 112).[67] Whereas the former by comparison comprises a "strict investigation" (*Dev.*, 110) "into facts which are external to us, present with us, and common to us all" (*Dev.*, 113),[68] the "less exact" method of history, theology, and the like, must argue to (and with) the facts by means of various antecedent considerations:

> In such science, we cannot rest upon mere facts, if we would, because we have not got them. We must do our best with what is given us, and look about for aid from any quarter; and in such circumstances the opinions of others, the traditions of ages, the prescriptions of authority, antecedent auguries, analogies, parallel

cases, these and the like, not indeed taken at random, but, like the evidence from the senses, sifted and scrutinized, obviously become of great importance (*Dev.*, 111).

This topical opposition of "science" and "moral subjects" is, of course, essentially the same as that encountered in the Oxford sermons and the *Grammar*, as is Newman's justification of reasoning by antecedent probabilities: in "all matters of human life, presumption verified by instances, is our ordinary instrument of proof, and, if the antecedent probability is great, it almost supersedes instances" (*Dev.*, 113–114). More fully, different subjects (erected on different principles) require different evidence and matter:

And, further, if we proceed on the hypothesis that a merciful Providence has supplied us with means of gaining such truth as concerns us, in different subject-matters, though with different instruments, then the simple question is, what those instruments are which are proper to a particular case. . . . The less exact methods of reasoning may do His work as well as the more perfect, if He blesses them. He may bless antecedent probabilities in ethical inquiries, who blesses experience and induction in the art of medicine (*Dev.*, 111–12).

Newman concludes: "The same principle is involved in the well-known maxim of Aristotle, that 'it is much the same to admit the probabilities of a mathematician, and to look for demonstration from an orator' " (*Dev.*, 113).

Just this need to select topics (antecedent probabilities) lies behind Newman's attack on historians like Milman and Gibbon, whose choices of *topoi* were in Newman's judgment reductionistic, or simply wrong,[69] and makes the conversion or the moral-intellectual state generally of the theologian so crucial an aspect of Newman's thought.[70] In fact, as indicated previously, Newman elsewhere goes so far as to identify his understanding of the importance of topical argument (and by implication persuasion) as one of his main achievements: " '. . . if I have brought out one truth in anything I have written, I consider it to be the *importance of antecedent probability* in conviction.' "[71] In the present case, this adverts to his reconstitution of the *status* of the question[72]—from static to dynamic "tradition"—and his efforts in Chapter II of the *Essay* to render the second term of his topic, "corruption-development," the greater antecedent probability.

It is not, however, topics that we need to consider, the selection and dialectical structuring of which should by now be discernible in practically all of Newman's formulations, so much as the data of historical inquiry, the methods of argument and interpretation, and the principles upon which Newman's choices rest. Since my purpose with the *Essay* is not to examine or test the argument itself, but to establish the nature and unity of Newman's thought, I intend no more than to explore selected lines of thought. In order to do so, however, we need to review the main parts at least of Newman's general argument, which are essentially as follows:

First, having rejected the Vincentian Canon as a "solution . . . as difficult as the original problem" (*Dev.*, 27)—the problem, namely, of the fact of doctrinal change—Newman suggests his hypothesis or "view" of the development of doctrine,

> *viz.* that the increase and expansion of the Christian Creed and Ritual, and the variations which have attended the process in the case of individual writers and Churches, are the necessary attendants on any philosophy or polity which takes possession of the intellect and heart, . . . that, from the nature of the human mind, time is necessary for the full comprehension and perfection of great ideas; and that the highest and most wonderful truths, though communicated to the world once for all by inspired teachers, could not be comprehended all at once by the recipients, but, as being received and tranmitted by minds not inspired and through media which were human, have required only the larger time and deeper thought for their elucidation (*Dev.*, 29–30).

Second, given the theoretically equal possibilities of "corruption" or "development" of doctrine (*topoi* that exhaust the range of "change"), Newman argues that, in principle at least, *all* significant ideas develop, and that, for that reason and others, development of Christian doctrine is "antecedently probable." Finally, by employing as criteria of genuine development various notes or signs, Newman attempts to argue by converging probabilities that what the Roman Church has proclaimed to be Apostolic doctrines are in actuality true developments.

In the first place, then, the data involved in Newman's notion of development of ideas are not restricted to *propositions*. They extend to include and indeed focus on the origins of propositions in and the "use to which they are put in the life, worship and witness of the church."[73] As "aspects" of and perspectives on what is taken to be reality, the kinds of ideas Newman studies are such as to "arrest and possess the mind," they "have life," and "attract and influence" in a real and not merely notional way:

[W]hen some great enunciation, whether true or false, about human nature, or present good, or government, or duty, or religion, is carried forward into the public throng of men and draws attention, then it is not merely received passively in this or that form into many minds, but it becomes an active principle within them, leading them to an ever-new contemplation of itself, to an application of it in various directions, and a propagation of it on every side (*Dev.*, 36).

In a word, such "living" (or persuasive) ideas are concrete; Christianity is a "fact in the world's history" (*Dev.*, 3), and ipso facto involved in "all" of the circumstances of historical and social life. Of the kinds of development, accordingly, Newman emphasizes those, like the "political," "in which 'doctrine' in the narrow sense plays a very small part."[74] "Historical" developments (for example) comprise "the gradual formation of opinion concerning persons, facts, and events" (*Dev.*, 46); "ethical" developments "are not properly matter for argument and controversy, but are natural and personal, substituting what is congruous, desirable, pious, appropriate, generous, for strictly logical inference" (*Dev.*, 47): "The development then of an idea is not like an investigation worked out on paper, in which each successive advance is a pure evolution from a foregoing, but it is carried on through and by means of communities of men and their leaders and guides; and it employs their minds as its instruments, and depends upon them, while it uses them" (*Dev.*, 38).

In accordance with Newman's view later articulated in the *Grammar*, then, that apprehension and inference in concrete matters are activities involving (more or less) the "whole man," Newman here situates ideas (and doctrines) and their development in terms of the "whole" life of the men whose ideas they are. *Practical* life of conduct, worship, rites, usages, polity, and even "superstition" is the ground and control of the theoretical formulation of doctrine. This same point is made another way in the above passage, in Newman's indication that doctrines are not the unique possession or product of "experts" (e.g., theologians or hierarchy), but dwell in "all" of the members of the relevant public or community. Theory thus combines again with practice, expert "leaders and guides" somehow combine with (Newman will later use the term "consult") a nonexpert laity—not certainly to formulate doctrine, but to ground doctrine in the real and concrete, and thereby to attempt to secure it from becoming "theoretical and unreal."

In sum, Newman is again concerned in the *Essay* (as he was in the *Via Media*, the *Apologia*, the *Grammar*) less with *what* is thought than with *how*—less with what doctrine is than what it does as a concrete rhetorical fact. Accordingly, the study of the concrete is itself concrete: history as a discipline is the attempt to apply, not abstract theory or "science," but prudence and judgment to know the concrete. As we have seen before, this means that all of the circumstances of the case (all available means of persuasion) need to be considered. Methodologically, this in turn means that the case itself can be located only by means of topics of discovery or their equivalent, and that the data will range across a more or less broad spectrum—in this case, of "political," "historical," "ethical" developments as well as conciliar propositions and inferences from them. It means, moreover, that we are involved necessarily with persuasion: for "ideas," first, are "living," and knowledge of them cannot abstract from their conditions of existence; and second, the concrete itself is not deducible a priori, but, as contingent, is perforce mediated by the probable and personal (or intersubjective) resources of the inquirer: "It will be a great mistake then to suppose that, because [Bacon] condemned presumption and prescription in inquiries into facts which are external to us, present with us, and common to us all, therefore authority, tradition, versimilitude, analogy, and the like, are mere 'idols of the den' or 'of the theatre' in history or ethics" (*Dev.*, 113).

This last point, of course, accounts for the pains Newman takes in Chapter II to establish the antecedent probability of "development" of doctrine (itself a concept with strictly analogical force). This attempt is difficult enough, requiring a host of "historical, philosophical, psychological and theological assumptions,"[75] "facts," and arguments to converge, such that, as in the development of doctrine itself, a "collection of weak evidences makes up a strong evidence" (*Dev.*, 107). This difficulty is compounded by the fact that the concreteness of history is itself a relative indeterminacy, not of the existence of doctrine, but of whether or not any given doctrine is a "development" from an earlier "idea." The question, then, is how one would know.

Newman's attempt to solve this problem divides the *Essay* into two unequal parts. In the first, as indicated above, he argues that ideas in general develop, that doctrines can therefore be expected to do so, and indeed even that what the Roman Church calls Apostolic truths are, granting a variety of "converging" arguments, the probable fulfillment of the expected developments. These, however, are all preliminary arguments that allow Newman to claim, as a result, that we are entitled—or rather bound—to use these probable developments as rules to interpret the ideas from which they derive, in much the same way as we use all prima facie acceptable opinions or alleged truths: "We prove them by using them, by applying them to the subject matter, or the evidence, or the body of circumstances, to which they belong, as if they gave its interpretation or colour . . ." (*Dev.*, 101).[76] As Lash summarizes, "If 'time is necessary for the full comprehension and perfection of great ideas,' then, according to Newman, later stages in the history of an idea may legitimately be used to interpret its comparatively obscure and ambiguous beginnings."[77] Now, this is clearly but the extension to a more restricted problem within the overall argument, of the method of arguing by antecedent probabilities (and the evidence they disclose) of historical theology itself—indeed, of all arguments and disciplines concerning concrete questions.

Thus, in Chapter IV of this first part of the *Essay*, regarding various "instances" of the method at work, Newman again employs topical pairs of terms to disclose phenomena and arguments at increasingly more concrete levels of analysis. On the question, for example, of whether the doctrine of the Papal Supremacy may not have developed from an earlier unarticulated apprehension of its truth, Newman first combines an "antecedent probability of a Popedom" with the "actual exemplification of it in the Post-Nicene Church" (*Dev.*, 154), as the "presumptive interpretation" of the earlier, Ante-Nicene Church. Such is his hypothesis or "presumption," which he next uses to seek further evidence:

> Starting with the evidence of Holy Scripture, . . . he moves on through the testimony of the Fathers, Pre-Nicene and Post-Nicene, who by their words and deeds evidence a powerful and convincing support of his theory. He is able to conclude that the clear evidence of the fourth century is proof of the historical continuation of Post-Nicene from the Pre-Nicene Church.[78]

And yet, even at this level of the "fact," Newman's case is not necessarily made, as he concedes in the next chapter:

> It may be said in answer to me that it is not enough that a certain large system of doctrine, such as that which goes by the name of Catholic, should admit of being referred to beliefs, opinions, and usages which prevailed among the first Christians, in order to my having a logical right to include a reception of the later teaching in the reception of the earlier . . . (*Dev.*, 169–70).

That is, "continuity" is not necessarily "development"; and it becomes "necessary in consequence to assign certain characteristics of faithful developments, which none but faithful developments have, and the presence of which serves as a test to discriminate between them and corruption" (*Dev.*, 170):

Taking this analogy [of "growth"] as a guide, I venture to set down seven Notes of varying cogency, independence and applicability, to discriminate healthy developments of an idea from its state of corruption and decay, as follows:—There is no corruption if it retains one and the same type, the same principles, the same organization; if its beginnings anticipate its subsequent phases, and its later phenomena protect and subserve its earlier; if it has a power of assimilation and survival, and a vigorous action from first to last (*Dev.*, 171).

Indeed, it is this last step, of combining alleged or seeming developments (i.e., "continuities") with notes of authenticity, that comprises the second and much larger "justificatory" part of the *Essay*. Schematically, the method is perfectly recognizable:

Earlier: Anti-Nicene Church   Analogy of
                 (its "words + acts")   "Growth"

             Ant. prob. + "evidence"

             Presumption   +   Evidence

Later: Continuity   +   Notes

                                          True Development

Better than anyone else, Lash has explored the great complexity of Newman's method of interpreting the "earlier by the later," only hinted at in the above schema, although he gives little attention to the role or adequacy of Newman's "notes" in the method. They are important, of course, for, just as "presumptive interpretation" is mere "viewiness" without evidence to support it, so "continuity" is viewiness unless controlled by factual signs of what is (supposedly) genuine development. On the other hand, Norris surely overstates the case, ignoring Newman's own admission of "varying cogency" and so on, by calling the notes "trenchant tests and definitive criteria";[79] on the contrary, they function rather as suggestive *topoi*, which can be used to call forth—from historical events,

136

the Fathers, Scripture, Councils (themselves all "loci" of truth, as Lash and Powell have each noted[80])—"facts and truths" pertinent to particular kinds of developments. As such, they run just as much risk of being irrelevant or misused as any other topics—perhaps more so, since their ground in the analogy of "growth," which constitutes the general problematic in the first place, provides no clear and unequivocal information on "what lines of argument" the analogy will be fruitful. Indeed, much of Newman's achievement is to have used the analogy at all; much of the value of the *Essay* is its function as a suggestive rhetoric of discovery of the conditions of dogmatic development.

The preceding, however, is merely to suggest in what ways rhetorical inquiry and argument can be exceedingly complex. Lash, again, has thoroughly analyzed many of the problems of the *Essay*. My purpose here, by contrast, is simply to conclude by briefly, even programmatically, suggesting how rhetorical principles and methods inform Newman's ecclesiological thought beyond the compass of the *Via Media* and the *Essay*.

In the first place, then, it is likely that Newman would have had little difficulty agreeing with Hans Küng that:

> It is essential for any church order inspired by the New Testament to exhibit, not a uniform, single-shaped ecclesiastical "hierarchy" ("sacred dominion," an expression first introduced by the person known as Dionysius the Areopagite in the fifth or sixth century), but a multiform, many-shaped ecclesiastical "diakonia" ("ministry" in the completely ordinary sense of "ministering to"): a "multiplicity of the church in the multiplicity of disciples, witnesses and ministers."[81]

For it is well known that Newman thought highly of the plurality of the theological "scholae" of the twelfth century and that it was to such intellectual dialogue and dialectic that he looked to stimulate (and control) the development of doctrine. As the following chapter indicates, Newman's "principle of antagonism," the notion that analogical God-talk is a "saying and unsaying to a positive result," applies as well to those who engage in such talk, for individuals, groups and "schools" can function as "sides" or voices *controlling* their partners in dialogue from the dangers of excessive self-importance or "abstraction." Since such "saying and unsaying," moreover, must be understood as relative to time and place, Newman accordingly stressed *freedom* for theologians in the prosecution of doctrinal formulation and *pluralism* of methods since each school or individual spoke from a unique perspective:

The Schola answers many purposes. It defends the dogma, and articulates it. Further than this, and since its teaching is far wider and fuller than the Apostolic dogma which is *de fide,* it protects it, as forming a large body of doctrine which must be got through before an attack can be made on the dogma. And it studies the opinion of the Church, embodying tradition and hindering frequent changes. And it is the arena on which questions of development and change are argued out. And again, if changes of opinion are to come, and false interpretations of Scripture, or false views of the dogma to be set right, it prepares the way. . . .[82]

In short, Newman construes the role of theologians and their relationships among themselves and to the hierarchy as he did the *topoi* that constitute discursive "views," as dialectical partners engaged in a dynamic *sic et non* directed to the unfolding of a relatively indeterminate Revelation. As one critic has noted, with regard to Newman's patient opposition to the authoritarian hierarchy of his own time, "The only cure Newman saw for the extreme centralization and control of thought was the advent of some great trial or purge for the whole Church out of which turmoil a renewed Papacy would emerge."[83]

In the second place, and even more significantly, Newman made clear throughout his life, but especially in his essay *On Consulting the Faithful in Matters of Doctrine,* that he looked to the laity of the Church to play an active and important role, to be a kind of "existential ground" for the Divine truth vouchsafed to the Church: for he held that it was not the hierarchy alone, but a *"conspiratio"* of hierarchy and laity that is the genuine residence of truth in the Church. While Newman personally accepted the doctrine of papal infallibility, it should be clear from the preceding chapters that, both dispositionally and methodologically, his first thoughts were of the ways in which the laity provided impetus for the development of doctrine and at the same time functioned as controls on and touchstones for the teaching office of the theologians and hierarchy. Thus, once again, we see at work a principle of antagonism in which both sides cooperatively compete in the maintaining and developing of the truth.

5

THOUGHT, WORD,
AND THING

*Thought and speech are inseparable from each
other. Matter and expression are parts of one:
style is a thinking out into language.*
"Literature,"
in *Idea*, 232

Newman's view of literature provides ready access to his larger thought on communication in general and its relation to method, already touched on in Chapter Three. In his most important essay on the subject,[1] he defines literature in the broadest of terms: ". . . by Letters or Literature is meant the expression of thought in language, where by 'thought' I mean the ideas, feelings, views, reasonings, and other operations of the human mind" (*Idea*, 243). The scope of this conception is significant, for it assimilates literature proper (poetry, drama, fiction) to literature as "expression of thought," an expansive formulation that will apply to all subject matters and disciplines except science.[2] To the degree that thought and expression are rhetorical—and we have already encountered, in several different discussions of method, why and how thought in concrete matters for Newman is necessarily rhetorical—it will be possible to close certain lines of argument begun in Chapter Two. First, study of the rhetorical nature and role of language will allow me to complete the preceding study of method in theology by reconsidering Newman's own use of language in inquiry and argument, as well as his conception of primary religious speech. Second, I can refer to further subject matters (such as literature proper) as well as to Newman's further uses of language, for under his architectonic conception of language-use fall all of the human sciences.

It will remain finally, to clarify the meaning and relative disposition of "things" in Newman's triad of thoughts-words-things, by indicating how even science under Newman's analysis usually receives a rhetorical interpretation. With the "circle of learning" thus closed, the *Idea of a University* will provide in the next chapter the high ground from which to view the whole, the "idea" of Newman's philosophy itself, under the aspect of liberal education, and to show how philosophizing is itself preeminently a rhetorical activity.

LANGUAGE AND LITERATURE: THE TWO-FOLD LOGOS:

A great author, Gentlemen, is not one who merely has a copia verborum, *whether in prose or verse, and can, as it were, turn on at his will any number of splendid*

139

phrases and swelling sentences; but he is one who has something to say and knows how to say it. . . . He is master of the two-fold Logos, the thought and the word, distinct, but inseparable from each other" (Idea, 243–44).

Implied in the definition of literature quoted previously is a ratio of terms whose meanings and relations will clarify what is at stake for Newman in language and communication. We can formulate the ratio this way: words (expression) are to thought (ideas), what thought is to the "real" that it seeks to represent: the more elusive and complex the reality, the more difficult for thought to circumscribe it; and the more complex the thought, the more difficult for words to express it. I indicated previously that, in the *Essay* on development, ideas are "aspects" of some far richer reality (also termed by Newman an "idea"), whose temporal unfolding under the guise of its many aspects is its development. In the same way that no single aspect is "deep enough to exhaust the contents of a real idea" (*Dev.*, 35), so words often fail to fathom the depths of thought: "thought is too deep and manifold, its sources are too remote and hidden, its path too personal, delicate, and circuitous, its subject matter too various and intricate, to admit of the trammels of any language, of whatever subtlety and of whatever compass" (*G.A.*, 185). Now, this is the pessimistic and skeptical view of language and its limited possibilities, expressed in the *Grammar*, that we encountered in the Oxford sermons written forty years before. But it is not the whole of Newman's view, for we saw in Chapter Three that in both of these works, as in others, Newman generalized the office of writer in more hopeful terms, and in terms that make sense of his own writings. As he says yet again in the *Idea of a University*, the writer is not one who "argues" theoretically, who coerces by abstract syllogisms, but one who excites thought in others, who wins over, stimulates, moves, and persuades: "literature does not argue, but declaims and insinuates. . . . it persuades instead of convincing, it seduces, it carries captive . . ." (*Idea*, 198).

Far from simply despairing of language, then, Newman rather asks that it evoke as accurately as possible (and he never underestimates the difficulty of this) the subtlety of thought in concrete matters. His writer-as-rhetorician must "paint" (*OUS*, 267), so to speak,[3] in his attempt to express "ideas, feelings, views, reasonings, and other operations of the human mind." Given this importance of rhetorical speech to thought and the "real," it comes as no surprise that Newman stands on its head the formula of his predecessor in rhetorical theory, Richard Whately, by

140

defining—not rhetoric as "an off-shoot from logic" as Whately does[4]—but logic as a "a sort of rhetoric, *bringing out to advantage*" (*OUS*, xii; emphasis added) in argument the reasoning of the mind. It is true that this reversal of terms suggests a contrast more stark than the reality; still, it points to the primacy of rhetoric, not merely in the communication but in the acquisition of truth.

Newman's view of the writer as rhetorician is elaborated in his essay titled "Literature" (1859), although an earlier account of literature in its more restricted sense ("Poetry, with Reference to Aristotle's *Poetics*," 1829[5]) sharply diverges from his mature conception. Far from understanding literature proper as pragmatic, persuasive, or didactic, Newman instead, as if correcting Aristotle, indirectly defines poetry (a category that includes fiction and drama) as the "free and unfettered effusion of genius" (*ECH*, I, 7), "the spontaneous exhibition of pathos or imagination" (*ECH*, I, 5). Whereas a rhetoricized poetics can be expected to feature the didactic, utilitarian, and communicative functions of art,[6] Newman here enlists against such a view, in what one critic properly calls "Romantic pseudo-Platonic fashion."[7] "The poetical mind," speculates Newman, "is one full of the eternal forms of beauty and perfection" (*ECH*, I, 10); its habits "lead to contemplation rather than to communication with others" (*ECH*, I, 24).

Again, although this early essay shows Newman to have been in this regard, like Shelley, almost Platonically antirhetorical, and, in Harrold's words, "at heart considerably a Romantic, there had nevertheless occurred in him a definite transition away from his earlier position."[8] Indeed, this change of view—from an emphasis on aesthetic beauty to a rhetorical interest in action and effect—parallels what Lash calls a "shift in emphasis" in Newman's theology, away from a deductive, rule-governed method suited to the quasi-Platonic ideal of an abstract immutable Tradition, to an inductive, personal, persuasive, and historical method. By 1878, "the shift in his conception of theological method allows him to use the term 'theology' in contexts where he had previously been unwilling to do so."[9] By 1858, he could use the term "literature" to apply both to persuasive speech and to communication in all concrete matters.

The above remarks give some background to understand the complex structure and the meaning and significance of Newman's Dublin lecture titled "Literature." By briefly considering this essay and other writings, it will be possible to see, first, how Newman redirects language, literature proper, and communication generally to the indeterminate and persuasive, in keeping with his rhetorical conception of apprehension, inference, and assent. Second, although much of his earlier writing appears to contradict this interpretation, in fact it supports my earlier contention regarding the latitude properly allowable to the application of his principles. And third, we will see how Newman's notion of "imagination," so astutely analyzed by John Coulson primarily in terms of metaphor, requires to be supplemented with the argument that, along with metaphorical language, topics are the primary linguistic devices of the imagination.

The complexity of Newman's distinctions and arguments pivots on his characteristic exploration of a few topical pairs. Simply, Newman in this essay turns successively in two opposed directions, testing uses of words against what they may be found, correctly or not, to have left out: on the one hand, he contrasts literature with "science" or "things;" on the other hand, with " 'laboured or polished periods,' " that is, with "mere words." "Literature," the "expression of thought in language," becomes a *via media* in which language as he defines it gains its rightful place as the source, as well as the communicator, of truth in concrete matters.

Examining these pairs more closely, we can see that Newman's first opposition, between "literature" and "science" (or "things"), is an attempt to establish a range, or rather *the* range, of language use; in fact, scientific language, used to express or convey "truth universal and eternal," is not properly "language" at all, but the use of words as counters for things or for the relations subsisting among things. "Such objects," Newman writes:

> become the matter of Science, and words indeed are used to express them, but such words are rather symbols than language, and however many we use, and however we may perpetuate them by writing, we never could make any kind of literature out of them, or call them by that name. Such, for instance, would be Euclid's Elements; they relate to truths universal and eternal; they are not mere thoughts, but things: they exist in themselves, not by virtue of our understanding them, not in dependence upon our will, but in what is called the *nature* of things, or at least on conditions external to us. The words, then, in which they are set forth are not language, speech, literature, but rather, as I have said, symbols (*Idea*, 230–31).

Lest there be some question as to what Newman meant to include under "science" here—certainly he meant to include mathematics, but, as he says, "What is true of mathematics is true also of every study, *so far forth as it is scientific*; it makes use of words as the mere vehicle of things. . . .

142

[T]hus metaphysics, ethics, law, political economy, chemistry, theology, cease to be literature in the *same degree* as they are capable of a severe scientific treatment" (*Idea*, 231; emphasis added). The trickier term, it seems, is "things," which apparently applies to objects, material or intellectual, capable of being treated in wholly circumscribed and unambiguous ways—capable, that is, of being reduced to terms used as notational counters and symbols. (As for "science," whose meaning Newman simply assumes his audience for this lecture knows, it is enough to indicate provisionally Newman's frequent equating of science with abstractions and generalizations from the concrete and with valid deductions from them.)

As I suggested previously, Newman postulates and explores his concept of "science" or "things" to determine what it fails to include. And what it fails to include he names "thought," that is, ideas and feelings (views, reasonings, and so on) that are not objective but "subjective," not impersonal but "personal," whose expression is "literature": "Science, then, has to do with things, literature with thoughts; science is universal, literature is personal; science uses words merely as symbols, but literature uses language in its full compass, as including phraseology, idiom, style, composition, rhythm, eloquence, and whatever other properties are included in it" (*Idea*, 231).

But what is "thought," and to what does it refer? We can, I believe, make swifter progress on this question by considering Newman's second opposition of terms. Having dispatched "things," he now contrasts thought with "mere words." Like science, which ideally makes a reduction of language to symbolic notation, "mere words" expresses a reduction of language to ornament and artifice, to "fine writing," and often to a hypertrophy of taste and desire for effect: "[T]he mere dealer in words cares little or nothing for the subject which he is embellishing, but can paint and gild anything whatever to order . . ." (*Idea*, 239). Significantly, Newman names Isocrates and "some of the sophists" as perpetrators: "[T]hey were set on words, to the neglect of thoughts or things" (*Idea*, 237). Literature, however, language "in its full compass," combines thought (now used in a more restricted sense of ideas) with feelings and effective speech: "[T]he artist, whom I am acknowledging, has his great or rich visions before him, and his only aim is to bring out what he thinks or what he feels in a way adequate to the thing spoken of, and appropriate to the speaker" (*Idea*, 239).

This combination in literature of the relatively abstract idea and the more personal, efficacious, and emotional word, is immediately reformulated by Newman in terms familiar to the rhetorical tradition.[10] Thought and feeling, and idea and word, now become "reason" and "speech:"

> This is what I have been laying down, and this is literature; not *things,* not the verbal symbols of things; not on the other hand mere *words;* but thoughts expressed in language. Call to mind, Gentlemen, the meaning of the Greek word which expresses this special prerogative of man over the feeble intelligence of the inferior animals. It is called Logos: what does Logos mean? it stands for *reason* and for *speech,* and it is difficult to say which it means more properly. It means both at once: why? because really they cannot be divided,—because they are in a true sense one (*Idea,* 232).

The terms I am isolating here, "thought" ("reason") and "speech" ("language in its full compass," "literature"), thus stand identified with each other, and opposed on either side by possible degeneracies of language. Like his view of what a view is, Newman's view of what language is opposes language, on the one hand, to the narrowness or specialism of abstract "things," which prescinds from personal feelings, values, and interpretations; and, on the other hand, to the "viewiness" of "mere words," which loses itself in expediency and sophistic effects. Literature is rather the feelingful, persuasive speech that reflects as well as possible the "inner man" (*Idea,* 236). Nevertheless, the question still remains as to what the reference of literature is—or rather, not literature, since its reference is "thought," but "thought" itself: what is thought such that it coincides with a persuasive "language in its full compass?"

The answer to this question is implied in Newman's opposition of thought with things, of literature with science, and is in keeping with the scope of definition that I have been concerned with from the start. To be sure, although the focus of this essay is on the man of letters ("Homer, or Pindar, or Shakespeare, or Dryden, or Walter Scott . . ." [*Idea,* 234]), "thought" reaches out to the "ideas, feelings, views, reasonings, and other operations of the human mind" (*Idea,* 243). Opposed to science, which elsewhere Newman identifies with abstraction from concrete facts, thought is precisely that through and by which the concrete is known. Conversely, the concrete, the "real," only exists (for us) "by virtue of our understanding," and "in dependence on our will" (*Idea,* 230): thought, then, is the interpretation of the concrete, and literature is its inseparable medium and expression. Of course, it is this inseparability that makes sense of Newman's emphasis on language "in its full compass," for this reason: the concrete is contingent and (relatively) indeterminate, requiring

144

an interpretation by persons using all the powers of their mind—will, feeling, and intellect. The language in which they think must therefore be intrinsically emotional, ethical, and persuasive; and in its expressive phase it must be "insinuative," for the thought it seeks to express is manifold, subtle, and intricate.

The ratio of terms with which I began further clarifies these concepts. Words are to thought (any ideation, not just that respecting concrete matters) what thought is to the real. Insofar as the real refers to fixed and unambiguous "things," physical or intellectual, ideation is relatively easy: abstractions can be circumscribed and made unambiguous and mediated by words used as symbols: "We speak of material objects," for example, "more freely than of ideas because our senses reveal material reality to us independently of the language used to describe it."[11] In discussing formal inference in the *Grammar,* where "logic," as we saw in Chapter Three, is construed as a kind of handmaiden to science, Newman continues this theme:

> [I]n other words, the nearer the propositions concerned in inference approach to being mental abstractions, and the less they have to do with the concrete reality, and the more closely they are made to express exact, intelligible, comprehensible, communicable notions, and the less they stand for objective things, that is, the more they are the subjects, not of real, but of notional apprehension,—so much the more suitable do they become for the purposes of Inference (*G.A.,* 172).[12]

With regard, however, to the real as concrete, dynamic, ambiguous— whether living and complex ideas of the sort discussed in the *Essay* or multiform problems and questions of life or study—the thought that strives to interpret it achieves only "aspects," interprets at risk and *ex confuso,* and is "unequal to a complete analysis of the motives which carry it on to a particular conclusion" (*G.A.,* 292). A fortiori the *expression* of such thought is unequal to the complex, intricate, often unconscious language or imagery in which it was conducted; it too will be a "calculus," though one possessed of "depth and breadth of associations," of "poetry" and "rhetoric" (*G.A.,* 267); these are all the more necessary to evoke the thought and the reality, and to "stimulate, in those to whom we address ourselves, a mode of thinking and trains of thought similar to our own" (*G.A.,* 200–01):

> The throng and succession of ideas, thoughts, feelings, imaginations, aspirations, which pass within him, the abstractions, the

juxtapositions, the comparisons, the discriminations, the conceptions, which are so original in him, his views of external things, his judgments upon life, manners, and history, the exercises of his wit, of his humour, of his depth, of his sagacity, all these innumerable and incessant creations, the very pulsation and throbbing of his intellect, does he image forth, to all does he give utterance, in a corresponding language, which is as multiform as this inward mental action itself and analogous to it . . . (*Idea*, 232).

The intrinsic difficulty language faces in approximating thought (for the above is a hopeful picture) accounts for the relation of analogy in which language stands to thought (it is a "calculus"). It accounts also for Newman's somewhat Janus-like skepticism about language and his more optimistic turn to what amounts to rhetoric as the closest approximation to thought and reality. Thus Cicero is instanced as one whose style is nothing less than the "development of the inner man"; and the great author in general is, again, not the sophist, "not one who merely has a *copia verborum* . . . but he is one who has something to say and knows how to say it" (*Idea*, 243).

In sum, thought approximates concrete reality, and rhetorical language and literature are its most effective medium of expression. As for literature in the restricted sense, as explicit persuasive argument, it is but an instance of Newman's overall philosophic method. We might think of literature proper as though it occupied a comparatively conservative place on the continuum of rhetorical activity, which ranges from a subtle, slow "conversion" to a more aggressive and argumentative "resolution." Though literature proper is less strictly argumentative, it is still conceived by Newman as directive and persuasive.[13] Thus, Newman in this essay and others turns, as he never does in his early essay on poetry, to the particularities of place and time as constitutive of literature's function. While not denying that literature possesses an aesthetic and transcendant nature, he also sees it as historical and indeterminate: "A literature, when it is formed, is a national and historical fact; . . ." national language and literature "are what they are, and cannot be anything else" (*Idea*, 255). (In much the same spirit, incidentally, he interprets the judgment of literature as properly indeterminate also, dependent in part on the state of mind of the judge at a given time.[14])

Again, for Newman, literature is not only the "expression" of the inner man, but the response of a powerful sensibility to a society and its crises:

146

The remark has been made that the history of an author is the history of his works; it is far more exact to say that, at least in the case of great writers, the history of their works is the history of their fortunes or their times. Each is, in his turn, the man of his age, the type of a generation, or the interpreter of a crisis. He is made for his day, and his day for him (*Idea*, 257).

Finally, it is significant that Newman insisted on literature's origin in sound. Walter Ong has noted that "for oral-aural man, utterance remains always of a piece with his life-situation. It is never remote."[15] Sound is "more real or existential" than writing, it is an "event," and a "special sensory key to interiority."[16] This stress on the practical and personal is precisely what Newman has in mind: "Now I insist on this, because it shows that speech, and therefore literature, which is its permanent record, is essentially a personal work" (*Idea*, 230). All of this appears the more natural when we recall that Newman at this time lectured on the rhetoric of preaching, citing rhetorical theory in a way that glosses his own thought and method: "Aristotle, then, in his celebrated treatise on Rhetoric, makes the very essence of the art lie in the precise recognition of a hearer. It is a relative art, and in this respect differs from Logic, which simply teaches the right use of reason, whereas Rhetoric is the art of persuasion, which implies a person who is to be persuaded" (*Idea*, 355).

THE CONSTRAINTS OF ACTION AND RELIGION

It is somewhat perplexing that Newman not only does not feature the pragmatic functions of literature and words generally, but that he so often appears to downplay them. He frequently urges, for example, that words need to be supplemented with "works" (attitudes or actions), with "thought," or with "things"—a position perhaps less surprising when we recall that Newman at these times is once again guarding against words becoming "mere words," words without content, or words cut off from the practical living-out of their meaning. Such words are themselves "abstract" and "theoretical."

In "The Usurpations of Reason" (1839), for instance, he claims that the sources of many religious errors is a willingness on the part of "theorists" to talk and speculate without having bothered to insure that such talk was rooted in their active lives, a need recognized again in one of the *Parochial and Plain Sermons:* "But let us, avoiding all refinements which lead to a display of words only, not to the improvement of our hearts and conduct, let us set to work practically . . ." (*PPS*, 5, 39); "That

147

a thing is true is no reason that it should be said, but that it should be done" (*PPS, 5*, 45). Similarly, "words" need to be grounded in an acquaintance with "things," for religious error also proceeds from theorists who "have rested their teaching on mere arguments," rather than on arguments wrought out of familiarity with subject matter (*OUS*, 62–4). In "Unreal Words" (1839), Newman makes his point by imagining the discourse of a blind man on color: "We should feel that he spoke on and from general principles, on fancy, or by deduction and argument, not from a real apprehension of the matters which he discussed. His remarks would be theoretical and unreal" (*PPS, 5*, 35).[17]

In a passage that ambiguously conflates his own views with popular sentiments, presumably shared by his audience, even literature is portrayed as no substitute for practical action: "Literature is almost in its essence unreal; for it is the exhibition of thought disjoined from practice. Its very home is supposed to be ease and retirement. . . . This indeed constitutes what is considered to be its true dignity and honour, *viz*. its abstraction from the actual affairs of men . . ." (*PPS, 5*, 42).

But the most damaging comments are those to be found in the "Tamworth Reading Room," a series of essays which sought to combat Sir Robert Peel's assertion that science and literature might best function in popular reading rooms to inculcate virtue, to teach. We seem to possess in this claim the rhetorical function of literature that I have just been attributing to Newman, and yet in fact Newman attacks Peel's thesis word for word.

In order to reconcile these views, I wish to consider briefly several of the ways Newman located these issues in his Dublin lectures. For instance, he concludes his essay on "Literature" by calling writers "the spokesmen and prophets of the *human* family (*Idea*, 245; emphasis added), a theme later developed in "English Catholic Literature" (1854): "National Literature is . . . the untutored movements of the reason, imagination, passions, and affections of the natural man . . ." (*Idea*, 261). Again, Discourse IX of the *Idea of a University* repeats this theme:

> Literature is to man in some sort what autobiography is to the individual; it is his Life and Remains. Moreover, he is this sentient, intelligent, creative, and operative being, quite independent from any extraordinary aid from Heaven, or any definite religious belief; and *as such*, as he is in himself, does Literature represent him; it is the Life and remains of the *natural* man . . . (*Idea*, 193–94).

Not quite explicit in this passage is a contrast between natural and supernatural, which Newman draws out in a later essay. There he "weighs

148

in the balance" the *literature of the natural man* and *religious faith and action.*[18] In slightly different form this topical pair appears in the second Discourse of the *Idea:* "In word indeed, and in idea, it is easy enough to divide Knowledge into human and divine, secular and religious, and to lay down that we will address ourselves to the one without interfering with the other; but it is impossible in fact" (*Idea,* 38).

Knowledge, then, may be divided into the human, natural, or secular on the one hand, and the divine, supernatural, or religious on the other ("Truth and Morality" in another formulation); analytically they are separable, though ultimately they belong to one and the same large fact. Thus the overlap that Newman notes in Discourse IX: "I do not mean to say that it is impossible in its very notion that literature should be tinctured by a religious spirit . . ." (*Idea,* 194). In other words, human and divine, or natural and supernatural, are opposing *topoi* that combine in the fullness of truth and morality but discriminate relatively separate concerns. What, then, of Peel's claims and the rhetoric of literature?

By looking more closely at further topical pairs in the ninth Discourse, we can see how Newman handles the problem. There he divides the natural or human realm into two areas: ". . . as Science is the reflection of nature, so is Literature also—the one, of Nature physical, the other, of Nature moral and social" (*Idea,* 194). Literature, it seems, does after all have something to do with man's moral life, especially in comparison to science, which has little or none at all. Thomas Vargish somewhat overstates the case: "[I]t is evident that literature, replete with moral and religious significance, does not suffer from this epistemological limitation of physical science."[19] We must bear in mind, however, that the moral life of the natural man is only part of his full moral life, which in its entirety consists both of the human and the divine, the secular and the religious. Very simply, then, to argue as Peel did, and Bloughram before him, that the literature and science of the "natural man" (even granting that they could lead one to act) would suffice to inculcate virtue *in its entirety,* is, in Newman's scheme, one-sided, hence "unreal." The human or natural morality of man is but part of the greater whole or "fact," and the lesser part at that; worse still, literature expresses human morality only fitfully and unsystematically. Even further removed from morality is "science," which accordingly takes the brunt of the attack in the Tamworth essays, for it is not only not moral, it does not lead to action, only "argument." As to "Why we are so constituted that Faith, not Knowledge or Argument, is our principle of action, [this] is a question with which I have nothing to do" ("Tamworth," 296).

149

In sum, to stress the personal, moral, and didactic functions of literature, as Peel and others did, must always be understood as one-sided, so long as one has in mind the salvation of the soul and the whole circle of truth. Newman naturally did have such concerns in mind, especially when facing auditors or opponents who did not. On the other hand, when he is able to focus on literature alone (as in his essay on the subject) and to speak of literature within its own sphere, not with respect to religion but simply as reason and speech, thought and word, idea and feeling—formulations his audience could be expected to have insufficiently appreciated—then Newman feels free to construe language in its full compass as directed to both the intellect and the heart of man. Literature offers "impressions," and although this may seem to be an innocuous concession, we recall that elsewhere Newman had pointed out that "impressions lead to action" ("Tamworth," 295). Such motives to action, it is true, are inadequate with respect to religion, but it does not then follow that they are not motives at all. In fact, only because literature is rhetorical and effective, only because it does concern itself with the moral and social, are men like Bloughram and Peel able to confuse literature's efficacy with a coherent motive to truth and morality. Kept in their places, however, and understood as mutually necessary components of truth and action, literature and religion are not irreconcilable foes, but a natural division of the one truth.

LITERATURE AND IMAGINATION

Thus far I have concentrated on the fact that Newman often downplayed the pathetic and effective dimensions of language, chiefly because he characteristically discussed language in topical opposition to the even more practical values of moral action and religion. Yet we have also seen that rhetorical speech—pathetic, ethical, persuasive—is a requirement of "thought" about the concrete. As part of the medium of concrete thinking, rhetorical speech is, moreover, logically and temporally primary, since such thought is the closest apprehension of the real. By contrast, "rational" or "scientific" thought and language are secondary, though not for that reason inferior, since they have their own tasks to perform: "science" abstracts from the real and allows unequivocal generalization and deduction. Newman's thought here and elsewhere is strikingly similar to Vico's, whose views on language Ernesto Grassi has summarized:

Language is divided into two fundamentally different forms of expression. One is purely rational, which. . . . is considered to be the measure of science, since it vouches for the objectivity of its statements with reasons, and these are not allowed to be clouded by subjective opinions. . . . It cannot be bound to times, places, or personalities; it is *unrhetorical.*

. . . The final consequence of rational speech is the demand for a mathematical symbolic language in which consequences can be drawn from the premises that we assume. Because its "scientific" nature consists in its strictly deductive character, . . . it can possess *no "inventive" character.* Such a language must restrict itself to finding what already is contained in the premises but not yet explicit or obvious.[20]

Rational language, then, abstracts from the given and confines itself to impersonal calculation, even ceasing at its furthest extreme to be language at all. On the other hand, language that facilitates our contact with the real, in real apprehension and assent, and our expression of it, is ipso facto rhetorical: it is probablistic, since the concrete is unique and contingent; it is "inventive," since the nature of the real is relatively indeterminate; and it is "pathetic" and ethical, since "It is in human nature to be more affected by the concrete than by the abstract" (*G.A.,* 31).

The question before us now is how we are to account for the pathetic, and especially for the inventive, character of concrete language and thought. For the answer we need to analyze "images," and more importantly "imagination." My intention is not to canvass Newman's writings for pertinent remarks on these concepts (in part because his practice is as illuminating as his explicit reflection), but briefly to consider some of the critical commentary in light of selected passages of Newman, with the purpose of suggesting in what ways and why that commentary is incomplete.

It is not difficult to understand, first of all, why images should be important to thought and language; given the priority Newman accords to real apprehension, images best evoke the concrete and are thus most pathetic. Indeed, in the *Grammar* real apprehension produces an "image" in the mind, a felt "impression" of the concrete existent (physical or mental), which is subsequently stored in the memory. What elicits such images (i.e., their linguistic counterparts) are "propositions embodying the notices of our history, of our pursuits and their results, of our friends, of our bereavements, of our illnesses, of our fortunes, which remain imprinted on our memory as sharply and deeply as is any recollection of sight" (*G.A.,* 24).

151

Secondly, "imagination," according to Thomas Vargish, is "like Aquinas's conserver of forms, a reservoir which stores up sense impressions;" as such it is "closely allied with memory."[21] Its inventive abilities seem to him (as to Jouett Powell) to be considerably limited, more akin to Coleridge's concept of "fancy" than to the profounder and more creative "imagination." We are reminded of the "constructive" ability of the imagination described in the *Grammar:* ". . . we are able by an inventive faculty, or, as I may call it, the faculty of composition, to follow the descriptions of things which have never come before us, and to form, out of such passive impressions as experience has heretofore left on our minds, new images . . ." (*G.A.,* 25).

Being impressions, images "stimulate the affections or motive powers to action;"[22] they are "real," and thus they present or re-present to the imagination what affects the mind and heart by their "vividness and effect" (*G.A.,* 25). Now, this point answers the simpler part of our question, for it is as vivid and effective (because affective) that images are rhetorical. As linguistic devices, moreover, images are rhetorical by virtue of their polysemous nature: the concrete that they image forth is itself determinable only within the broader horizon of interpretation postulated by the inquirer. Images themselves give choices.

In these two characteristics, then, their polysemousness and their affectivity, resides the power of images, for good as well as for ill. Their dangerousness arises in two ways. First, they are ambiguous: not only are they unsuitable for "scientific" work, but as rhetoric they are liable to confuse and mislead, to "assail" the imagination (*OUS,* 132). Second, their emotional power is no guarantee alone of their truth, for "distinctness of the images, required for real assent, is no warrant for the existence of the objects which those images represent. A proposition, be it ever so keenly apprehended, may be true or may be false" (*G.A.,* 58). Hence Newman's statement in the *Apologia* that he desired, when struggling with the difficulties precipitated by the collapse of the *Via Media,* to be "guided, not by my imagination, but by my reason" (*Apo.,* 100): "If we simply put aside all inferential information, such as is derived from testimony, from general belief, from the concurrence of the senses, from common sense, or otherwise, we have no right to consider that we have apprehended a truth, merely because of the strength of our mental impression of it" (*G.A.,* 58).

Newman frequently warned against this vulnerability of the imagination to falsehood or to the force of "the world," mere "things." The better part of the Oxford sermon "Contest between Faith and Sight" (1839) is devoted to this theme, which is reiterated in the sixth Discourse of the *Idea of a University*. Vargish cites numerous sermons in which Newman expostulates against images. In his *Theological Papers* Newman sees his cherished argument from analogy to be potentially "dangerous as indulging the imagination;" indeed, he goes so far as to speculate that "imagination, not reason, is the great enemy of religion" (*T. P.*, 47).

Nevertheless, Vargish, and especially Powell, indicate the positive role images can play in religious life. According to Powell, images and imagination are the mainstay for Newman of "living the faith:"

> I would suggest that the concept "imagination" most often served as a tool for describing the way in which the Christian faith molds the life of its followers. He [Newman] did speak of the way in which the facts of the Christian revelation strike the imagination of the religious inquirer and gain a foothold in his consciousness. But the consequences of this foothold are Newman's primary interest. . . . In that regard, he noted, imagination stirs the motive powers of the man who adopts a given image. . . .[23]

In the end, however, Vargish, Powell, and others explore the roles of images and imagination far less penetratingly than John Coulson, chiefly because, as an epistemological concept, "imagination" is erroneously restricted by them to its functions as "conserver of forms," or, at best, as "combiner of images" and instigator to action. Coulson, by contrast, starting from Newman's original intention to speak not of "real" but of "imaginative" apprehension and assent, shows that the imagination for Newman is, at its most inventive, an ability of mind distinct from but not opposed to "reason," that can *reach forward, perceive, and assent to truth*. It does so in one complex act of apprehension, inference, and assent: "When we 'use imagination,' we begin to see our world differently. Our standpoint or focus changes, but this act of imagination remains incomplete until spontaneously and creatively we gain an enlarged sense of reality." On this analysis, imagination may be distinguished from discursive "reason" only in that its own reasonableness is implicit, its act of inference *"per modum unius"* (*G.A.*, 196). "Reason" proper—that is, explicit reflection, rhetorical or otherwise—authenticates the insights of imagination. Coulson writes:

> When we investigate . . . our imaginative convictions, our purpose is both to establish their reality, and to know that we know. We do so within a structure or context—in religion that of tradition—which determines the nature of the evidence. . . . Predisposed as we are to accept this evidence as "reliable" we notice that when it is taken

together it converges or coalesces (as in legal logic) rather than demonstrates its necessity (as in scientific logic). . . . What began as "an impression on the Imagination has become a system or creed in the Reason."[24]

At the end of this quotation is an excerpt from the *Essay* on development that succinctly summarizes the present concern: at times imagination *assents to* an "impression" or complex image, a "living" idea, which only subsequent theological reflection lifts to certitude (or disconfirms). To the question *how,* by what linguistic means does the imagination apprehend truth, Coulson answers by analyzing Newman's deep respect for the original language of Scripture and its truth-saying power, in light of Coleridgean and other notions of metaphor, symbol, story, image, and myth. Like the simpler (linguistic) "image" discussed above, metaphor for example—and in particular "dense"[25] metaphor, as found in Shakespeare and the Bible—is pathetic, ethical, imagistic, and polysemous, characteristics required if language is to grasp the concrete. For Coleridge, Newman, Arnold, and others, what I am calling rhetorical language is "re-presentative"[26] of our primary experience of reality; Scripture, for example, is the irreducible language of the experience of God, always inadequate but nevertheless to be cherished and safeguarded: "The metaphors by which [doctrines] are signified are not mere symbols of ideas which exist independently of them, but their meaning is coincident and identical with the ideas" (*OUS*, 338). For Coulson,

By such means, by the accumulation of analogies, the order of the Universe or the moral law is *apprehended* as distinct from being *comprehended.* That is to say, we believe in or grasp *how* it is, rather than understand *why* it is so; but by such belief we gain what comprehension we can. . . . this is the sensibility which T. S. Eliot terms 'associated,' one in which both feeling and thought are immediately one.[27]

Following Newman's own focus on locating and justifying real or imaginative apprehension, inference, and assent, however, John Coulson concentrates on the *reasonableness* of metaphor and myth in Newmanian terms of implicit converging probabilities interpreted within the "fiduciary framework"[28] of the relevant community of interpreters (i.e., within and by means of the relevant postulated *topoi*). This is clearly a focus on proof and judgment. But just as I argued in Chapter Two that the *Grammar* (and subsequent Newman critics) ignores questions of *inquiry* and invention of cases—the companion value to proof and judgment, and logically and temporally prior—so here the relatively unexamined side of metaphor and imagination is its inventive value for inquiry. This side Coulson does not treat. By exploring it along fairly restricted lines of argument, I believe that the philosophical, as distinct from the more restricted religious and theological, significance and justification of Newman's ideas can be made clearer.

First, as a primary vehicle of imagination, metaphor can be seen to be inventive, topical, and transformative in the following ways: First, the "analogical leap" effected by the transfer of a term from a familiar to an unfamiliar field "informs our discovery"[29] of what the unfamiliar is and means, creating a new understanding by means of an initial absurdity in and tension of interpretations of the metaphoric juxtaposition; this I take to be the essence of metaphor.[30] But metaphorical transfer presupposes an insight into the similarity between fields.[31] The question then becomes what it is to "see," to have an "insight" into the similar. In a penetrating essay on inductive inference in Hume, Karl Popper goes behind Hume's rather cavalier analysis of the "repetition" of "similar cases" that provides the basis of such induction, summarizing many of the points which are, I think, implicit in Newman's views on analogy, metaphor, imagination, and philosophic method:

> The kind of repetition envisaged by Hume can never be perfect; the cases he has in mind cannot be cases of perfect sameness; they can only be cases of similarity. Thus *they are repetitions only from a certain point of view.* (What has the effect upon me of a repetition may not have this effect upon a spider.) But this means that, for logical reasons, there must always be a point of view—such as a system of expectations, anticipations, assumptions, or interests— *before* there can be a repetition; which point of view, consequently, cannot be merely the result of repetition.[32]

Second, on this analysis, as on Newman's own, we "interpret" sensory (and for Newman, of course, spiritual) reality by means of a point of "view"—of interests or "experience" broadly conceived. Now this is really to make two points: first, we see the similar (perhaps only dimly, by anticipation or imaginative vision) by an original constitutive act of insight that metaphor conveys. In this regard, John Coulson approvingly cites Kierkegaard, who "sees imagination as 'what providence uses to get men into reality. . . .' "[33] Second, "resemblance" is always "for-us," in just the way that Newman argues that all real apprehension of the concrete is relative to first principles, beliefs, experience, and so on.

155

Indeed, resemblance and meaning in metaphor are *"for people"*[34] in the further sense that construction and interpretation of metaphor implicitly rely on intersubjective meanings, values, beliefs, and so on. Metaphor, therefore, is itself a topic in two ways: it is a place or frame of reference where meaning, even a "surplus of meaning,"[35] arises, partially structuring what is complex and indeterminate; and it is a place relative to the metaphorist's and his interpreters' horizons of interpretation: "Thus, while metaphor may guide perception of a situation, it is itself intimately connected with the situation in which it is uttered. Metaphor draws its materials from communal knowledge, achieves its effects through the active cooperation of the auditor, and assumes its form in relation to a particular context. . . ."[36]

In all of these ways, metaphor is preeminently rhetorical in the fullest sense: it is ethical and emotional transposition of complex images in an original attempt to determine persuasively a more or less hidden and incoherent fact, independent of any prior cognitive act to warrant its findings: it grasps the real "on the basis of an immediate act or 'view.' "[37] As such, metaphor can even be "world constitutive," revealing not just a local, specific, circumscribable situation, but the nature or structure of reality itself, and "transforming" or "converting" those who participate in it.[38]

Equally as important as metaphor, however, *topics* for Newman are what might be called the discursive tools of the imagination. With his eye trained on instances of "literary" imagination (dense metaphor, story, parable, myth, and the like), and later on the reasonableness of imaginative assent, Coulson simply overlooks the fact that by far the most common *uses* of imagination in Newman's works (as distinct from Newman's talk about the primary language of imagination in, for example, Scripture) are his postulations of dialectically structured *topoi* to constitute the real. Not all such postulations are equally imaginative. To consider a statement or proposal, first "in theory" and then "in practice," for instance, is normally less imaginative than commonsensical. But then some metaphors are less revealing than others, as Coulson's discussion of "primary" and "secondary" metaphors—based on Coleridge's distinction between imagination and fancy—attests.[39] Nevertheless, many choices of topical pairs will require as great an imaginative "insight" into the similarity of cases, and into the potential for discovery (invention) by the topics, as the creation of many metaphors. In turn, the discovery that the topics make possible will also require imagination, for topics are the very means by which the concrete is to be known; topics "find arguments,"[40] or in Newman's words find the "mass of probabilities" (*G.A.*, 190), all of the "particular circumstances" (*G.A.*, 197), of the concrete existent.

Further, Newman's own philosophical position requires topics or their equivalent to perform this inventive and "world-constitutive" activity: if the concrete is both indeterminate and relative to the true and correct interests of inquirers, then a personal "way in" to reality is necessary. For this reason, Newman indicts the powerlessness of logic to establish its premises or touch the concrete: "As to Logic, its chain of conclusions hangs loose at both ends; both the point from which the proof should start, and the points at which it should arrive, are beyond its reach; it comes short both of first principles and of concrete issues" (*G.A.*, 185). By contrast, truth in the concrete is a "personal question" (*G.A.*, 310)—more accurately, an interpersonal question—that cannot be deduced a priori. In just the way that Newman exposes the inadequacy of "logic" and "science," Vico attacked the rationalism of Descartes: "The problem which concerns Vico as to the philosophical significance of topics . . . centers on the question of whether the rational process is adequate as a key to phenomena. The original "finding," the *invenire,* never can occur within a deductive process because it cannot reach beyond its premises."[41]

Like Vico, Newman conceives of the *invenire* as the function of topics and metaphor. A particularly good example of this is Newman's conception of "conscience:" it is constructed of topically paired terms, "moral sense" and "duty," and it constitutes at the same time a metaphor, drawn from an individual's experience of human relationships, for his relationship to God. Conscience (1) avoids predetermining the concrete case by being conceived as relative to times, places, and people; (2) its mutual values control each other from a reductive one-sidedness; (3) each term is a place for the discovery of arguments; (4) as a metaphor, it allows a "shaping" of the divine by the human;[42] and (5) as a topic it is preeminently ethical, persuasive, and imagistic.[43]

Topics, then, range across the middle ground of imagination, between earthbound facts and high-flying metaphors, myths, and the rest. Quite rightly, Newman speaks of topics as providing a "view," a perspective affording insight into the real—whether into complex and "multiform" ideas or local, more specific cases. Sometimes a view, as an "impression on the Imagination" (*OUS*, 329; *Dev.*, 53), is held as a true belief and given a real assent, and one seeks to "realize" it (*Dev.*, 37) through time by exploring its meanings and coherences with other truths, by adjusting it to views held by others, and generally by "investigating" its inferential support (*G.A.*, 208). Sometimes one does not believe as yet, but postulates *topoi* more or less tentatively, hypothesizes, guesses, and then "realizes" his view in the sense that he explores it, weighs opposing facts and truths, tests it, "inquires" rather than "investigates,"[44] and perhaps ends by rejecting what had previously looked hopeful. And sometimes a view—whether held as possible, probable, or true—is held only intellectually and is given only an armchair wave—a "notional" assent—and "realizing" it means contacting "all of its circumstances" and, by mediating its truth through one's "whole" being, making "real" what before was an unreal belief.

In my analysis of the *Via Media* I discussed, under the "aspect" of the structuring and exploring of topics, how the "realization" of an idea could be pursued both creatively and systematically. Now it is possible to show that a single principle rules Newman's entire methodological practice and theory.[45] By briefly discussing what Newman called his principle or "method of antagonism" (*T.P.*, 102), seeing how it is both an impetus to and a check on Scriptural analogy and metaphor, we ourselves can gain a larger view of the Newman corpus, one that fully exposes both how and why Newman's is a "complex unity"[46] of rhetorical invention and judgment.

NEWMAN'S PRINCIPLE OF ANTAGONISM

For Newman Scriptural language, like all rhetorical thought and speech, is by definition original, polysemous, ethical, and imagistic; by means of it, we apprehend the real, seeing how it is and not why. But we must ask, with Coulson, "How do we know that there is a reality to correspond to what may be a mere metaphor?"[47] And we must ask, with Newman, how we are to reconcile the contradictions, fathom the ambiguity, and in general "hazard the development" (*OUS*, 327) of the primary symbolic language in order to raise faith to dogmatic statement and certitude. For "How can teaching and intercourse, how can human words, how can earthly images, convey to the mind an idea of the Invisible" (*OUS*, 338)? The language of Scripture is a persuasive language, which is, however, at best only an "economy or accommodation," a "calculus" (*OUS*, 334) that must finally break down: "[A]t length our instrument of discovery issues in some great impossibility or contradiction, or what we call in religion, a mystery" (*OUS*, 345):

> [F]rom the nature of the case, all our language about Almighty God, so far as it is affirmative, is analogical and figurative. We can only

speak of Him, whom we reason about but have not seen, in the terms of our experience. When we reflect on Him and put into words our thoughts about Him, we are forced to transfer to a new meaning ready made words, which primarily belong to objects of time and place. We are aware, while doing so, that they are inadequate, but we have the alternative of doing so, or doing nothing at all (*T.P.*, 102).

Newman's answer to this predicament is methodologically quite characteristic: in just the way that topical invention is controlled by, and finds its integrity in, an "oscillative"[48] movement, a back-and-forth exploration, not only of competing or correlative places for argument, but of the interpreter and his material, so metaphor finds in the same method its own integrity and control:

We can do no more than to put ourselves on the guard as to our own proceeding, and protest against it, while we do <frame> <adhere> to it. We can only set right one error of expression by another. By this method of antagonism we steady our minds, not so as to reach their object, but to point them in the right direction; as in an algebraical process we might add and subtract in series, approximating little by little, by saying and unsaying, to a positive result (*T.P.*, 102).

Coulson rightly makes much of this "saying and unsaying to a positive result." Metaphors, like topics, "enable us to see, initially, by juxtaposition rather than by logical sequence: their meaning emerges as they are taken together—a resolution which has been variously described as a holding in polar tension, or seeing stereoscopically . . . or correction by opposite strokes."[49] For Newman there is no more offensive a stance than dogmatic adherence or reduction to a single method or subject when more is involved. In the concrete, what is at stake is indeterminate and ambiguous, and one must attend to both sides of the question, risk opposing interpretations, pursue the interaction of terms, and allow for complementary persons or groups. This is obviously the principle behind Newman's assiduous cultivation of the *scholae* of the Church, which pluralistically function, or "cooperatively compete" as opposing *topoi* for theological discovery. It is the principle behind Newman's dialogical view of the Church, in which the laity is a nonexpert partner supplementing the knowledge and actions of an "expert" hierarchy, who likewise control the laity: "Newman rejected the idea that the infallibility of the Church resided exclusively in the Magisterium. Neither did he maintain that infallibility resided in the laity apart from the teaching office. He viewed infallibility residing, rather, in the Church as such, in the expression of a unity between Magisterium and faithful."[50] It is the principle that structures the Church as distinct but mutually dependent "offices" (*V.M.,* Preface, xlff.); that provides the framework for the *Idea of a University,* in terms of "sacred and secular" knowledge, and of "memory" and "reason;" and that ultimately informs the presiding *topos* of Newman's life and work—that of the "two and two only absolute and luminously self evident beings, myself and my Creator" (*Apo.,* 16). Less obviously but no less really, it is the principle behind "Growth the only evidence of Life" (*Apo.,* 17) and "probability the guide of life," for each implies conflict. In short, the principle of antagonism is a key to Newman's rhetorical method— which, however, like all rhetorical principles, requires "a very various application according as persons and circumstances vary, and must be thrown into new shapes . . ." (*Dev.,* 58).

In this context the truth of a metaphor is a hard-won result of the conflict of interpretations over time. In an insightful way, Newman foreshadows the need for continual testing of one's tradition, for ideology-critique and a hermeneutics of suspicion, by emphasizing the critical and corrective roles of theologians and laity within the Church, and, outside of it, of a pluralism of thought and method (in, to give an example, the university). On the other hand, this critical path itself has limits, for an impatience to criticize, debunk, and control, like that fretful reaching after fact and reason in coming to faith, can undermine the original enterprise. Thus, when Newman seeks "all of the circumstances" or facts, a *methodological* caution prevents him from pretending that rhetoric is ever anything but limited, selective, and contestable; for this same reason, Aristotle confined the end of rhetoric to persuasion *as far as possible* under the circumstances (*Rhetoric* 1355b). One seeks to *see* as much as one can—given his principles, the aspect under which he sees, and the powers and limits of his group, time, and place. Similarly, one seeks to *say* what one can—given the audience, one's purpose, materials, and occasion: hence Newman's great interest in "economy" (itself based on the principle of antagonism, broadly understood), as a rhetorical strategy of response sensitive to a complex convergence of audience, purpose, occasion, and truth.

The answer to Coulson's question, then, as to how we know whether metaphor (or any concrete claim) is true, is that we first (negatively) beware the man possessed of only one idea. "Newman's account of assent reveals the extent to which *all* assents and beliefs raise the question of truth within a complex and not a simple form. . . ."[51] More positively, we pursue a great number and variety of tests and seek "field-dependent"[52] criteria of adequacy for existential verification, as adumbrated in Chapter Three.[53]

THE ENDS OF RHETORIC

The question of its own final adequacy aside, the principle of antagonism, in reality a diversity of safeguards, controls, and tests suited to different concrete problems, gives the lie to John Holloway's accusation that Newman thought little about how the "whole man" might reason unsoundly. Quite the contrary, Newman keenly appreciated the fact that there existed "fallacies as well as valid operations" in rhetorical reasoning.[54] Moreover, Newman frequently insisted upon a conservative estimate of the force of his own arguments and writings. In the *Essay* most notably, Newman's structuring analogy of "development" is accorded, initially at least, a negative and not a positive value. What he had to say in the *Grammar* about Butler's argument fully applies to his own:

> Butler's argument in his *Analogy* is such a presumption used negatively. Objection being brought against certain characteristics of Christianity, he meets it by the presumption in their favour derived from their parallels as discoverable in the order of nature. . . . he could not adduce it as a positive and direct proof of the Divine origin of the Christian doctrines that they had their parallels in nature, or at the utmost as more than a recommendation of them to the religious inquirer (*G.A.*, 246).

Analogy, then, primarily functions as a means of invention and argument for which only further corroborative evidence will provide more positive force. And this is the case not only with analogy, but more or less with all argument by antecedent probability, insofar as it seeks "to create a broad presumption in favour"[55] of a thesis. Rhetorically, Newman's arguments, whether analogical or enthymematic, may be said to "clear a place," to *locate or establish a site within which the reader may stand* to consider all of the circumstances of the question. On this analysis, all of Newman's works are, in a special sense, negative, and even, somewhat paradoxically, noncontroversial—not that they do not advocate a position, but that the end of such advocacy is less to establish the truth so much as the reasonableness of entertaining the view. One is invited to stop and look. This analysis is quite in keeping with Newman's own insistence on the limits of the power of language and on the fact that change, of people no less than doctrines or ideas, is a slow, moral growth. It is in keeping

161

also with Coulson's appreciation of the tentativeness and interrogative nature of Newman's thought in preparing the *Grammar:*

> In the *Grammar of Assent* as we have it Newman is working within certain limits, and it is now possible to supplement his treatment with material from the *Letters* and *Philosophical Notebook.* It is also possible to see how much subtler and more wide-ranging Newman's discussion is than is usually supposed. It is, as it should be philosophically, much more tentative. Yet even his published work on Assent is entitled "an essay in aid of a grammar. . . ."[56]

The ends of such rhetoric as Newman theorized about and practiced, whose specific strategies and devices Holloway has analyzed so well, are not, then, reducible to persuasion in any simple sense, to resolution of "local" cases. At any given moment, such resolution might be possible; the *Essay,* for instance, is in part an extended sorites aimed at a very specific conclusion. But in the larger scheme of things Newman is far more interested in what we can call the rhetoric of conversion or transformation. This is the reason why, using a phrase of Coleridge, he refers to the *Grammar* as offering "aids to reflection" (*GA,* 198). Such rhetoric aims at edifying the reader and at "realizing" a place where one might himself realize—develop, actualize, explore, and "really" apprehend if not assent to—the facts and truths submitted to him. "Newman was only saying that when we are seeking to present a complete overview, . . . we have no warrant for arbitrary selection."[57] *Seeing* is thus the end of this rhetoric; reality is meant to be revealed. "It is difficult for me to take a step without what I should call *a view*" (*L.D., XIX,* 26).

THE RHETORIC OF SCIENCE

A few remarks are in order by way of introduction. Like other Victorians, Newman sometimes used the word science to refer to all systematic bodies of knowledge, as in the *Idea of a University,* and sometimes to refer to the natural sciences only. Similarly, scientific method sometimes meant deductive, "logical," formal, and rationalist methods (theology was often called a deductive science), and sometimes experimental, inductive, "informal" ones, as in physics, for example. Naturally, which meanings Newman intended will be indicated here, although the primary focus is on natural science.

Newman's various *dicta* on the natural sciences are fugitive and unsystematic (he engaged in no hard scientific studies himself), although some of his "occasional" Dublin lectures and the ninth Discourse of the *Idea* express typical views (his own and others') on the relation of the physical sciences to religion. Here one finds what appears to confound somewhat my approach to Newman's thought as rhetorical, namely, his characterizations of scientific methods and subject matters as impersonal, autonomous, rule-bound, and positivistic. It would, however, be sadly one-sided to maintain that, for Newman, the *Geisteswissenschaften* are rhetorical, while the *Naturwissenschaften* are strictly empirical. On the contrary, in just the same way that Newman, in reacting to the evidentialist school, did not simply deny evidence and argument in the human sciences, but incorporated them into a larger view of reason, truth, and method; so here it is at least antecedently probable that in contrasting the natural sciences to more rhetorical ones, Newman does not simply deny rhetoric but rather allows for rhetorical dimensions to scientific inquiry, argument, and judgment. This becomes all the more plausible when we recall that his audience is given to the popular notion of the strictness of empirical science, in which case we might expect Newman to actively seek out the counterpart of such strictness, namely the "rhetoric of science"— *conceding* all of the necessary distinctions between natural and moral studies and then *leading to* further considerations.

That, at least, is the thesis here. Theoretically, no such strict oppositions are possible in Newman's philosophical stance, and in practice Newman *does* locate in all fields—not, it is true, on each and every occasion, but when his purpose and the rhetorical situation allow—the rhetorical components of various subject matters and methods.

In Discourse III of the *Idea,* Newman explains how each body of knowledge or science stands relative to others and to that truth or complex whole of which each is an integral part: "All that exists, as contemplated by the human mind, forms one large system or complex fact, and this of course resolves itself into an indefinite number of particular facts . . ." (*Idea,* 52). Insofar as each science is only part of that "one integral subject" (*Idea,* 52) of contemplation, of "truth," each science is only an "aspect" or "abstraction"[58] of the whole. Moreover, inasmuch as each study more or less seeks to "arrange and classify" the facts (themselves only aspects of the original "fact") with which it is concerned, we can say that each study more or less severely tends, in the language of the *Grammar,* to notional propositions and formal inferences respecting them. On the other hand, on starting at least, sciences begin with facts as "real apprehensions" of things, and those will be more or less determinate, depending on the subject matter. Determinacy, as Newman noted in the *Philosophical Notebook* (1855) is what makes "science" in its broad sense possible at all:

> Such then is the process by which the mind generally, without any particular gift is able to form sciences, or to exercise a principle of forming abstractions from contemplating an object before it. That faculty is brought into exercise, and is directed by the *evident differences and sympathies* of the attributes which any one object possesses, evident, that is, as they are to ordinary abilities (*P.N.*, II, 21; emphasis added).

No matter how determinate or indeterminate on starting, however, as any study rises to second-stage abstractions and inferences from them, it will achieve further fixity and determinateness.

In the preceding section on literature, we saw that Newman represented the physical sciences, "things" as opposed to "thought," as considerably unvarying and exact: "[N]ature physical remains fixed in its laws" (*Idea*, 194). In the Dublin lectures to which we now turn, however, Newman rhetorically emphasizes either determinateness *or* indeterminateness in the physical sciences, depending on what he is comparing them with and what his purpose and audience require.

The purpose of these lectures on the relation of science to religion is to show that no antagonism exists between the "truths"—the methods and conclusions—of the one and the other: "I propose, then, to discuss the antagonism which is popularly supposed to exist between Physics and Theology; and to show, first, that such antagonism does not really exist, and, next, to account for the circumstance that so groundless an imagination should have got abroad" (*Idea*, 346). As one critic has stated it, Newman's project was to "sell" science to theologians and theology to scientists—a characteristically rhetorical aim that depends for its success on his showing the one-sidedness of seeing the natural world only, or the supernatural world only, as the whole truth. "Truth," we know, comprised for Newman both the secular and the sacred: those who fixate on the world of "science" need to consider the moral and religious; those enamoured with the "immutable" truths of abstract theology need to consider the contingencies of this world.[59] Now, what is important to focus on is that Newman's strategy is to contrast science and religion or theology as starkly as possible, with a view to showing that they are not antagonistic on the simple basis that they deal with utterly different kinds of things:

These two great circles of knowledge, as I have said, intersect; first, as far as supernatural knowledge includes truths and facts of the natural world, and secondly, as far as truths and facts of the natural world are on the other hand data for inferences about the supernatural. Still, allowing this interference to the full, it will be found, on the whole, that the two worlds and the two kinds of knowledge respectively are separated off from each other; and that, therefore, as being separate, they cannot on the whole contradict each other (*Idea*, 347–48).

As I mentioned, this contrast between the two is extended to their methods:

The method of Physics . . . has hardly any principles or truths to start with . . . It has to commence with sight and touch; it has to handle, weigh, and measure its own exuberant *sylva* of phenomena. . . . Physical Science is the richer, Theology the more exact; Physics the bolder, Theology the surer; Physics progressive, Theology, in comparison, stationary; Theology is loyal to the past, Physics has visions of the future (*Idea*, 356).

In this view, clearly, theology is an "exact" science of deduction, while physics, being richer and bolder, is less exact—though still, it would seem, able to be brought under a rule by being "measured and weighed."

Note, however, how thus muted exactness or determinacy of the method of inductive science is now played up when compared with, not theology, but the subtle movement involved in coming-to-faith:

You will observe, then, Gentlemen, that those higher sciences of which I have spoken, Morals and Religion, are not represented to the intelligence of the world by intimations and notices strong and obvious, such as those which are the foundation of Physical Science. The physical nature lies before us, patent to the sight, ready to the touch, appealing to the senses in so unequivocal a way that the science which is founded upon it is real to us as the fact of our personal existence (*Idea*, 412).

Depending, then, upon the context and purpose, Newman exploits the range of possibilities intrinsic to any idea, activity, or fact. Chiefly because his purpose is to contrast science and theology, or science and faith, Newman alternately emphasizes science as indeterminate, open-ended, and unstable, or as stable, fixed, and exact. In principle, at least, this is not equivocation, but the location of ideas in terms of concrete considerations, not the least of which is the audience: "Newman's writings in general, and the *Essay* in particular, eloquently illustrate the truth of the principle that 'The public statements of Victorian critics and essayists . . . are often best regarded as refutation, qualification, or approval' DeLaura [1969], xi)."[60]

But let us consider more positive arguments. Quoting earlier from the *Philosophical Notebook*, I noted Newman's attention to the determinate in thought and sense; but the full passage from which I excerpted confirms Newman's broader sensitivity to the *relative* determinacy indicated above:

> Such then is the process by which the mind generally, without any particular gift is able to form sciences, or to exercise a principle of forming abstractions from contemplating an object before it. That faculty is brought into exercise, and is directed by the evident difference (and sympathies) of the attributes which any one object possesses, that is, as they are to ordinary abilities. *But it may be* these sympathies and differences lie *not* on the surface of the object—yet really exist. Here then is the exercise of originality or genius, to find out such conditions, which are not suspected by men in general (*P.N.* II, 21; emphasis added).

Thus Lash is correct to note that "although Newman is concerned to defend methodological pluralism in general . . . he does not posit an absolute disjunction between historical and scientific method."[61] Lash quotes Newman himself on this point: " '[S]urely sciences there are, in which genius is everything, and rules all but nothing.' "[62] That remark shows an insight into the nature of scientific discovery that has perhaps been generally appropriated only in our day.

In what ways, then, are rules and other stable characteristics of scientific method and interpretation supplemented by or otherwise adjusted to methodological strategies of an "extra-scientific" stamp? It should be noted that it is not only in "discovery" that we seek these, but in all stages of scientific inquiry and argument. To what extent, for example, did Newman recognize an indeterminacy in the very facts themselves of science and thus in its very nature?

In its experimental and inductive character science deals with facts about which it has real apprehensions, in an attempt to ascertain the structures and function of phenomena and to establish the laws that govern them.[63] Further, with respect now to the scientist, science aims at "substituting scientific methods, such as all may use, for the action of individual genius" (*G.A.*, 192). But, as we saw, scientific method can never

166

wholly transcend *personal* effort and art; this was, in fact, a theme of the Oxford sermons, where explicit reasoning was understood to be rooted in reasoning "not by rule, but an inward faculty" (*OUS*, 257). A parallel turn to the *person*—not over and against definiteness of method, but in combination with it—can be seen in Newman's stressing of the point that scientists need "modesty, patience, caution;" for these are,

> . . . dispositions of mind quite as requisite in philosophical inquiries as seriousness and earnestness, though not so obviously requisite. Rashness of assertion, hastiness in drawing conclusions, unhesitating reliance on our own powers of reasoning, are inconsistent with the homage which nature exacts of those who would know her hidden wonders. She refuses to reveal her mysteries to those who come otherwise than in humble and reverential spirit of learners and disciples (*OUS*, 8–9).

Newman also extends the range of this injunction by warning scientific inquirers against "excessive attachment to system" (*OUS*, 9), since he describes the personal art of discovery, and personal familiarity with and judgment of facts, as the "true healthy action of our ratiocinative powers" in *all* fields: "Thus a proof, except in abstract demonstration, has always in it, *more or less*, an element of the personal, because 'prudence' is not a constituent part of our nature, but a personal endowment" (*G.A.*, 205; emphasis added).

In short, not only with respect to "thought" but also with respect to "things," Newman counters abstract theory with personally apprehended facts and combines objective determinacy of external realities with crucial internal qualities of inquirers, the most important of which is "personal judgment."

In a similar way, Newman interprets the physical as grounded in the personal experience of "will": "[O]f these two senses of the word 'cause,' *viz.* that which brings a thing to be, and that on which a thing under given circumstances follows, the former is that of which our experience is the earlier and more intimate. . . . Starting, then, from experience, I consider cause to be an effective Will . . ." (*G.A.*, 50–51).[64]

Again, nature's laws, although uniform, are not invariable:

> A law is not a cause, but a fact; but when we come to the question of cause, then, as I have said, we have no experience of any cause but Will. If, then, I must answer the question, What is to alter the order of nature? I reply, That which willed it;—That which willed it, can unwill it; and the invariableness of law depends on the unchangeableness of that Will (*G.A.*, 53).

It is really only in the *Grammar of Assent,* where he explicitly appropriates "experimental science" to informal inference, that Newman succeeds in methodologically locating the rhetorical dimensions of science that I have been instancing. Even in this work, however, the deeper precariousness and indeterminacy of science must be inferred, since he never addressed the question squarely (having had no particular call to, and having conceded as much to logic and science as possible). Like all reasoning in the concrete, science too originates with real apprehensions, which by definition are more or less indeterminate; for while science may deal for the most part with facts common and accessible to all, still there is no guarantee that any given object of study, viewed under a certain aspect, will surrender all of its relevant information all at once to all inquirers, or (for that matter) that all inquirers will always share the same criteria of relevancy. As an induction upon facts, moreover, such science deals with probabilities, not only in the sense that material phenomena are contingent, but in the sense that an inquirer may interpret the meaning or significance of a fact differently: scientific judgment of evidence, scientific argument, even the decision to trust the evidence of one's fellow inquirers are all "committed to the personal action of the ratiocinative faculty" (*G.A.,* 223).

We have already seen how Newman referred these matters to what he generally called "genius," but now I am suggesting that it follows from these hints in the *Grammar* that, in the physical as well as the moral or human sciences, the inquirer uses general topics and "resources" to *constitute* his problems and data. Granting that his possibilities for statement may sometimes be severely constrained by readily indentifiable facts, we can nevertheless see that even the locations of facts common to all may depend upon the questions scientists are asking at a given time; and in all cases a personal judgment will enter to some degree: "The aspect under which we view things [including "the familiar objects of sense"; *G.A.,* 241] is often intensely personal. . . . Each of us looks at the world in his own way, and does not know that it is perhaps characteristically his own" (*G.A.,* 240).

Most importantly, the resources employed by the inquirer must be recognized as socially generated and validated "truths and facts." Just as the historian, for example, relies on a variety of prepossessions to order an inchoate reality, so will the scientist rely on "tacit understandings" (*G.A.,* 237) in knowing: "It is by . . . ungrudging, prompt assents" to the "informations" of the age "that we become possessed of the principles,

168

doctrines, sentiments, facts, which constitute useful . . . knowledge"
(G.A., 41–2).

But now we are approaching the limits of how clear Newman was about the rhetoric of science. What is clear is that Newman envisioned no sharp separation between the physical and the human sciences, and that his "thing-thought" dichotomies were more rhetorically determined formulations than final pronouncements.

6

"A COMPREHENSIVE VIEW":
The Role of Rhetoric in Liberal Education

*The function of a University is to enable you to shed
details in favour of principles.*
A. N. Whitehead,
The Aims of Education

1

INTRODUCTION

UNANSWERED QUESTIONS

In the seventh of the original *Discourses on the Scope and Nature of University Education,* published February 2, 1853 and later reconstituted as the first part of *The Idea of a University* (1873),[1] Newman elected to take up the controversy, begun nearly a half century earlier in the *Edinburgh Review,*[2] as to whether liberal education was properly to be established on the Benthamite principle of "utility." This is, of course, a controversy that we continue to thread our own way through today, made all the more complex by the rise of the modern research university and, more recently, the "multiversity."[3] In Newman's time, "like a spirit, every where pervading and penetrating" the age (*Idea,* 123), utility normally signified either usefulness to an individual's future calling, as formerly it had in Locke,[4] or usefulness to society at large (by way of training in "science"), as in the arguments of the "Edinburgh Reviewers" that Newman sought to counter. Up to this point in the text, and at length in Discourse Five, Newman had argued his well-known thesis that knowledge or liberal education "is capable of being its own end. Such is the constitution of the human mind, that any kind of knowledge, if it be really such, is its own reward" (*Idea,* 97). Naturally, what such knowledge is, when it really is such, and how one proceeds to get it are further questions. Newman's point here is simply that liberal learning stands on its own worth and is not to be subordinated to anything beyond it. This is a repeated theme of the *Idea,* announced again at the beginning of Discourse Seven: "[T]his is what some great men are very slow to allow; they insist that Education should be confined to some particular and narrow end, and should issue in some definite work, which can be weighed and measured. . . . This they call making Education and Instruction 'useful,' and 'Utility' becomes their watchword" (*Idea,* 135).[5]

Soon after this Newman concedes that, after all, "what has its *end* in

170

itself, has its *use* in itself also" (*Idea*, 142); and he proceeds to observe further that the Edinburgh Reviewers ("in their better moments"; *Idea*, 142) appear likewise to mean by "useful" what he means by "liberal" and "good in itself"—namely, "the cultivation of the 'understanding,' of a 'talent for speculation and original inquiry,' and of 'the habit of pushing things up to their first principles' " (*Idea*, 143)—in which case what had threatened to freeze into opposition could be read as a verbal dispute and dropped.

Characteristically, Newman is not content to stop with such an "obvious answer" to those "who urge upon us the claims of Utility in our plans of Education" (*Idea*, 143). Indeed, unlike those theorists who assume that liberal education, if it is not "useful," must therefore be "useless,"[6] Newman is prepared to concede far more to his opponents than mere words:

> I am not going to leave the subject here: I mean to take a wider view of it. Let us take "useful," as Locke takes it, in its proper and popular sense, and then we enter upon a large field of thought. . . . I say, let us take "useful" to mean, not what is simply good, but what *tends* to good, or is the *instrument* of good; and in this sense also, Gentlemen, I will show you how a liberal education is truly and fully a useful, though it be not a professional, education. "Good" indeed means one thing, and "useful" means another; but I lay it down as a principle, which will save us a great deal of anxiety, that, though the useful is not always good, the good is always useful (*Idea*, 143–44).

Although this further concession may seem rhetorically confusing,[7] there is no inconsistency in saying that what is good in itself can generate further goods. It may be admitted, nevertheless, that Newman takes up a practical tone and argument here that contrast noticeably with his previous line. According to Culler, with this pragmatic appeal Newman needlessly obscures and even reverses his basic principle that knowledge is its own end, and more importantly he commits a category mistake, assigning to Aristotle's class of the "useful and good" what should more properly be termed "good simply": "It could not be called useful because, although it redounds with all possible goods, which indeed it contains, these goods are all less worthy than itself. Nothing that it produces is so desirable as that which it is."[8]

Disregarding the rather superficial issue of rhetorical obscurity and blunting of effect, we would do better to ask the more substantive question: What is the purpose of this Discourse? Is the argument good or bad? Culler, for one, is not impressed:

Such is the conclusion, the rather grudging conclusion, of New-man's seventh discourse. "If one *must* have a utilitarian end to education, this is it." But why "must" one have such an end? The whole burden of the fifth discourse was that one must not, that liberal knowledge is its own end, and now, under the guise of carrying the argument a step further, Newman has actually reversed it.[9]

In this chapter, as part of an attempt to view the *Idea* in its theory and practice from the vantage of the whole of Newman's writings, I propose that the Fifth, Sixth, and Seventh Discourses, on the "good in itself" and the "useful," are not only compatible but present mutually necessary sides of the truth as Newman understands it.[10] If indeed the *Idea* is "the perfect handling of a theory," as Pater proclaimed,[11] then we need to ask why the argument of a major contested portion of that theory—the Seventh Discourse—is sound, and how it fits into and advances the work as a whole. The argument here is that Newman accommodates the rampant util-itarianism of nineteenth-century "science" by referring it to its deeper rhetorical roots: behind his concessions to utility extends a long tradition in which *"honestas"* and *"utilitas"* are not opposed but united.[12] This means that liberal education is neither anti-specialist nor antiutilitarian, though it does suggest that specialist technique and utility must be re-defined within the enterprise of cultivating the arts of the mind. Technique and special knowledge are not ends in themselves, but they are indispens-able conditions for the one who would be a *generalist,* capable "of entering with comparative ease into any subject of thought, and of taking up with aptitude any science or profession" (*Idea,* 11).

The Seventh Discourse best illustrates these matters, and for this reason I choose to begin and end with it. I do so on the premise that it is, in Kenneth Burke's phrase, a "representative anecdote" of the *Idea* as a whole, and indeed of Newman's theory and practice of intellectual inquiry as a whole.[13] Accordingly, I feature Discourses Five to Seven; focus on Newman's concern with "utility" (or, more generally stated, "practice") as the key to his method of thought; and, sideways as it were, bring in morality and religion—what Newman named the "integrity" as distinct from and supplemental to the "essence" of a university—to put in propor-tion and to qualify his own intellectual emphasis.

To frame the discussion in this way, featuring "philosophy" in New-man's sense,[14] uncovers several unanswered and even unasked questions. What is Newman's method in the *Idea* and how does it relate to his method elsewhere?[15] What did Newman mean by "judgment" in the Seventh Discourse? How does judgment relate both to that "liberal education" of which it is the culmination and perfection, and to the faculty of "judgment," which elsewhere Newman calls the architectonic faculty (*G.A.*, 221)? Because "judgment" is a dynamic commonplace in the debate over the nature and function of liberal education from the sophists on, we should be mindful that one has choices about how to give the term meaning with respect to one's subject matter and audience. In particular, the interplay of prudence and rhetoric touched on in Chapter Two can be seen to lie just below the surface of the *Idea,* so that we need to ask how Newman uses and transforms his cultural inheritance to give "judgment" meaning. Indeed, given the subtle but unquestionable emphasis Newman places, in the *Idea* as in all of his works, on "action," historical change, and intellectual transformation in general, we are constrained to challenge those of his critics who see him as privileging the permanent and unchanging and who consider his conception of knowledge in the *Idea* as speculative, purely notional, and even "strictly static."[16]

Above all, what does Newman mean by "knowledge" or "liberal education," "the cultivation of the intellect, as such" (*Idea,* 111), which he variously designates as "philosophy, philosophic knowledge, enlargement of mind, or illumination" (*Idea,* 114), or again as "liberal learning," "liberal knowledge," "*philosophia prima,*" and "the science of sciences"? It may indeed by wondered whether a good many readers of the *Idea* are not permanently frustrated with so general an account of what this science of sciences is supposed to be. Newman tells us that it is a "sort of science" and "in some sense a science of sciences" (*Idea,* 57), but it is never specified in what sense or of what sort, or what constitutes it as a "science" in the first place. Nor does Newman ever clearly relate this alleged science to judgment or utility, much less indicate whether it can actually be taught.

These questions are important if we are to take seriously Newman's claim that "from first to last, education, in [the] large sense of the word, has been my line" (*A.W.,* 259).[17] In the *Autobiographical Writings,* Newman likens education to "giving . . . juster *views*" (*A.W.,* 259), and in the *Idea* to getting "a connected *view* of old and new, past and present, far and near" (*Idea,* 121; emphasis added), and a "habit of *viewing* . . ." (*Idea,* 75; emphasis added). In truth, however, these allusions to education and to "viewing" will remain vague until we consider them as self-instantiated in the text itself.[18]

To put all of this as radically as possible: we misunderstand Newman unless we understand him *differently* from the way his audience understood him.[19] That audience had a variety of interests, needs and expectations, just as Newman sought to achieve certain goals regarding them—in particular, to place theology in the university curriculum and to recommend knowledge for its own sake, and in general to open up sites for reflection about education.[20] But to reduce the meaning of the Discourses to this historical context, or to separate Newman's theory of education from his practice of philosophizing in the *Idea,* is to deny Newman's own fundamental tenets of philosophical interpretation and liberal learning. Instead, we must apply his theory and practice to our own situation by seeing that theory and practice as a whole, and in light of our own grasp of the fate of "utility" in education. Only then will we have combined, as Newman argued that we should, theory and practice, the liberal and useful.

For Newman is well aware that he is practicing in this work what he preaches as a philosophic idea and ideal, namely, to combine, in a "judicious admixture," knowing and acting, theory and practice. Several times he states or implies that he is writing "philosophically,"[21] that is, seeking to establish "mutual and true relations" among "facts" by constructing "a comprehensive view" of his subject. In particular, the Seventh Discourse, with its explicit wedding of knowing and acting, theory and practice (in this case the good-in-itself and the useful), is only the most conspicuous embodiment among many others in these discourses of his more encompassing ideal.

What I am proposing, then, is a similar comprehensive (or generalist's) view of Newman's theory and practice, now from the aspect of "philosophy" itself.[22] In the following two sections, accordingly, we seek to identify what Newman means by "philosophy," specifically, its province or scope, its general methodological principles, and the qualities of mind it requires and cultivates. This attempt to grasp his "idea" will lead, then, in the last two sections, to a more active appropriation of his principles and methods of philosophic judgment, in which it will be possible to see why and how Newman concretely specified the abstract principles we have located, and how his praxis exemplifies that sense of "judgment" forwarded as the aim of education in the Seventh Discourse.

2

PHILOSOPHY

THE STRUCTURE OF THE IDEA

To appreciate what Newman is doing in this text and why, we need to get a preliminary sense of the larger topical oppositions or "root-topics" that structure this work, and specifically of what Newman means by its central concept of "philosophy." Two overriding issues can be discerned—the place among the secular sciences for theology (the secular-sacred *topos*), and the relationship of the liberal to the useful (the liberal-utility *topos*). Three divisions among the discourses can also be discerned:

1. Discourses One to Four establish the scope or matter of a university education, first opposing the secular sciences to theology and then uniting them as mutual values, the "secular" and the "sacred," of a single truth;

2. Discourses Five to Seven establish first the form and then the end of liberal education or philosophy, in two stages: Discourses Five and Six first oppose and then unite "memory" and "reason"; and Discourse Seven first opposes and then unites the "useful" and the "liberal";

3. Discourses Eight and Nine establish, relative to each other, the agents of philosopy and truth, first opposing and then uniting the secular ideal of the "gentleman" (*Idea,* 159–61) within the secular university and the "religious ideal" of the Catholic intellectual.

We need briefly to clarify here several different relations between "liberal education" and "utility." First, as noted previously, the two can be understood as synonyms if "what has its *end* in itself, has its *use* in itself also" (*Idea,* 142); but this is the least interesting possibility, rejected by Newman himself. Second, liberal education can be understood to be unequivocally opposed to utility if by the latter is meant "some particular and narrow end" (*Idea,* 135). From first to last, Newman rejects those who "argue as if every thing, as well as every person, has its price; and that where there has been a great outlay, they have a right to expect a return in kind. This they call making Education and Instruction 'useful' . . ." (*Idea,* 135).

Third, liberal education can be understood to require—or, more accurately, *society* requires for its proper functioning—both the liberally educated and the "useful" individual, where "useful" means the full range of "professional interests" and the division of labor generally:

There is a duty we owe to society as such, to the state to which we belong, to the sphere in which we move, to the individuals towards whom we are variously related, and whom we successively encoun-

175

ter in life; and that philosophical or liberal education, as I have called it, which is the proper function of a University, if it refuses the foremost place to professional interests, does but postpone them to the formation of the citizen . . . (*Idea*, 146).[23]

But we need to realize that Newman ends in yet another, further place, wherein both the liberally educated and the competent worker, the transformed individual and the good member of society, the good in itself and the good for others, are the mutual and interdependent values of both the secular ideal, the gentleman, and the sacred ideal, the Christian humanist: "This, then, is how I should solve the fallacy. . . . I say that a cultivated intellect, because it is good in itself, brings with it a power and a grace to every work and occupation which it undertakes" (*Idea*, 146).

On this analysis Newman concedes to his opponents various "facts and truths," ultimately reconstituting the controversy by qualifying and completing what he alleges to be otherwise a potentially debilitating view. We will need to ask how he effects this new unity and in asking will necessarily encroach upon, and thus will also need to discuss, further seeming oppositions that readers have inclined to reify, but that are better kept as soluble concepts that separate and combine according to context and application. To give an example: in "The Tamworth Reading Room" (1840), Newman had inflicted serious damage on the notion that intellectual study alone was sufficient to stimulate, mold, and control moral and religious character. A decade later, he eloquently reaffirms this thesis in the *Idea:* "Quarry the granite rock with razors, or moor the vessel with a thread of silk; then may you hope with such keen and delicate instruments as human knowledge and human reason to contend against those giants, the passion and the pride of man" (*Idea*, 111). Some critics have taken this discrimination of the intellectual and moral to be an opposition, by overlooking or disregarding Newman's statements that, although the "essence" of the university may be discriminated from its "integrity," both together constitute the university as a whole (*Idea*, 5).[24] Moreover, the failure to recognize this unity-in-difference, this discrimination of "integrity" and "essence" as well as their combination, has prevented otherwise discerning readers from recognizing, in Newman's ideal of the "gentleman," the modern equivalent of Quintilian's *vir bonus dicendi peritus,* the good man skilled in speaking. To be sure, the moral charge is less pronounced in Newman, but the function of Newman's "gentleman" and Quintilian's orator—as generalists capable of handling all subjects, locating values, making connections, resolving ambiguities—is the same.[25]

More than one commentator on the *Idea* has cast Newman's "gentleman" in a far less grandiose role, dismissing him as either a leisured dilettante or jack-of-all-trades or as a social or epistemological elitist disdainful of the common man's "opinion," as well as the common man.[26] Yet, though it is a fact that the tradition of the gentleman-scholar has always been bound up with money, status, and power, the argument here is that it is "theoretical and unreal" to elevate historical features over the principles that Newman espouses. This is not to say that money and power are simply insignificant or easily extricable accidents of liberal education, but it is to say that they are not constitutive of Newman's ideal. The task, then, is to distinguish the jack-of-all-trades from the disciplined generalist, and the aspirant to an elite "clerisy" from the philosophical humanist.

THE PROVINCE OF PHILOSOPHY

The province of philosophy is commonly accepted to be all knowledge, and Newman exerts much effort in the first four discourses to show that this includes sacred as well as secular; the task of the university is to teach all knowledge, and theology is a species of knowledge: therefore it must teach theology. But what does it mean to say that "philosophy" covers "all knowledge?" Whereas the individual sciences parcel out among themselves "larger or smaller portions of the field of knowledge" (*Idea*, 53), philosophy is of the whole.[27] But what does this mean? In the first place, it does not mean that philosophy must speak of all things at once in some set of vast metaphysical abstractions, for Newman states clearly in Discourse Six that in philosophizing, "It matters not whether our field of operation be wide or limited . . ." (*Idea*, 125). The suggestion seems to be that, unlike a science concerned with a specific subject matter, philosophy sweeps across all disciplinary boundaries, attempting now larger, now smaller, discriminations and appropriations of the concrete fact of reality.[28]

In the second place, one philosophizes by taking a "view":[29] "That only is true enlargement of mind which is the power of viewing many things at once as one whole, of referring them severally to their true place in the universal system, of understanding their respective values, and determining their mutual dependence . . ." (*Idea*, 122).[30]

In this regard, interestingly, philosophy is akin to science: "[F]or I suppose Science and Philosophy, in their elementary idea, are nothing else but this habit of *viewing*" (*Idea*, 75). The difference is that a particular science *abstracts* its subject matter from the concrete whole of reality, and then further abstracts its covering laws and theories from this part, seeking knowledge more about the relations among things than about the concrete things themselves—so that we can say that no single science fully "enlightens the mind in the knowledge of things, as they are . . ." (*Idea*, 54). Philosophy, on the contrary, seeks to "determine the concrete" (*Idea*, 39), "in its concreteness,"[31] in its parts, and as a whole. It hunts out "real things."[32]

Merely to recount this, however, to repeat what Newman says philosophy includes, is not adequate for communicating that philosophy, since, like Plato, Newman believed that "philosophy" could not be taught, that is, it was not a "something" that could be handed over to another. To be sure, one can state abstract principles, but principles need to be applied in concrete situations if they are to be anything more than bloodless notions. Merely to repeat a train of thought is for Newman to reduce it to inert "knowledge," things lacking the life of "reason." Indeed, in merely repeating Newman's own doctrines, the commentator on the *Idea* will fail to account for how Newman himself enlivens ideas with reason; he will thus fail to communicate that thought:

> The [true] enlargement [of mind] consists, not merely in the passive reception into the mind of a number of ideas hitherto unknown to it, but in the mind's energetic and simultaneous action upon and towards and among those new ideas, which are rushing in upon it. It is the action of a formative power, reducing to order and meaning the matter of our acquirements; it is a making the objects of our knowledge subjectively our own . . . (*Idea*, 120).

Because we are seeking to make the objects of Newman's view of "philosophy" subjectively our own, we must be *active* in that appropriation. The goal of such a philosophical "view" of liberal education and philosophy, however, is not to treat the *Idea* "technically," as one working out all of the details might. Since a view by definition is comprehensive, connective, and seminal, we are seeking rather, "philosophically," to resituate and redefine the importance of the work for our own time, by taking "a connected view of old and new, past and present, far and near, . . . which has an insight into the influence of all these one on another; without which there is no whole, and no centre" (*Idea*, 121).

In Chapter Four, I analyzed briefly Newman's view of what a "view" is, citing various topical pairs—reason-memory, system-fact, topics-*copia*—as constitutive principles of a view in the abstract. In practice, of course, we saw that Newman relied on issue-specific or special topics to locate the facts of whatever problem was under review. In the *Idea* we return to Newman's theroetical discussion of what it means to get a view, to do philosophy, not in its technical but in its generalist sense; here his special topics, "knowledge" and "reason" (in relation to "secular" and "sacred," and "liberal" and "useful") are also the common topics of his thought as a whole. Thus the *Idea* offers a unique moment of intersection in which we can readily shift from the *Idea* as a self-instantiating whole to the *Idea* as part of the larger corpus of theory and practice, and do so by appropriating "knowledge" and "reason" (and "secular-sacred," "liberal-useful") as Newman intended them to be taken, as *indeterminate and open-ended* "first principles" of liberal education and of his thought as a whole:

> Knowledge is called by the name of Science or Philosophy, when it is acted upon, informed, or if I may use a strong figure, impregnated by Reason. Reason is the principle of that intrinsic fecundity of Knowledge, which, to those who possess it, is its especial value, and which dispenses with the necessity of their looking abroad for any end to rest upon external to itself (*Idea*, 103).

We can envision Newman's range of philosophy as extending from secular to sacred knowledge, with the unity or combination of memory and reason as the means of appropriation of such knowledge. Newman's focus, in turn, is on "reason," which in turn combines the liberal and the useful (and, as we will see presently, the determinate and the indeterminate).

THE METHOD OF PHILOSOPHY

At the heart of this philosophy is the indivisible unity of all things[33]—of man's powers of knowing; of the knower and the known;[34] of the known and the language in which it is expressed; and of the world in itself and in relation to its ontological ground in God.[35] As Holloway summarizes it, Newman *"believed that reality is a great ordered system with the Creator at its apex,"*[36] a notion the *Idea* frequently reiterates: "All that exists, as contemplated by the human mind, forms one large system or complex fact" (*Idea*, 52); "All knowledge forms one whole, because its subject—matter is one; for the universe in its length and breadth is so intimately knit together, that we cannot separate off portion from portion, . . . except by a mental abstraction" (*Idea*, 57); "I have hitherto been engaged in showing that all the sciences come to us as one" (*Idea*, 64); "Nature and Grace, Reason and Revelation, come from the same Divine Author, whose works cannot contradict each other" (*Idea*, 187). It is the task of philosophy, accordingly, to "map out" (*Idea*, 105)

179

the whole by discriminating the "countless relations" subsisting among its countless "facts":

> Knowledge is the apprehension of these facts, whether in themselves, or in their mutual positions and bearings. And, as all taken together form one integral subject for contemplation, so there are no natural or real limits between part and part; one is ever running into another; all, as viewed by the mind, are combined together, and possess a correlative character one with another . . . (*Idea*, 52).

This idea of unity or order, widespread among the Victorians,[37] is of course an extremely fruitful one. It has been, moreover, a theme throughout our readings of Newman's works, for on reflection it is possible to make out what is a consistent unity of ideas about precisely this idea of unity, regardless of Newman's particular subject of inquiry. We would do well to examine this theme more closely if we are to grasp its implications for liberal education.

In the two works that flank his career, first of all—the Oxford sermons and the *Grammar of Assent*—Newman highlights the unity of the knowing subject *in himself,* as a being of intellectual, emotional, ethical, spiritual, and imaginative powers;[38] and the unity of the knowing subject and the reality the knower seeks to know. In each of these works, further, "knowing" is constituted as itself a unity of two kinds of "reason:" reason, as logical, explicit, a posteriori, "objective"; and reason$_2$, which reappropriates reason$_1$ and "combines" it with "conscience," "moral feelings," and "antecedent considerations" (or topics). In fact, in Discourse Four of the *Idea,* Newman thematizes just the means by which one achieves unity, namely "combination," itself a notion that combines, according to Newman, the concepts of "compromise" and "principle." "Compromise," he writes in this Discourse, "is the first Principle of combination." Yet compromise should never sacrifice "the main object of the combination, in the concessions which are mutually made. Any sacrifice which compromises that object is destructive of the principle of combination" (*Idea*, 35–6).

Now, the idea of an epistemological unity, or combination, of the powers of the mind is exemplified in the *Idea* in the notion of philosophy or liberal education as itself a combination (according to the circumstances of the kind of problem under consideration) of "reason" and "fact;" or again, Newman speaks of the *matter* of philosophy as a unity or combination of "mind" and "world." Similarly, in both the *Via Media* and the *Apologia,* Newman's reconstitution of the status of each controversy—from objective doctrines to rhetorical modes of "inventing" doctrines, and from Kingsley's demand for explicit and objective "reasons" to Newman's shift to the "whole man"—similarly instantiates this idea of unity. So, again, does the *Essay* on development, where a highly formalized sense of "reason" (as explicit doctrine) is united for the first time with the "historical" life of the whole Church, and the essay "Literature," in which "thought" is cast as the twofold *logos* of "reason" and "speech."

From this perspective one can begin to see that Newman has constituted each of his major works in much the same manner, though from different "aspects" and with changing formulations. Each work articulates a comprehensive unity of "reason" with whatever correlative value is appropriate to the problem. What is more, not only is each work articulated philosophically, as a nontechnical view of a concrete whole, but each work itself *articulates* philosophy, or what it is, to know.

In featuring this unity of knower and known, however, a unity that stresses what might be called the indeterminacy of the real, Newman is still able to allow that reality is not, in all of its aspects and for all of our own purposes in knowing, equally indeterminate, hence equally mediated by the subjectivity (or intersubjectivity) of the knowing agent: "[I]t is not every science which equally, nor any one which fully, enlightens the mind in the knowledge of things, as they are, or brings home to it the external object on which it wishes to gaze" (*Idea*, 54). To speak of this inequality of the sciences is to assert that some sciences, in particular the human sciences, more fully express the range of possibilities, significance, and meaning of a given reality. Biology does perfectly well analyzing cells, and physics the conversion of mass to energy; but a birch tree (to take an example) is more than cells, and writing a poem about birches more than an exercise in entropy. Literature, religion, history, ethics—to cite studies Newman privileges in Discourse Seven (*Idea*, 152)—more fully take cognizance of such "facts" (and their potential values) than the natural sciences either can or aim to do, for the former are intrinsically more ambiguous and value-laden; hence they are also interconnected to each other and to the external world they represent. As a result, as Holloway puts this crucial point: "[I]f complete knowledge is a complex order which contains many kinds of knowledge, the nothing is more likely than that some knowledge will come by logical [or empirical, statistical, mathematical] proof and some will not."[39]

It may be thought that the point here is simply that the relatively more determinate methods of the *Naturwissenschaften* must make way for the greater indeterminacies of the *Geisteswissenschaften*. In part, at least, this is true. To give a parallel, Matthew Arnold, in his polemics over education with Thomas Huxley, features, as is well known, "poetry" and "eloquence" (or rhetoric) and even (like Newman himself) gives pride of place to these human or "moral" sciences. In his essay "Literature and Science" (1882), Arnold argues that, whereas science merely locates facts, poetry and rhetoric assign them value, and thus place them for use in a human framework of experience and conduct, an experience and conduct that, after all, as he says in *Literature and Dogma,* comprise "three-quarters of life."

What Arnold fails to recognize clearly, or at least to articulate consistently, is that, in the first instance at least, the "facts" of the *Naturwissenschaften,* or the all-encompassing "fact" of concrete reality as such, are not an a priori given, but a radical indeterminacy.[40] As such they require nothing less than the "whole man" to know them, since it is only his own wholeness that will include all that may be necessary to any given act of knowing.

This last point might be made another way. Even if a given datum or problem can or should (for certain purposes) be studied "objectively," as a determinate fixity, by "bracketing"[41] to some degree the full scope of our powers and resources as human beings, nevertheless such a datum or problem can only first be recognized as such against the full range of possibilities as to its existence and meaning and thus necessarily against the full range of *man's* powers and resources—cognitive, emotional, ethical, and so on. We cannot do any bracketing unless there exists something to bracket and unless that "something" extends beyond the sphere of relevance dictated by the chosen features of the object under study. In other words, the aim of liberal education and philosophy is knowledge of the "whole" of reality, understood as a guiding ideal, not as an actual aim or even a possibility; it follows that the training of the intellect must be above all a cultivation of the ability to discriminate relative indeterminacies with respect, not only to the matter of indeterminacy, but to any range of possibilities one wishes to investigate; and this requires, again, the full range of our powers and resources. Anything less, even if *per accidens* suitable to a given problem, can never be adequate to the whole that is the ultimate object of philosophic inquiry. This adequacy (albeit at best asymptotic) resides in the power of discriminating "all" the possibilities inherent in something—even if that something proves to be a determinate recurrency (say, planetary motion, or the course of a disease) that does not require the "whole man" in order to be known as such. Still, even in such cases (to follow this through), all such determinate problems can and must, as Arnold points out, be referred back to the larger context of human life and conduct beyond them: nuclear fission may be in the first instance a problem for theoretical physics, but not in the second instance: quickly it becomes a problem for statesmen, revolutionaries, poets, novelists, theologians, ethicists, political philosophers—in the large sense of the word, rhetoricians all.

Thus we are returned once more to the complete range of man's powers as the only possible foundation for liberal education. When we further recall that "value" and "conduct" are "three-quarters of life," we may conclude a fortiori to the cultivation of the whole man through "rhetoric" as inventional and discriminative excellence. For this reason Newman's intellectual and educational ideal—the "imperial intellect"—is at the same time emotional, ethical, spiritual, and imaginative, just as the Oxford sermons earlier, and the *Grammar of Assent* later made clear (and for this reason Arnold too denominates his version of the same ideal as "imaginative reason").

We can summarize the matter and method of philosophy in the following way: philosophy as liberal education is the ability to view the whole of reality, not all at once, but piecemeal, "as far as the finite mind can embrace [it]" (*Idea,* 124), moving from part to part but with respect to elucidating the whole. It is the taking a connected view of things as concrete, for their own sake, whether the view at any moment is large or small: " . . . the clear, calm, accurate vision and comprehension of all things, as far as the finite mind can embrace them, each in its place, and with its own characteristics upon it" (*Idea,* 124).[42] As Walter Ong has put it, "It becomes evident at this point that his [Newman's] insistence on the value of a liberal education is integral to [his] opposition to the antidogmatic mind of his age. For by a general enlargement of mind, by a familiarity with principles educed at various levels from matter—a familiarity which is acquired by allowing the mind to range at large over the entire field of being—man is saved from the cramping which pinches the positivist outlook on life."[43]

It remains to say specifically, then, to what qualities of mind it is that one is attempting to educate.[44]

3

QUALITIES OF THE PHILOSOPHIC MIND

Samuel Johnson was no doubt correct when he observed that "It is, indeed, the faculty of remembrance, which may be said to place us in the class of moral agents;" and so was Wordsworth, who located in the memories of childhood (and the imaginative use of them) the authentic self of the mature man. But Hobbes and Bacon stress the inadequacy of memory alone to true learning, and Newman later also stresses the need to go beyond "inert" ideas, the "measure[ment] of knowledge by bulk" (*Idea*, 125), to a higher "reason," as *active and personal appropriation* of subject matter: "a smattering of a hundred things or a memory for detail, is not a philosophical or a comprehensive view" (*Idea*, 128); "a great memory . . . does not make a philosopher" (*Idea*, 121).[45]

But in highlighting this habit of "reason" as an active and personal appropriation of "facts," distinct from the more abstract processes and results of the individual sciences, Newman should not be understood to have intended a simple equivalence between liberal learning and what he later called real apprehension, informal inference, and real assent. Were that the case, it would imply that the individual sciences, not being in themselves philosophical or liberal (and thus not "real"), were therefore necessarily notional. Yet this is not necessarily the case, since a given study—religion, literature, history—can be pursued in a "real" *or* a "notional" way and is normally a combination of the two.

In the *Grammar of Assent,* moreover, Newman explicitly equated liberal learning and the "furniture of the mind" it provides, with "credences," a species of *notions:* "This is what is called, with a special appositeness, a gentleman's knowledge, as contrasted with that of a professional man, and is neither worthless nor despisable, if used for its proper ends; but it is never more than the furniture of the mind, as I have called it; it never is thoroughly assimilated" with it (*G.A.,* 42). Furthermore, liberal learning at the university level is simply too comprehensive to admit of very much depth or concreteness: "Even the most practised and ernest minds must needs be superficial in the greater part of their attainments" (*G.A.,* 42). There cannot be, therefore, any simple equivalence between liberal knowledge and real apprehension or assent. Nevertheless, liberal learning cannot be purely notional either, since such abstraction involves a departure both from the "whole" and from that aspect from which one views the whole.

The solution as to what Newman intends by stressing the active and personal character of learning in face of its undeniable notional dimension (this latter a result of the scope and connectedness of vision that liberal learning entails) is given rhetorically in the concept of the topics. Throughout the present work, we have taken the topic to be a general, quasi-notional instrument that represents a perspective one lives in as well as thinks with, a horizon shared with others. It comprises an angle or perspective, a "view" we take of the concrete; hence it is a wedge or opening, so to speak, into reality. As we attempt to constitute the concrete by selecting topics for exploration, we "place" ourselves and our world in that attempt. We are not yet at the level of particulars here, much less of specialized study of them, but somewhat above them, mapping out their possibilities, relations, and meanings.[46] Nevertheless, we are also not dealing with pure "notions," which are abstractions from facts that remain abstractions. Topics function more as ideational templates that open up and direct us toward facts, not away from them.

For the purposes of liberal education, then, when we attempt to get students "thinking like" historians, anthropologists, lawyers, literary critics, even econometricians and biologists, we are not aiming chiefly at cultivating their ability to observe facts, catalogue fixed relations, generalize laws from given data, or memorize and manipulate rules. To be sure, these abilities are indispensable conditions for and components of liberal education: "Suffice it, then, to say here, that I hold very strongly that the first step in intellectual training is to impress upon a boy's mind the idea of science, method, order, principle, and system" (*Idea*, 12).[47] But we need to bear in mind that the primary task of such education for Newman is to cultivate the art of determining the indeterminate "fact" of the whole (and thus of any part) of reality. To prepare students to do that means developing in them habits of personal intellectual appropriation of the field-variant *topoi* of their respective studies. In other words, it means providing students with controlled opportunities to address indeterminate and ambiguous problems, problems that require, from the student's own changing and developing knowledge and experience, the deployment of ideas (topics) that promise to constitute the issue adequately, disclose its circumstances for understanding, interpret meanings, and assess its value and truth. Topics constitute our horizons, as well as the parameters of subject matters and their problems, and liberal education is the cultivation of the arts of inquiry and proof, understanding and judgment, through gradual mastery of the symbolic means of knowing and acting in the world—a mastery of "rhetoric."

In sum, we expect students to know details, but we expect them finally to "shed details in favour of principles,"[48]—to infuse facts with reason. But here again, "details" and "facts," "principles" and "reason," are for Newman not themselves fixed and stable entities or processes, known objectively prior to engagement with particular cases. They are topics to be given meaning only in the context of historically situated inquirers and problems. Once more we are moving in a midlevel range between pure theory and pure facts, where the active mind, while not in immediate possession of things in all of their circumstances, possesses instruments to contact things even in some detail and depth, without losing contact with that comprehensiveness and scope crucial for "philosophy," and without lapsing into abstract "science" in the process.

Putting things this way opens up a perspective implied not only in the *Idea,* and particularly in the Seventh Discourse, but in all of Newman's theory and parctice; namely, the view that the liberally educated individual is first and foremost a generalist.[49] Elsewhere we have seen that Newman's own work was resolutely nontechnical; this holds, of course, for the *Idea* as well.[50] Though the question of "generalism" involves many themes, serious misconceptions about both what a generalist is and what Newman must have meant are too widespread and longstanding not to be addressed here. Four theses need to be argued: (1) "Philosophy" is not specialism but generalism; yet the two are not opposed, but are mutually constitutive concepts; (2) the generalist as "gentleman" is neither a specialist manqué nor a disengaged elitist, but a disciplined intellectual whose *techne* is beyond "science" as such; (3) the generalist, who is many-sided and even "whole," can approach the whole of reality at different levels of inclusiveness; and (4) the science of sciences known by the generalist both informs and reflects on these levels.

1. *Philosophy as general.* If the liberal knower or philosopher in Newman's sense is active and mediatorial, because the reality he seeks to know is more or less indeterminate, it follows that the philosophy he requires to know and practice, if it is to enable him to encounter the novel and changing in creative and true ways, cannot be technical, expert, or "specialized" in the way that an abstract science must be.[51] In its twofold orientation to the indeterminacy of the real and to the whole of what is real, philosophy seeks neither facts as such—"not mere knowledge, or knowledge considered in its matter" (*Idea,* 117)—nor systematic abstraction apart from the whole and from the real—"assigning predicates to subjects"[52] (*Idea,* 53)—but general and changing relations among unique, concrete, and infinitely complex particulars: "All that exists . . . resolves itself into an indefinite number of particular facts, which, as being portions of a whole, have countless relations of every kind, one towards another. Knowledge [philosophy] is the apprehension of these facts, whether in themselves, or in their mutual portions and bearings" (*Idea,* 52).[53]

It may be objected that any science seeks concrete facts; yet it will be recalled that it does so only to abstract laws from them, not to dwell on their individual characters. Any particular science also studies relations, but only the relations of concrete facts idealized into commonalities, treated as ideal types, and restricted to that selection of the facts that comprise that science. As Aristotle says in the *Nicomachean Ethics,* "And so the man who has been educated in a subject is a good judge of that subject, and the man who has received an all-round education is a good judge in general" (1095a 2).

Now it is "philosophy" that cultivates the "good judge in general." The concrete facts and relations constituting the whole that philosophy studies, as both subjectively mediated and "realized"[54] and as unrestricted to any field, are simply not discoverable in either that allegedly pure empiricism or pure abstractionism about which science boasted to itself in Newman's time. Aristotle suggests both this universality and indeterminacy in the *Rhetoric:* "As for the particular *topoi,* the better [i.e., the more exact] our choice of propositions, the more we imperceptibly glide into some discipline other than Dialectic or Rhetoric" (*Rhetoric,* 1359b).

Historically, of course, the generalist has been pitted against the specialist to the great detriment of the former, but it is possible to see first, that room exists for both types in Newman's economy, and second, that generalism and specialism do not oppose each other: within limits, the specialist can, and for the purposes of liberal education should, be general or liberal, and the generalist to some extent can, indeed must, be technical. The first point, that room exists for both, Newman addressed again and again: "I say, you must use human methods in their place, and there they are useful; but they are worse than useless out of their place":

> I have no fanatical wish to deny any whatever subject of thought or method of reason a place altogether, if it chooses to claim it, in the cultivation of the mind. Bentham may despise verse-making, or Mr. Dugald Stewart logic, but the great and true maxim is to sacrifice none—*to combine,* and therefore to adjust, all (D.A., 189–90; emphasis added).

We might say that the specialist seeks what James Clerk Maxwell called the *"particular go"* of something, while the generalist seeks to *place* the thing, to relate it to other things, to explore its value for himself and others, to map out its possibilities and meanings, to trace its effects, and to assess its truth:

> [T]he philosophy of an imperial intellect . . . is based, not so much on simplification as on discrimination. Its true representative de-

187

fines, rather than analyzes. He aims at no complete catalogue, or interpretation of the subjects of knowledge, but a following out, as far as man can, what in its fulness is mysterious and unfathomable. Taking into his charge all sciences, methods, collections of facts, principles, truths, which are the reflexions of the universe upon the human intellect, he admits them all, he disregards none, and, as disregarding none, he allows none to exceed or encroach. His watchword is, Live and let live (*Idea*, "Christianity and Scientific Investigation," 371–72).

   The second point, that the specialist and the generalist presuppose each other, indeed share each other's qualities, emerges from Newman's explicit awareness of the importance to a university of specialized subject matter disciplines (and by implication, research): "[L]et me not be supposed, Gentlemen, to be disrepsectful towards particular studies, or arts, or vocations, and those who are engaged in them. In saying that Law or Medicine is not the *end* of a University course, I do not mean to imply that the University does not teach Law or Medicine." Liberal learning does not mean the avoidance of details or particular studies: "What indeed can it teach at all, if it does not teach something particular" (*Idea*, 145)? Accordingly, philosophy arises out of, requires, and orders specific studies, just as the idea of a special study presupposes a whole from which it abstracts. And there is more than this, for the specialist will himself be more adept in his own specialty if he is at the same time a generalist.[55]

   The specialist and generalist, therefore, must not be set in opposition to each other, for each supplements and presupposes the other.[56] At the same time it is the generalist who is the proper object of university education, since only the orientation to indeterminacy and wholeness equips the individual to discriminate the constitution of reality *at any "place" in the whole:* science or specialism as such cannot do that. Hence it is altogether a further question whether or to what extent the generalist proceeds to become a true specialist, though of course he can so proceed, and it is perhaps hoped that he will, without loss to what is liberal in him so long as he continues to pursue the whole: "Yet of course there is nothing to hinder those who have even the largest stock of such [liberal knowledge or "notions"] from devoting themselves to one or other of the subjects to which the notions belong . . ." (*G.A.*, 42). Thus the professor who has specialized "will just know where he and his science stand, he has come to it, as it were, from a height, he has taken a survey of all knowledge, he is kept from extravagance by the very rivalry of other studies, he has gained from them a special illumination and largeness of

mind . . . which belongs not to the study itself, but to his liberal education" (*Idea,* 146). Again, "all knowledge" here is a metaphor for that
dynamic ambiguity and need for connection that is Newman's ideal.
Hence even science itself within its own domain presupposes that generalism cultivated by the university as a whole.

It is unreal, therefore, to insist antecedently that Newman must have
discountenanced specialism and research simply because he advocated
generalism. In point of fact, he had no trouble with the idea, for example,
of a college "major," but only feared—and he has hardly been embar-
rassed on this score—that the one-sidedness of specialization and the
mercantile sense of utility would usurp the idea of integrity or wholeness:
"Unit [wholeness] and essence are equivalent. . . . This is quite consistent
with holding that we cannot fully *attain* to the essence" (*P.N.,* II, 8).[57]

2. *The "gentleman" as generalist.* It follows that our language is
ideologically skewed when we define the generalist merely negatively as a
"nonspecialist"; a generalist is not a failed specialist unless we are prepared to hold that a specialist is a failed generalist. For some purposes, it
may be useful to consider either one in this fashion, but neither one
aspires to the calling of the other. The question is rather, in what does the
generalist's calling, his practice of the "science of sciences," consist?

Before we can answer this question, we face prior confusions about
Newman's "philosopher," whom Newman describes in the later discourses as a "gentleman." Weighted down as this term is with con-
notations of class and privilege, indeed with the traditions of the
aristocrat, the courtier, the philosopher-king, it has dragged attention
away from Newman's real point, which is resolutely intellectual, not
social.[58] Liberal education "is the education which gives a man a clear
conscious view of his own opinions and judgments, a truth in developing
them, an eloquence in expressing them, and a force in urging them. It
teaches him to see things as they are, to go right to the point, to disen-
tangle a skein of thought, to detect what is sophistical, and to disregard
what is irrelevant. It prepares him to fill any post with credit, and to
master any subject with facility" (*Idea,* 154–55).[59] One problem is that
many critics have equated Newman's gentleman-philosopher with either
an epistemological or social elitist, or with the nonspecialist jack-of-all-
trades, the dilettante. We need briefly to consider each of these charges in
turn, beginning with the last.

That the gentleman is not a specialist, and was not meant to be, has
already been defended; but the generalist must not be forced too far in the
opposite direction and confused with the dilettante: "All I say is, call

189

things by their right names, and do not confuse together ideas which are essentially different. A thorough knowledge of one science and a superficial acquaintance with many, are not the same thing; a smattering of a hundred things or a memory for detail is not a philosophical or comprehensive view" (*Idea*, 128).

To get a clearer idea of what sort of knowledge might exist in between specialized knowledge of a science and a smattering of a hundred things, we might consider the boast of Newman's mentor Richard Whately that, though he had specialized in none of the disciplines, nevertheless he knew them all in the sense that he knew their fundamental principles. According to Culler, Whately distinguished a superficial "smattering" from an equally limited, but fundamental, knowledge:

> My own learning [he admitted] is of a very singular kind, being more purely elementary than anyone's I know. I am acquainted with the elements of most things, and that more accurately than many who are much versed in them, but I know nothing thoroughly, except such studies as are intrinsically of an elementary character, *viz.* grammar, logic, metaphysics, ethics, rhetoric.[60]

The difference between the jack-of-all-trades and the generalist, we might venture, is that the former in effect is unprincipled: that is, the problem is that he is without principles, or that he has too many and cannot choose among them consistently. He is intellectually adrift. He may be good at reasoning, arguing, and concocting visions, even true visions, but it is all as it were randomly, and as though ignorant of where, when, and how ideas occur. Newman describes him as one who is merely "viewy":

> Those on the other hand who have no object or principle whatever to hold by, lose their way, every step they take. They are thrown out, and do not know what to think or say, at every fresh juncture; they have no view of persons, or occurrences, or facts, which come suddenly upon them, and they hang on the opinion of others, for want of internal resources (*Idea*, 123).[61]

In contrast the generalist, by virtue of his systematic and disciplined exposure to both a comprehensive range of problems and to problems requiring a comprehensive range of principles for their solution, is principled without being either dogmatically one-sided (overspecialized) or pseudo-tolerant and merely fashionable. In short, the jack-of-all-trades is intellectually orphaned; the philosopher-as-generalist is judiciously principled.

190

Somewhat less clear and more difficult to address is the way in which the generalist-philosopher is to be discriminated from the social or epistemological elitist, since the tradition of the gentleman-scholar virtually gags on its ties to money, leisure, power relationships, class divisions, ideological hegemony, liberation from the senses, indulgence of the senses, and the condescension of the philosopher-king. Critics of Newman's ideal are at sixes and sevens about its exact shortcomings, but they fall generally into two groups. Ben Knights, for example, finds it paradoxical that an ideal intended to lead society should be accessible only to an intellectual elite oriented to "a world of transcendent (and hence unarguable, uncontaminated) values. . . ."[62] P. A. Dale, on the other hand, argues that, unlike Arnold, Newman had no desire to make culture prevail among the masses.[63] In a similar vein, Clark Kerr refers to Newman's ideal as a "village with its priests," and Timothy Corcoran alleges that Newman embraced the uselessness of liberal learning.[64] For Dwight B. Heath, as for Dale and Kerr, " . . . it is clear that [Newman] was referring to the perfection only of a socially and intellectualy elite stratum, and not to the entire national society of his time. On the contrary, he would undoubtedly have been scandalized at the suggestion that education should be a right of all, rather than the privilege of a few."[65]

These criticisms, however, are a priori and simply do not square with the facts. Though geared to the middle and upper classes of Dublin, for example, the university over which Newman presided was responsive to the needs for evening and continuing education for all classes of society. Newman is perfectly explicit on this point:

> It must not be supposed that . . . I have some sort of fear of the education of the people: on the contrary, the more education they have, the better, so that it is really education. Nor am I an enemy to cheap publication of scientific and *literary* works, which is now in vogue: on the contrary, I consider it a great advantage, convenience, and gain; that is, to those whom education has given a capacity for using them (*Idea*, 127–28).[66]

Moreover, Newman's portrait of the gentleman in Discourse Seven is not a class statement but an ethical and intellectual one and is no more reducible to this or that historical exemplification of a type than similar portraits and statements of ideals in the Greek and Roman rhetoricians.[67]

In the second place, Newman's conception of knowledge, and of intellectual inquiry generally, far from featuring static, transcendent universals untouched by human hands and historical change, is, we have seen, thoroughly historical, nonexpert, and nontechnical, conceived by and for the generalist.[68] The *Idea* itself addresses a nonspecialized audience with a nontechnical vocabulary useful for transforming a particular moment in the history of liberal education.

What Newman's ideal most reminds us of, then, is not the philosopher-king, but the Ciceronian orator (with whom Newman was thoroughly familiar) who knew what to do with the knowledge a special pursuit presents; who himself was, in effect, a specialist in versatility and adaptation; who had mastered, not all things, but the arts of discovery and invention of intellectual principles and methods necessary to address and eventually take up any calling; and who was oriented to the whole as his own special gift and calling, not against the specialist, but as the one who "places" specialism and generalism alike.

If there is any fear, then, about liberal education, it is the fear on Newman's part of modern man drowning in an age of information, unfamiliar with lifesaving techniques that would allow him to enlist special knowledge for humane purposes and enterprises. Needless to say, such a fear is wholly realistic. Liberal education is intended to supply the surest safeguard against elitism, for it directs the individual outward toward the whole, away from dogmatism and one-sidedness, on the one hand, and superficiality on the other.

3. *Liberal Education at Different Levels.* Although the specialist and the generalist do not in principle oppose each other, the threat of unbridled specialism, of runaway "utility," is obviously so culturally pressing that Newman repeatedly warns against the one-sidedness of the "devotees of any science . . . to the exclusion of others" (*Idea*, 56). To one who equates, as Newman does, "reason" with *"perception"* (*P.N.*, II, 35, 73),[69] narrowness of vision is the gravest of errors, for it results in a denial of *what is*, hence is the antithesis of the liberal ideal. The specialist who lacks philosophy "becomes, what is commonly called, a man of one idea; which properly means a man of one science, and of the view, partly true, but subordinate, partly false, which is all that can proceed out of anything so partial" (*Idea*, 76).[70]

If the ideal is not to be one-sided but to be "whole," nevertheless it is not self-evident what it can mean to perceive the "whole" of reality. Culler, for example, is skeptical that this has much meaning at all.[71] Undoubtedly Newman's formulation is troublesome, since any whole less than the ultimate whole can be considered a part from a higher perspective and since, in any case, Newman frequently spoke as though we apprehend wholes to begin with; so it is a bit unclear what sort of ideal this is supposed to be. It is useful to distinguish apprehending some whole all at once—as when I apprehend, say, a saltshaker—and apprehending a whole only dimly and vaguely over time. Newman clearly has in mind the latter type, for education for him is a *process*.[72] Nevertheless we must still ask, how much of the infinite whole of reality the finite human being must apprehend, however dimly, in order for us to say that he knows the whole—in order, that is, for us to say that he knows in a "liberal" and not a technical way. When one studies biology or chemistry or any special subject matter, what distinguishes one's pursuit as "liberal," besides the fact that one is seeking knowledge "for its own sake" (since, after all, a specialist also can consider knowledge for its own sake)?

The answer Newman gives is that one is involved "philosophically" in "getting a view" when one attempts to relate concrete facts into meaningful connections, for their own sake, and *regardless of the expanse of vision* so long as this intellectual activity is informed by an orientation to reality *as a totality*. But what can it mean to be oriented to reality as a totality? Newman writes: "That only is true enlargement of mind which is the power of viewing many things at once as one whole, of referring them severally to their true place in the universal system, of understanding their respective values, and determining their mutual dependence" (*Idea*, 122–23).

Newman is clear, first of all, that "viewing" is a gradual and ongoing process, indeed a historical process, of assimilation, and we are reminded that the "assimilative power" was his third "note" of a true development of doctrine in the *Essay* on development. As historical, doctrines are in an important sense relative to times and places; nevertheless they also "percolate, as it were, through different minds" (*Dev.*, 365), assimilating, taking up into themselves, past attempts to articulate truths they express anew. As ideas, Christian doctrines do not differ from the subjects of a liberal curriculum. These latter must also be seen as historicallly relative; hence there is no position from which to view or grasp "*the* whole" *sub specie aeternitatis*. Newman means, rather, that we are (metaphorically) "whole" to the extent that, "[p]ossessed of this real illumination, the mind never views any part of the extended subject-matter of Knowledge *without recollecting that it is but a part, or without the associations that spring from this recollection*" (*Idea*, 123; emphasis added).

In other words, precisely because knowledge is historical, there is no ahistorical place to stand to grasp the whole; "viewing" is not a bid for either omniscience or eternity. It follows that the attempt to grasp the whole is not an achievable aim but a pragmatic posture and direction. It is the ability to assimilate new details, to transform them within one's existing knowledge, to refer them to principles, to create new structures of relationships, and always to attempt to build outward toward still more comprehensive relationships.[73]

4. *The science of sciences.* Finally, there is a metalevel implied in Newman's conception of the science of sciences, the level on which we attempt to get views of what it might mean, "to get a view." Here we try to sophisticate theoretically the viewing we exercise on the other three levels. Most recently, Kuhn, Feyerabend, Rorty, Toulmin, Habermas, and Foucault in the sciences and philosophy; Gadamer, Ricoeur, Tracy, and Kaufman in hermeneutics and theology; Burke, Booth, Perelman, Grassi, Valesio, and Fisher in rhetoric are theoreticians of the science of sciences—much as Newman himself was. All of them pursue a relativistic, nonscientistic conception of knowledge and of "method." The question that faces us, then, is what, for Newman, is this method or mode of knowing?

4

PRINCIPLES AND METHODS

MODES OF INQUIRY

There are two ways we might approach this question of what it means to know philosophically: through a discussion of principles and a discussion of methods.[74] Principles articulate the kinds of data as well as the parameters of subject matters, so that by learning principles (or by learning only those principles that are presupposed by subject matters and their principles, i.e., the first principles of metaphysics) one could be said to know, at least implicitly, those subject matters, and thus be said to possess "universality." An example of this is Whately's focus on the foundations of the disciplines mentioned earlier. Methods are the rules and devices by which we transform subject matters into wholes or products. Plato held that "dialectic" was the method of methods applicable to all philosophic problems, but Aristotle taught that priniciples and methods differ from art to art and science to science. Like Plato, Cicero embraced an architectonic art of arts, but unlike Plato and like Plato's rival, Isocrates, he found it not in dialectic but in rhetoric. Subsequent formulations of architectonic and subordinate arts and sciences constitute the history of the idea of liberal education, a history that has recently been summarized as a conflict between the "philosophic" (and later "scientific") and rhetorical (or "oratorical") traditions.[75] The question here is how Newman understood philosophy to gain universality.

In the first place, it is widely received among commentators on the *Idea* that some version of "metaphysics" underwrote Newman's intellectual ideal. For example, in view of the influence exerted on Newman by the Alexandrian Platonists or by Coleridge, Ben Knights and Harold Weatherby refer Newman's intellectual program and epistemology generally to Platonic philosophy.[76] A. Dwight Culler and Martin Svaglic, in contrast, trace Newman's interest in first principles to Aristotle's *Metaphysics*.[77] As we have learned, however, "first principles" is a tricky concept in Newman's thought, one that bears far closer resemblance to rhetorical *topoi* than to determinate universals—Platonic, Aristotelian, or otherwise. While one can exaggerate the conflict between the rhetorical and philosophical (as metaphysical) by overlooking the attempts made by each intellectual tradition to accommodate each other, nevertheless Newman's use of and theorizing about "reason" place him more squarely in the camp of Cicero and Quintilian, Vico, Vives, and Gibbon, with their interest in the practical and expedient, than with either the Plato of the Forms or the Aristotle of the first philosophy. Newman suggests in the *Idea* that at bottom we are all Aristotelians (*Idea,* 102), and little question remains that his reference points are the *Poetics, Ethics,* and *Rhetoric*.[78]

Indeed, "Reason" itself for Newman was an indeterminate first principle of philosophy, given precise meaning only when articulated with reference to specific, concrete problems. In this respect, it is telling that "reason" in the *Idea* gets defined as "judgment" (and all that that term entails) in the Seventh Discourse, where the controversy over "utility" contextualizes the previous abstractions surrounding the "liberal" and the "good in itself." More specifically, "reason" is understood as the ability to create and recreate meaning in the discrimination of concrete experience. There is nothing here regarding *theoria* as the perception of metaphysical essences—which is, however, not the same as saying that such perception is not a *part* of what Newman means.

In fact, we need to guard against that very one-sidedness that would lead us to reject an abstract metaphysics. We need only recall that the "range" of reason extended for Newman from the more fixed and technical to the more indeterminate and dynamic. While Newman concentrated on the latter, his ideal of philosophy necessarily includes (in some fashion) the methods and principles of the former, since without them the student is not equipped to make that very discrimination between fixed and unfixed, immutable and mutable (and all of the further discrimina-

195

tions that these make possible), that is necessary to philosophic viewing. Hence his rhetorical philosophy cannot deny, has no wish to deny, metaphysics as such. What is objectionable about the various attempts to enfranchise Newman's thought to Aristotelian or Platonic metaphysics is, first, their failure to grasp "first principles" primarily as indeterminate resources for invention and argument, and second, their failure to subordinate subject matter disciplines and more technical means of treating them, to apprehension of the concrete. As abstract, metaphysics, or any science, is first grounded in and relative to the concrete life from which it rises: " . . . metaphysics is a conditional science, conditional on the truth of those starting points [which] commend themselves to me, and not perhaps to another" (P.N., II, 89). This relativity (which is not mere "subjectivity") of first principles accounts for Newman's paradox that "egotism is modesty in metaphysical discussion" (T.P., 48). In short, an abstract science of any sort is in itself a plausible and valuable enterprise, but it is a technical, specialist enterprise, subject to all of the limitations that such abstraction imposes (while enjoying, to be sure, a comparative intellectual purity of terms and techniques). For this reason metaphysics is subordinate to the philosophy of the whole person in his "intelligent subjectivity."[79]

Another way to achieve universality in philosophy is to concentrate not on principles but on methods. Since the Renaissance, the rise of inductive procedure has done most to displace and thwart rhetoric as a universal method, and "logic" in many forms—Cartesian rationalism, British empiricism, Whatelian syllogistic, logical positivism—has claimed an enormous range of application through its mastery of the forms of reasoning. "Logic" was a recurring concern for some nineteenth-century thinkers, but Newman is skeptical:

> . . . to remove the original dimness of the mind's eye; to strengthen and perfect its vision . . . to give the mind clearness, accuracy, precision; to enable it to use words aright; to understand what it says, to conceive justly what it thinks about, to abstract, compare, analyze, divide, define, and reason, correctly. There is a particular science which takes these matters in hand, and it is called logic; but it is not by logic, certainly not by logic alone, that the faculty I speak of is acquired (Idea, 272–73).

Newman's imagery for the mind here, the eye and vision, recalls his central interest in "viewing"; clearly, seeing is not in the first instance logical, and for that reason cannot furnish the primary means for liberal education. Newman's contemporary, William Whewell, agrees that seeing is not reasoning, but draws quite different conclusions from this fact, for viewing, according to Whewell, is itself *unteachable:* ". . . the new and true idea suited to the emergency, the happy guess, no teaching can give the student. . . . We cannot teach men to invent new truths."[80] According to Whewell, the proper instrument for training the mind is not inductive logic, which requires imaginative vision, but deductive reasoning, best exemplified in mathematics. The inductive sciences are still too new to provide sufficient discipline. Greek and Latin literature convey the past and are valuable for that reason. But literature as such is too vague, and, worse yet, philosophy is far too unstable and shifting to provide a basis for knowledge and education. By contrast, "Mathematical doctrines are fixed and permanent; no new system of geometry can supersede the old."[81]

We can locate Newman's very different views of this matter by comparing them in passing to those of the sixteenth-century Spanish humanist, Juan Luis Vives, whose *De Tradendis Disciplinis* ("On the Transmission of Learning") mapped out the most comprehensive vision of education since Quintilian,[82] and is strikingly similar to Newman's. Like Newman three centuries later, Vives combines the *topoi* of "secular" and "sacred," "God" and "man," "piety" and "wisdom," "knowledge" and "eloquence." The goal of education is "practical wisdom"—Ciceronian *prudentia* modified by Christian *caritas*—of which "judgment" is the architectonic faculty, and rhetoric, in the narrow sense, as an art of speech, the art "which, least of all, it becomes good or wise men to neglect."[83] In formulations after Vives', judgment or prudence is termed "manners" or "taste,"[84] but, as R. S. Crane has noted, these are but "new name[s] for the old discipline of rhetoric."[85] It has been argued that Jane Austen extends this tradition of "taste," transforming it into moral "conversation,"[86] but A. Dwight Culler, precisely because he sees in "conversation" little more than social politeness, is unable to see how Newman's interest in conversation in the *Idea* is connected to these deeper dimensions of rhetoric.[87]

In short, "rhetoric" in both senses, as a narrow art of literary excellence and as a general faculty of judgment and discrimination, is for Newman the centerpiece of liberal education, quite as it was for Vives. The curriculum, text-oriented and steeped in the study of language, seeks to cultivate the power of appreciation and judging. To clarify Newman's own instantiation of this tradition, we must turn once more to the Seventh Discourse.

JUDGMENT IN PHILOSOPHY: THE SEVENTH DISCOURSE

Let us recall that in the *Grammar of Assent* Newman extends Aristotle's concept of *phronesis* from the realm of moral conduct to that of actional thought in concrete matters, making *phronesis,* or what he calls the illative sense, the excellence of the faculty of judging: "Thus the Illative Sense, that is, the reasoning faculty, as exercised by gifted, or by educated or otherwise well-prepared minds, has its function in the beginning, middle, and end of all verbal discussion and inquiry, and in every step of the process" (*G.A.,* 233).[88] The idea here seems to be that the illative sense is the perfection of the larger faculty of judgment. This faculty includes but reaches beyond the sense of *krisis* or *judicatio*—the decision rendered at the terminus of inquiry by the spectators or judges[89]—to oversee *all* the stages of inquiry and thought: "Judgment then in all concrete matter is the architectonic faculty; and what may be called the Illative Sense, or right judgment in ratiocination, is one branch of it" (*G.A.,* 221; *Idea,* 87).

There are in the *Idea* innumerable judgments rendered, of course, but two moments may be said to be summational: Discourse Nine, when the "sacred" and the "secular" are brought to a consummation in the idea of the Catholic university and the Catholic intellectual, and Discourse Seven, where the "liberal" and the "useful" undergo an equivalent marriage of minds under the banner of "judgment." In the formation and transformation of an individual's judgment, what had been forwarded as an independent good is also shown to implicate practical action and utility in the broad sense of the word. What, then, is this judgment that liberal education seeks?

In this Discourse, Newman calls "judgment" the aim of education.[90] The term implies that range of inquiry, argument, and assent that it later assumed in the *Grammar,* but here the focus is on inquiry and discovery *(inventio):* " 'Of the intellectual powers, the judgment is that which takes the foremost lead in life. How to form it to the two habits it ought to possess, of exactness and vigour' "—the equivalents of Newman's (or Gibbon's) term "fact" and "reason" (*Idea,* 453)—" ; is the problem' ":

> Judgment does not stand here for a certain homely, useful quality of intellect, that guards a person from committing mistakes to the injury of his fortunes or common reputation; but for that master-principle of business, literature, and talent, which gives him strength in any subject he chooses to grapple with, and enables him to *seize the strong point* in it (*Idea,* 151–52).

Now, what receives Newman's emphasis here is the ability to see, inquire, discover, and discriminate (elsewhere, in the *Philosophical Notebooks* he equates "reasoning" with "seeing;" *P.N.*, II, 35). To seize the strong point is to choose based upon one's past experience—to be persuaded and thus to persuade. It shares little with the Carlylean or Emersonian *seeing through* symbols to immutable transcendent ideas and ideals, but points rather to the persuasive postulation of first principles as possible constitutions of contingent realities and to effective argument from them. This is that dimension of rhetorical *inventio* and demonstration in *phronesis:* "Thus a proof, except in abstract demonstration, has always in it, more or less, an element of the personal, because 'prudence' is not a constituent part of our nature, but a personal endowment" (*G.A.*, 205).

Just as the *Grammar,* in keeping with its focus on assent, features judgment as the terminus of inference, so the *Idea,* in keeping with its thematic of "viewing," stresses inquiry as invention and discrimination.

QUALITIES OF THE CURRICULUM

We might get at this matter of judgment in another way, by reflecting on the kinds of courses that Newman says best cultivate that faculty and by asking further questions about the liberal curriculum as best as we can reconstruct it here. It is necessary to quote Newman's own quotation of fellow-Oxonian Davison at some length:

" . . . it will not be denied, that in order to do any good to the judgment, the mind most be employed on such subjects as come within the cognizance of that faculty, and give some real exercise to its perceptions. Here we have a rule of selection by which the different parts of learning may be classed for our purpose. Those which belong to the province of the judgment are *religion (in its evidences and interpretation), ethics, history, eloquence, poetry, theories of general speculation, the fine arts, and works of wit.* Great as the variety of these large divisions of learning may appear, they are all held in union by two capital principles of connexion. First, they are all quarried out of one and the same great subject of man's moral, social, and feeling nature. And, secondly, they are all under the control (more or less strict) of the same power of moral reason. If these powers . . . be such as give a direct play and exercise to the faculty of the judgment, then they are the true basis of education for the active and inventive powers . . . (*Idea,* 152; emphasis added).

Now, this passage raises enduring questions: is Newman denying a place to the natural sciences, or to the social sciences or mathematics, in liberal education? Can one identify a core curriculum? Does Newman lock into a specific curriculum, or does he recognize the need for change? We cannot do justice here to these sweeping questions, but we can try to dispel some of the erroneous interpretations of Newman's enterprise.

Quoting Davison, Newman does point to a specific "core" of subjects that are especially liberal—religion, history, ethics, eloquence, and so on. It has been suggested (along the lines that Newman pursues a static realm of ideals) that with "the enormous self-confidence of an Englishman of the Victorian age," Newman virtually equated human civilization with European civilization and in effect had little appreciation for the historical relativity of a liberal curriculum. Combined with the misconception that he promoted an aristocratic clerisy or elite, it is not difficult to cast this Catholic cardinal as reactionary, a dogmatic promoter of the classics blinded by the self-satisfaction of the Victorian period.[91]

A more careful reading of the *Idea*, however, and a consulting of Newman's other writings on education, show unequivocally that the opposite is the case. Indeed, Newman begins the entire Discourses with his characteristic interest in practice and change: "It will serve to remind you, Gentlemen, that I am concerned with questions, not simply of immutable truth, but of practice and experience." Or again:

> Even the question of the union of Theology with the secular Sciences, which is the religious side [of his subject], simple as it is of solution in the abstract, has, according to difference of circumstances, been at different times differently decided. Necessity has no law, and expedience is often one form of necessity. . . . Thus a system of what is called secular Education, in which Theology and the Sciences are taught separately, may, in a particular place or time, be the least of evils . . . (*Idea*, 24–5).[92]

If Newman could see so controversial a subject as mixed education as relative to time and place, it is not implausible that he could see the content of the curriculum as similarly relative. But we need not be limited here to antecedent probabilities. Having first expounded on the enduring nature of the "liberal" in Discourse Five, Newman typically proceeds to balance this emphasis: "There have indeed been differences of opinion from time to time, as to what pursuits and what arts came under [the idea of liberal education], but such differences are but an additional evidence of its reality. . . .:"

200

[T]hough its subjects vary with the age, it varies not itself. The palaestra may seem a liberal exercise to Lycurgus, and illiberal to Seneca; coach-driving and prize-fighting may be recognized in Elis, and be condemned England; music may be despicable in the eyes of certain moderns, and be in the highest place with Aristotle and Plato . . . still these variations imply, instead of discrediting, the archetypal idea . . . by means of which issue is joined between contending opinions, and without which there would be nothing to dispute about (*Idea*, 102–03).[93]

Another way to grasp this is to recall the central point of the *Essay on the Development of Christian Doctrine*: namely, *ideas develop*. This means that the "idea" of a university (as both institution and as "philosophy") and its curricular designs will change, as Newman explicitly avowed they will. They will be mediated by the horizons of new educators who will refashion and rethink the stable principles of philosophy. But this means in turn that we can never possess "the" immutable acount of "reason" or "philosophy." Any attempt historically to fix absolutely the idea of man's intellectual perfection is to contradict the goal one aspires to as one who is liberally educated, for it presumes to render man's nature— by definition indeterminate—determinate.

More positively, since the intelligent subjectivity of man's reason covers a broad band of possibilities, from the concreteness of real apprehension and informal inference to the abstraction of notional thought, any discourse about man that aspires to be complete must somehow account for this range. To be sure, any such discourse may itself be real or notional, rhetorical or "scientific," even strictly metaphysical. But any broad "philosophical" account, in Newman's sense of the term, must, in accounting for that range, decide how much to weight one end of that range over the other. Precisely because "philosophy" is rhetorical and concrete, this decision will be unreal to the extent that it is made apart from the full reality—historical, social, political, ethical, religious, and so on—of the inquirers whose question it is. Thus Newman himself, for example, in formulating reason as "judgment," weights the practical and persuasive in order to *redress* what was to him (and to others) the obvious abstractionism of the empiricists and utilitarians (just as he weights the role of theology to redress the misconception that it had no place in knowledge at all). These are instances of just that philosophical-thought-as-concrete, the seizing the strong point in a contingent matter, that Newman describes in the Seventh Discourse. On Newman's own analysis, such philosophy requires a similar concrete act of appropriation (or "application") on the part of new inquirers forming for themselves the questions of the perfection of the intellect, the nature of philosophy and education, and the role of the university. We can never stop asking, or answering, these questions because, in principle, formulations and emphases other than Newman's own may well be required by new problems, people, and perspectives. In exploring the new in this way, by using the old as guidelines or topics that provide a general stability from which to effect change, those inquiring will be practicing Newman's rhetorical art of discrimination at the very moment that they emphasize something other than discrimination. However much one weights either the concrete or the abstract within the concrete whole of man's indeterminate nature, the range itself enables us to be open-minded as to the character of and means to its perfection.

5

JUDGMENT

THE DISCIPLINE OF PHILOSOPHY

On the analysis given above, human nature is not susceptible of a priori determination of "the" truth and method; yet any attempt to dictate method or curriculum (in other than a provisional way) would be guilty of just such a determination. This is one of the chief reasons why Newman did not spell out what he meant by "Reason" in the *Idea*—a fact that evidently disturbs A. Dwight Culler: "Philosophy . . . merely emerges out of the particular sciences as a kind of *tertium quid* of the intellectual world—and much beyond this Newman is unable to go." I. T. Ker similarly argues that Newman had nothing specific in mind, that his science of sciences meant nothing more than "a well-trained mind."[94] Both of these statements are correct enough as far as they go, but they are also one-sided and potentially misleading, and we need to make two points to avoid misunderstanding.

First, we have now had many occasions to see that all of Newman's views are equally, because intentionally, general. Only George Levine seems to have caught on to the peculiarly notional manner in which Newman treats the concrete: "[H]is commitment to the particular and concrete as opposed to the theoretical and general is itself strongly theoretical."[95] The reason for this is that Newman's primary concern has

202

always been more to locate principles, to open up views, to create new places (topics) for perception and discrimination, than to work out the details. What he himself says of original minds in the *Grammar* applies reflexively to himself: "[T]he great discoverers of principles do not reason. . . . It is the second-rate men, though most useful in their place, who prove, reconcile, finish, explain" (*G.A.*, 245).[96] So in the *Idea* Newman does not "finish" and "explain" philosophy; since this is perforce an everchanging task of application, Newman stays at the level between pure theory disconnected from circumstances and pure pedagogical doctrine enmeshed in details.

But this raises the second point, which is that Newman was hardly unclear himself regarding how one might go about teaching or learning the activity of philosophy he was describing. By drawing on the method he himself used, Newman might have gotten as concrete as he liked. He need merely have detailed his own procedure, a feat of self-reflection to which he was obviously equal. True, Newman's "philosophy" was, from one angle—that of explicit statement in the *Idea*—a *tertium quid,* little more than "a well-trained mind." But then this is just the point: precisely because Newman recognized that his exemplification of philosophic method does not exhaust that method, is indeed only one possibility among others, any move on his part to submit his own procedure as "the" model to follow would have instanced just that abstraction from the concrete fact that he was arguing against in the Seventh Discourse. It would be tantamount to dictating curricular design, or "fixing" a canonic list of texts, or dogmatically pronouncing which courses could be liberal and which not. But Newman's purpose was neither to specify the conditions under which intellect was to be perfected nor to articulate *sub specie aeternitatis* some one canon, curriculum, or truth. It was, rather, to locate *topoi* for thought about the life of the mind, which later technical inquiry could elaborate; so that what Newman said of John Davison applies equally well to himself, that he was "a teacher of *principles* [rather] than of *doctrines*" (*ECH,* II, 407). To his immediate audience, these topics could be little more than the most general of sites for reflection; to his age, they were apparently hardly even that, given the obscurity into which these writings promptly fell. For us, who can take a larger view, they can be more, if we wish to use them (for we may reject the "idea" they constitute). In any case, we can see in them just that distaste for self-disclosure that Newman expressed in the *Apologia*. He who praised "egotism" in philosophy, who was unquestionably intrigued by his own mind and person-

203

ality, nevertheless here, as in all of his works, exhibits the character of the true rhetorician, whose business it is to find common, not private, places to constitute and explore the real.

What Culler says of the university as an institution, then—that it offers a *"methodos"* or *"way"* to truth—applies equally well to *The Idea of a University* as text—it is a method, specifically a "rhetoric" of liberal education, meaningful only in context and in application.[97] As itself a new *organon* of philosophy, it not only discriminates knowledge but advances it as well in its continuing reformulation of education and philosophy. This same idea has recently been expressed by Charles Wegener in *Liberal Education and the Modern University:*

> The disciplines of thought are as much concerned with the tactful discrimination of the ways in which thought may . . . function in relation to all our problems, activities, and satisfactions as they are with the constitution of objects and activities of which intelligence may be wholly constitutive. *Its architectonic function emerges in that process of tactful discrimination. . . .*[98]

Newman's art of discrimination, then, is a pluralistic rhetoric of invention requiring the on-going discovery and formulation of a developing truth understood from the perspective of concrete existence; its persuasive articulation and presentation in language directed at securing the realization, identification, and adherence of audiences; and its justification by means of a practical judgment amidst material probabilities and uncertainties: "It is the education which gives a man a clear conscious view of his own opinions and judgments, a truth in developing them, an eloquence in expressing them, and a force in urging them" (*Idea,* 154). For this reason, Newman avoids the essentialist question, What does one need to know in order to be liberally educated? (a wholly intelligible question from another perspective), in favor of the rhetorical and existentialist question, How does one know liberally? The answer Newman gives is "realization" and topics;[99] what might be called philosophy in a low key but in a human vein, gaining in existential depth what it foregoes in linguistic purity and rule-governed technique.

Harrold Zyskind formulates such a philosophy this way: "Rhetoric always has been an art of reading or posting signs, and its contemporary value in this regard could lie in its insistence on treating some of them as principles which, as such, need to be examined in the large rather than to be passed over into what they signify."[100] To characterize rhetoric in this fashion is not to endorse an incompetent means of philosophizing. On the contrary, within limits of its own (its necessary refusal to become technical, hence its "simplicity" regarding such specialization), rhetoric-as-philosophical adapts its principles and methods to the kinds of questions it asks and to its subject matters as constituted by those questions. Not the specialist's details, but the generalist's ability to read, interpret, and relate principles-as-signs is among the rhetorician's special competencies and gifts, and one especially needed given the dangers facing our own hyper-specialized age. These are competencies that we need all the more in proportion as we are tempted to ignore, denigrate, or simply misunderstand whatever is outside of what we *can* understand, namely subject-matter disciplines. Within the disciplines, moreover, these competencies are just the ones we do in fact attempt to cultivate in the literary critic, historian, anthropologist, sociologist, biologist, though often without articulating to ourselves the basis of our need and aim. For this reason, Newman rightly concentrates in the *Idea* not on the object of knowledge, but on the inventional powers of the knowing agent and on the correlative personal realization of judgment: "There is no enlargement, unless there be a comparison of ideas one with another, as they come before the mind, and a systematizing of them:"

> We feel our minds to be growing and expanding *then,* when we not only learn, but refer what we learn to what we already know. It is not the mere addition to our knowledge that is the illumination; but the locomotion, the movement onwards, of that mental centre, to which both what we know (the accumulating mass of our acquirements) and what we are learning, gravitates (*Idea,* 120–21).

In sum, liberal education is the cultivation of habits of invention, interpretation, argument, and judgment aimed at the realization (the personal grasp, development, and concretization) of knowledge from the perspective of the historical, concrete individual in relation to his "conscience" and to others. "Philosophy" is less a specific set of subject matters or activities than the capacity for discovery and discrimination among particulars. For this reason, the natural and social sciences, though not as maximally indeterminate as the humanities, are themselves, on Newman's own principles, perfectly acceptable as opportunities to engage in liberal education, so long as they are taught (1) with respect to the whole, (2) for their own sake, not to cultivate technical competencies, and (3) as (relative) indeterminacies requiring the active discrimination of their principles and parts.

THE SEVENTH DISCOURSE REDIVIVA

Newman's reformulation of philosophy as judgment, and more specifically as an ability to choose what will give intelligibility to a concrete problem, enables us to pose a final set of questions. If, as Newman asserts, the philosopher is one who can seize the strong point by means of "moral reason" in " 'the same great subject of man's moral, social, and feeling nature' " (*Idea*, 152); if he is one who in concrete questions "realizes" true relations among facts; and if he is one who discovers "real things," infers not only by means of a smart syllogism but by a thought and language "in its full compass," and decides or judges the fact by means of a more or less free illative sense—then, we must ask, does Newman in the *Idea* prove himself to be a good philosopher? What of his *own* judgment? Was it good judgment to seize upon utility as a strong point for controversy? More pointedly, was his "concession" to those upholding utility wise? Or was it rather, as Culler concludes, a distraction from and subversion of Newman's own best judgment? Why concede what could as easily have been ignored?

First, it should be clear by now that Newman is "doing philosophy" in just the way he describes it in the text, or, more accurately, his performance is a plausible example of the "idea" of philosophy without claiming to exhaust it. Why is it a plausible example? A complete answer would require considerable reference to historical conditions, the audience, its presuppositions and the like. In lieu of that, it is possible to mount above such facts and venture the following thesis: Newman's principles— "secular-sacred," "liberal-useful," "narrow utility-wide utility," "the gentleman-the Christian humanist," and many others—function to open up ranges of thought and experience to be used as places (1) to test the argument that Newman makes against one's own thought and experience; (2) to explore that thought and experience further, in the context of changing historical conditions, needs, and so on; and, it may be, (3) to solve at a general level, and only for a specific set of circumstances, the problem that the inquiry names—in this case, the problem of the nature and scope of liberal education. The Seventh Discourse can serve as a representative anecdote (for in fact all of the discourses function in the same way) to make these claims clearer.

We have said that the discourse pivots on the root-topic of the liberal and useful, but it should be observed how these values operate. The areas of thought and experience they point to are and already have been problems for Newman's audience, and more generally for his age. They are problems, of course, that are very much with us still. This is not in itself, however, a fact likely to impress anyone, for at this level we might want to say that Newman's principles and strong points are trivialities, mere commonplaces of an ongoing debate. So they are; but Newman uses

206

them to do two things. First, they concretize enduring, abstract values, lest the discussion remain cut off from human experience: as topical abstractions they are in search of facts. Second, by means of them Newman drives a wedge, as it were, between the dogmatic adherent (whether liberal or utilitarian) and that to which he dogmatically adheres on the ground that either alone will pervert the reality.

It is interesting to see how Newman goes about doing this. By conceding the full value and reality of what it is his interlocutors cherish, namely utility, Newman is then able to point towards a further reality that they themselves presuppose, but that they have not yet discerned, much less reflected on. Utility as a narrow pursuit is a plausible goal, one crucial to the social good. But broader means to that good are also plausible, in fact more so, for in the long run is not the social good better served by excellent minds able to address all problems? The answer to this question, it should be noted, is not self-evident, and it is not intended by Newman to be deduced from previously established premises. The answer depends rather on the willingness of the audience to stop, turn around, and explore its own values and beliefs; and of course the audience may reject Newman's invitation, as well as his conclusion. But this risk Newman appears willing to run, in the belief that philosophy simply does not exist apart from such values. Thus, by addressing common places, the common sense of both sides of the debate, Newman contacts the only thing that can give thought reality, namely, the experience of the *whole man* who is thinking. From the perspective of a (soft) utilitarian, to give an example, the stress on the "liberal" will irritate, just as, from the perspective of the (pure) humanist, the stress on the "useful" will confound and threaten. But all of this irritation and fear can be changed to something more tolerable—indeed, "liberating"—when it is recognized that a narrow utility destroys itself because it destroys the idea of the whole that it presupposes and that only a broader sense of utility, a more liberal sense, upholds the values the utilitarian prizes. By the same token, when it is recognized that one who seeks the liberal in Newman's sense already lives in a world of utilities, and that the values he prizes exist only within such utilities, then the sense that he is speaking to *barbaroi* diffuses, for the "barbarian" is already within the gates—or more accurately, the walls and gates have come down, and there is no conflict between the academy and the "wild" beyond. A university education, Newman summarizes, is "the great ordinary means to a great but ordinary end; it aims at raising the intellectual tone of society, at cultivating the public mind, at purifying the national taste, at supplying true principles to popular enthusiasm and fixed aims to popular aspirations, at giving enlargement and sobriety to the ideas of the age, at facilitating the exercise of political power, and refining the intercourse of private life" (*Idea*, 154). All this, not over and apart from the perfection of the intellect, but on the premise that the liberal is inseparable from the context of real concrete existence—lest education and the university become abstract, "theoretical," and "unreal" pursuits.

Note, more closely, how Newman drives a wedge into the concept of utility, discriminating the narrow from the broad, and arguing the ultimate absurdity of the former for the purposes of education, but *allowing for* utilitarian interests in the long-range fulfillment of the latter. He is then in a position to reconstitute the whole question by combining this new sense of the useful with the liberal. And the liberal, in turn, takes on a new, more concrete meaning, facilitating a parallel transformation of those who had dogmatically held to an abstract liberalness, bringing them to a more concrete sense of their own values. This is not verbal sleight-of-hand, since it explicitly appeals to the experience of those involved: the "transformations" are places where incompatibilities are disclosed and extensions or restrictions of outlook suggested.[101]

Finally, precisely because philosophy or reason is a concrete response of the whole man, Newman's own attempt to articulate that philosophy is itself intentionally "realized" in the concrete experience of his auditors (it is for this reason that it can still speak eloquently today), appealed to as a ground and test; in historical needs and conditions as he interprets them, appealed to as guides regarding the degree of emphasis to be placed on either side of (say) the "liberal-useful" topic; and in Newman's own pastoral intentions, appealed to as means of transforming those who are constrained by overly dogmatic interests. This is the justification of the Seventh Discourse, the reason why Newman makes seeming concessions, and the reason why, in doing so, his argument is philosophical: without such *address*, first of all, reason is not made concrete; without such *concessions*, secondly, no one is likely to move; and without such *interests* to move them to, thirdly, movement or transformation is meaningless. What Newman does is to use the terms of his auditors or readers as expandable and restrictable "fields" of interest that, when explored from the perspective of other fields, shift the grounds of those who occupy them. This is the reason why philosophy cannot be repeated: for it is not a set of static doctrines, but a dynamic, innovative, and opportunistic thought interpreting and reinterpreting enduring values and achievements of "the whole man."

PHILOSOPHIC RHETORIC

The ubiquity of rhetoric, indeed, is unlimited.
Hans-Georg Gadamer,
"On the Scope and Function of
Hermeneutical Reflection"

NEWMAN IN THE RHETORICAL TRADITION

In previous chapters I had occasion to refer Newman's thought to the larger rhetorical tradition (or traditions) behind it, without attempting, however, to explore all of the places of mutual convergence and illumination. In this chapter, I turn to rhetorical theorizing after Newman, and particularly to what is called philosophic or "epistemic"[1] rhetoric, to suggest how Newman's own philosophic rhetoric presents us with opportunities for rethinking certain central topics of contemporary rhetorical theory. Certainly two of the most important of those topics are "action," as in the term "symbolic action," and "certainty"—or, in other words, the first principle of nearly all contemporary rhetorical theory and the question of its epistemic status. The most incisive rhetorical theorists on these issues are Kenneth Burke and Stephen Toulmin, to whose work therefore we will turn presently, in the belief that Newman can both correct their excesses and enrich their thought. Before doing so, however, it may be useful, as a way of providing context for that discussion, to reflect briefly on what we have learned about Newman's relationship to previous rhetorical theory.

One of the most significant facts that has emerged from our study is that Newman's rhetorical theorizing subsumes Aristotelian rhetoric and the major rhetorical tradition deriving from Aristotle within more comprehensive ranges of concerns. Aristotle's rhetoric, for example, is "enthymematic" in lodging persuasion in the enthymeme; "deliberative" in the sense that future political action is the paradigm of the types of oratory; and "resolutive" in that the subjects of deliberation are relatively well circumscribed in their aims (consider, as examples of the type, the speeches by Cleon and Diodotus over the fate of Mytilene in Thucydides). Newman's rhetoric, by contrast, though fully allowing for such concerns, still is not enthymematic but inductive or jurisprudential, stressing the complexity and subtlety of proofs in the justification of beliefs; not deliberative but philosophical or epistemic, expanding the realm of rhetoric far beyond practical action; and not chiefly resolutive but transformative, concerned with long-term and thorough-going change (and "development") of an individual's entire outlook on life. In contrast to his predecessors, Whately and Campbell, Newman does not reject classical doctrine, but assimilates it within more comprehensive topical structures (enthymematic-inductive, deliberative-epistemic, resolutive-transformative).

Regarding specifically these different emphases in Aristotle and Newman, undoubtedly the most significant shift is from the deliberative to the epistemic. In this Newman draws closer to Cicero in the following way. Because "experience" (in the large sense) mediates perception and understanding, knowledge is ineluctably both probable and persuasive; only thought and word together can possibly comprise philosophy. Whereas Aristotle emphasizes the difference between demonstration on the one hand and dialectic and rhetoric on the other, or again between dialectic on the one hand and rhetoric on the other, Cicero and Newman stress the rhetorical component in *all* knowing. At the same time, we must beware of simply identifying Newman's project with the Ciceronian reduction of Aristotelian distinctions to rhetorical principles and methods. For the fact is that, although rhetorical reasoning for Newman is present in all thought, all thought is not exclusively, but only more or less, rhetorical. And the "less" in that formulation is real enough in Newman's eyes to warrant a distinction between two kinds of question: "First, those whose answers are already determinate and are to be found and established by appeals to evidence and logic; and, second, those whose answers are not fully determinate, for which answers must be created rhetorically."[2] Thus, for example, as Jouett Powell is right to point out,[3] Newman distinguishes formal or notional theology from the original religious experience and speech it attempted to articulate and from the rhetorical theology he himself practised. Or again, Newman recognizes that rhetorical persuasion is a relatively marginal factor in metaphysical arguments. In this respect he differs from Cicero and the Stoics, for whom resignation to probable arguments on either side of a question was the sum and substance of philosophy. For Newman, such argument was foundational to but not equally present in all inquiry.

Here again, however, we have to keep up with Newman's almost metronomic attending to either side of a case, for it is equally true that Newman himself always stressed, as a counterweight to the age, the rhetoric present in just those more determinate problems and disciplines. It is on this basis, in fact, that I have suggested throughout the present work that rhetoric is "architectonic" in Newman's thought, meaning not that it is the only legitimate mode of inquiry or proof, but rather that it is ever the focus of his approach to all inquiry and argument. Rhetoric for

210

Newman provides a unique perspective on the human element in all knowing and believing. But it is never understood to be the only approach, nor thought to be equally illuminating on all questions. Certain generic limits to rhetoric are fully implied and often stated in his work: the ambiguity of the language of rhetoric, rhetoric's dependency on probabilities, its susceptibility to corruption or superstition or authority (ideology), its tendency to oversimplification, its lack of hard-and-fast criteria for judgment. And yet, given his own specific audience and aims—to fight "liberalism" in religion, low-level empiricism in science, positivism in history, rationalism in philosophy and theology—rhetoric was the natural counterperspective for Newman to assume.

Furthermore, his insight that all knowing is more or less rhetorical separates Newman from his empiricist predecessors, Whately, Campbell, and Hume. Whately, we know, differed from Campbell on the question of the "utility" of the syllogism, considering it not as an ancillary aid but as the *only* form of reasoning ("induction" was not considered to be an independent form of argument but the observation of particulars).[4] Moreover, concerned as he was with arming Christian apologists against attacks on the faith, Whately saw in the syllogism a clean and lightweight weapon, not for converting innocent unbelievers but for scattering the sceptics among them. But Newman saw beyond the syllogism and grasped what Whately only dimly appreciated: that the differences in men's interpretations reside not in their logical machinery but in the substantive adequacy of their arguments. In this respect, far from rejecting logic, Newman constructs a range for "reason" that includes attention to the concrete "facts" and their interpretations as well as to logical forms.

In this latter regard Newman draws closer to Hume and Campbell. Like them he concentrates on the experimental and inductive basis of reasoning. But here too Newman goes beyond without rejecting what he has learned, for he furthers the empiricist project and its mechanical association of ideas by recognizing the centrality of antecedent considerations—topics and persuasives—to argumentation.[5] Here Newman joins forces with the romantics, but again balancing their interest in "genius" with a due appreciation of the strengths and limits of explicit argumentation and logic.[6] In short, Newman emerges as nothing less than the first modern epistemic rhetorician, incorporating classical, empiricist, and romantic interests in a theory of belief and practice of persuasion that anticipates modern developments in rhetoric and hermeneutical philosophy and theology.

The preceding placement of Newman, though adequate for my limited purposes, is clearly inadequate to the actual issues involved. Equally as important, my own account is in danger of overessentializing Newman's principles in the way I have sometimes claimed others tend to do, by thinking of his theory as a set of static "givens" rather than as topical resources for further thought. What those resources are cannot be discovered simply by formulating what Newman said; instead we must turn Newman reflexively on himself, on his practice in, for example, the *Grammar of Assent*. When we do that, we can see the outline of a model for rhetorical theory itself: the first half on "apprehension" locates the first principles of epistemic rhetoric; the section on "inference" adumbrates the nature of rhetorical justification; and the section on "assent" and "certitude" locates the judgment involved in rhetorical belief and knowledge. Newman's thought, in other words, can be seen to provide a comprehensive overview of philosophy and rhetoric.

Although it is not possible here to make explicit what I understand Newman's pluralistic philosophic rhetoric to comprise, it is possible, first, to inquire into the ground or first principle of Newman's philosophy, and to show how such a ground provides opportunities for rethinking another philosophic rhetoric, that of Kenneth Burke; and second, it is possible to show that Newman's thought on the epistemic status of principles, and assents generally, foreshadows the work of Stephen Toulmin in *The Uses of Argument*. These two inquiries will indicate how Newman's work is genuinely significant for contemporary rhetorical theory.

THE ONTOLOGICAL BASIS AND SCOPE OF RHETORIC RECONSIDERED

As long as we make the necessary distinctions, it is plausible, I think, to say that "action" in some sense or other is the essential ground or topic of all rhetorical theory and practice. As such it is worthy of serious attention as to its meaning and scope, for these will partly determine the characteristic features and range of a given rhetoric. Needless to say, the meaning (and scope) of "action" has undergone many alterations since Aristotle, although most of them have been made within the Aristotelian tradition itself, and are, on that basis, distinguishable from senses of action generated not so much outside the tradition as beyond it. Thus, the Aristotelian tradition may be fairly said to focus on the realm of *practical* action, where action means primarily deliberation, and features terms like act, will, choice, decision, consequence, effect. In Cicero, at least when philosophy is in view, this is less the case; but Bacon places rhetoric in the realm of the known and directs it to "the better moving of the will";

Hume contends that rhetoric is given its fullest scope in the political deliberations of Parliament; and George Campbell and Richard Whately emphasize persuasion to practical action (whether such rhetoric is delivered from the pulpit or the legislator's chair). By contrast, the major trend in modern philosophy and rhetoric is to extend the realm of rhetoric far beyond the realm of deliberation. Rhetoric is considered as a mode of knowing, and its key terms are belief, knowledge, prejudice, judgment (or, in the deconstructive mode, rhetoric is an exercise in troping, and its key terms are absence, differance, social practices, community). To understand this is to grasp that the ground of rhetoric is still "action," but now meant in the way I used that term with respect to Newman; that is, as synonymous with the "practical" generally, and as shorthand for the combination of "theory" and "practice," of "knowing" and "acting" in their various guises, with the latter terms given priority: both terms of this dialectic are necessary, as we have seen, but "practice" or "action" as the personal, persuasive, experiential, effective, remain the ground of rhetoric-as-philosophy. Thus Newman, of course, but also Chaim Perleman, Stephen Toulmin, Kenneth Burke, Paolo Valesio, Wayne Booth, Richard McKeon (and many others who have been or could be cited from other disciplines) understand rhetoric as philosophic and as grounded in action. The question now, it would seem, is not the scope but the precise meaning of action in various epistemic rhetorics: is it the same for any two such rhetorical theorists? This question, I submit, is central for contemporary rhetorical theory and practice.

In this section, and without hoping to exhaust it, I would like briefly to pursue that question regarding both Newman and the most visible of contemporary rhetoricians, Kenneth Burke. My own view is that action, and thus rhetoric, though they often appear to be for Burke what they are for Newman (and though genuine tensions exist in Burke's many formulations), are significantly different and for the most part unrecognized in their difference. My ultimate intention here is to throw this central topic into (or out of) perspective, to render it problematic and a place to be fought over in rhetorical theory, and thus to develop our powers of discrimination and judgment not only about Newman or Burke, but about philosophic rhetoric in general.

"Action" as Rhetorical Reason. In the *Grammar of Assent,* Newman establishes three components of knowing and believing—namely, apprehension, inference, and assent—and he conducts his exploration of each of these by means of the well-known distinction of the "real" and the "notional."[7] Since apprehension is discussed in the first half of the *Gram-*

213

mar only as a necessary logical and psychological condition of assent, and since, in turn, assent may be said to be reasonable only when supported by implicit or explicit inferences, it is "inference" that stands at the center of the *Grammar*.[8] There Newman realizes his aim of locating the kinds of evidence and arguments for nondemonstrable belief in indeterminate matters, and of showing that one can legitimately believe what he cannot actually prove. Accordingly, it becomes easy to see that the structuring *topoi* of the *Grammar of Assent* are "formal" (notional) and "informal" (real) inference. This is the comprehensive range Newman has postulated for "reasoning," in response to the excessive and one-sided cultivation of "science" and "logic," and as an attempt to locate man's full rationality and thus, it will be seen, his essence or nature. Of course, these two kinds of inference are not given equal weight, since, again, informal inference is that mode of reasoning that justified the kind of belief Newman was concerned with (and which he employed in the writing of the *Grammar* itself). Thus, the *Grammar* is both a discussion about and an instance of rhetorical reason and man's rhetorical nature.

Now, this range of man's faculties generated in this work (and elsewhere) is explicitly equated by Newman with man's own *nature* in Chapter IX: "What is the peculiarity of our nature, in contrast with the inferior animals around us? It is that, though man cannot change what he is born with, he is a being of progress with relation to his perfection and characteristic good" (*G.A.*, 225). But in what does this perfection and good consist? "[H]ere I am brought to the bearing of these remarks upon my subject. For this law of progress is carried out by means of the acquisition of knowledge, of which inference and assent are the immediate instruments" (*G.A.*, 225). In other words, it is man's capacity for "imaginative" inference and assent which constitutes his essence, and is, by the same token, the essence of the rhetorical "act": for Newman it is man's rationality in a broad sense of the word, understood as comprising intellectual thought, but also man's emotional, moral, and spiritual contemplations as well, that is the meaning of "action," of rhetoric, and of man philosophically considered:

> After all, man is not [in the narrow sense] a reasoning animal; he is a seeing, feeling, contemplating animal. . . .
> Life is for action. If we insist on proofs for everything, we shall never come to action: to act you must assume, and that assumption is faith. . . . (*G.A.*, 94–5).

To speak of "action" in this way, as a coherent synthesis of theory and practice in informal inference (and real assent), is obviously not to deny a place to formal inference, or to the fact that "practice" sometimes entails not "reasoning" per se but acting, doing, fulfilling one's duties, performing just deeds. But these senses of practice are easily accommodated, since informal inference itself is never wholly a discursive process, and in any event fully involves the "whole man," or woman, who reasons. It therefore involves all that he does as well as all that he thinks. Indeed, the whole point is that these are ultimately inseparable. Given this meaning of "action," then, as the fundamental point of Newman's rhetoric, what is its scope? What are the ultimate referents of informal inference and real assent? As a way of rounding out the present analysis of Newman's thought, and as a way of answering these questions, I wish to consider, very briefly, two points: the open-endedness of man's nature and the corresponding pluralism implied by Newman's views, his responsiveness to what may be called the indeterminacy of the real.

The first point is usually approached, not surprisingly, in the light of Newman's theology, which grounds man's nature, and thus his ultimate end or perfection, in the providence of God: Providence renders man's perfection not only a mystery but a "project."[9] This theology pervades Newman's works, of course, but it is crystallized for a moment in the *Apologia*, where Newman recounts his "early mistrust of material reality" as a final limit to this life, and of his "resting in the thought of two and two only absolute and luminously self-evident beings, myself and my Creator. . . . (*Apo.*, 18).

In the *Grammar of Assent,* however, which is in the first instance a philosophical and not a theological analysis,[10] man's nature is, first, a self-justifying fact to be taken as such and an *indeterminacy in itself,* a question and problem to be solved—"a being of progress with relation to his perfection and characteristic good." This good, we have seen, is a function of "reason" as defined above, but philosophically it is also an *indeterminate* end: "Other beings are complete from their first existence, in that line of excellence which is allotted to them; but man begins with nothing realized (to use the word), and he has to make capital for himself by the exercise of those faculties which are his natural inheritance. Thus he gradually advances to the fulness of his original destiny" (*G.A.*, 225).[11] In short, as ongoing and "indeterminate"—in the sense that man *shapes* his inchoate self and world (the pragmatic focus on deliberation and will) and in the sense that human formulations of transcendent truths are by definition dynamic, ambiguous, intersubjective, and developing (the Newmanian focus on knowing and saying)—man's scope for "action" is indefinitely extended along what, to use Newman's own topics, we may call a "secular-sacred" range.

215

My second point, alluded to in the previous section, is that Newman, in keeping with this view of the indeterminacy of man and the "real" generally and in keeping with his rhetorical method of generating "all" of the topics and means of persuasion by which to disclose what is indeterminate, implicitly formulates in the *Grammar* a pluralism for "action" by admonishing men to begin with themselves and their experience, with what they are or believe themselves to be: "Such as I am, it is my all; this is my essential standpoint, and must be taken for granted" (*G.A.*, 224):

> What I have to ascertain is the laws under which I live. My first elementary lesson of duty is that of resignation to the laws of my nature, whatever they are; my first disobedience is to be impatient at what I am, and to indulge an ambitious aspiration after what I cannot be, to cherish a distrust of my powers, and to desire to change laws which are identical with myself (*G.A.*, 224).

Newman's essential standpoint here signifies what may be called the *maximizing of voices*—of conscience, reasoning, and judgment—along the indefinite, "secular-sacred" range of man's action, not in the belief that all claims to represent man's nature will truly do so, but in order to generate as diverse and exhaustive a set of topics as possible to *discover* truth. Anything less than such a pluralism (which, incidentally, applies fully as much to Newman's views on the diversity of religions) risks predetermining man's nature, and as such would be theoretical and unreal.

By way of conclusion, finally, it should be noted that this fundamental standpoint or principle—what I have identified as the act of rhetorical reason—is not merely a psychological but a normative, philosophical-as-rhetorical position. Our mental powers constitute our very natures, and we are therefore under the necessity of *using* those powers: to put them in doubt is implicitly to assert the validity of the nature that is being questioned and is thus self-contradictory. "Our being, with its faculties, mind and body, is a fact not admitting of question, all things being of necessity referred to it, not it to other things" (*G.A.*, 224). In itself, of course, this argument (though its logic is inescapable) proves nothing about the mind or body, being only a reductio ad absurdum of an opposing view. As Walgrave has noted, however, Newman is really making the practical and "common sense" argument that, if we wish to know ourselves as human beings, then we have no choice but to use those powers that constitute our essence.[12] Such an argument is circular, of course—a fact that Newman himself fully recognizes: "I cannot think, reflect or judge about my being, without starting from the very point which I aim at concluding. My ideas are all assumptions, and I am ever moving in a circle" (*G.A.*, 347). On Newman's own rhetorical analysis of mind, however, the theoretical difficulty of this circular reasoning dissolves in the solution of the practical and persuasive force we feel in it, as well as in the gain we realize. In short, it "works," that is, its truth is established in what it discloses, in its own consistency and simplicity, and in the harmony it reveals. These criteria of adequacy to truth are everywhere implied in the *Grammar*:

> It is . . . by objections overcome, by adverse theories neutralized, by difficulties gradually clearing up, by exceptions proving the rule, by unlooked-for correlations found with received truths, by suspense and delay in the process issuing in triumphant reactions,—by all these ways, and many others, it is that the practiced and experienced mind is able to make a sure divination that a conclusion is inevitable, of which his lines of reasoning do not actually put him in possession (*G.A.*, 208).

All the way down to its foundations, namely the integrity of our nature and our duty to abide by it (the "knowing"-"acting" topic again structuring Newman's argument), Newman's rhetorical philosophy subordinates theory to practice in the concrete realm, where "action" is *imaginative inference and assent* in the search for truth.

"Action" as Analysis and Appropriation. To turn now to an analysis, even if only a suggestive one, of Kenneth Burke's philosophic rhetoric, is to meet with concerns superficially similar to Newman's, but on a second look, not only different from but opposed to the meaning and scope of "action" for which Newman argued.[13] To be sure, this opposition is equivocal and conflicted, but a bias is clearly discernible, I think, toward what we can simply name, for now, a sophistic version of epistemic rhetoric. The purpose, to repeat, of juxtaposing these two theorists is to create what Burke calls a "perspective by incongruity" to disclose the problematic status of "action," to discriminate ranges of philosophic rhetoric, and to suggest lines of argument regarding inadequacies in Burke not before recognized.[14]

In the first place, then, whereas Newman had constituted the range of being by means of his "real-notional" and "formal-informal" pairs, Burke's system similarly turns on his distinction between "motion" and "action:" each term (as in Newman) is necessary for a full account of what is; but the former, lacking any dimension of "choice" or "purpose," is adequate only to describe movement in space. "Action," however, does imply choice, hence it is more appropriate to account for "what people are doing and why they are doing it."[15] Although not equivalent pairs,

217

motion and action, formal and informal, and notional and real were paired in response to a perceived overconcern of the times with "science." In the *Grammar of Motives* (1945), and especially in the earlier *Permanence and Change* (1935), Burke had argued against behavioristic reductions of human life to causal necessity on the ground that such vocabularies (which feature "motion") cannot handle man's ability to *choose*.[16] In opposition to these, he argues that man's ultimate "situation" or "motive," his "characteristic pattern" is to express purpose or choice *by means of our linguistic ability* (later, "symbolic action"): that is, it is language specifically that provides us with the wherewithal to choose: " . . . speech in its essence is not neutral. Far from aiming at suspended judgment, the spontaneous speech of a people is loaded with judgments. It is 'intensely moral' " (*PC*, 176–77). Thus, generically, "action" is ethical choice: man "lives by purpose—and purpose is basically *preference*" (*PC*, 235; emphasis added). This last point is farreaching in its implications, for "preference" above all is a matter of having "attitudes," fundamental attachments and aversions that are intrinsically hortatory and directive, so that *symbolic* action is the "dancing of an attitude."[17] At the same time, symbolic action is one's "charting" (*PLF*, 7) of an objective "situation," which is but another word for motives (*PLF*, 18) in keeping with one's fundamental attitudes and interests. These two functions, "attitudinizing" and "charting," the *catharsis* of one's feelings[18] via the linguistic specification (directed by those feelings) of objective motives— are the obverse sides of *symbolic action,* or "rhetoric," which is the "representative anecdote" for action generally and thus for man's essence or "substance." What we now need to know is how, specifically, Burke argues these claims.

To ask this question is really to inquire more closely into what it means to say that man's substance is language. In the *Grammar of Motives* Burke argues that *any* attribution of substance necessarily involves one, whether philosopher, poet, or scientist, in linguistic incompatibilities, because "substance" refers to "something that stands beneath or supports the person or thing" (*GM*, 22) being defined. As a consequence, the definition involves simultaneously, and paradoxically, speaking of the object (or person or event) in terms of what it is not, its context: "That is, though used to designate something *within* the thing, *intrinsic* to it, the word etymologically refers to something *outside* the thing, *extrinsic* to it" (*GM*, 23): "To tell what a thing is, you place it in terms of something else. This idea of locating, or placing, is implicit in our very word for definition itself: to *define,* or *determine* a thing, is to mark its boundaries, hence to use terms that possess, implicitly at least, contextual reference" (*GM*, 24). As Burke proceeds to show, language accordingly provides various strategies (and thus choices) by which to define—for example, placing things in terms of their "scenic" contexts, or the contexts of their origins or ends, three general sources of "motives" or determinants of meaning that "cause" a thing to be what it is. What does it mean, then, to define man in terms of the very means by which we name motives, namely, "terms" themselves?

To state the matter as succinctly as possible, to define man's nature *in terms of language itself,* Burke argues, is *to account more fully* than any other definitional strategy for this nature. To name man as the "symbol-using animal" whose language use is itself a motive not reducible to other motives (of "scene," "agent," "agency" or "purpose," all derived from the key term "act"), is to say that his nature *is* the act by which any naming of substance occurs. "Language" is the only "context" that mitigates the "paradox of [attributing] substance" by attributing to man both *extrinsic* motives (all those motives that language can name) and *intrinsic* motives (language itself, which is unique to man). To come at this from a slightly different angle: "substance" is itself an "act" word (a term that designates how something characteristically acts; *GM*, 227). To say that man's substance is language is to say that man's characteristic act is precisely his ability to "attitudinize" (choose) and "chart" (name substance) through language. Since language is intrinsically ethical and evaluative, and thus expressive of attitudes that both locate and recommend motives, man's ability to use words is simultaneously an attitudinizing and an analyzing of what is and what is desired. Language is thus man's "universal motive" or situation, and the pentad, Burke's five grammatical-rhetorical coordinates for analyzing motivation, are his "perpetual-motion machine"[19] for operationalizing this capacity to designate motives and thus substance. Hence, Burke's focus on language does not deny other motives, economic, physical, psychological, technological and so on; but it argues that such motives are "filtered" and evaluated (this will ultimately be a function of our attitudes) by the terms we use to name them. The world impinges upon us, but it gets reflected, deflected, and selected by our divergent "terministic screens" (*LSA*, 46). These screens are the means by which we find and judge reality in keeping with our essential interests and attitudes, the "yes-es" and "no-es" we feel as natural, social, verbal and "extra-verbal" creatures.[20] Lastly, Burke's own turn to symbolic action to "name" man is itself a function of his own attitude, which, as constitutive of the system, is really an "attitude of attitudes," namely, his desire to

219

avoid the dangerous "fanaticism" of perfecting one motive at the expense of others, or the equally dangerous "dissipation" of lapsing into self-serving narcissism (*GM,* 318). Instead, Burke exhorts to the "humbler satisfactions" (*GM,* 317) of his own method, which is more humane, pluralistic, and "realistic" regarding attitudes and motives since it attends equally, one might say democratically, to all.

I indicated above that Burke's choice of symbolic action to account for man's nature is a function of his own most basic "attitude." This choice is what, in *Permanence and Change* and in the *Grammar of Motives,* Burke called an "act of faith," meaning the fundamental presupposition that constitutes any philosophic system and directs attention to some things and not others, determines what will be considered "proof" and what will not, and so on (*PC,* 235–36; *GM,* 84). By briefly examining Burke's own presupposition more closely, and by using it as a guide to what Burke features in his system, I can disclose further aspects of his thought that indicate it is not as amenable as one might have supposed to Newman's version of epistemic rhetoric. It is this argument, as brief and general as it is, that can help us to discriminate two varieties of rhetorical "action," and thus varieties of philosophic rhetoric itself, and that will suggest the ways Newman's position effectively subsumes Burke's "dramatism" and "logology."

First of all, the significance of Burke's fundamental presupposition that it is language more than anything else—more than "reason," or economic necessities, or psychological drives, or technology, or God— that accounts for man's nature, for his ability to choose, might best be measured by contrasting it to what is dramatistically quite close to it, the Aristotelian (and Newmanian) concept of the "act" and the "entelechy." Whereas "act" for Aristotle is in principle teleological, directed to the fullest development of that which acts (and is thus also, in principle, "idealistic" and "progressive"), Burke transforms this idea of an "end-oriented act" in favor of a *functional analysis of linguistic motives,* in which an "act" is always the sum total of the "causes" that constitute it. Burke enacts this transformation on the ground that the Aristotelian conception, although dramatistic, is too hierarchial—too progressive— and thus not attitudinally and methodologically sensitive enough to the need to qualify all such hierarchizing with what might be called a "democracy of functions," namely, the pentad (or, if we include "attitude," the hexad). It follows, then, that the principle of the entelechy is not one for Burke of "development"—which is impossible in the dramatistic calculus since the "perfection" of an act can only be the implicit, *static* ("logical") relations existing among all of the five sources of motives constituting it—but a principle rather of *complete description or analysis* of all of its motives. Now, what this in turn signifies is that Burke's method, indeed the philosophy as a whole, is primarily concerned with the *analysis* of the interaction of existing motives; hence "action" for Burke is not, as for Newman (and Aristotle) "reason," but rather the citing or observing of motives and their logical relations (for "clusters" of terms "imply" one another and thus can be "derived" from and "substituted for" each other); and the motives and relations themselves are thought of as both "forces" and "fixities." As he says in his article "Dramatism": "Dramatism is a method of analysis and a corresponding critique of terminology designed to show that the most direct route to the study of human relations and human motives is via a methodical inquiry into cycles or clusters of terms and their functions."[21]

In such linguistic analysis, furthermore, one does not "choose" motives so much as "identify" them ("identification" is, of course, the term that replaces "persuasion" in the *Rhetoric of Motives*); indeed, even the "attitudinizing" of wishes can be, in principle, indifferent to *which* motives embody them. In keeping with the "paradox of substance," Burke's concern with act (and thus choice) tends to disappear into the terms of what it is *not,* viz., the other four sources of motivation. Thus, Burke's own "attitude of attitudes"—the skeptical subversion of linguistic accounts of "motivation" aimed at preventing the unjust tyranny of any one account—paradoxically leads to the *systematic avoidance* of terms like "reason" and "choice" in favor of "analysis," "attitude," and "act" as "caused substance," in keeping with the genius of the system.[22] But, again—for this is the ultimate point to be clarified—to say as much is to diverge considerably from Aristotle (and Newman), as well as from the "new rhetoric" of such men as Stephen Toulmin and Chaim Perelman, Wayne Booth and Walter Fisher. Instead of Burke the defender of multiple views, we catch a glimpse here of Burke the totalizing analyst.[23]

To be sure, what I am arguing here is to some extent a question of emphasis and degree. "In principle," Burke's system fully permits terms like reason, choice, probability, argument, design, purpose; but *in fact* they are rarely featured. Beyond the heavy ethical language of *Permanence and Change* (language that is pretty much dropped subsequently), the only real exception to what I am arguing—an exception that does more to prove the rule than to negate it—is Burke's "representative anecdote" for dramatism, the "enactment of a constitution." As a social framework for belief (and even here the Newmanian ring of the term "belief" refers more

221

to "attitudes" and "wishes" than to the naming of substance; *GM*, 360, 365, 373), a constitution is a partial representation (*GM*, 362, 372) of the wishes of those in a specific time and place, which serves thenceforward to canalize action and thought, express generalized will, and provide "coordinates" for future action: "[C]onstitutions are important in singling out certain directives for special attention, and thus in bringing them more clearly to men's consciousness" (*GM*, 367). In the first place, then, a constitution represents, once more, Burke's own philosophic ground in attitudes and desires, for a constitution not only institutionalizes various divergent attitudes, but itself possesses an attitude toward those attitudes, one of tolerance for and resignation to the "Scramble" among "directives" (motives) for a hearing—a state of affairs less orderly, but also less dangerous, than the "perfecting" of one (inadequate) language of motivation over all of the others. And, in the second place, a constitution is a model for negotiation, argument, and compromise while also providing an "order" of its own that culminates in the democratic "attitude of attitudes"—hence it is a model for motivational rhetoric itself.

Regarding just this last point, however, Burke's actual treatment of the constitution as a model tends to downplay "argument" and reason,"[24] and to use expressions such as "centering attention" and "raising to men's consciousness"—expressions, in other words, that treat what is at stake as already existing and "given" and needing only to be observed or analyzed. Burke sums up this tendency himself:

> In sum: There are principles in the sense of wishes, and there are principles in the sense of interrelationships among the wishes. Principles as wishes are voluntary or arbitrary, inasmuch as men can meet in conference and decide how many and what kind of wishes they shall subscribe to. But once you have agreed upon a list of wishes, the interrelationships among those wishes are necessary or inevitable (*GM*, 375).

It is true, on the other hand, that Burke can also speak of constitutions as calculi "encouraging men to evaluate their public acts" (*GM*, 368) in one way and not another, which is another way of talking about men "interpreting" and "reasoning" together. But my point is that the whole thrust of dramatistic analysis and attitudizing is to concentrate on the priority of wishes, and the atemporal spinning-out of motives, and not on the messy but also more realistic problem of putting such analysis to the test; for although Burke's system can disclose all of the "logical" possibilities, it is singularly inept at talking about real-life "probabilities," "decisions," "purposes," and the like. Or perhaps more accurately, while the system itself could be turned to such concerns, Burke himself thinks of such things as either logical or empirical (causal) fixities.

This can be seen, finally, in Burke's own terms for what it is to get at motives. In *The Philosophy of Literary Form*, for example, it is significant that motives are understood to "chart" an objective situation, for this is to understand them, in the first instance, as biological, social, or linguistic "givens" or fixities that primarily need to be mapped out. Thus, Burke's literary analyses in that work are spoken of as "indexes," "catalogues," and even "statistics." Similarly, in *Language as Symbolic Action*, "terministic screens" are said to "select, reflect, and deflect" reality, as though reality is a fixed set of forces that can only be harnessed or shunted off, not reasoned over as probabilities and problems of interpretation. This tendency is best seen, however, in Burke's innumerable analyses of "equational clusters" of terms (a particularly good example is his analysis of the "order" cluster in *The Rhetoric of Religion*), where motives are timeless, unchanging forces. Because such fixities all serve Burke's god-terms of "act" and "attitude," we can say that (as with Newman) "knowing" is subordinate to "practice" and "acting." But because "action," in turn, is primarily *attitudinizing by means of the analysis of motives,* "theory-practice" and "knowing-acting" are strangely adjusted back to the side of theory and knowing, that is, of *what is.* This *epistemic* turn, however, is emphatically not that of Newman, since "what is" for Burke is itself a function of desire, and knowledge is thus *moralized* "towards a better life: "For it is essentially a realism of the *act:* moral, persuasive—and acts are not 'true' or 'false' in the sense that the propositions of 'scientific realism' are" (*RM,* 44).[25] In other words, for Burke the universe is not to be known as something that is "true," but is rather something to be *taken on and analyzed* in terms of what R. M. Hare has called a "blik": that is, as an ultimately nonrational choice (for Burke, an "act of faith"), which has better or worse consequences. And for Burke, of course, his own "attitude of attitudes" is a blik intended to "purify war" through verbal adjustment. For Newman, on the other hand, the world is not in the first place "feeling" but something to be known as "true," by means of *rational, rhetorical* criteria of adequacy for argument (of just the sort Basil Mitchell has sketched out in response to Hare).[26]

As a way of concluding this discussion, then, it may be helpful if I recapitulate the leading points and venture a few final generalizations about these two philosophic rhetorics. In the first place, I have suggested that Newman can be of some importance for contemporary rhetorical theorizing, for, among other things, he can help us to see how central the concept of "action" is, and help us also to articulate the meaning and scope of that term. For Newman himself, we have seen, "action," and thus "rhetoric," is *imaginative reason and assent amidst an indefinite range of man's indeterminacy*. For Burke, on the contrary, symbolic action is the *analysis of motives in service of a humane attitude of skeptical resignation to man's determinacy*. And it is just this restriction of man's essence to human language that marks the "scope" of action for Burke and that leads me to call his rhetoric "sophistic." For whereas, philosophically, man *may not* be the measure of man in Newman's rhetoric, since the rhetorically indeterminate is maximized as far as possible without sacrificing claims to being reasonable, man *is* the measure of all things for Burke and language is his means of calculation: rhetoric is thus, as in Newman, a pluralism of voices or "perspectives," but it is so only within the range of human and not divine "motivation." Indeed, Burke himself points to these limits of his philosophic rhetoric.[27] In this way, Burke *arbitrarily*, in accordance with his original choice of blik (to use the word), *cuts off religious talk as such*, and can readmit it only as language about language itself ("logology"), whereas for Newman *rhetoric legitimates and maximizes the religious and rhetorical interpretation of reality*. In short, on this analysis, Burke is finally less rhetorical and thus less pluralistic than Newman, whose own philosophy can fully admit dramatism and logology without either doing violence to their meaning or subverting his own claims.

But we need not at this time choose between them. Rather, we can and should appreciate the subtle but very important differences they embody for philosophic rhetoric: Newman as fully able to incorporate the main concerns of the Aristotelian tradition, but also as jurisprudential, transformative, epistemic, idealistic, tragic (in his recognition of sin), open-ended and dynamic; and Burke as able, in principle, also to include Aristotelian preoccupations but primarily focused on a rhetoric that is attitudinal, analytic, associative, epistemic-as-sophistic, functional, "comic," epideictic, static, and ultimately dogmatic. These terms and others are meant merely to suggest ways to discriminate the complexities of philosophic rhetoric and to suggest also how so removed, and even so seemingly conventional a figure as Newman, is in fact a neglected giant able to encompass even so imposing a figure as Burke. Regardless, finally, of whether we think him right or wrong, Newman presents a powerful version of philosophic rhetoric.

THE QUEST FOR CERTAINTY

I have argued in the preceding section that Newman's philosophic rhetoric is grounded in a concept of action that coherently assimilates theory to practice and throws into relief the comparatively fixed and (ultimately) dogmatic ways in which Burke construes his own first principle, symbolic action, and its scope. My intention has been to suggest that, although this is not by any means the only possible reading of Newman and Burke, nevertheless the present focus on action in Newman is a useful way of making problematic Burke's highly visible and often too readily accepted starting point for philosophic rhetoric.

In this section, it remains to explore a fairly restricted question about rhetorical judgment, namely, whether or not it makes sense to say that rhetoric can properly generate certainty and not just probability in its conclusions. Though the choice of this problem is not absolutely dictated by the preceding inquiry, but arises rather in part out of my interest in showing how Newman either anticipates or brings into question aspects of contemporary rhetorical theory, nevertheless the question does refer back to first principles by asking after the epistemological status of a concept like action. The current development of rhetorical epistemology by many rhetoricians ignores the issue of the cognitive status of belief and certainty, while discussions in other fields, such as philosophy, and positions such as that of H. H. Price, ignore or misrepresent one of the more sophisticated views taken on the problem since Locke, namely, Newman's own. The question, again, seems to be this: can belief that is less than demonstrable knowledge but more than ungrounded "enthusiasm" reasonably command from the one who holds it an unqualified, unconditional assent? Or must we, like Price, hold with John Locke that all concrete beliefs, since they are supported only by probabilities, rank only a less-than-total commitment, along the lines of "as if" or "practical" certainty endorsed by Bishop Butler, Whately, and others? In order to clarify how Newman anticipates Toulmin on this issue, it is necessary first to recall Newman's account of "logic," since the solution to the epistemological problem in the *Grammar* depends on (and is in part marred by) Newman's (mis)understanding of the role of logic. We can then turn to the *Grammar* itself and to Toulmin's approach in *The Uses of Argument*.

Now, it is known that the *Grammar of Assent* was written as an attempt to articulate the position Newman had been developing for years, partly in letters to his lifelong friend, the freethinker William Froude, against the latter's skepticism about religious faith and, indeed, about certainty in general. The question turned on whether or not in matters of fact it can correctly be said that it is possible for one to achieve certainty.[28] The problem is that argument in such matters was comprised of premises that were only probable, so that any conclusion drawn from them was not demonstratively entailed with regard to its truth (i.e., its negative was not logically contradictory). Froude held that "even the highest attainable probability does not justify the mind in discarding the residuum of doubt":

> More strongly than I believe anything else I believe this—that no subject whatever—distinctly not in the region of ordinary facts with which our daily experience is consonant—distinctly not in the domain of history or of politics, and yet again a fortiori, not in that of theology, is my mind (or as far as I can take the mind of any human being,) capable of arriving at an absolutely certain conclusion.[29]

As is known, Froude's "ethic of belief" so widely shared by his contemporaries followed the Lockean principle that one adjusts his *degree* of assent to the evidence. Locke himself believed the existence of God could be demonstrated, but while he conceded cases where propositions approximated so closely to certainty that "we assent to them as firmly . . . as if they were infallibly demonstrated,"[30] he considered these cases to be few in number and compelled by common sense. Newman, by contrast, considered such cases "to be found throughout the range of concrete matter" (*G.A.*, 317) and not compelled, but rather somehow decided or committed to. Newman, then, was concerned with justifying what Locke had castigated as a "surplusage" of belief over proof.[31]

Newman's defense of absolute adherence to materially probable propositions may be summarized briefly. In the first chapter of the *Grammar*, Newman distinguishes three ways of holding propositions, either by "doubting" them (in which case there is a "suspense of mind" [*G.A.*, 7] about them), "inferring" them, or "assenting" to them. Dismissing doubt as more or less irrelevant to his concerns, Newman distinguishes inferring and assenting on the basis that the former is a "conditional" and the latter an "unconditional" acceptance of a proposition; assent (when it is legitimate) presupposes inference as a sine qua non (*G.A.*, 189), but it is otherwise distinct from inference. The "conditionality" of inference means that a conclusion is held on the basis of the premises that support it and thus varies in strength in the degree with which one accepts those premises—whereas an assent does *not* vary because it does not depend on (though it presupposes) premises. The question, then, is how it comes to happen that assent can transcend conditionality:

What presents some difficulty is this, how it is that a conditional acceptance of a proposition,—such as is an act of inference,—is able to lead as it does, to an unconditional acceptance of it,—such as is assent; how it is that a proposition that is not, and cannot be, demonstrated, which at the highest can only be proved to be truth-like, not true, such as "I shall die," nevertheless claims and receives our unqualified adhesion.

Most assents are unconsciously arrived at (*G.A.*, 189), but those that are explicitly examined and reaffirmed constitute "complex" assents, or "certitudes" (*G.A.*, 196ff.). How, again, can both assents and certitudes deserve "unqualified adhesion?"

Newman is aware, of course, that the probable *content* of premises will never entail the truth of a conclusion in concrete matters, that the syllogism in these matters only leads to probabilities. Newman's answer to the question, therefore, is that assent follows upon but is independent of premises, that it is through the *personal* estimate of a convergence of myriad probabilities that one is not only allowed but morally obligated to assent. Regarding such a concrete proposition, "We are considered to feel, rather than to see, its cogency; and we decide, not that the conclusion must be, but that it cannot be otherwise"; "the conclusion in a real or concrete question is foreseen and predicted rather than actually attained; foreseen in the number and direction of accumulated premises, which all converge to it, and as the result of their combination, approach it more nearly than any assignable difference, yet do not touch it logically . . ." (G.A., 321).

Now, such an account does not deny the Lockean insight that on many questions we hold conclusions in varying degrees, but only asserts that when we assent, and not simply infer, the act is unconditional because we "feel" our way beyond the material probability of the premises to the truth of the conclusion.[32] *Logically* the conclusion is (necessary but) uncertain, as it is materially; but personally, psychologically, and epistemologically, it is held to be true. Newman provides many examples of such absolute assent (the best known being his "Great Britian is an island" example[33] [cf. G.A., pp. 161–64, 322–29]). James Livingston cites W. G. Ward's agreement with Newman regarding the attack on what Ward called " 'equationism,' the Lockean principle which enjoins the moral obligation of effecting an 'equation' between the strength of one's conviction and the amount of proof on which it rests." Jamie Ferreira treats this issue with great effectiveness.[34]

In sum, Newman holds that by virtue of converging probabilities "too fine to avail separately, too subtle and circuitous to be convertible into syllogisms" (*G.A.*, 288), which "vary both in their number and their separate estimated value" (*G.A.*, 293), the proof is, to the mind properly estimating it, "equal" to the assent—again, not logically, but materially and psychologically: "Certitude is a mental state; certainty is a quality of propositions" (*G.A.*, 344): "It follows that what to one intellect is a proof is not so to another, and that the certainty of a proposition does properly consist for assent in the certitude of the mind which contemplates it" (*G.A.*, 293). It should be clear from preceding chapters, moreover, that this view does not result in radical subjectivism—the notion that what appears to one to be probable or true necessarily *is* so—since one may be said to legitimately reach certitude only when his claims are grounded in arguments perceived to be sufficient, despite the fact that "not all men discriminate . . . in the same way" (*G.A.*, 293). Thus, the ultimate court of appeal is an illative sense, sufficient unto itself for final judgment, but morally bound to consider "all" of the relevant considerations. The illative sense, Newman writes, is:

> a rule itself, and appeals to no judgment beyond its own; and attends upon the whole course of thought from antecedents to consequents, with a minute diligence and unwearied presence, which is impossible to a cumbrous apparatus of verbal reasoning, though, in communicating with others, words are the only instrument we possess, and a serviceable, though imperfect instrument (*G.A.*, 361–62).

In *The Uses of Argument* Stephen Toulmin provides a contemporary confirmation of Newman's argument that certainty (certitude) is *normatively* acceptable under the proper circumstances. In that work Toulmin is interested in showing that the universal premise of a categorical syllogism (All A's are B's) disguises the fact that the *content* of the conclusion of such a syllogism "goes beyond" (in some sense) the content of the premises. He is able to show this by distinguishing "warrants" (general law-like statements sanctioning inferences from data to claims[35]) from the "backing" for such warrants (the information necessary to support the warrant, [*UA*, 103]). Because one cannot determine merely from the linguistic form of the universal premise whether or not the *backing* entails (i.e., includes as part of its content) the conclusion, it is impossible to tell if the conclusion "goes beyond" the content of the premises.

The significance of this distinction emerges only slowly. First, Toulmin shows (*UA*, 123) that most formally valid deductive arguments are deconstructable in this way, that is, the backing of most warrants in everyday arguments and in the academic disciplines do not include the conclusions. These arguments Toulmin calls "substantial," meaning that a logical type-jump occurs between the premises and the conclusion. A logical "type" refers to the different kinds of data constituting premises and conclusions (assertions, for example, about "present and past events, predictions about the future, verdicts of criminal guilt, aesthetic commendations, geometrical axioms and so on;" *UA*, 13). A type-jump signifies the fact that the content of a conclusion in a deductive argument is not strictly (substantially) contained in the premises, hence not, in Toulmin's sense, "analytically entailed." This kind of argument, the "substantial," is therefore distinguished by Toulmin from one that is "analytic": "An argument from D to C [data to claim] will be called analytic if and only if the backing for the warrant authorising it includes, explicitly or implicitly, the information conveyed in the conclusion itself" (*UA*, 125).

Although it is Toulmin's prerogative to stipulate definitions, I wish to suggest that his main ones, in particular "substantial" and "analytic," create more confusion than they are worth. Note that "analytic" refers to the *content* of arguments, to the fact that the backing includes the content of the conclusion. Now, Toulmin equates this sense of analytic (analytic-as-content) with what it is logicians care about: "In many treatises on formal logic . . . the term deduction is reserved for arguments in which the data *and backing* positively entail the conclusion—in which, that is to say, to state all the data and backing and yet to deny the conclusion would land one in a positive inconsistency or contradiction" (*UA*, 122; emphasis added). Since this would require all arguments to be analytic to be acceptable, and since most arguments are not analytic but substantial, Toulmin seeks to dissociate deductions from formally valid arguments. On pp. 119–20, he shows how the substitution of the backing for a warrant creates a quasi-syllogism that he proceeds to *call* "deductive," and one that is clearly acceptable as an argument but is not formally valid, concluding that the "shuffling of terms," which he understands logical validity to consist in (*UA*, 118), is no necessary part of deduction and thus (we are left to infer) is irrelevant as a criterion. Toulmin subsequently renames validity in the sense that he applies the term, not to the form, but to the content of arguments. To be sure, as far as content goes, Toulmin is correct to say that formal validity is irrelevant. But then, as only a glimpse into logic texts will show—even Whately can be cited on this score[36]— formal validity has nothing to do with semantic considerations, the content of premises, or any sense of entailment other than linguistic form.[37]

229

Toulmin himself seems to be aware of this (he subsequently argued that it was not his intention to attack formal logic[38]), and, strictly speaking, his attack is less against logical validity than it is against the danger that logic will be confused with analyticity-as-content. Indeed, he says as much:

> Nothing is decided by merely putting a case in proper form, but rather a situation is created in which we can begin to ask rational questions. . . .
> So long as no more than this is meant by the phrases "logically possible, impossible and necessary," they are innocuous and acceptable enough: yet the danger remains of confusing logical possibility, impossibility and necessity with other sorts. . . . Logical considerations are not more than formal considerations, that is, they are considerations having to do with the preliminary formalities of argument-stating . . . (*UA*, 172–73).

Toulmin's real target, therefore, is an *ideal* of analyticity-as-content that would insist that all substantial arguments, though sometimes (or always) able to be expressed in valid form, are nevertheless inferior to arguments that are not only formally but substantially analytic. Hume, of course, is the godfather to this "analytic paradigm": "If one follows Hume, one ends by allowing the Court of Reason to adjudicate only in cases where analytic arguments can properly be demanded" (*UA*, 175). This is an extreme view of Humean skepticism, I think, belied in part by Hume's work in morals, criticisms, and history, but the moral is true so far as it goes, namely, that if one's only criterion is analyticity-as-content, most of what flies under the banner of "good reasons" is decidedly lacking rigor.

As I have tried to suggest, however, the alleged inferiority of substantial arguments containing a type-jump (what Toulmin elsewhere calls a "logical gulf" [*UA*, 224] between premises and conclusion) necessarily follows only if one allows analyticity to refer to content, as it does on Toulmin's analysis of analytic and substantial (distinctions themselves made necessary only because of the warrant-backing distinction). If, however, these latter distinctions are not introduced (and the confusions they give rise to regarding what is or is not "data" or a "warrant" are well known), then a formally valid argument *is* an analytic argument, since the conclusion does not "go beyond" the premises in the only really meaningful sense of "go beyond": if you admit the premises, it is consistent to admit the conclusion and inconsistent not to. As for the *truth* or *soundness* of an argument, logicians recognize those as problems outside their jurisdiction, and Toulmin would have been much clearer had he abided by the validity/soundness distinction. The "logical gulf" he is talking about, therefore, derives from an *epistemological* criterion concerned ultimately with self-evident truths, relations of ideas, and the like, which, when made the premises of syllogisms, yield certain truth (analytic in form and content). To confuse this analytic paradigm with mere formal validity is the risk incurred by Toulmin's distinctions.

In short, Toulmin argues against the analytic paradigm by invoking what amounts to the conventional distinction between validity and sound-ness (*UA*, 185), that is, by showing that modal qualifiers like "possibly," "presumably," "probably" and so on are field-dependent, noncompelled judgments (when not reducible to statistical computation) regarding the degree of sufficiency of evidence and thus the kind of qualifier that it deserves. Although the "force" of such qualifiers—the practical implica-tions of their use—are field-invariant, the "criteria" of their use (*UA*, 30) are dependent on the fields in which they occur: "The things we must point to in showing that something is possible will depend entirely on whether we are concerned with a problem in pure mathematics, a prob-lem of team-selection, a problem in aesthetics, or what; and features which make something a possibility from one standpoint will be totally irrelevant from another" (*UA*, 37).

More importantly, however, this also means that a modal qualifier like "probably" cannot be reduced to field-invariant criteria, and that "probability" will shift from calculability in one field to something like "reliable judgment" in another, as Newman himself had argued in the Oxford sermons and the *Grammar*. At the same time, "probability" as a personal estimate or reliable judgment *can* avoid subjectivism because it is interpersonal and grounded in standards of judgment beyond mere agree-ment:

> Rational discussion in any field accordingly depends on the pos-sibility of *establishing* inference-warrants in that field: to the extent that there are common and understood interpersonal procedures for testing warrants in any particular field, a judicial approach to our problems will be possible. . . . Two people who accept common procedures for testing warrants in any field can begin comparing the merits of arguments in that field (*UA*, 175–76).

Finally, since modal qualifiers are generated by the critical judgment of inquirers, it follows that "certainty" in the sense of "absolute adhesion" forwarded by Newman is no different from other modal qualifiers and is normatively appropriate provided the circumstances (arguments) sanction it. Toulmin suggests that we simply need to reject the analytic paradigm as irrelevant to most rational discussion and to see "certainty" not as a leap across a logical gulf, but rather as a "change of posture" (*UA*, 254) in the order of viewing. In concrete matters of fact, "a time comes when we have produced in support of our conclusions data and warrants full and strong enough, in the context, for further investigation to be unnecessary" (*UA*, 234).

The similarity of this line of reasoning to Newman's need not be belabored. After we adjust their positions on the nature of logic, we find that logical validity is an acceptable and necessary control on truth, but one subordinate to field-dependent and intersubjectively validated criteria:

> In logic as in morals, the real problem of rational assessment—telling sound arguments from untrustworthy ones, rather than consistent from inconsistent ones—requires experience, insight and judgement, and mathematical calculations (in the form of statistics and the like) can never be more than one tool among others of use in this task (*UA*, 188).

By contrast, Victorians like Froude and Clifford followed Whately, Butler, Hume, and Locke in recognizing only an "as-if" or "practical" certainty—being willing to act as though a conclusion were certain when, *logically*, it was not—and thus indirectly subscribing to the analytic paradigm. Newman is the first to break through this abstract position, and in so doing is the first to create a comprehensive range for "judgments," which few rhetoricians even today seem to recognize. In this way, and in many others not yet explored, Newman makes significant and lasting contributions to philosophic rhetoric.

CONCLUSION

In this work I have tried to show that Newman offers us a coherent rhetorical theory and an innovating rhetorical practice that belie conceptions of him as dogmatic, elitist, and reactionary on the one hand, or merely skeptical, subjective, and equivocating on the other. In fact, Newman combines a cathedral-like unity and sweep of vision with a modern sensibility for change and adaptation. His epistemic rhetoric is notable in several respects: it marks a decisive break with its immediate past and a *reprise* of the classical rhetorical tradition; it is grounded philosophically in the conscience and the self, which could provide contemporary the-

232

orists with a much-needed complement to the newly fashionable so-
ciological slant of the American pragmatist tradition (in which Booth and
Burke, for example, clearly stand); and it argues in a serious way for both
the legitimacy of rhetorical certitude (as distinct from logical certainty),
and the (rhetorical) plausibility of and need for the concept of the transcendent as the limit of rhetorical invention. In Newman's rhetorical
philosophy, faith and commitment are rhetorically defensible, as they are
in the philosophy of Michael Polanyi, or in the theology of Peter Berger,
who finds in what he calls "signals [i.e., rhetorical signs] of transcendence" the type of evidence necessary for an "inductive faith."[39] Whether
avowedly religious or not, thinkers like Newman, Polanyi and Berger offer
a post-Enlightenment foundation for belief and knowledge that is its own
via media between an impossible mirroring of nature and metaphysics of
presence and an equally impossible relativism. To support rhetoric upon
rhetorical foundations may appear hopelessly circular, but I have tried to
indicate that the rhetorical circle need not be vicious if the circle is big
enough. Moreover, as Michael Novak has argued:

> Every argument about deciding on the criteria by which to conduct
> one's inquiries and one's actions is of necessity circular: it begins
> from and returns to one's idea of one's self. To justify a theory about
> what knowing is, one must have a theory about the knower, i.e., the
> self. The circularity may be broken only at one point. In intelligent
> self-consciousness, a man may be able to criticize his justifications
> and his way of knowing, and try alternatives.[40]

Such a rhetoric as we discover in Newman, Berger, Novak, Polanyi,
and Burke presupposes, furthermore, the centrality of what Michael
Polanyi calls the "fiduciary framework," the more or less implicit and
unarticulated set of "encased knowns" that provide relatively stable sets of
assumptions, beliefs, and so on to interpret the world. Given the framework (or horizon, paradigm, view) we inhabit, we use what is at hand
until we have reason to doubt. We pursue, in other words, a systematic
rhetoric of assent:[41]

> We must now recognize belief once more as the source of all
> knowledge. Tacit assent and intellectual passions, the sharing of an
> idiom and of a cultural heritage, affiliation to a like-minded com-
> munity: such are the impulses which shape our vision of the nature
> of things on which we rely for our mastery of things. No intelligence,
> however critical or original, can operate outside such a fiduciary
> framework.[42]

233

On this point, Newman could not be more explicitly anti-Cartesian: "Of the two, I would rather have to maintain that we ought to begin with believing everything that is offered to our acceptance, than that it is our duty to doubt of everything. The former, indeed, seems the true way of learning. In that case we soon discover and discard what is contradictory to itself . . ." (*G.A.*, 243). However, whereas Newman and Burke, for example, agree on the necessity for views, frameworks, perspectives, and on the need for systematic assent, they stress different things. Newman alludes to the notion of a view or framework most often in the context of historical "tradition." Burke, in contrast, looks to the authority of dramatism itself. Said otherwise, Newman (like Polanyi and Gadamer) may operate between theory and fact, but he has his eye on the historical and diachronic. Burke, for all of his extraordinary sensitivity to the concrete, achieves his greatest insights into *universal* (not historical) strategies of motivation implicit in constitutions, terministic clusters, or religion.

A great deal more remains to be learned about Newman's theory and practice of rhetorical assent. Here I wish to end by suggesting two important topics for exploration—Newman's pluralism and his ethics of rhetoric. I have suggested that Newman grounds his philosophy in the individual (who, we recall, is in part at least constituted in and by his community and tradition). Specifically, the individual conscience is for Newman the *locus classicus,* the topic of topics, for the discovery, interpretation, presentation, and assessment of what is real, across the range of the secular and the sacred (or transcendent). "Conscience" may appear a merely quaint term, yet it is closely aligned (to give but one strand of argument) with Polanyi's sense of "conscientiousness," which he (Polanyi) sees as the grounding value for the search for truth.[43] Nor need conscience founder on the Freudian critique of religion, which sees in conscience merely the introjection of external authority. As Hans Kung, Peter Berger, and even Newman himself have noted, it is no argument against the evidence for God that we project onto our understanding of the divine our own significant human influences. On the contrary, our mothers and fathers may rather be seen as *topoi* that open us up to the transcendent.[44] Moreover, teleological conceptions of self, such as those of Adler, Jung, Karen Horney, Carl Rogers, and Erik Erikson, suggest a very different picture of "the self" and how the conscience might be formulated. Newman's conception is by no means identical with these, but there is an important area of overlap and convergence with (for example) the God-archtype for Jung, or the "real self" for Horney or Rogers. Contemporary rhetoricians are silent about how the "self" and its possibility for transcendence suggest new formulations for rhetorical invention.

Second, we have in Newman's rhetorical philosophy an ethic of belief that contrasts noticeably with those of his predecessors, Whately and Campbell, while it looks forward to the ethical metaphors of dialogue, conversation, and friendship in Buber, Gadamer, Rorty, Carl Rogers, and Wayne Booth. Where Whately's rhetoric is subject-oriented, geared to clear language and straightforward presentation of facts, centered on private judgment, and relatively indifferent to audience,[45] Newman's is a far more nuanced ethic of assent and even hope, geared to "economies" of expression in accordance with the nature of the audience, to the centrality of ethos, and to the sometimes straightforward, sometimes circuitous presentation of *interpreted* facts in appropriate language. In the Newmanian world, moreover, the audience has serious ethical responsibilities for reaching out, critically but first sympathetically, to hear and understand. Like Gadamer, Newman seeks a fusion of horizons where private judgment, now more important, now less, merges with the judgments of others in tradition and reflection. In these and many other ways Newman can be heard to speak heart to heart to so rhetorical an age as our own. The theory and practice of belief and invention that he offers is not only his own personal achievement, but a considerable rhetorical resource for us in our own search for innovation as a way of realizing the past, present, and future.

NOTES

PREFACE

1. Nancy S. Struever, "The Conversable World: Eighteenth Century Transformations of the Relation of Rhetoric and Truth," in Nancy S. Struever and Brian Vickers, eds., *Rhetoric and the Pursuit of Truth: Language and Change in the Seventeenth and Eighteenth Century* (Los Angeles: University of California, 1985), pp. 77–119.

2. Struever, "Conversable World," p. 100.

CHAPTER ONE

1. John Henry Newman, "The Tamworth Reading Room" in *D.A.*, pp. 254–305.

2. Jouett Lynn Powell, *Three Uses of Christian Discourse in John Henry Newman: An Example of Non-Reductive Reflection on the Christian Faith*, Diss. Series No. 10 (Missoula, Montana: Scholars' Press, 1975), pp. 23ff.

3. See esp. his note, "Liberalism" in *Apo.*, pp. 254–62; see also *Idea*, pp. 310–27; *ECH*, I, pp. 30–9; *ECH*, II, pp. 336–74; *PPS*, 2, pp. 206–16; *PPS*, 4, pp. 295–306; *PPS*, 6, pp. 327–42; *V.M.*, I, pp. 128–44; *DMC*, pp. 192–213, 214–37.

4. See, for example, "Religious Emotion," in *PPS*, 1, pp. 177–89; also *Apo.*, p. 31, on Newman's dissatisfaction with Keble's more emotional account of faith: "I did not at all dispute this view of the matter, for I made use of it myself; but I was dissatisfied, because it did not go to the root of the difficulty. It was beautiful and religious, but it did not even profess to be logical."

5. Harold Zyskind, "A Case Study in Philosophic Rhetoric: Theodore Roosevelt," *Philosophy and Rhetoric*, 1 (1968), p. 233; cf. "Some Philosophic Strands in Popular Rhetoric," in Howard E. Kiefer and Milton K. Munitz, eds., *Perspectives in Education, Religion, and the Arts* (Albany: State University of New York Press, 1970), pp. 373–95.

6. On Newman's combining theory and practice, and knowing and acting, see, for example, Father James, O.F.M., Cap., "Newman as a Philosopher," in Michael Tierney, ed., *A Tribute to Newman: Essays on Aspects of His Life and Thought* (Dublin: Browne and Nolan, Limited, 1945), pp. 232–33: "There is in his thought and work, as in his life, a wedding of theory and practice which, as he saw the matter, is consummated in action;" Henry Tristram, "Two Leaders—Newman and Carlyle," *Cornhill Magazine* (1928), p. 370: "Newman, it would appear, was essentially a man of action." Wilfrid Ward also speaks of Newman's "intense practicalness" (*Last Lectures*, 1918; repr. Freeport, New York: Books for Libraries Press, Inc., 1967, p. 8), and of the pragmatic drive in his thought (p. 74). See also Geoffrey and Kathleen Tillotson, *Mid-Victorian Studies* (University of London: Athalone Press, 1965), p. 259; and L.A.G. Strong, "Was Newman A Failure?" *The Nineteenth Century* (May 1933), p. 626, who condemns Newman precisely because he *was* a rhetorician.

7. Cf. Edward Sillem, *P.N.*, I, p. 74: "Logic, he [Newman] held, is a servant, not a master; it is the individual who thinks and controls his thinking, not logic."

8. One is forever running across new claims about Newman's alleged irrationalism; most recently see, for example, John Finlay, "The Dark Rooms of the Enlightenment," *The Southern Review*, 23 (April 1987), pp. 311, 327, 331; and Malcolm Woodfield, *R. H. Hutton, Critic and Theologian* (Oxford: Clarendon Press, 1986), p. 64: "[The *Grammar* of Assent] is anti-intellectual, it attacks intellectual convictions and rational conclusions."

9. In "Newman as a Philosopher," *International Philosophical Quarterly*, XVI, 3 (September 1976), pp. 263–64, Johannes Artz distinguishes Newman's philosophical enterprise in these two works: "According to the *Idea* . . . philosophy is understood in the broader sense of the word: as the forming and arranging power for the matters of knowledge and the special sciences, as a habit and attitude forming the whole mind of man and its personal judgment," whereas more properly philosophy refers, according to Artz, to specific contributions to "metaphysics, epistemology, logic, psychology, etc." Given his purposes Artz's distinction is proper and useful, but in the present work I am interested in, among other things, exploring the continuity between these works, and in demonstrating that they can be mutually illuminating.

10. The reader should note the use of "method" and "methods" as denoting respectively Newman's overall philosophical orientation, and his various techniques of inquiry, argument, and interpretation.

11. See especially J. M. Cameron, "Newman and Empiricism," in *The Night Battle: Essays* (Baltimore: Helicon Press, 1962), pp. 219–43; William R. Fey, OFM Cap., *Faith and Doubt: The Unfolding of Newman's Thought on Certainty* (Sheperdstown, West Virginia: Patmos Press, 1976); Thomas Vargish, *Newman: The Contemplation of Mind* (Oxford: Clarendon Press, 1970), pp. 16–24; Edward Sillem, *P.N.*, I, pp. 192–226. We might apply to Newman what R.S. Crane ("Shifting Definitions and Evaluations of the Humanities from the Renaissance to the Present," in *The Idea of the Humanities,* 2 vols. [Chicago: The University of Chicago Press, 1967], I, pp. 55–6) says of the sixteenth-century humanists generally: "What is important for our present purposes . . . is that . . . the context in which the values of the classics and the various arts are discussed is that of a 'philosophy' oriented directly, not to the discovery of truth about *things* but to the guidance of human *actions*—a philosophy which is not necessarily hostile to natural science (as was particularly clear in Vives) but tends to view natural science mainly as a means to ends that are not scientific (Vives, Erasmus). . . ."

12. Nicholas Lash, "Literature and Theory: Did Newman Have a 'Theory' of Development?" in James D. Bastable, ed., *Newman and Gladstone: Centennial Essays* (Dublin: Veritas Publications, 1978), p. 162. In a letter to the author (June 19, 1985), Professor Lash refers to this essay as indicating "something of my own understanding of the way in which Newman's work exemplifies a particular tradition of rhetorical practice."

13. To my knowledge the only essay on Newman as a rhetorical *theorist* is E. P. J. Corbett, "Some Rhetorical Lessons from John Henry Newman," *College Composition and Communication* (December 1980), 402–11. In *Human Communication as Narration: Toward a Philosophy of Reason, Value, and Action* (Columbia: University of South Carolina Press, 1987), p. 53 n. 74, Walter Fisher notes that the *Grammar of Assent* "is a work deserving more attention than it has received from scholars concerned with logic and rhetoric;" and David Tracy, in *The Analogical Imagination: Christian Theology and the Culture of Pluralism* (New York: Crossroad Publishing Co., 1981), p. 86 n. 33, writes: "Indeed an analysis of Newman's project in the *Grammar* in the light of the present distinctions among dialectics, rhetoric-poetics and ethics-politics would perhaps prove a more enlightening setting forth of the complexities at stake than one more round of the W. C. Clifford-William James debate on 'the will to believe'." Otherwise see David F. Rea, "John Henry Newman's Conception of Rhetoric" (Master's Thesis, Fordham University, 1956); Sr. Mariella Gable, O.S.B., "The Rhetoric of John Henry Newman's *Parochial and Plain Sermons,* with Special Reference to his Dependence on Aristotle's *Rhetoric*," Diss. Cornell 1934; and Rev. James H. Loughery, "The Rhetorical Theory of John Henry Newman," Diss.

University of Michigan 1951. On rhetoric in the nineteenth century, see Winifred Bryan Horner, ed., *The Present State of Scholarship in Historical and Contemporary Rhetoric* (Columbia: University of Missouri Press, 1983).

14. Another advantage is that it discloses a coherent set of principles and methods of philosophical inquiry, argument, interpretation and judgment in a more concise and simple way than previously. As indispensable as earlier commentary is, and as valid as it is given its purposes and methods, certain works separate issues that belong together, such as reasoning and arguing, thought and expression (e.g., Jouett Lynn Powell, *Three Uses of Christian Discourse in John Henry Newman,* and Jay Newman, *The Mental Philosophy of John Henry Newman* [Waterloo, Ontario: The Wilfrid Laurier University Press, 1986]). Others, which deal with reasoning at length, fail to notice altogether that Newman is presenting in effect a theory of rhetorical persuasion (e.g., A. J. Boekraad, *The Personal Conquest of Truth According to John Henry Newman* [Louvain: Editions Nauwelaerts, 1955]; Fr. P. Zeno, O.F.M., Cap., *Our Way to Certitude: An Introduction to Newman's Psychological Discovery: The Illative Sense and His Grammar of Assent* [Leiden: E. J. Brill, 1957]; Sylvester P. Juergens, *Newman on the Psychology of the Faith in the Individual* [New York: The Macmillan Company, 1928]; David Pailin, *The Way to Faith: An Examination of Newman's 'Grammar of Assent' as a Response to the Search for Certainty in Faith* [London: Epworth Press, 1969]). And still others, while often brilliantly analyzing problems that often overlap on those treated here, do so within a fairly restricted compass (e.g., John Coulson, *Religion and Imagination* [Oxford: Clarendon Press, 1981]; Nicholas Lash, *Newman on Development: The Search for an Explanation in History* [Shepherdstown, West Virginia: Patmos Press, 1975]; Stephen Prickett, *Romanticism and Religion* [Cambridge: Cambridge University Press, 1976]; Thomas J. Norris, *Newman and His Theological Method* [Leiden: E. J. Brill, 1977]). An extended study of Newman's rhetorical method is called for to synthesize previous insights, to adjust those judgments that have insufficiently accounted for the rhetorical factor, and to advance into new areas.

15. Consider the studies by Lash, Norris and Jay Newman, or that by Harold L. Weatherby, *Cardinal Newman in His Age: His Place in English Theology and Literature* (Nashville: Vanderbilt University Press, 1973), esp. chs. VIII and X.

16. For example, it is typical of much of the commentary to see "real" and "notional" apprehension, or "formal" and "informal" inference, as contrasting and fixed categories (or as poor excuses for such), whereas in fact they are intended only as guidelines to phenomena that are fluid, overlapping, and impossible to identify rigorously prior to particular instances. Or again, Thomas J. Norris construes Newman's "signs" of genuine developments of doctrine as "definitive criteria" (Norris, *Method,* p. 73), whereas they are intended rather as general "criteria of adequacy" that simply cannot be made more exact without sacrificing their applicability to the changing, uncertain nature of such developments.

17. To ask these questions raises the more fundamental issue of how one can or should read Victorian nonfictional prose, nonfiction generally, or even literature. My own position is pluralistic, best articulated by Wayne C. Booth, *Critical Understanding: The Powers and Limits of Pluralism* (Chicago: The University of Chicago Press, 1979), and Tracy, *The Analogical Imagination.* On the problem of reading Victorian nonfiction see, for example, A Dwight Culler, "Method in the Study of Victorian Prose," *The Victorian Newsletter,* 9 (Spring 1956), pp. 1–4; Martin Svaglic, "Method in the Study of Victorian Prose: Another View," *The Victorian Newsletter,* 2 (Spring 1957), pp. 1–4; George Levine, "Non-Fiction as Art," *The Victorian Newsletter* (Fall 1966), pp. 1–4; Patrick J. McCarthy, "Reading Victorian Prose: Arnold's 'Culture and Its Enemies,'" *University of Toronto Quarterly,* XL

238

(Winter 1971), pp. 119–35; Jerome H. Buckley, "Looking Backward: Victorian Poetry and Prose," *The Victorian Newsletter*, 65 (Spring 1984), pp. 1–3. Only after the present work was essentially finished did I discover Jonathan Loesberg, *Fictions of Consciousness: Mill, Newman, and the Reading of Victorian Prose* (New Brunswick: Rutgers University Press, 1986).

18. Jay Newman, *Mental Philosophy*, p. 9; cf. Adrian J. Boekraad and Henry Tristram, *The Argument from Conscience to the Existence of God* (Louvain: Editions Nauwelaerts, 1961), esp. pp. 48–9.

19. *Night Battle*, pp. 236–37. Cf. Juergens, *Psychology of the Faith*, p. 167: "There is a complete absence of scientific formalism, of adequate definitions and divisions, of clearcut distinctions and a strictly logical order;" and Charles Frederick Harrold, *John Henry Newman: An Expository and Critical Study of His Mind, Thought and Art* (New York: Longmans, Green and Co., 1945), pp. 130–31: "It [Newman's method] is not only arbitrary and personal, but also sometimes quite loose, and very frequently 'old-fashioned'." But see also Leslie Stephen, "Newman's Theory of Belief," in *An Agnostic's Apology* (n.p., n.d.), p. 179: "Newman is, like Mill, a lover of the broad daylight; of clear, definite, tangible statements. There is no danger with him of losing ourselves in that mystical haze which the ordinary common-sense of mankind irritates and bewilders."

20. Harrold, *John Henry Newman*, p. 251; see also A. Dwight Culler, *The Imperial Intellect* (New Haven: Yale University Press, 1955), pp. 2, 5, 7, 9, 23, 30–33.

21. Sillem, *P.N.*, I, p. 151.

22. Edward Copleston, *A Reply to the Calumnies of the Edinburgh Reviewers* (London: J. Cooke, J. Palmer and J. MacKinley, 1810), pp. 26–7, 141–42. For further information on Copleston see, for example, Geoffrey Faber, *Oxford Apostles* (London: Faber and Faber, 1974), pp. 98–105. For further information on Newman's Oxford, and on the rhetorical nature of the eighteenth century background, see Charles Edward Mallet, *A History of the University of Oxford*, 3 vols. (New York: Longmans, Green and Co., 1928), and Crane, "Shifting Definitions," pp. 89–122. Also Svaglic, "Method in Victorian Prose," p. 3: "After all, with the possible exception of the *Nicomachean Ethics*, there was hardly a more important book in the old Oxford curriculum than the *Rhetoric* of Aristotle, which exerted a profound influence on some of the greatest Victorian writers;" Gerard Verdeke, "Aristotelian Roots of Newman's Illative Sense," in *Newman and Gladstone: Centennial Essays* (Dublin: Veritas Publications, 1978), p. 177: "Undoubtedly the problem of persuasion on almost any subject was one of the main concerns of Newman's intellectual reflection;" and Loughery, "Rhetorical Theory," pp. 323–24. Consider also the remark of Thomas Arnold, Headmaster of Rugby, in A. P. Stanley, *Life and Correspondence of Thomas Arnold* (London: B. Fellowes, 1844), II, p. 260: "We have been reading some of the *Rhetoric* [of Aristotle] in the Sixth Form this half year [1841], and its immense value struck me again so forcibly that I could not consent to send my son to an University where he would lose it altogether."

23. Thus Macaulay claims ("Lord Bacon," in Thomas Babington Macaulay *Critical, Historical, and Miscellaneous Essays and Poems* [N.Y.: Lovell, Cornell, & Co., n.d.], II, p. 238): "The old systems of rhetoric were never regarded by the most experienced judges as of any use for the purpose of forming an orator." As for logic, W. R. Ward, *Victorian Oxford* (New York: Barnes and Noble, 1965), p. 57, reports that it was "the most unpopular compulsory subject," and calls Copleston and Whately "extinct volcanoes in their championship of logic in religion" (p. 17).

24. Culler, *Imperial Intellect*, p. 12.

25. Richard Whately, *Elements of Rhetoric*. Edited, with an Introduction Douglas Ehninger (Carbondale: Southern Illinois University Press, 1963); hereafter cited as *Rhetoric*.

26. See Gable, "Rhetoric of John Henry Newman," p. 16.

27. Quoted in Henry Tristram, "Two Leaders—Newman and Carlyle," p. 371.

28. Richard Whately, *Elements of Logic* (Delmar, New York: Scholars' Facsimiles and Reprints, 1975); hereafter cited as *Logic*. For an analysis and commentary see John Stuart Mill, "Whately's Elements of Logic" in *Collected Works of John Stuart Mill*, ed. by J. M. Robson (Toronto: University of Toronto Press, 1978), XI, pp. 3–35. On Whately's method of composing see *A.W.*, p. 67, and Faber, *Apostles*, p. 102. For an account of Newman's role in composing the *Logic*, see his letter to William Monsell, October 1852, in *L.D.*, XV, pp. 175–79.

29. For support for this claim see Franz Michel Willam, *Die Erkenntnislehre Kardinal Newmans* (Frankfurt: Gerhard Kaffke, 1969), pp. 66–7, and Sr. Mariella Gable, p. 16; see also Whately's letter to Newman, 11 November, 1834, in *L.D.*, IV, p. 356, alluding to the time when, as friends, "we consulted together about so many practical measures and about almost all the principal points in my publications;" *A.W.*, p. 67: "It was a peculiarity of Whately to compose his books by the medium of other brains;" and Ray E. McKerrow, " 'Method of Composition': Whately's Earliest Rhetoric," *Philosophy and Rhetoric*, 11 (Winter 1978), pp. 43–58.

30. Joseph Butler, *The Analogy of Religion* (London: J.M. Dent and Co., n.d.), p. 2.

31. Faber, *Apostles*, p. 100; see, for example, Richard Whately, *Historic Doubts Relative to Napolean Buonaparte* (Andover: William F. Draper, 1874). On Whately as a practicing rhetorician, see Ray E. McKerrow, "Richard Whately: Religious Controversialist of the Nineteenth Century," *Prose Studies: 1800–1900*, 2 (1979), pp. 160–87, and Lois J. Einhorn, "Richard Whately's Public Persuasion: The Relationship Between His Rhetorical Theory and His Rhetorical Practice," *Rhetorica*, IV (Winter 1986), pp. 47–65.

32. See Willam, *Erkenntnislehre*, p. 67: "Die Bedeuting der 'Elemente der Rhetorik" fur die späteren erkenntnis-philosophischen Untersuchungen Newmans kann kaum uberschätet werden."

33. Mary Rosner, "Reflections on Cicero in Nineteenth Century England and America," *Rhetorica*, IV (Spring 1986), p. 169. Cf. "Personal and Literary Character of Cicero" (1824), *H.S.*, I, pp. 239–300.

34. Cf. Vincent F. Blehl, "Newman, the Fathers and Education," *Thought* (Summer 1970), p. 200.

35. See Charles Frederick Harrold, "Newman and the Alexandrian Platonists," *Modern Philology*, XXXVII (February 1940), pp. 279–90. See also H. I. Marrou, *Saint Augustin et la fin de la culture antique* (Paris: E. D. Bocard, 1938); Ernest L. Fortin, "Augustine and the Problem of Christian Rhetoric," *Augustinian Studies*, 5 (1974), pp. 85–100; Raymond DiLorenzo, " '*NON PIE QUAERUNT*: Rhetoric, Dialectic, and the Discovery of the True in Augustine's *Confessions*," *Augustinian Studies*, 14 (1983), pp. 117–27; Mary C. Preus, *Eloquence and Ignorance in Augustine's On the Nature and Origin of the Soul* (Atlanta, Ga.: Scholars' Press, 1985), esp. ch. 1. What W. R. Johnson ("Isocrates Flowering: The Rhetoric of Augustine," *Philosophy and Rhetoric*, 9 [1976], p. 228) has to say about Augustine may usefully be applied to Newman: "The more one reads the *Confessions* and the *Civitas* the harder it becomes to distinguish the philosophy from the theology, the theology from the Isocratean rhetoric, the rhetoric from the Ciceronian humanism. . . . contemplation and action so completely interanimate one another, end in such total interdependence, that in his books as in his life they are all but identical."

36. See, for example, *Ari.*, pp. 25–38, 110, passim.

37. As a younger man (and tractarian), Newman was less accommodating, as evidenced in his letter to Samuel Rickards of May 30, 1837 in *L.D.*, VI, p. 74: "The age is so very sluggish that it will not hear unless you bawl—you must first tread on its toes, and then apologize"; and to Richard Hurrell Froude, September 18, 1833, in *L.D.*, IV, p. 52: "Men are made of glass—the sooner we break them and get it over, the better."

38. On these particular concepts see Robin C. Selby, *The Principle of Reserve in the Writings of John Henry Cardinal Newman* (Oxford: Oxford University Press, 1975), esp ch. 2; and *P.N.*, II, pp. 111–19.

39. Thomas De Quincey, "Rhetoric," in David Masson, ed., *The Collected Writings of Thomas De Quincey* (Edinburgh, 1889–1890; Rpr. New York: AMS Press, 1968), X, p. 81. See also Rene Wellek, "De Quincy's Status in the History of Ideas," *Philological Quarterly,* XXIII (July 1944), pp. 248–72, and Paul M. Talley, "De Quincey on Persuasion, Invention, and Style," *Central States Speech Journal,* XVI (November 1965), pp. 243–54. For Newman's own understanding or use of the term rhetoric as style or sophistry, see, for example, *V.M.*, I, pp. xxvii, xxxii; *VM*, II, p. 101; *D.A.*, p. 263; *Ari*, pp. 25–38; *ECH*, II, p. 42; *H.S.*, III, "The Sophists," pp. 47–59; *Prepos.*, pp. 45, 225, 231; *Dev.*, pp. 7, 106; *L.D.*, XVI, p. 9; *On Con*, p. 60; *Letter*, pp. 77–8.

40. For further analysis of Whately's thought see Ray E. McKerrow, "Richard Whately on the Nature of Human Knowledge in Relation to Ideas of His Contemporaries," *Journal of the History of Ideas,* XLII (1981), pp. 439–55, and "Richard Whately's Theory of Rhetoric," in Ray E. McKerrow, ed., *Explorations in Rhetoric: Studies in Honor of Douglas Ehninger,* (Glenview, IL: Scott, Foresman and Co., 1981), pp. 137–56.

41. See Wilbur Samuel Howell, *Eighteenth Century British Logic and Rhetoric* (Princeton: Princeton University Press, 1970), esp. chs. 5 and 6; and Walter Jackson Bate, *From Classic to Romantic* (New York: Harper & Row, 1946).

42. Cf. *Idea,* p. 335: "It [rhetoric] is a relative art, and in that respect differs from Logic, which simply teaches the right use of reason, whereas rhetoric is the art of persuasion, which implies a person who is to be persuaded." Cf. De Quincey, *Collected Writings,* X, p. 92: "Rhetoric is the art of aggrandizing and bringing out into strong relief, by means of various and striking thoughts, some aspect of truth which of itself is supported by no spontaneous feelings, and therefore rests upon artificial aids."

43. Cf. *T.P.,* p. 90: "Contrast between the corpus and the individual motivum" of belief. The one is "conscious, objective etc. the other latent, implicit, etc., the one logical, the other rhetorical. . . ."

44. Zyskind, "Case Study," p. 230.

45. Thomas Carlyle, "Characteristics," in *Collected Works,* 30 vols. (London: Chapman and Hall, 1870), VIII, p. 333; see also "Inaugural Address at Edinburgh," XI, pp. 320ff., and *Heroes and Hero-Worship,* XII, p. 5.

46. The literature on Newman as rhetorician is rather large. The reader would do best to begin with the bibliographies by Martin J. Svaglic, "John Henry Newman: Man and Humanist," in *Victorian Prose: A Guide to Research* (New York: The Modern Language Association of America, 1973), pp. 115–65, and John R. Griffen, *Newman: A Bibliography of Secondary Sources* (Front Royal, VA: Christendom College Press, 1980), pp. 63–9. The most important book or chapter-length studies include the following: Lewis E. Gates, "Newman as a Prose Writer," in *Three Studies in Literature* (New York: The Macmillan Company, 1899), pp. 64–123; Walter Houghton, *The Art of Newman's Apologia* (Hamden, CT: Archon Books, 1970); John Holloway, *The Victorian Sage: Studies in Argument* (New

York: W. W. Norton and Co., Inc., 1953), pp. 158–201; George Levine, "Newman and the Threat of Experience," in *The Boundaries of Fiction* (Princeton: Princeton University Press, 1968), pp. 164–258; A. Dwight Culler, *Imperial Intellect*, ch. 6; William R. Siebenschuh, "What is Art and What is Evidence: Newman's *Apologia Pro Vita Sua*," in *Fictional Techniques and Factual Works* (Athens, GA: University of Georgia Press, 1983), pp. 10–27; Wilfrid Ward, "The Sources of Newman's Style," in *Last Lectures*, pp. 49–71; Fernande Tardivel, *La Personnalité Literraire de Newman* (Paris: Gabriel Beauchesne et Ses Fils 1937); and articles on various aspects of the *Apologia* included in the edition by David J. DeLaura (New York: W. W. Norton and Co., 1968), pp. 373–508, and in Vincent Blehl and Francis X. Connolly, eds., *Newman's Apologia: A Classic Re-Considered* (New York: Harcourt, Brace and World, Inc., 1964). See also the works listed in note 13 above.

47. Lewis E. Gates, "Newman as a Prose Writer," pp. 79–81. See also Robert A. Colby, "The Structure of Newman's *Apologia Pro Vita Sua* in Relation to His Theory of Assent," *The Dublin Review*, 460 (Summer 1953), pp. 140–56.

48. David J. DeLaura, "Newman's Apologia as Prophecy," in DeLaura, ed., *Apologia*, p. 494.

49. *Victorian Sage*, pp. 8–9; cf. Ward, "Newman's Psychological Insight," in *Last Lectures*, p. 144: "But he [Newman] was at times so preoccupied with the psychology of actual reasoning as to seem almost to lose sight of the distinction between accurate spontaneous reasoning and inaccurate." Interestingly, Holloway is in a more tolerant mood when it comes to appraising rhetorical method as used by Carlyle; see pp. 51–2: "[E]motions are not always and necessarily evoked by trickery, and a criterion can be found to distinguish genuine from sophistical evocation. For though language can evoke emotions, so can things themselves; and language, even when it fails to state or describe, has a legitimate emotive power if it operates not independently, in a beautiful though empty mist, but by re-directing our attention to objects, concentrating it upon them, and thereby making us notice aspects of them that previously we have overlooked." Cf. DeLaura, "Newman's Apologia as Prophecy," in *Apologia*, p. 494.

50. J.-H. Walgrave, *Newman the Theologian*. Translated by A. V. Littledale (New York: Sheed and Ward, 1960), p. 367; see also pp. 234–38.

51. *Boundaries*, pp. 5–6, 179–80, 183, 191, 193, 244.

52. *Art of Newman's Apologia*, pp. 40, 53, 86, 193.

53. Culler, "Method in Victorian Prose;" Weatherby, *Newman in His Age*, esp. chs. VIII and X; and Harold L. Weatherby, "Style and Its Consequence: Newman's Language of Religion," in Bastable, ed., *Newman and Gladstone: Centennial Essays*, p. 296: "The chief virtue of Houghton's analysis [in *The Art of Newman's Apologia*] is the skill with which he shows how Newman's style is adapted to convey those states of mind at the expense of rational . . . propositions."

54. "Newman and the Romantic Sensibility," in Hugh Sykes Davies and George Watson, eds., *The English Mind: Studies in the English Moralists Presented to Basil Willey* (Cambridge: At the Cambridge Press, 1964), pp. 193–218. Cf. Harrold on Newman as a romantic, *John Henry Newman* p. 249: "Though his mind was Aristotelian, his heart was Romantic–Platonic." It is very doubtful that this mind–heart dichotomy is helpful in Newman's case.

55. *Mental Philosophy* p. 7. Cf. Vargish, *Contemplation of Mind*, p. 26: "As Henry Tristram remarks, 'It is always well to observe precisely [Newman's] nuances of expression.' A *logical* microscope, however, would not be our most suitable instrument."

56. *Last Lectures*, pp. 122–23.

57. *John Henry Newman,* p. 372. Harrold's words here are very much those of Ward in "Newman and His Critics," in *Last Lectures,* p. 12.

58. C. Sarolea, quoted in Harrold, *John Henry Newman,* p. 369.

59. *Newman the Theologian,* pp. 234ff.

60. See, for example, Svaglic, "Newman: Man and Humanist," pp. 153–54.

61. See *Topics,* in Aristotle, *The Organon, or Logical Treatises of Aristotle.* 2 vols. Edited by Octavius Freire Owen (London: Henry G. Bohn, 1853), II, pp. 359–69; and *Posterior Analytics,* B19, in Owen, ed., *Organon,* p. 9. For excellent discussions of the intricacies involved, see for example J. D. G. Evans, *Aristotle's Concept of Dialectic* (Cambridge: Cambridge University Press, 1977); and G. E. L. Owen, ed., *Aristotle on Dialectic* (Oxford: Clarendon Press, 1968).

62. Aristotle, *Rhetoric.* Translated by John Henry Freese (Cambridge: Harvard University Press, 1982). Cf. *Nicomachean Ethics.* Translated, with introduction and notes, by Martin Ostwald (Indianapolis: Bobbs-Merill, 1962), 1140a10–20. See also Larry Arnhart's commentary on the *Rhetoric, Aristotle on Political Reasoning* (DeKalb, IL: University of Northern Illinois Press, 1981), esp. pp. 15–16; and William M. A. Grimaldi, S. J., *Studies in the Philosophy of Aristotle's Rhetoric* (Wiesbaden: Franz Steiner Verlag GMBH, 1972), ch. 1.

63. See, for example, *De Oratore,* 2. 41. 178 (note that it is Antonius who is speaking here, whereas it is Crassus who is generally considered to be Cicero's most reliable spokesman); *Brutus,* 89, 279; *Orator,* 128. Gadamer is aware of this reduction ("On the Scope and Function of Hermeneutical Reflection," in *Philosophical Hermeneutics.* Translated and edited by David E. Linge [Berkeley: University of California Press, 1976, p. 23], but see pp. 24ff.).

64. At least, this is how Aristotle is regularly construed. But the *Rhetoric* admits of another interpretation. Aristotle notes that the special *topoi (eide)* are drawn from sciences like politics and ethics, and he suggests that these sciences themselves use persuasion. What prevents us from arguing that Aristotle recognizes the role of persuasive argument by enthymemes in principled inquiries—recognizes, that is, the "rhetoric of" politics or ethics—but that he wishes to focus on persuasion *outside* of special disciplines? For support for this view, see Quintilian, *Institutes of Oratory,* translated by H. E. Butler. 4 vols. (Cambridge: Harvard University Press, 1980), 2. 15. 16: "Aristotle seems to have implied that the sphere of the orator was all-inclusive when he defined rhetoric as the *power to detect every element in any given subject which might conduce to persuasion . . .;*" also Grimaldi, *Studies,* pp. 92–3, and Valesio, *Novantiqua,* pp. 28, 32, passim.

65. *De Inventione,* 1. 6. 8 reflects the early Cicero's separation of the "general" questions of the philosopher from "the business of the orator," but the mature Cicero in *De Oratore,* 3. 142–43 reverses this position (see also *De Oratore,* 1. 5 and *Orator,* 45). According to Antonius, *all* questions are "general" (*De Oratore,* 2. 134). See Marrou, *Education in Antiquity,* p. 211. On Cicero's thought and legacy, see, for example, M. L. Clark, *Rhetoric at Rome* (London: Cohen and West, 1953), ch. V; Richard McKeon, *Introduction to the Philosophy of Cicero* (Chicago: The University of Chicago Press, 1950); Jerrold E. Siegal, *Rhetoric and Philosophy in Renaissance Humanism* (Princeton: Princeton University Press, 1968), ch. 1; Victoria Kahn, *Rhetoric, Prudence and Skepticism in the Renaissance* (Ithaca: Cornell University Press, 1985), ch. 2. On Isocrates' views, see for example, *Antidosis,* in *Isocrates,* 3 vols. (Cambridge: Harvard University Press, 1968), II, pp. 181–365.

66. Quintilian, *Institutes,* 1. Preface, 9ff. 5. Introduction.

67. See *Institutes,* 2. 21, 4; 2. 21, 23; and Cicero, *De Oratore,* 1. 5. 17; 1. 6. 20.

68. For classical rhetoricians the kinds of discourse were three: deliberative, concerning persuasion to or dissuasion from future thought, attitude or action; epideictic, involving praise or blame of some agent or act; and forensic, concerning accusation or defense in a court of law.

69. See Aristotle, *Rhetoric,* II, 2–17; cf. Robert C. Solomon, *The Passions: The Myth and Nature of Human Emotion* (Notre Dame: University of Notre Dame Press, 1983); William W. Fortenbaugh, *Aristotle on Emotion* (New York: Barnes and Noble, 1975); Arnhart, *Political Reasoning,* pp. 9–10, 116–18, passim; Grimaldi, *Studies,* pp. 24–7. The enthymeme is not the preferable vehicle to express or generate emotion (*Rhetoric,* 1418a 8), but all emotion is a result in part of a process of (usually unconscious) reasoning.

70. For helpful expositions of the topic see, for example, Richard McKeon, "Creativity and the Commonplace," *Philosophy and Rhetoric,* 6 (1973), pp. 199–210, and "Arts of Invention and Arts of Memory: Creation and Criticism," *Critical Inquiry,* I (June 1975), pp. 723–39; Ernesto Grassi, *Rhetoric as Philosophy* (University Park: The Pennsylvania State University Press, 1980); Sister Joan Marie Lechner, O.S.U., *Renaissance Concepts of the Commonplaces* (New York: Pageant Press, 1962); Michael C. Leff, "The Topics of Argumentative Invention in Latin Rhetorical Theory from Cicero to Boethius," *Rhetorica,* I (Spring 1983), pp. 23–44; Carolyn R. Miller, "Aristotle's 'Special Topics' in Rhetorical Practice and Pedagogy," *Rhetoric Society Quarterly,* XVII (Winter 1987), pp. 61–70; Scott Consigny, "Rhetoric and Its Situations," *Philosophy and Rhetoric,* 7 (1974), pp. 175–86; W. A. De Pater, S. C. J., "La fonction du lieu et de l'instrument dans les *Topiques,*" in G. E. L. Owen, ed., *Dialectic,* pp. 164–88; Grimaldi, *Studies,* pp. 115–35; Arnhart, *Political Reasoning,* passim; Walter J. Ong, *Ramus, Method and the Decay of Dialogue* (New York: Octagon Books, 1979); Nancy S. Struever, "Topics in History," *History and Theory,* 19 (1980), pp. 66–79; Otto Bird, "The Tradition of the Logical Topics: Aristotle to Ockham," *Journal of the History of Ideas,* XXIII (1962), pp. 307–23, and "The Re-Discovery of the Topics," *Mind,* 70 (October 1961), pp. 534–39; Thomas M. Conley, "'Logical Hylomorphism' and Aristotle's *Koinoi Topoi,*" *Central States Speech Journal* 29 (Summer 1978), pp. 92–7; Donovan J. Ochs, "Aristotle's Concept of Formal Topics," *Speech Monographs,* 46 (Winter, 1969), pp. 419–25, and "Cicero's *Topica:* A Process View of Invention," in McKerrow, ed., *Exploration in Rhetoric,* pp. 107–18.

71. See De Pater, "La Fonction de Lieu," p. 173; Kenneth Burke, *A Rhetoric of Motives* (Berkeley: University of California Press, 1969), p. 56; and Leff, "Topics of Argumentative Invention."

72. See Cicero, *De Oratore,* 2. 166; *Topica,* 2. 8; 4. 23; Quintilian, *Institutes,* 5. 10. 20. Francis Bacon, *De Augmentis,* in *The Works of Francis Bacon,* ed. James Spedding, Robert Leslie Ellis, and Douglas Denon Heath, 7 vols. (London: Longman and Co. et. al., 1858), IV, pp. 424, 423.

73. *De Augmentis,* in *Works,* IV, p. 424; cf. Aristotle, *Rhetoric* 139b18.

74. Cf. Consigny, "Rhetoric and Its Situations," pp. 182–83: "I construe the topic as a formal opposition of two (or more) terms which can be used to structure the heteronomous matter of a particular situation." My account of the topic tends perhaps to make the tradition of the topics seem uniform and unproblematic, whereas in fact it is ambiguous and paradoxical. Among many distinctions that could be made, two are pertinent here. The first is the distinction between topics as devices of invention and innovation, and as devices of memory, as "set pieces" for a given purpose or occasion. In the present work I am concerned

244

exclusively with topics of the first sort. But here a further distinction is necessary, between inventional topics as inferential forms, and inventional topics as material sources (or re-sources) to locate the *content* of one's subject or problem. Grimaldi, for example ("The Aristotelian Topics," *Traditio,* 14 (1958), pp. 1–16), distinguishes Aristotle's topics of invention as being of two kinds: the "general" topics, which are "forms of inference," and the "particular" topics, which are "sources for material." Leff, on the other hand ("Topics of Argumentative Invention," p. 26), considers *both* kinds of Aristotelian topics as inferential, and the Ciceronian topics of "act" and "person" (and their sub–topics) in the *De Inventione* as material. My own practice in this work is to consider the topic as a (Baconian) "re-source" for discovering *what* can be said about a (more or less) indeterminate subject; cf. Paolo A. Cherchi, "Tradition and *Topoi* in Midieval Literature," *Critical Inquiry,* 3 (Winter 1976), pp. 281–94.

75. Hans-Georg Gadamer, *Truth and Method* (New York: Crossroad Publishing Company, 1986), p. 269: "The horizon is the range of vision that includes everything that can be seen from a particular vantage point."

76. See *Rhetoric,* 1359b 4–7. Cf. John Henry Newman, "University Preaching," in *Idea,* p. 338: "To say nothing else, common-places are but blunt weapons; whereas it is particular topics that penetrate and reach their mark."

77. See Ochs, "Aristotle's Concept of Formal Topics." For the typology of the topics that I use here, see James H. McBurney, "The Place of the Enthymeme in Rhetorical Theory," *Speech Monographs,* 3 (1936), pp. 49–74; and George Kennedy, *The Art of Persuasion in Greece* (Princeton: Princeton University Press, 1963), pp. 100–1.

78. *Novum Organum* in *Works,* IV; cf. McKeon, "Creativity and the Commonplace," p. 203.

79. *De Augmentis,* in *Works,* IV, p. 421.

80. Cf. McKeon, "Creativity," p. 201.

81. In keeping with her stress on rhetoric as an art oriented to *civil* questions, Nancy S. Struever ("Topics in History") stresses the commonality and accessibility of topics as their distinguishing feature. My *epistemological* concern (in keeping with Newman's) requires that the stress be placed on their indeterminacy.

82. See W. B. Gallie, "Essentially Contested Concepts," *Proceedings of the Aristotelian Society,* 56 (1957), reprinted in Max Black, ed., *The Importance of Language* (Ithaca: Cornell University Press, 1962), pp. 120–46.; also Eugene Garver, "Rhetoric and Essentially Contested Arguments," *Philosophy and Rhetoric,* 11 (1978), pp. 156–72.

83. John Dewey, *The Public and Its Problems* (Athens, Ohio: Swallow Press, 1954), pp. 20, 34.

84. *Public and Its Problems,* p. 33.

85. *Public and Its Problems,* p. 33.

86. The term topic has not been unfairly imposed on Newman here; along with ἦθος (ethos), τόπος (topos, topoi) was a rhetorical term that Newman (and fellow Oxonians like Hurrell Froude) used with ease and some frequency; see, for example, *L.D.,* II, p. 259; IV, p. 269; V, p. 292; XII, p. 338; and XII, pp. 354–55; and *T.P.,* p. 94, where he calls the "notes" of the church "heads of arguments."

87. So Newman writes to Henry Wilberforce on March 3, 1855, in *L.D.,* XVII, p. 400: "How inconsistent one is or rather one sided! Here am I desirous of peace and thinking war will upset the constitution—which I *do* think—but then, when the very chance of peace comes, rises the chance of an English know-nothing-ism."

88. *Novantiqua*, p. 38.

89. Charles Stephen Dessain, Cardinal Newman on the Theory and Practice of Knowledge. The Purpose of the Grammar of Assent," *Downside Review*, 75 (1957), p. 3.

90. Cf. *G.A.,* p. 218: "What I have been saying of Ratiocination, may be said of Taste, and is confirmed by the obvious analogy between the two. Taste, skill, invention in the fine arts—and so, again, discretion or judgment in conduct—are exerted spontaneously, when once acquired, and could not give a clear account of themselves, or of their mode of proceeding. They do not go by rule, though to a certain point their exercise may be analyzed, and may take the shape of an art or method." For an excellent discussion of the relations between rhetoric and taste at which Newman only hints here, see Streuver, "The Conversable World: Eighteenth Century Transformations of the Relation of Rhetoric and Truth," in *Rhetoric and the Pursuit of Truth*, pp. 77–119.

91. Corbett, "Some Rhetorical Lessons," p. 402.

92. See Philip Snyder, "Newman's Way with the Reader in a *Grammar of Assent*," *The Victorian Newsletter*, 56 (Fall 1979) pp. 1–6; cf. Jay Newman, *Mental Philosophy, ch. 1, sec. 7, "The Grammar* as an attempt at self–vindication," pp. 18–21.

93. *Kenneth Burke, A Rhetoric of Motives* (Berkeley: University of California Press, 1962), p. 172.

94. Kenneth Burke, *A Rhetoric of Motives*, p. 43.

95. Cf. Walter Davis, *The Act of Interpretation* (Chicago: The University of Chicago Press, 1978), p. 24: "Communication, for Burke, is a far more complex affair than traditional rhetorical theory . . . is able to handle. For rather than simply presenting a body of abstract commonplaces or quasi–propositional themes that are enhanced but in no way essentially altered by the writer's verbal and mimetic power, communication is an inherently dramatic activity involving the basic social needs and functions of the psyche and transpiring primarily through our engagement in symbolic actions."

96. Cf. Frank Lentricchia, *Criticism and Social Change* (Chicago: University of Chicago Press, 1983), esp. chapter 5.

97. I refer in particular to those essays collected in *Rhetoric*. Edited with an introduction by Mark Backman (Woodbridge, CT.: OX Bow Press, 1987). For a summary of McKeon's position, see Backman's introduction, and Gerard A. Hauser and Donald P. Cushman, "McKeon's Philosophy of Communication: The Architectonic and Interdisciplinary Arts," *Philosophy and Rhetoric*, 6 (Fall 1973), pp. 211–34.

It is obvious that I am resisting the impossible task of defining "rhetoric" once and for all. My own conception in this work is closest to those architectonic conceptions of Cicero and McKeon, for whom rhetoric is a total orientation towards language and the arts of inquiry, argument, interpretation, and judgment. These conceptions include—they do not reject—the idea of rhetoric as an art of persuasion in the civic realm (Aristotle, Bacon, Hume); as the study of argumentative techniques in probable matters (Perelman); as the persuasive dimension of all symbolic action (Burke). I would liken my conception to that of Wayne Booth in *Modern Dogma and the Rhetoric of Assent* (Chicago: The University of Chicago Press, 1974)—"the art of discovering warrantable beliefs and improving those beliefs in shared discourse" (p. xiii)—except that the Toulminian ring of "warrants" *suggests,* at least (what is clearly not Booth's intention), that rhetoric focuses on explicit "arguments" set forth in some recognizable syllogistic form. In fact Booth in this work anticipates Walter Fisher's notion of the "narrative paradigm" or narrative mode of discourse *(Human Communication as Narration),* which one can also see anticipated by Cicero and Quintilian, as indeed by Newman.

246

98. "Introduction" in *Rhetoric,* p. xx.

99. "Introduction" in *Rhetoric,* p. ix. See Rorty, *Philosophy and the Mirror of Nature* (Princeton: Princeton University Press, 1978), esp. pp. 357–94.

100. "Modern Sophistic and the Unity of Rhetoric," in John S. Nelson et. al., eds., *The Rhetoric of the Human Sciences* (Madison: The University of Wisconsin Press, 1987), pp. 19–37.

101. *Plurality and Ambiguity: Hermeneutics, Religion, Hope* (San Francisco: Harper and Row, 1987), p. 122 n. 8.

CHAPTER TWO

1. See, for example, *Apo.,* p. 1; *L.D.,* XII, p. 158; XV, pp. 165, 398; XVI, p. 165; XVII, p. 316.

2. See *Apo.,* pp. 340–464.

3. Samuel Wilberforce, "Review of Newman's *Apologia Pro Vita Sua,*" *Quarterly Review,* 116 (October 1864), p. 546; cf. Meriol Trevor, *The Pillar of the Cloud* (New York: Doubleday and Co., 1962), p. 82; and DeLaura, ed., *Apologia,* p. 493.

4. Quoted in R. W. Church, *The Oxford Movement: Twelve Years, 1833–1845* Edited with an Introduction by Geoffrey Best (Chicago: University of Chicago Press, 1970), p. 55.

5. Kenneth Burke, *Attitudes Toward History* (Los Altos, California: Hermes Publications, 1959), p. 306.

6. See Thomas Babington Macaulay, *Critical, Historical,* and *Miscellaneous Essays and Poems,* 3 vols. (New York: Lovell, Coryell, and Co., n.d.), II, pp. 142–254, and I, pp. 193–230.

7. Jane Millgate, *Macaulay* (London: Routledge and Kegan Paul, 1973), pp. 44, 192–93.

8. On Arnold as rhetorician, see Everett Lee Hunt, "Matthew Arnold: The Critic as Rhetorician," *Quarterly Journal of Speech,* XX (November 1934), pp. 483–507; and James A. Berlin, "Matthew Arnold's Rhetoric: The Method of an Elegant Jeremiah," *Rhetoric Society Quarterly,* XIII (Winter 1983), pp. 29–40. See also James C. Livingston, *Matthew Arnold and Christianity: His Religious Prose Writings* (Columbia; University of South Carolina Press, 1986), pp. 64–5, 71, passim.

9. Matthew Arnold, *The Complete Prose Works of Matthew Arnold,* 11 vols. Edited by R. H. Super (Ann Arbor: University of Michigan Press, 1961–77), V, p. 202.

10. See Bernard Semmel, "T. B. Macaulay: The Active and Contemplative Lives," in Richard A. Levine, ed., *The Victorian Experience: The Prose Writers* (Athens, Ohio: Ohio University Press, 1982), p. 24.

11. Walter J. Hipple, Jr., "Matthew Arnold, Dialectician," *University of Toronto Quarterly,* XXXII (October 1962), pp. 1–26. Recall T. S. Eliot's description of Arnold as "an undergraduate in philosophy," so specialized had "philosophy" grown during the course of the nineteenth century. See also Livingston, *Matthew Arnold and Christianity,* p. 71. It might be noted that Hipple's and Berlin's attempts to cast Arnold in the image of Plato simply fail to recognize how rhetorical topics function in "dialectical" structures. As Hipple himself notes (p. 6), "But in comparing Arnold with Plato, a crucial difference must not be overlooked. For Arnold's thought, if judged by the system of Plato himself, is an incomplete dialectic. There is in Arnold nothing to correspond with the highest of the levels of the divided line of *The Republic;* there is no "reason" in Plato's sense, and no eternal forms for reason to intuit," Rather than force Arnold on this Procrustean bed of dialectic, we need to take him as the rhetorician Hunt correctly said he was.

Notes to Chapter 2

12. Quoted in Hipple, "Matthew Arnold, Dialectician," p. 1.

13. Walter Houghton, "The Rhetoric of T. H. Huxley," *University of Toronto Quarterly*, XVIII (1949), p. 166: "What has happened here is fairly common in Victorian writing. . . . The difficulty stems from an inability to stand far enough off, with enough detachment to contemplate different and perhaps mutually exclusive elements in a given situation at one and the same time. Arnold observed 'our want of flexibility . . . our inaptitude for seeing more than one side of a thing . . . .' " See also Houghton, *The Victorian Frame of Mind* (New Haven: Yale University Press, 1957), p. 161: "By and large, the Victorian mind was rigid. It tended to follow one line of thought, to look at objects from a single point of view, to shut out wide interests."

14. Cf. Anthony Ward, *Walter Pater: The Idea in Nature* (Worcester: MacGibbon and Kee, 1966), p. 175.

15. Basil Willey, *Nineteenth Century Studies* (Cambridge: Cambridge University Press, 1980), p. 205.

16. Willey, *Studies*, pp. 89, 85–6.

17. Gillian R. Evans, " 'An Organon More Delicate, Versatile and Elastic': John Henry Newman and Whately's *Logic*," *The Downside Review*, 99 (July 1979), p. 176.

18. We will also use two lesser collections, the *Philosophical Notebook* (1859–1887) and the *Theological Papers of J. H. Newman on Faith and Certainty* (1853–1885).

19. Newman usually spoke of faith from a strictly human point of view; as a typical example see his letter to Mrs. William Froude, 27 June 1848, in *L.D.*, XII, p. 228: "I wish you would consider whether you have a right notion how to gain faith. It is, we know, the Gift of God, but I am speaking of it as a human process and attained by human means. Faith then is not a conclusion from premises i.e., a *strictly* logical inference, but the result of an act of the *will*, following upon a *conviction* that to believe is a *duty*."

20. Cf. D. M. MacKinnon, "Introduction," in *OUS*, p. 17.

21. See, for example, *PPS*, 2, XV, "Self-Contemplation," p. 166; XIV, "Saving Knowledge," pp. 153ff.; XXII, "The Gospel, A Savings Trust Committed to Us," p. 258: "By the Faith is evidently meant, as St. Paul's words show, some definite doctrine; not a mere temper of mind or principle of action. . . ." Cf. *Apo.*, p. 54; "[R]eligion, as a mere sentiment, is to me a dream and a mockery." Also *Apo.*, p. 98; *A.W.*, p. 142; *P.N.*, II, p. 167.

22. J. D. Holmes, "Introduction," in *OUS*, p, 25. Cf. Lee H. Yearley, *The Ideas of Newman*, (University Park: Pennsylvania State University Press, 1978), p. 19.

23. Holmes, "Introduction," p. 25.

24. A third alternative, that faith was knowledge gained by "intuition, intellectual forms, and the like" (*G.A.*, 222), Newman rejected out of hand as an unreal account of how men in fact come to know divine truths. Newman's alleged "Platonism" notwithstanding, such a position helps us to measure the distance between a Newman and a Carlyle.

25. See William Paley, *A View of the Evidences of Christianity*. In Three Parts, with Annotations by Richard Whately (New York: James Miller, 1865). See also Richard Whately, *Introductory Lessons on Christian Evidences* (Philadelphia: H. Hooker, 1856).

26. In the *Parochial and Plain Sermons* Newman often refers to the "speculative age," the "educated age," an "age of established religion," referring to this pronounced appeal to "secular" reason.

27. See, for example, *G.A.*, p. 273–74: "I think Paley's argument clear, clever and powerful . . . but in this matter some exertion on the part of the persons whom I am to convert is a condition of a true conversion. . . . if he has longed for a revelation to enlighten

him and to cleanse his heart, why may he not use, in his inquiries after it, that just and reasonable anticipation of its probability, which such longing has opened the way to his entertaining?" Also *E.S.*, II, p. 204.

28. Cf. *OUS*, pp. xv-xvi.

29. Unlike Paley's position, Whately's is more nuanced than that portrayed in the Oxford sermons (or later by Sillem, *P.N.*, I, pp. 28–9). In fact Whately recognized the role that antecedent moral dispositions play in coming to faith (See *The Use and Abuse of Party–Feeling* [London: John W. Parker and Son, 1859], pp. 351–52, hereafter referred to as the *Bampton Lectures*.) Nevertheless there is no question that, in his writings generally, Whately stresses the centrality of evidence and logical reasoning.

30. Cf. *OUS*, p. 63: "It is absurd to argue men, as to torture them, into believing." In fact such arguments distract from genuine religious impulses: see *G.A.*, p. 274: "Men are too well inclined to sit at home, instead of stirring themselves to inquire whether a revelation has been given; they expect its evidences to come to them without their trouble; they act, not as suppliants, but as judges. Modes of argument such as Paley's, encourage this state of mind." Indeed, evidences "draw men away from the true view of Christianity," leading them "to think that Faith is mainly the result of argument" (*OUS*, p. 198); and they interfere with devotional contemplation of divine facts (*OUS*, p. 22).

31. Cf. *OUS*, p. 179: "If Faith be such a principle, how is it novel and strange?"

32. Cf. *Dev.*, p. 351; *P.N.*, II, pp. 30, 43–60, 65–7. On the corruptibility of conscience see, for example, *G.A.*, p. 80; *Letter*, pp. 127–38; *PPS*, 3, IX.

33. See *OUS*, p. 187: "Faith, then . . . does not demand evidence so strong as is necessary for what is commonly called a rational conviction, or belief on the ground of reason; and why? For this reason, because it is mainly swayed by antecedent considerations." A contemporary Catholic theologian expresses the same idea this way:

When the reality of man is understood correctly, there exists an inescapable circle between his horizons of understanding and what is said, heard and understood. Ultimately the two mutually presuppose each other. Consequently, intertwined in this specific way, Christianity assumes that these presuppositions which it makes are inescapably and necessarily present in the ultimate depths of human existence, even when this existence is interpreted differently in its reflexive self-interpretation, and that at the same time the Christian message itself creates these presuppositions by its call.

Karl Rahner, *Foundations of Christian Faith: An Introduction to the Idea of Christianity* (New York: Crossroad Publishing Company, 1987), p. 24.

34. Cf. *OUS*, p. 227: "[F]ew men are in a condition to weigh things in an accurate balance, and to decide, after calm and complete investigation."

35. This is a central tenet of Newman's philosophy and can be found throughout his works. See, for example, his letter to Blanco White, 1 March, 1828, in *L.D.*, II, p. 60: "And I agree with you too in feeling the incommensurability (so to speak) of the human mind—we cannot gauge and measure by any common rule the varieties of thought and opinion. We all look at things with our own eyes—and invest the whole face of nature with colors of our own.—Each mind pursues its own course and is actuated in that course by tenthousand [sic] indescribable incommunicable feelings and imaginings." Also *PPS*, 2, XIV, p. 153; *OUS*, p. 267; *P.N.*, II, p. 21; *G.A.*, p. 240: "The aspect under which we view things is often intensely personal. . . . Each of us looks at the world in his own way. . . .;" *PPS*, 1, XXIV, p. 317: "Religion, it has been well observed, is something *relative to use*. . . ."

36. See Newman's letter to Samuel Wilberforce, 4 February 1835, in *L.D.,* V, p. 21: "The ordinances etc. of the Spirit of regeneration are the persuasions of the Gospel . . ." (see also p. 47); and *OUS,* p. 200: "mere facts persuade no one."

37. See *OUS,* p. 191: "Not that it has no grounds in Reason, that is, in evidence; but that it is satisfied with so much less than would be necessary, were it not for the bias of the mind, that to the world its evidence seems like nothing."

38. Cf. Edward T. Channing, "General View of Rhetoric," in *Lectures Read to the Seniors in Harvard College.* Edited by Dorothy I. Anderson and Waldo W. Braden (Carbondale: Southern Illinois University Press, 1968), pp. 38–9:

> [P]ersuasion is said to be heated and reckless, and bent upon setting people above or beyond reason, so that they may be ruled by impulse. Yet persuasion has its proper topics and method, not less than the coolest addresses to the understanding, and is, for the most part, a brief and informal kind of reasoning. This siren or this fury is often reason herself, kindled and inspired. Persuasion has, indeed, little appearance of proving and convincing; but this is so, probably, because feeling makes perception so rapid that steps and processes are not required. The heart leaps over the space required for full, formal statements, whether of proofs or reasonings, and feels all their force without stopping for them.

39. "Implicit" and "explicit" are, therefore, somewhat misleading terms. Insofar as they distinguish persuasive reasonings from scientific and logically-cast ones, implicit must be taken to contrast with explicit. But to the degree that explicit reflection does recover "*all* of the grounds" of faith, no quarrel exists between them: one is still implicit and the other explicit, but both deal in persuasion. Cf. Powell, *Three Uses of Christian Discourse,* p. 77.

40. In Chapter Four below I attempt to clarify and back this claim more fully. Newman's position was in fact nuanced and dialectical, for while he allowed and usually spoke of theology (as distinct from religious experience and language) as a systematic and deductive enterprise, his own impulse (and practice) was to explore its practical and rhetorical dimensions. Theology and religion do not, then, embody a simple fixed contrast between real and notional, rhetorical and dialectical, but they exhibit the mutual influence and interplay of these two dimensions. Consider the following: *Idea,* pp. 190, 230–31, 355; Owen Chadwick, *From Bossuet to Newman: The Idea of Doctrinal Development* (Cambridge: Cambridge University Press, 1957), p. 166: "His own approach to theology was historical and philosophical. See also Gabriel Daly, "Newman and Modernism," in Mary Jo Weaver, ed., *Newman and the Modernists* (Lanham, MD: University Press of America, 1985), pp. 187–88; " 'Theology' was widely understood, by both integralists and Modernists, to apply only to scholastic modes of thought. George Tyrrell frequently used the term 'theology' in this sense. He, Blondel, and Newman all described themselves as not being theologians, meaning scholastics. Something is seriously wrong with received theology when some of the finest christian minds of their age find it necessary to disclaim their status as theologians"; T. M. Schoof, *A Survey of Catholic Theology: 1800–1970* (Paramus, N.J.: Paulist Newman Press, 1970), p. 41: "He regarded himself neither as a theologian nor as a philosopher in the sense in which these were understood in the Church of his time;" Adrian J. Boekraad and Henry Tristram, *The Argument from Conscience to the Existence of God, According to J. H. Newman* (Louvain: Editions Nauwelaerts, 1961), p. 47, quoting Maurice Nédoncelle: C'est un penseur sans denomination. Et par consequent, lorsqu'il est philosophe, c'est sans le savoir." Contemporary rhetoricians and theologians have begun to catch up to this insight. See, for example, Samuel Isjelling, *Rhetoric and Philosophy in Conflict* (The Hague: Martinus Nijhoff, 1976), ch. XI; Grassi, *Rhetoric as Philosophy,* ch.

5; Gordon D. Kaufman, *An Essay On Theological Method* (Missoula, Montana: Scholars Press, 1975); Sallie MacFague, *Metaphorical Theology: Models of God in Religious Language* (Philadelphia: Fortress Press, 1982); Tracy, The *Analogical Imagination;* The Reverend Mark Schoof, O.P., "The Theological Roots of Christian Dogmatism," *Downside Review,* 94 (July 1976), pp. 178–96; Frank Burch Brown, *Transfiguration: Poetic Metaphor and the Language of Religious Belief* (Chapel Hill: University of North Carolina Press, 1983).

41. The term is ambiguous, sometimes referring (as here) to the conclusion of an argument as a conjecture antecedent to confirmation in fact, sometimes to the (major) premise, and sometimes to the argument as a whole. (In addition, an antecedent probability—as a conclusion of one argument—can combine with evidence to create a further argument.) Newman usually used the term in the first sense, to refer to a conclusion (e.g., "the antecedent probability that a revelation will be given"), but having been steeped in Whately, Copleston, and Aldrich, he was aware that such probabilities derive from what Whately called "a priori" or "antecedent" probabilities. See Whately, *Rhetoric,* pp. 46–52; Henry Aldrich, *Artis Logicae Rudimenta* (Oxford: Henry Hammans, 1862), p. 209, note b: "The eikos is clearly regarded by Aristotle as a *general proposition,* employed as a premise. In the *Rhetoric,* 1.2.15, he describes it as having the same relation to its conclusion as an universal to a particular. In another sense, any proposition may be called probable, which can *as a conclusion* be supported upon (morally) reasonable grounds. . . ." Cf. *Prepos.,* p. 227; Ray McKerrow, "Probable Argument and Proof in Whately's Theory of Rhetoric," *Central States Speech Journal* 26 (Winter, 1975), p. 261. In 1860 Newman sketched out the following for Book II of the *Grammar:* "Chapter 1. There are two kinds of argument for a fact εἰκονα and σήμεια. On their respective provinces. Versimilitude or likehood and probable [sic] rising to moral certainty."

"Of these two the personal argument is mainly founded on the former *[eikota],* though of course the latter *[semeia]* ever must be the direct ground of conviction, but the former so heightens even a low probability as to make it enough. Bring out all this fully." (*T.P.,* p. 91).

42. Elsewhere Newman refers to antecedent probabilities as "versimilitudes" (*OUS,* Preface of 1870, p. xiii), recalling Cicero's use of *versimile* for such probabilities in *De Inventione.* Cf. also *T. P.,* pp. 108–9.

43. Cf. *L.D.,* XII, p. 31. On this concept see F. E. Peters, *Greek Philosophical Terms* (New York: New York University Press, 1967), pp. 52–5; Arnhart, *Political Reasoning,* passim. On the *eikos* see Aristotle, *Rhetoric,* 1357a15ff.; Grimaldi, *Studies,* pp. 107–10; Arnhart, pp. 43–5, 108–9, 158–60.

44. In *The Realm of Rhetoric* (Notre Dame: University of Notre Dame Press, 1982), p. 2, Perelman notes that the "acceptable" *(eulogos)* "has a qualitative aspect" that cannot be reduced to "calculable probability." Cf. Aristotle, *Topics,* 100b20–22; Willam, *Erkenntnislehre,* pp. 43–4. Thus De Quincey (*Works,* X, p. 86) writes: "It could not be by accident that the topics, or general heads of argument, were never in an absolute and unconditional sense true, but contained so much of plausible or colorable truth as is expressed in the original meaning of the word *probable.* A *ratio probabilis,* in the Latin use of the word *probabilis,* is that ground of assent—not which the understanding can solemnly approve and abide by—but the very opposite to this; one which it can submit to for a moment, and countenance as within the limits of plausible." This "softer" sense of probable as plausible, Campbell (*Philosophy of Rhetoric,* p. 82) rejects, whereas Whately (*Rhetoric,* p. 47) accepts it as just that, a softer species of the harder probability he prefers.

45. *Minor Attic Orators,* 2 vols., with an English translation by K. J. Maidment, M. A.

(Cambridge: Harvard University Press, 1968), I, p. 53. Newman's use of "prepossession" and "prejudice" in their positive senses reaches back through Edmund Burke to Cicero's *praesumptio* (in *De Inventione*), and forward to Gadamer's reclamation of the term in *Truth and Method*. Thus Newman writes in *Prepos,* pp. 227–28: "Prejudice, you know, means properly a pre-judgment, or judgment by anticipation; a judgment which is formed prior to the particular question submitted to us, yet is made to bear upon it. . . . Now there is nothing unfair in . . . this; what is past naturally bears on the future; from what has been, we conjecture what will be; it is reasonable and rational to do so." Cf. Edmund Burke, *Reflections on the Revolution in France* (Indianapolis: Bobbs–Merrill, 1955), p. 99, on "just prejudice": ". . . prejudice, with its reason, has a motive to give action to that reason, and an affection which will give it permanence. Prejudice is of ready application in the emergency; it previously engages the mind in a steady course of wisdom and virtue and does not leave the man hesitating in the moment of decision skeptical, puzzled, and unresolved. Prejudice renders a man's virtue his habit, and not a series of unconnected acts. Through just prejudice, his duty becomes a part of his nature."

46. *Minor Attic Orators,* I, p. 55.

47. Cicero, *Cicero,* 28 vols. (Cambridge: Harvard University Press, 1967), X, p. 57.

48. Cf. *DMC,* pp. 277–79. Selby provides several useful examples of antecedent probability in Newman's works, pp. 82–8; see also Chapter 4 below.

49. Mackinnon rightly notes ("Introduction" in *OUS,* p. 25) that Newman was "fascinated by induction."

50. The companion syllogism (enthymeme) based on our natural neediness and depravity would be thus. Major: God would not abandon us to state of depravity; Minor: we are in such a state; and so on.

51. Thus Sillem is not correct when he states that "As he [Newman] uses the term, 'probability' refers to the conclusion of a deductive line of reasoning considered formally as a conclusion; he never uses it of a state of mind." Cf. *L.D.,* XI, pp. 288–89; and Sillem, *P.N.,* I, pp. 176–79.

52. In DeLaura, ed., *Victorian Prose,* p. 139, Martin J. Svaglic observes of the two-fold or dialogical nature of Newman's thought: "This is a major aspect of Newman's writing that should well repay further study."

53. Otis M. Walter, "On the Varieties of Rhetorical Criticism," in Thomas R. Nilsen, ed., *Essays on Rhetorical Criticism* (New York: Random House, 1968), p. 166.

54. Cf. also *L.D.,* XII, p. 5, and XI, p. 293; and *T.P.,* p. 11.

55. Cf. Willam, *Erkenntnislehre,* pp. 66–85; and Selby, *The Principle of Reserve,* pp. 76–8.

56. Whately, *Rhetoric,* p. 51. Cf. *L.D.,* XII, p. 31.

57. See McKerrow, "Probable Argument and Proof in Whately's Theory of Rhetoric," p. 261.

58. De Quincey (*Works,* X, p. 82) takes a decided stand against Whately's alleged reduction of rhetoric to a base in "conviction," and his reduction of conviction to empirical proofs: "All [of the formal teachers of rhetoric] agree that Rhetoric may be defined *the art of persuasion.* But, if we inquire what *is* persuasion, we find them vague and indefinite or even contradictory. . . . Dr. Whately, in the work before us *[The Elements of Rhetoric],* insists upon the *conviction* of the understanding as 'an essential part of persuasion'. . . . We, for our parts, have [another view]. Where conviction begins, the field of Rhetoric ends. . . ." De Quincey here fails to appreciate that Whately allowed for *degrees* of conviction.

59. David Hume, *An Enquiry Concerning Human Understanding* (Indianapolis: Bobbs-Merrill, 1955), pp. 58–9.

60. Aristotle admits that we may engage in internal rhetoric with ourselves (*Rhetoric,* 1391b), but here too the suggestion is that we use publicly-sanctioned materials in doing so.

61. See Whately, *Logic,* pp. 222–52; *Rhetoric,* pp. 39–40, *passim;* McKerrow, "Richard Whately's Theory of Rhetoric," p. 142; McKerrow, "Richard Whately on the Nature of Human Knowledge," p. 543.

62. Cf. *Bampton Lectures,* chs. 1–2.

63. Cf. Richard Whately, "On the Love of Truth," in *Essays [Second Series] on Some of the Difficulties in the Writings of the Apostle Paul* (London: John W. Parker and Son, 1854), pp. 11, 27.

64. Whately, "On the Love of Truth," in *Essays,* p. 12. ˙

65. Whately, *Rhetoric,* p. 15. See also Evans, "John Henry Newman and Whately's *Rhetoric,*" pp. 176ff.; and Wilbur S. Howell, *Eighteenth Century British Logic and Rhetoric* (Princeton: Princeton University Press, 1971), pp. 707–12.

66. Whately, "Introduction," in Paley, *A View of the Evidences of Christianity,* p. 4.

67. See John Locke, *An Essay Concerning Human Understanding,* Alexander Campbell Fraser, ed. 2 vols. (New York: Dover Publications, 1959), II, p. 373 n. 1.

68. I. A. Richards, *The Philosophy of Rhetoric* (London: Oxford University Press, 1936), pp. 5–8.

69. Cf. Wilbur S. Howell, "Renaissance Rhetoric and Modern Rhetoric: A Study in Change," in D. C. Bryant, ed., *The Rhetorical Idiom: Essays in Rhetoric, Oratory, Language and Drama, Presented to Herbert August Wichelns* (Ithaca: Cornell University Press, 1958), p. 62; Ray McKerrow, "Richard Whately's Theory of Rhetoric," pp. 150–52; Donald C. Bryant, ed., *The Rhetorical Idiom: Essays in Rhetoric, Oratory, Language and Dramas, Presented to Herbert August Wichelns* (Ithaca: Cornell University Press, 1958), p. 62.

70. Whately, *Bampton Lectures,* pp. 351–52: ". . . our notions of the moral attributes of the Deity are not derived (as Dr. Paley contends they are) from a bare contemplation of the created universe, without any notions of what is antecedently probable, to direct and aid our observations. . . . The truth I conceive is exactly the reverse of this; *viz.* that man having in himself a moral faculty . . . is thence disposed and inclined antecedently, to attribute to the Creator . . . moral qualities. . . ."

71. Cf. Bacon, *Novum Organum,* in *Works,* VI, p. 54.

72. Cf. *OUS,* pp. 213, 200: "Half the controversies in the world are verbal ones; and could they be brought to a plain issue, they would be brought to a prompt termination. Parties engaged in them would perceive, either that in substance they agreed together, or that their difference was one of first principles."

73. See, for example, Walgrave, Boekraad, Pailin, Casey, Ferreira.

74. *Victorian Sage,* p. 173. For similar views see, P. J. FitzPatrick, "Newman's *Apologia:* Was Kingsley Right?" in T. R. Wright, ed., *John Henry Newman: A Man for Our Time?* (Newcastle upon Tyne: Grevatt and Grevatt, 1983), pp. 27–36; and Inge, Weatherby, O'Donoghue, Jay Newman, Leslie Stephen, Henry Wilberforce.

75. Cf. *G.A.,* pp. 175–80, 202, 217, 321. In his *Discourse on Method* (in *Philosophical Essays.* Translated, with an Introduction and Notes, by Laurence J. LaFleur [Indianapolis: Bobbs–Merrill, 1977]), Descartes recounts his gradual attainment to the insight that correct method in philosophy requires casting off the yoke of "custom and example" (p. 13) in favor of individual certification of what could not help but be true: ". . . we need only refrain from accepting as true that which is not true, and carefully follow the order necessary to deduce each subsequent proposition from the others" (pp. 15–16); ". . . I should . . . reject as absolutely false anything of which I could have the least doubt . . ." (p. 24). Such universal doubt was to lead to knowledge of what was absolutely *certain,* and certain to all men alike

so long as they exercised their rational facaulties, in all times and places. Knowledge was of the immutable and eternal; all mere belief and probability, accordingly, is to be rejected— history, poetry, eloquence, though he "esteemed them highly" (p. 7), are not knowledge. All depends on unshakeable foundations, a "first truth," untainted by circumstance, probability, opinion, change. Paticular cases, if they are the subject of knowledge at all, are but instantiations of universals.

On the other hand, while Newman accepted the *Cogito* and himself appealed to "first principles" that could not be doubted without self- contradiction, nevertheless he highlights first principles of a quite different sort. First principles are often not eternal verities essentially unconnected to, and unchanged by, particular cases, but time–bound concepts whose effectiveness, and truth, reside in their (rhetorical) ability to order data in ways that make optimal sense. First principles are contingent and indemonstrable, known more by an intellectualized version of Aristotelian *phronesis* (working overtime, as it were, beyond the moral realm), called by Newman the illative sense, than by *nous* or Cartesian intuition.

76. Cf. Hans–Georg Gadamer, *Truth and Method* (New York: The Crossroad Publishing Co., 1986), p. 240: ". . . 'prejudice' means a judgment that is given before all the elements that determine a situation have been finally examined."

77. *Truth and Method,* pp. 245–49.

78. Michael Polyani, *Personal Knowledge* (Chicago: University of Chicago Press, 1962), ch. 10.

79. M. Jamie Ferreira, *Skepticism and Reasonable Doubt* (Oxford: Clarendon Press, 1986), pp. 149–71.

80. Walgrave, *Newman the Theologian,* p. 116.

81. Cf. *Idea,* "Christianity and Physical Sciences," pp. 346–67.

82. See Chapter Four below. I follow Owen Chadwick's practice of referring to the *Essay On the Development of Christian Doctrine* as the *Essay*.

83. Philip Wheelwright, *Metaphor and Reality* (Bloomington: Indiana University Press, 1962), p. 170. For a recent formulation of "perspectivism" along Newmanian lines, see Richard A. Cherwitz and James W. Hikins, *Communication and Knowledge: An Investigation in Rhetorical Epistemology* (Columbia: University of South Carolina Press, 1986); and Van A. Harvey, *The Historian and the Believer* (Philadelphia: Westminister Press, 1966), esp. ch. VII.

84. Giambattista Vico, *On the Study Methods of Our Times.* Translated, with an Introduction and Notes, by Elio Gianturco (Indianapolis: Bobbs–Merrill, 1965), pp. 15–16.

85. Michael Polanyi, *Science, Faith and Society* (Chicago: University of Chicago Press, 1946), esp. ch. II.

86. For this term see Douglas Ehninger, "Introduction," in Richard Whately, *Rhetoric,* p. xxv.

87. Ehninger, "Introduction," p. xiv.

88. *Imperial Intellect,* p. 197.

CHAPTER THREE

1. Since Newman's time, of course, the subject has hardly faded away. Bernard Longergan, Basil Mitchell, Paul Tillich, Michael Novak, Peter Berger, Gordon Kaufman, David Tracy, to name only a few, have tackled the problem in ways implicitly or explicitly along Newmanian lines.

2. See A.W., p. 270: "These attempts, though some of them close upon others, were, I think, all distinct. They were like attempts to get into a labyrinth, or to find the weak point in the defences of a fortified place."

3. See Jay Newman, *Mental Philosophy*, p. 99.

4. Pailin, *The Way to Faith,*, p. 109.

5. See H.H. Price, *Belief* (London: George Allen and Unwin Ltd, 1969), p. 316, and Artz, "Newman as Philosopher," pp. 276–77. Cf. John Dewey, "What Pragmatism Means by Practical," in *Essays in Experimental Logic* (New York: Dover Publications, n.d. Rpr. University of Chicago Press, 1916), p. 327: "Now the moment the complicity of the personal factor in our philosophic valuations is recognized, is recognized fully, frankly, and generally, that moment a new era in philosophy will begin." Also Valesio, *Novantiqua*, p. 32: "We can express reality only through selections or stylization. This is the root of rhetoric, this is what explains its essential importance for all the sciences of man and society."

6. This is unquestionably a troublesome formulation; for an elaboration see the following note.

7. This is the case (1) irrespective of whether such things actually exist or not. I may have a real apprehension that "My neighbor's dog is a cocker-spanial" whereas in fact my neighbor owns no dog, and (2) regardless of whether subject and predicate are compatible. I can "impose a sense on" "Epistemology ran down the street" (for this example see Jay Newman, *Mental Philosophy*, p. 42), though "formally" or objectively it may be senseless. For Newman's distinction between "formal" and "logical" propositions, see *T.P.*, pp. 102–3: "By a logical assertion, I mean one in which the wording is intelligible; by a formal one in which there is an intelligible sense." This is not the same as saying that Newman's account of apprehending meaning is correct; in fact there are serious problems with it, but these lie beyond the present concerns.

It should be noted in passing here that Newman's distinction between real and notional is not equivalent to saying that real apprehension is nonconceptual. On the contrary, real apprehension is an *"interpretation"* (*G.A.*, 13; emphasis added) of a predicate in terms of relevant concrete "facts" and of whatever antecedent truths, probabilities and so on frame these facts and give them meaning. Real apprehension is thus inextricably conceptual and intrinsically constituted by *antecedent* "probabilities."

8. Phillip Wheelwright, *The Burning Fountain* (Bloomington: Indiana University Press, 1954), pp. 25–9; *Metaphor and Reality*, p. 33.

9. That theology could be characterized as "concrete" is, as noted in the previous chapter (note 39), rather confusing, given Newman's earlier definitions of theology as notional (esp., *G.A.*, ch. 5). The confusion is mostly verbal, depending on what Newman, in keeping with his times, was willing to call theology, as distinct from what theologians today would include under that term. We will see that ample room exists in Newman's thought for a theological reflection that is both real and notional. See Nicholas Lash, "Was Newman a Theologian?," *The Heythrop Journal*, XXVII (July 1976), pp. 322–25. For a contemporary version of Newman's approach, see The Revd. Mark Schoof, O.P., "The Theological Roots of Christian Dogmatism," *The Downside Review*, 94 (July 1976), p. 195: "I am not suggesting that theology should cease to be a science. . . . But is there not also a case for a more direct form of practising theology . . . from non-scientific reservoirs of 'real' experience, and in a language which is imaginative or 'real' rather than technical . . .?"

10. Cf. I.T. Ker, "Introduction," in *G.A.*, p. lx. Hence the term "concrete" and its synonyms—"fact," "thing," "reality," "the real," "the particular case," "practice"—refer to the particular phenomena from which the generalizations, laws, rules, and so on of the

sciences are drawn (*OUS*, p. 259). This is not to indict those more determinate procedures of (for instance) mathematics or physics. Newman was aware of a far greater fixity in their subject matters, both in the sense that they do not normally require mediation by the "whole" person in the way other subjects do, and in the sense that certain aspects of nature and man are recurring and stable, hence more easily generalizable. The traditional self-understanding of sociology, for example, has been to formulate laws as explanatory and predictive accounts of its concrete phenomena, that is to say, to treat the concrete abstractly. In the Oxford sermons Newman notes the irrelevance to such a study of "the purity and acuteness of the moral sense" (*OUS*, p. 59).

11. As Lash has noted (*Newman on Development*, p. 48): "Newman's conception of 'things' or 'facts existing' is wide enough to include theoretical systems."

12. See, for example, Jay Newman, *Mental Philosophy*, p. 45. Powell (*Three Uses of Christian Discourse in John Henry Newman*) rightly argues that in some contexts *notions* are more important.

13. See J.D. Bastable, "Cardinal Newman's Philosophy of Belief," *Philosophical Studies*, 5 (December 1955), 48–9; M. Jamie Ferreira, "Newman and William James on Religious Experience: The Theory and the Concrete," *The Heythrop Journal*, XXIX (1988), 44–57; Price, *Belief*, pp. 330–34; Jay Newman, *Mental Philosophy*, pp. 39–48; also Ker, "Introduction," in *G.A.*, p. lvii; and N. D. O'Donoghue, "Newman and the Privileged Access to Truth," *Irish Theological Quarterly*, 42 (1975) p. 257.

14. Nicholas Lash, *Change in Focus: A Story of Doctrinal Change and Continuity* (London: Sheed and Ward, 1973), p. 84, emphasis added.

15. Cf. F. Nicolina, quoted in Ernesto Grassi, "Critical Philosophy or Topical Philosophy? Meditations on the *De nostri temporis studiorum ratione,*" in Giorgio Tagliacozzo and Hayden V. White, eds., *Giambattista Vico: An International Symposium* (Baltimore: Johns Hopkins University Press, 1969), p. 49: " '[Vico] considers the three famous operations of the mind, perception, judgment, and reasoning, which he divides into topics, criticism, and method; *so that topics appears as the faculty or art of apprehending.* . . . (emphasis added).' " See also Paolo Valesio, *Novantiqua: Rhetorics as a Contemporary Theory* (Bloomington: Indiana University Press, 1980), p. 33: ". . . topoi had already seen to it, so to speak, that speech would not approach reality—the referential world—directly, but only through them. . . ."

16. *Belief*, p. 331.

17. This charge is variously brought by Leslie Stephen, William Ralph Inge (*Faith and Its Psychology* [New York: Charles Scribner's Sons, 1910]), Jay Newman, N.D. O'Donoghue, and Harold Weatherby, among others.

18. Cf. *PN*, II, p. 87, note of Dec. 1, 1859: "All I am at is to draw out a *case*, or a *probable* doctrine. . . ." Newman never specifies what degree of apprehension of a predicate is necessary to apprehend a proposition (and ultimately therefore to assent to it), but not because he prefers to traffic in "fuzzy, imprecise" notions out of philosophical inadequacy as has been alleged (Jay Newman, *Mental Philosophy*, p. 45), nor because the question is irrelevant to the kinds of *religious* questions he has in mind (for example, "What the Church says is true" would not require a nuanced account of the degree of apprehension of the predicate involved). The answer, rather, is that Newman is acutely aware that the question is *contingent*, dependent on the specific case, on one's purposes, one's needs, and so on. As Jay Newman himself has noted, such a question is not referable to a single standard. "Sufficient" cannot be legislated ahead of time, and Newman rightly refrains from attempting to do so. In

fact, Newman here anticipates Polanyi's argument in *The Tacit Dimension* (Garden City, New York: Anchor Books, 1966) that apprehension of a whole is a personal judgment, relying on myriad "tacit" particulars not susceptible of quantification or exhaustive explication. Such a personal dimension precludes measurement, and Newman's lack of such specification suggests an appropriate philosophical sensitivity to the concrete, not naiveté to theoretical fine distinctions.

19. See Jay Newman, *Mental Philosophy*, p. 57.

20. Cf. Lash, "Did Newman Have a 'Theory' of Development?"

21. See, for example, Weatherby, *Cardinal Newman in His Age*, chs. 6 and 8; and Strong, "Was Newman a Failure?" p. 627.

22. *Belief*, p. 316.

23. Jay Newman, *Mental Philosophy*, p. 47. Similarly, in *The New Rhetoric and the Humanities* (Dordrecht: D. Reidel, 1979), p. 4. Chaim Perelman wrongly links Newman with the "old tradition" of rhetoric—the empiricist tradition of Locke, Hume, Campbell and Whately—"in which the theory of invention is reduced to a minimum." My argument here, of course, is that Newman significantly *alters* that tradition, forging new links with the rhetorical theories of Aristotle and Cicero much as Perelman himself did, but doing so a century earlier.

24. Cf. Howell, *Eighteenth-Century British Logic and Rhetoric*, pp. 372–437.

25. *Philosophy of Rhetoric*, p. xliii.

26. See *L.D.*, I, pp. 306–7; *L.D.*, XV, pp. 175–79; *A.W.*, pp. 67–8.

27. See *Logic*, pp. xxxviii, xxix; *Rhetoric*, p. 15.

28. *Logic*, p. xv.

29. *Logic*, pp. 252–61; on Copleston, see Raymie E. McKerrow's unpublished "Richard Whately and the Revival of Rhetoric in England," Southern Speech Communication Association Convention, Houston, Texas, April, 1986.

30. *Logic*, p. 60.

31. Cf. McKerrow, "Richard Whately's Theory of Rhetoric," p. 142.

32. Cf. Evans, "Newman and Whately's Logic," pp. 175–91; Vargish, *Contemplation of Mind*, p. 15.

33. *Rhetoric*, Parts I and II.

34. Cf. Howell, *Eighteenth-Century British Logic and Rhetoric*, pp. 695ff., and Bate, *From Classic to Romantic*, ch. 5.

35. Cf. David Hume, *A Treatise of Human Nature* (Oxford: Clarendon Press, 1978), p. 84ff.

36. Hume, *Treatise*, p. 629.

37. *Philosophy of Rhetoric*, pp. 274, 285ff.

38. See *Philosophy of Rhetoric*, Book II, chs. VI–IX.

39. Wheelwright, *Metaphor and Reality*, p. 33.

40. Cf. Locke, *Essay Concerning Human Understanding*, 2 vols. (New York: Dover Publications, 1959), II, p. 146.

41. O'Donoghue, "Privileged Access," p. 247.

42. Cf. Artz, "Newman as Philosopher," p. 286; and *G.A.*, p. 190: "It follows that what to one intellect is a proof is not to another, and that the certainty of a prosposition does properly consist in the certitude of the mind which contemplates it. And this of course may be said without prejudice to the objective truth or falsehood of propositions. . . ."

43. In a letter to Simeon Lloyd Pope, 15 August 1830, in *L.D.*, II, p. 264, Newman

writes: "Practical matters . . . are determined by the ηθος of the agent—who (whether he be correct or not) still adopts his measures, not on a process of reasoning which words will do justice to, but on feeling, on the dictates of an internal unproduceable sense."

44. On the illative sense and *phronesis,* see Verdeke, "Aristotelian Roots of Newman's Illative Sense," in Bastable, ed., *Newman and Gladstone,* pp. 177–95. For relevant discussions of the sort of rhetoric Newman develops, see, for example, Victoria Kahn, *Rhetoric, Prudence and Skepticism in the Renaissance;* Jerrold Siegel, *Rhetoric and Philosophy in Renaissance Humanism: The Unity of Eloquence and Wisdom* (Princeton: Princeton University Press, 1968); and Eugene Garver, *Machiavelli and the History of Prudence* (Madison: University of Wisconsin Press, 1987).

45. Cf. Cicero, *De Oratore,* 1. 18. 83; 2. 16. 60; 1.31. 122; *De Officiis,* 1. 27. 94; 2. 3. 9–10; 3.3. 11. See Quintilian, *Institutes,* Preface, 9.

46. See for example Valesio, *Novantiqua,* esp. pp. 61–144.

47. See for example Arnhart, *Political Reasoning;* Grimaldi, *Studies;* Lois Self, "Rhetoric and *Phronesis:* The Aristotelian Idea," *Philosophy and Rhetoric* (Spring 1979), 130–43; Christopher Lyle Johnstone, "An Aristotelian Trilogy: Ethics, Rhetoric, Politics, and the Search for Moral Truth," *Philosophy and Rhetoric,* 13 (Winter 1980), pp. 1–24; Robert C. Rowland and Deanna F. Womack, "Aristotle's View of Ethical Rhetoric," *Rhetoric Society Quarterly,* XV (Winter and Spring 1985), pp. 13–31. See also Kahn, Siegel and Garver.

48. *Nichomachean Ethics.* Translated, with an introduction and notes, by Martin Ostwald (Indianapolis: Bobbs–Merrill, 1962).

49. *Nichomachean Ethics,* 1144a29–1144b 1: "Without virtue or excellence, this eye of the soul. [intelligence,] [nous] does not acquire the characteristic [of practical wisdom]. . . . But whatever the true end good may be, only a good man can judge it correctly. For wickedness distorts and causes us to be completely mistaken about the fundamental principles of action. Hence it is clear that a man cannot have practical wisdom unless he is good."

50. Thus W. W. Fortenbaugh, *Aristotle on Emotion* (New York: Barnes and Noble, 1975), p. 77: "[M]oral virtue ensures a correct goal, while practical wisdom as a perfection of man's logical side is responsible for correct means-end deliberations." For Aristotle the rhetor and the *phronimos* can be distinguished, since the rhetor *may* not be ethically good, while the *phronimos* is so by definition. The *ethical* rhetor, moreover, may not be practically wise, since he may fail in his attempt to find the good in the concrete. Only the ethical rhetor who is guided by *phronesis* in seeking the good is equal to the *phronimos.* As Victoria Kahn shows, these distinctions are collapsed for Cicero and Quintilian, for whom the prudent man and the orator "are ideally the same. . . . Cicero's point is not simply that the orator has the rhetorical skills of persuasion that will enable the prudent man to achieve a particular end, but that the latter is prudent precisely by being an orator" (*Rhetoric, Prudence and Skepticism in the Renaissance,* p. 35).

51. Even in his early essay on Cicero (*H.S.,* I, p. 258) Newman is well aware of the need to adapt to circumstance: "[Cicero] considered it to be actually the duty of a statesman to accommodate theoretical principle to the exigencies of existing circumstances."

52. Cf. *Rhetoric,* 1378a 8: "The emotions are all those affections which cause men to change their opinions in regard to their judgments, and are accompanied by pleasure and pain."

53. *Studies,* p. 16. Thus Fortenbaugh (*Aristotle on Emotion,* p. 18) writes: "Viewed as an affliction divorced from cognition, emotion was naturally opposed to reason and conceived of as something hostile to thoughtful judgment. It was Aristotle's contribution to have

offered a very different view of emotion, so that emotional appeal would no longer be viewed as an extra-rational enchantment." See also William James, "The Sentiment of Rationality," in John J. McDermott, ed., *The Writings of William James* (Chicago: University of Chicago Press, 1977), p. 334: "It is utterly hopeless to try to exorcise such sensitiveness by calling it the disturbing subjective factor, and branding it as the root of all evil. 'Subjective' be it called! and 'disturbing' to those whom it foils! But if it helps those who, as Cicero says, *'vim naturae magis sentiunt,'* it is good and not evil. Pretend what we may, the whole man within us is at work when we form our philosophical opinions. Intellect, will, taste, and passion co—operate just as they do in practical affairs"; and Carlyle, "Characteristics," in *Works,* VIII, p. 330: ". . . when we feel ourselves as we wish to be, we say that we are *whole."*

54. Cf. Verdeke, "Aristotelian Roots," p. 178: "[T]his close co-operation between New-man and Whately does not mean that both scholars always agreed on philosophical matters; on the contrary they even dissented on such important questions as the meaning and value of the Aristotelian philosophy for the intellectual climate of that time." Also Sillem, *P.N.,* I, pp. 161–62.

55. The difference between Newman and Aristotle is perhaps more apparent than real on this point, inasmuch as the kinds of truth-questions Aristotle had in mind were those relatively circumscribed problems of the *polis* and its citizens in the Aeropagus or law courts, problems that could be expected to be resolved within the framework of those institutions and the argumentation they allowed; whereas Newman (for whom the question of religious faith was never far off) cast his net much farther, intent on those more recondite questions of value and belief and faith lying beyond the ken of institutional negotiation and formal debate. See *L.D.,* XII, p. 159: "If I might generalize, I should say I always dislike a polemical paper from which you can pick out choice expressions like a plum"; and *L.D.,* IV, p. 274, where Newman worries that readers of "Tracts for the Times" will not be able to *"realize* the arguments." Even the pulpit, he observes in another letter, "makes one unreal, rhetorical" (*L.D.,* II, p. 337). See also *OUS,* pp. 88–9: "It is only necessary for Reason to ask many questions; and, while the other party is investigating the real answer to each in detail, to claim the victory, which spectators will not be slow to award, fancying (as in the manner of men) that clear and ready speech is the test of Truth."

56. Cf. *Prepos.* p. 85: "[F]act and argument are the tests of truth and error." This is a passage which, read in the context of Newman's mistrust of controversy, requires that we distinguish the powers and limits of controversy. For more on this theme see Jan Derek Holmes, "Personal Influence and Religious Conviction—Newman and Controversy," in *Newman Studien,* X (Heroldsberg bei Nürnberg: Glock und Lutz, 1978), pp. 26–46; and Wilfrid Ward, "Personality in Apologetic" in *Last Lectures,* p. 104: "Arguments were, for most minds, in his judgment auxiliary and medicinal—no more. Medicine cures a living body that is diseased; it does not take the place of diet."

57. Cf. Ward, *Last Lectures,* p. 104: "If the complicated network of associations, which enshrine for a living mind and for a society its fundamental beliefs, were once broken up by disturbing argumentative discussion, it could not possibly be replaced by mere arguments."

58. Artistotle, *Rhetoric,* 1356a 4; *see Idea, p. 271;* see also Cicero, *De Oratore,* 2. 84. 323; *Orator,* 4. 21. 401; Quintilian, *Institutes,* 1. 6. 5.

59. Cf. Newman's letter to Simeon Lloyd Pope, August 15, 1830 in *L.D.,* II, p. 264: "I am amused at your wishing me to give you *in two lines* my reasons for quoting the B. [Bible] Society—when it is well, if by a thousand one approximates toward conveying one's meaning to another on any question of practice—Practical matters cannot be defended by argument, or explained on paper—(i.e., except accidentally)—they are determined by the ηθος [ethos]

259

of the agent. . . . Were I with you a fortnight . . . I should be able by the end of it, to explain to you *what I mean* on the subject of the B.S . . . but as to drawing up a formula, I am quite unequal to throwing my reasonings into the form of $y^2 = px + x^2$. See *G.A.*, pp. 245–46: "In like manner, good character goes far in destroying the force of even plausible charges. There is indeed a degree of evidence in support of an allegation, against which reputation is no defence; but it must be singularly strong to overcome an established antecedent probability which stands opposed to it." See also *T.P.*, pp. 17–18, 26.

60. One can see this principle applied throughout his works; for example, in the way he sought "big names" to attract students to the fledgling Catholic University of Dublin, see his letter to J.B. Dunne, 25 July, 1854 in *L.D.*, XVI, p. 206.

61. See also *OUS*, p. 275; *Prepos*, p. 45; *Ari*, pp. 136–37; *V.M.*, II, p. 103: "The arguments, then, which we use, must be such as are likely to convince serious and earnest minds, who are really seeking for the truth, not amusing themselves with intellectual combats, or desiring to support an existing opinion anyhow;" and *On Con*, p. 61: "Drill sergeants think much of deportment; hard logicians come down with a sledge-hammer even on a Plato who does not happen to enumerate in his beautiful sentences all the argumentative considerations which go to make up his conclusion. . . ."

62. *Agnostic's Apology*, p. 229. But see *G.A.*, p. 185: "Every exercise of nature or of art is good in its place; and the uses of this logical inference are manifold."

63. See *P.N.*, II, p. 73 n. 2; *T. P.*, p. 51; and Brian Wicker, "Newman and Logic," *Newman–Studien*, V (Nurnberg: Glock und Lutz, 1972), 251–52:

> The logical writers whose influence Newman absorbed as an undergraduate and a fellow [of] Oriel in the early 19th century, were all more or less wedded to a psychological theory of the nature of logical subject–matter. That is to say, they held that the object of logical study was to determine the possibilities and limitations of mental processes, and to exhibit the rules by which such processes worked. The logician's materials—terms, propositions and syllogisms—were of interest first and foremost because they reflected mental processes of apprehending, conceiving, inferring, etc., and it was these processes which logic attempted to regulate.

See also Culler, *Imperial Intellect*, pp. 40–41; Sillem, *P.N.*, I, p. 157.

64,. See *T. P.*, p. 53: "Whately considers that the syllogism is the only form or analysis of reasoning—consequently the laws of syllogising are with him nearly the whole of Logic; and he hardly recognizes any doctrine about the use of terms or of propositions except with reference to syllogisms." Also *T. P.*, p. 52: "Different definitions of Logic. The widest is Tandel's—*'Scientia tractans de veritate cognitionis humanae.'* . . . The narrowest is Whately's—'The art of reasoning.' " Newman's falls in between: *T. P.*, p. 53: "In such a diversity of opinions, I must choose my own. Now I have a definite meaning which I shall give it myself—viz 'The Science of Proof or Inference.' This definition is wider than Whately's. . . ."

65. *Logic*, p. 35.

66. "Newman and Logic," pp. 251–68.

67. Wicker, "Newman and Logic," p. 254.

68. Aginst Newman's view, see Wicker, "Newman and Logic," p. 252: "To put the matter briefly, it is by giving his variables *concrete values* that the logician shows the relevance of formal logic to living arguments about the world . . . (emphasis added)." See *T. P.*, p. 55, where Newman includes under logic "Ideas, Names, Classifications, Definitions, Divisions, Judgment, Categories, Propositions, and Ratiocination." The last-named is actually the focus, but the idea is that reasoning is clearest when the "ideas, names, classifications," and so on are clearest, that is, unambiguous and abstract. For similar views (though

Newman never quotes them), see Richard Kirwan, *Logick; or, An Essay on the Elements, Principles, and Different Modes of Reasoning* (London: Payne and MacKinlay, 1807); and John Gillies, *Aristotle's Ethics and Politics, Comprising His Practical Philosophy* (London: T. Cadell and W. Davies, 1804).

69. *Posterior Analytics,* 1, 10, 76b 25; *T. P.,* p. 53.

70. Cf. Ward, *Last Lectures,* p. 85: "Does Newman then, it will be asked, simply set aside logic. . . ? He is not so foolish"; and Bastable, "Newman's Philosophy of Belief," p. 57: "Aristotle would accept his [Newman's] critique of the syllogism calmly."

71. In *The Uses of Argument* (Cambridge: Cambridge University Press, 1958), esp. pp. 123–35 and 248–52, Stephen Toulmin distinguishes substantial and analytical syllogisms on the basis that only the latter analytically entail their conclusions, that is, presuppose the information contained in the conclusion in their major premises. Substantial arguments involve a "type–jump" between the data in the premises and those in the conclusion. In these arguments, according to Toulmin, a logical "gap" exists between premises and conclusion, hence there is no analytical entailment. Newman recognizes much the same thing when he writes in *G.A.,* p. 208: "In like manner, the conclusion in a real or concrete question is foreseen and predicted rather than actually attained; foreseen in the number and direction of accumulated premisses, which all converge to it, and as the result of their combination, approach it more nearly than any assignable difference, yet do not touch it logically (though only not touching it,) on account of the nature of its subject matter. . . ." For the confusions in Toulmin's view, see Chapter Seven.

72. See Toulmin, *The Uses of Argument,* p. 15.

73. These others include, for example, John Wisdom, "Gods," in *Philosophy and Psycho–Analysis* (New York: Philosophical Library, 1953), pp. 149–68; John Dewey, *How We Think* (Boston: D.C. Heath and Co., 1933), and *Logic: The Theory of Inquiry* (New York: Henry Holt and Co., 1938), esp. Part II; Walter Fisher, *Human Communication as Narration.*

74. See Jay Newman, *Mental Philosophy,* pp. 145–60. Wicker, "Newman and Logic," p. 252, writes: "Newman is here contrasting thinking in words from thinking without words, *or perhaps beyond the capacity of words* (emphasis added)."

75. Newman never clarified the relations holding among words, concepts and images. It is, I think, fair to say that Newman suggests that concepts depend upon language, but also that imagery (of various kinds) can substitute for, while it exceeds the reach of, both. Consider his account of music in *OUS,* pp. 346–47; and of language, pp. 341–42:

> Again, what impediments do the diversities of language place in the way of communicating ideas! Language is a sort of analysis of thought; and, since ideas are infinite, and infinitely combined, and infinitely modified, whereas language is a method definite and limited, and confined to an arbitrary selection of a certain number of these innumerable materials, it were idle to expect that the courses of thought marked out in one language should, except in their general outlines and main centres, correspond to those of another. Multitudes of ideas expressed in the one do not even enter into the other, and can only be conveyed by some economy or accommodation, by circumlocutions, phrases, limiting words, figures, or some bold and happy expedient.

See also *G.A.,* p. 185: ". . . thought is too keen and manifold, its sources are too remote and hidden, its path too personal, delicate, and circuitous, its subject–matter too various and intricate, to admit of the trammels of any language, of whatever subtlety and of whatever compass."

76. Cf. Gerard Casey, *Natural Reason: A Study of the Notions of Inference, Assent, Intuition, and First Principles in the Philosophy of John Henry Cardinal Newman* (New York: Peter Lang, 1984), p. 6: "It is my contention that Newman is wrong in insisting upon such a sharp dichotomy between types of inference." I would say that Newman in fact does not insist, at least not consistently, on this seeming separation. Generally we might say that, as "logic" stands to formal inference, "rhetoric" stands to informal.

77. He cites, for example, "Bonelli, Dmowski, Gerdil. Balmez, St. Sulpice course, Ubaghs, Mill, Whewell, Brown, Reid, Hamilton" (*T.P.*, p. 51), in addition to Whately.

78. See also *G.A.*, pp. 181, 184: "So much on logical argumentation; and in thus speaking of the syllogism, I speak of all inferential processes whatever, as expressed in language, *(if they are such as to be reducible to science)* . . . (emphasis added)."

79. More accurately, they can be really and notionally apprehended at once: *G. A.*, p. 14: ". . . in the same mind and at the same time, the same proposition may express both what is notional and what is real." See also *T.P.*, p. 138.

80. *Works*, VII, p. 333. See also *Sartor Resartus* in *Works*, I, pp. 50ff. In the "Preface to the Third Edition" (1871) of the Oxford Sermons Newman goes so far as to assimilate logic to rhetoric: "The process of reasoning, whether implicit or explicit, is the act of one and the same faculty, to which also belongs the power of analysing that process, and of thereby passing from implicit to explicit. Reasoning, thus retrospectively employed in analyzing itself, results in a specific science or art, called logic, which is a sort of rhetoric, bringing out to advantage the implicit acts on which it has proceeded (pp. xi–xii)." Cf. Harrold, *John Henry Newman*, p. 128: "And Newman's book [the *Grammar of Assent*] might well bear the title, *An Essay in Aid of a Rhetoric of Belief: or How to Hold One's Belief Most Cogently and to Express It Most Persuasively.*"

81. For a more modern view of logic, see, for example, Irving M. Copi, *Introduction to Logic* (New York: The Macmillan Company, 1953); Morris R. Cohen and Ernest Nagel, *An Introduction to Logic and Scientific Method* (London: Routledge and Kegan Paul Ltd, 1961); Richard B. Angell, *Reasoning and Logic* (New York: Meredith Publishing Company, 1964).

82. See, for example, *P.N.*, II, p. 126: "On the scientific method compared with what may be called the personal. It is analgous to the legal;" also Toulmin, *The Uses of Argument*, p. 7: "Logic (we may say) is generalised jurisprudence." See also *Wisdom*, "Gods," p. 157, and Perelman, "The New Rhetoric: A Theory of Practical Reasoning," in *The New Rhetoric and the Humanities* (Dordrecht: D. Reidel, 1979), p. 34.

83. Julius Stone, *Legal Systems and Lawyers' Reasonings* (Stanford: Stanford University Press, 1964), pp. 301–37, *passim*. Interestingly, Stone cites Newman's *Grammar of Assent* (p. 327 n. 124) amidst texts on rhetorical theory, and argues at length about the connections between rhetoric and law (particularly with respect to *topoi*). For similar views on law and legal reasoning, see, for example, Benjamin N. Cardozo, *The Nature of the Judicial Process* (New Haven: Yale University Press, 1921); Edward H. Levi, *An Introduction to Legal Reasoning* (Chicago: The University of Chicago Press, 1949); James Boyd White, *The Legal Imagination*, Abridged Edition (Chicago: The University of Chicago Press, 1984), esp. Ch. 4; and White, *Heracles' Bow: Essays on the Rhetoric and Poetics of the Law* (Madison: The University of Wisconsin Press, 1985).

84. Stone, *Legal Systems*, p. 303. Also see, for example, Richard E. Crable, "Models of Argumentation and Judicial Judgment," *The Journal of the American Forensic Association*, XII (Winter 1976), 113–20.

85. Rupert Cross, quoted in Stone, *Legal Systems*, p. 315. Law is not in the first instance

a deduction from rules for several reasons: (1) precedents usually compete, and the judge has discretion to choose among them; (2) statutes and precedents are often ambiguous, and it is difficult or impossible to establish what the rule (under which the case at bar will provide a minor premise) even is; (3) the level to which the previous *ratio* is generalized is arbitrary; (4) past *dicta* are not binding.

86. Levi, *Legal Reasoning,* p. 2.

87. Stone, *Legal Systems,* p. 316. See also John Dewey, "Logical Method and Law" and Edwin W. Patterson, "Logic in the Law," in Ray D. Hensen, ed., *Landmarks of Law* (Boston: Beacon Press, 1960), pp. 127–57.

88. Stone, *Legal Systems,* p. 315.

89. See Stone, *Legal Systems,* p. 301, n. 3.

90. On various types of inductive inference, see S.F. Barker, "Must Every Inference Be Either Deductive or Inductive?" in Max Black, ed., *Philosophy in America* (Ithaca: Cornell University Press, 1965), pp. 58–73. See also *G.A.,* p. 209.

91. John Stuart Mill, *A System of Logic.* Edited by J. M. Robson. Vols. VII and VIII in *Collected Works* (Toronto: University of Toronto Press, 1963).

92. See, for example, Angell, *Reasoning and Logic,* pp. 281–96. Cf. Walter J. Ong, S.J., "Newman's Essay on Development in Its Intellectual Milieu," in Joseph Houppert, ed., *John Henry Newman* (St. Louis: B. Herder Book Company, n.d.), p. 43: "The parallel between the inductive process and the steps which, under grace, precede that act of faith as Newman described them . . . is of course not exact. Unlike a real induction, this process leads to a singular: 'God has revealed.' But it does suggest an induction in that it is a process leading to a higher level of intelligibility. . . .: Cf. *G.A.,* p. 209.

93. See M. Jamie Ferreira, *Scepticism and Reasonable Doubt* (Oxford: Clarendon Press, 1986), p. 182; *L. D.,* XXI, p. 146; *Wisdom,* "Gods," p. 157; see also Quintilian, *Institutes,* V, 12, 4–6; and Chaim Perelman and L. Olbrechts-Tyteca, *The New Rhetoric* (Notre Dame: University of Notre Dame press, 1969), pp. 471–74.

94. See *T. P.,* pp. 106–12; *G. A.,* pp. 239–41.

95. *Studies,* p. 58. I am aware that the nature of the enthymeme has been hotly contested by rhetoricians (and some philosophers) over the past few decades. I find Arnhart and Grimaldi the most persuasive. For a counter–statement, see Thomas M. Conley, "The Enthymeme in Perspective," *Quarterly Journal of Speech* (May 1984), pp. 168–87.

96. Raphael Demos, "On Persuasion," *The Journal of Philosophy,* XXIX (April 1932), p. 228. See also Michael Polanyi, *Personal Knowledge* (Chicago: University of Chicago Press, 1958), p. 267: "This then is our liberation from objectivism: to realize that we can voice our ultimate convictions only from within . . . the whole system of acceptances that are logically prior to any particular assertion of our own. . . ."

97. "On Persuasion," p. 229.

98. "On Persuasion," p. 230. See also note 109 below.

99. See Wayne Brockriede, "Where is Argument?" *The Journal of the American Forensic Association,* IX (Spring 1975), pp. 179–82, who reminds us that arguments "are not in statements but in people" (p. 179); see also *T. P.,* p. 56: "To say words *mean* things is incorrect for *words* can mean nothing. *I* mean."

100. *Mental Philosophy,* p. 152.

101. Cf. *G.A.,* p. 200, where Newman comments on a certain argument on behalf of the truth of Christianity: "Many have been converted and sustained in their faith by this argument, which admits of being powerfully stated; but still such statement is after all only intended to be a vehicle of thought, and to open the mind to the apprehension of the facts of

the case, and to trace them and their implications in outline, not to convince by the logic of its mere wording." See Fisher, *Human Communication*, pp. 88–9; and the excellent example of what I am arguing here in Michael Leff, "Topical Invention and Metaphorical Interaction," *The Southern Speech Communication Journal*, XLVIII (Spring 1983), p. 226: ". . . the metaphor fills out and completes the tendencies of the propositional logic."

102. On this point see Charles W. Kneupper, "On Argument and Diagrams," *The Journal of the American Forensic Association*, XIV (Spring 1978), p. 183: ". . . [N]o theorist/critic can expect a diagram to [capture the full persuasive effect of an argument] when abstacted from the . . . context in which it is utilized."

103. Jay Newman, *Mental Philosophy*, p. 152.

104. Richard Rorty, *Philosophy and the Mirror of Nature* (Princeton: Princeton University Press, 1979), p. 316.

105. See also *G.A.*, p. 228: ". . . the individual is supreme, and responsible to himself, nay, under circumstances, may be justified in opposing himself to the judgment of the whole world. . . ." See also Polanyi, *Personal Knowledge*, p. 265: "I have insisted on this before on diverse occasions: pointing out repeatedly that we must accredit our own judgment as the paramount arbiter of all our intellectual performances."

106. This appeal to *sensus communis* is similar to that in *Truth and Method*, (p. 22), where Gadamer, endorsing the principle as it occurs in Vico, writes: "For Vico . . . the *sensus communis* is the sense of the right and the general good that is to be found in all men, moreover, a sense that is acquired through living in the community and is determined by its structures and aims."

107. See also *G.A.*, p. 197: "I should determine the particular case by its particular circumstances, by the combination of many uncatalogued experiences floating in my memory, of many reflections, variously produced, felt rather than capable of statement; *and if I had them not, I should go to those who had*" (emphasis added).

108. Among the many one might cite, see, for example, Stanley Fish, *Is There a Text in This Class? The Authority of Interpretive Communities* (Cambridge: Harvard University Press, 1980), who argues for a radical indeterminacy in texts on the basis that all reading is interpretation and all interpretation is self-confirming (because there are no "facts" to appeal to outside of interpretations); see for example ch. 15, "What Makes an Interpretation Acceptable?" For a similar view among philosophers see Richard Rorty. Among rhetoricians one might cite Paolo Valesio and even Kenneth Burke. For an early and not wholly adequate response to deconstructionist, Fishian and other claims for radical indeterminacy, see M.H. Abrams, "How to Do Things with Texts", *Partisan Review*, XLVI (1979), pp. 566–88. More recently (and persuasively) see Wayne C. Booth, *The Company We Keep: Ethical Criticism and the Ethics of Reading* (Berkeley: The University of California Press, 1988), esp. Part I.

109. "Pragmatism's Conception of Truth," in John J. McDermott, ed., *The Writings of William James*, pp. 431, 435.

110. Van A. Harvey, *The Historian and the Believer*, pp. 204–45. If we drop the idea that such systems are *simply* arbitrary we have a position similar to that of Rorty. I thoroughly agree with Richard J. Bernstein's conclusion that Rorty is *farther* from the pragmatists (like Dewey) whom he appeals to than are Gadamer and Habermas; see "Philosophy in the Conversation of Mankind," in *Philosophical Profiles* (Philadelphia: University of Pennsylvania Press, 1986), pp. 55–6: ". . . once we realize that we are dealing with forms of discourse which differ from each other in degree and not in kind, once we realize that effective rationality is always a form of *rational* persuasion which can never attain a definitive ahistorical closure, then the reflective task would seem to be to clarify the

different forms of *phronesis* and *rational* persuasion." Apart from its contemporary tone, this sentence (note the combination of prudence and rhetoric) could easily be Newman's.

111. In *Literature Against Itself: Literary Ideas in Modern Society* (Chicago: The University of Chicago Press, 1979), p. 202, Gerald Graff makes a similar argument to the one pursued here:

> It may be true, as Wittgenstein says, that all seeing is *seeing as,* and that the aspect under which we see things is determined by our "language games." But I cannot decide to see my four walls or typewriter or this page in front of me as something wholly other than what they are—as the Pacific Ocean, say—or not to see them at all, whereas I can decide, if I like, not to be a philosophical realist in my interpretation of these experiences. My experience of my room is *given* and *unrefusable* in a way that my attempt to interpret this experience philosophically cannot be, though both my experience and my interpretation of it are constructions.

Thus Kenneth Burke refers to the "recalcitrance" of experience in *Permanence and Change* (Indianapolis: Bobbs–Merrill, 1965), p. 256: "Each approaches the universe from a different 'point of view,' and the difference in point of view will reveal a corresponding difference in the discovery of relevant 'facts.' Such a position does not involve us in subjectivism, or solipsism. It does not imply that the universe is merely the product of our interpretations. For the interpretations themselves must be altered as the universe displays various orders of recalcitrance to them." Newman would argue that much about *human nature* comprises one of those orders, that is, is *rhetorically* unrefusable in the way much of external reality is. For an illuminating study of this "sanction of the natural," see Ferreira, *Scepticism and Reasonable Doubt,* esp. chs. 7–9.

112. Graff, *Literature Against Itself,* pp. 202, 203; emphasis added.

113. See *Prepos.,* pp. 293–95. Similar general criteria are advanced by Thomas Kuhn, quoted in Basil Mitchell, *The Justification of Religious Belief* (New York: Oxford University Press, 1981), pp. 80ff.; John Wisdom, "Gods," in *Philosophy and Psycho-Analysis*; and Wayne C. Booth, *Critical Understanding: The Powers and Limits of Pluralism* (Chicago: University of Chicago Press, 1979), esp. pp. 219–32.

114. Richard J. Bernstein, *Beyond Objectivism and Relativism: Science, Hermeneutics, and Praxis* (Philadelphia: University of Pennsylvania Press, 1983), p. 155. Cf. Raymond Williams, *Marxism and Literature* (London: Oxford University Press, 1977), pp. 115–16:

> Most versions of 'tradition' can be quickly shown to be radically selective. From a whole possible area of past and present, in a particular culture, certain meanings and practices are are selected for emphasis and certain other meanings and practices are neglected or excluded. Yet, within a particular hegemony, and as one of its decisive processes, this selection is presented and usually successfully passed off as 'the tradition,' 'the significant past.' What has then to be said about any tradition is that it is in this sense an aspect of *contemporary* social and cultural organization, in the interest of the dominance of a specific class.

But note also Booth's response to such an argument in *Critical Understanding,* p. 232: "That's precisely what the effort of human understanding is based on: the assumption that one code *will* dominate over another in such a way as to establish the superiority, in a given setting, of some readings over some other readings."

115. "A Review of Gadamer's Truth and Method," in Fred R. Dallmayr and Thomas A. McCarthy, *Understanding and Social Inquiry* (Notre Dame: University of Notre Dame Press, 1977), p. 358.

116. *Beyond Objectivism and Relativism,* p. 156.

117. "Interpretation and Its Discontents," in Stanley B. Messer, Louis A. Sass, and Robert L. Woolfolk, eds., *Hermeneutics and Psychological Theory* (New Brunswick: Rutgers University Press, 1988), pp. 89–90.

CHAPTER FOUR

1. See, for example, *Prepos.* p. 57; *Dev.*, pp. 110–12; Lash, *Newman on Development,* ch. 2.

2. The question whether Newman was a "true" historian will find different answers, depending on different philosophies of history. Harrold is more or less correct to answer this question negatively, inasmuch as Newman never took up history "professionally," as "intrinsically interesting" (*John Henry Newman,* p. 223), and Harold correctly contrasts Newman's "critical and polemical" work with the writing of history as such. But see Chadwick, *From Bossuet to Newman,* p. 99, for a more positive assessment of Newman's historical sense.

3. *John Henry Newman,* p. 223; also pp. 223–24: "Yet it remains true that, regardless of the moral or polemical aims in these essays [i.e., *Historical Sketches,*], Newman's historical writings hold our interest as narratives."

4. Although Newman denies *copia* of ideas and so on to the writer or speaker as such (*Idea,* p. 243), the man or woman of good illative judgment would necessarily possess such in order to be able to judge probabilities and cases. Cf. J. Derek Holmes, "Cardinal Newman's Apologetic Use of History," *Louvain Studies,* 55 (Fall 1973), 338–49.

5. The sort of historical enterprise alluded to is described by Carl Hempel in "The Function of General Laws in History," *The Journal of Philosophy,* 39 (January 1943), pp. 35–7.

6. *John Henry Newman,* pp. 224–25.

7. For a comparable juxtaposition of "insight" *(ingenium)* as imaginative apprehension of the real, topics as instruments of discovery and invention, and *copia* as that upon which topics work, see John D. Schaeffer, "Vico's Rhetorical Model of the Mind: Sensus Communis in the *De nostri temporis studiorum ratione," Philosophy and Rhetoric,* 14 (Summer 1981), pp. 158: ". . . one can say that the topics are a method by which ingenuity can exhaust the probable arguments on a subject, and *copia* is the store of words and experiences upon which ingenuity works."

8. *Method,* p. 75.

9. Specifically, Norris wrongly reduces what were antecedent "considerations" for Newman, to antecedent "probabilities"; many "considerations" are not probable at all (e.g., God, Church, dogma), but are held as truths. Norris further reduces "antecedent probabilities" to "hypotheses," again wrongly, since many such probabilities are used, not just *tentatively* to locate possible relevancies, but *positively* to assess the status of further evidence or facts—to "colour the facts" (*OUS,* 227). These errors derive from Norris's incomplete grasp of "real apprehension" and from his mistaken belief that the method of the *Essay* exhausts what is actually a richer and more comprehensive notion of method, adumbrated in the *Grammar.* Real apprehension of a concrete fact for Norris is always (mistakenly) of a "totality"—while apprehension, depending upon its clarity, could function as a hypothesis—it is more common to "really apprehend" an object in only *some* of its (infinite) aspects. It is misleading for Norris to separate "experience" and "data of the problem" from apprehension proper; data themselves, after all, must be apprehended, and so as must a "problem." As a result of these errors, Norris's formulation of real apprehension

and informal inference cannot cope with the way Newman talks of moving from an incomplete to a more complete grasp of a fact. Nor does Norris have anything specific to say about the persuasive nature of Newman's method.

10. Newman's primary concern, after all, was defending the legitimacy of religious judgment, not exploring strategies of rhetorical invention.

11. Lash, *Newman on Development* p. 35.

12. Lash, *Newman on Development*, p. 36.

13. See "Note A: Liberalism" in *Apo.*, p. 261, especially proposition 9: "There is a right of Private Judgment: that is, there is no existing authority on earth competent to interfere with the liberty of individuals in reasoning and judging for themselves about the Bible and its contents, as they severally please;" also *V.M.*, I, Lectures V and VI.

14. See *Apo.*, p. 53; also *V.M.*, I, p. 40.

15. See Walgrave, *Newman the Theologian*, p. 45: "In it [the *Via Media*] he aims at setting out the doctrinal basis of his theology. . . . He treats mainly the sources and rules of the faith."

16. Cf. Chadwick, *From Bossuet to Newman*, p. 88 (but see also p. 12 for a more nuanced view of the Protestant position). What Chadwick refers to as theoretical and empirical levels, Newman calls the theoretical and practical. On the theoretical level he attacks the Protestant's "antecedent notion" ("that, when God speaks by inspiration, all other external means" of judgment, besides Scripture alone, "are superseded") as "self-inconsistent" and "arbitrary" (*V.M.*, I, 131). On the practical level he points to actual facts, and to consequences (i.e., Latitudinarianism) deriving from their position, which serve to subvert it. These latter are clearly the more important and decisive, in keeping with Newman's view that, unless some ultimate principle is at stake (such as the Church itself), consequences, actions, facts, and so on, are the test of "theory": "The primacy of the ancient Church, and the stability of its teaching and practice—these are the basis of the Tractarian theory of authority. . ." (Chadwick, p. 88).

17. Cf. *V.M.*, I, p. 35: "If then we would leave ourselves room for proving that Scripture is inspired, we must not reject the notion and principle of the argument from tradition and from Antiquity. . . . In other words, to refuse to listen to these informants because we have a written word [Scripture], is a self–destructive course, inasmuch as the written word itself is proved to be such mainly by these very informants which, as if to do honour to it, we reject."

18. See *V.M.*, I, p. 48: ". . . there is striking dissimilarity, or even inconsistency between their system as quiescent, and as in action, in its abstract principles, and its reasonings and discussion on particular points." Cf. *Apo.*, p. 101.

19. Cf. *V.M.*, I, "Preface to the Third Edition" (1877), p. xxii:

Such is an hypothesis; and, to come to the subject of these Lectures, such also is the *Via Media,* a possible road, lying between a mountain and a morass, to be driven through formidable obstacles, if it is to exist, by the boldness and skill of the engineers. It is projected and planned for a definite necessity, the necessity of the Anglican position. . . . And this dressing up of an hypothesis being the scope of the Author's undertaking here, it is not wonderful, . . . that he should aim at consistency in his statements rather than at proof founded on evidence. . . .

20. See *V.M.*, I, pp. 46–7.

21. Since my purpose here, and in general, is to explain the coherence of Newman's thought and method—that is, to "get a view," a "lie of the country"—the danger is too *many* details, whether with respect to "infallibility," the "prophetical office," the Oxford Move-

ment, or anything else. What is needed is to rise above these facts without losing sight of them, as Newman suggests in the previous note.

22. Church, *The Oxford Movement*, p. 91: "Thus had been started [in the Tracts] . . . a great enterprise. . . . There was no thought as yet of acting on the middle classes, or on the ignorance and wretchedness of the great towns, though Newman had laid down that the Church must rest on the people. . . ." Cf. also *Apo.*, p. 48, quoted in the previous chapter: "No great work was done by a system; whereas systems rise out of individual exertions."

23. To expound, or worse, merely to reiterate abstract truths would be doubly unreal, denying two crucial aspects of the concrete fact—the audience, whose views concretize the problem of religion, and the question of how such truths are originally won.

24. This is what Newman really means when he says in the *Apologia* that it was his method to jump *in medias res;* this is not just a "custom" (Norris, *Method*, p. 58), but a methological device.

25. Principles control facts just as facts control principles; see Walgrave, *Newman the Theologian*, p. 114.

26. Cf. *V.M.*, I, p. 147: "Do you really mean to say, that men and women, as we find them in life, are able to reduce these doctrines from Scripture, to determine how far Scripture goes in implying them, to decide upon the exact force of its terms, and the danger of this or that derivation from them?"

27. Cf. *Apo.*, p. 101: ". . . in my Prophetical Office, I view as simply separate ideas, Rome quiescent, and Rome in action." "I drew a parallel distinction between Anglicism quiescent, and Anglicanism in action."

28. Quoted in Culler, *Imperial Intellect*, p. 196.

29. *Imperial Intellect*, p. 197; cf. also Yearley, *The Ideas of Newman*, pp. 8–9.

30. *Newman on Development*, pp. 42–4.

31. Culler, *Imperial Intellect*, p. 197.

32. Cf. *Apo.*, p. 100: "I have said already that, though the object of the Movement was to withstand the Liberalism of the day, I found and felt this could not be done by mere negatives. It was necessary for us to have a positive Church theory erected on a definite basis. This took me to the great Anglican divines; and then of course I found at once that it was impossible to form any such theory, without cutting across the teaching of the Church of Rome. Thus came in the Roman controversy."

33. Bishop Butler, quoted in Lash, *Newman on Development*, p. 35.

34. *Apo.*, p. 92. See Rev. Edmund Darvil Benard, *A Preface to Newman's Theology* (St. Louis: B. Herder Book Company, 1946), p. 31, who says that Newman was "painfully fair" to his opponents. For an example of how Newman combines the concede–and–lead with the *reductio absurdum*, see *Apo* p. 51: "I was not unwilling to draw an opponent on step by step, by virtue of his own opinions, to the brink of some intellectual absurdity, and to leave him to get back as he could." See also *Dev.*, p. viii: "Perhaps his confidence in the truth and availableness of this view has sometimes led the author to be careless and over–liberal in his concessions to Protestants of historical fact."

35. See Gunter Biemer, *Newman on Tradition* (London: Herder and Herder, 1967), p. 54.

36. Again, one can say of the *Via Media* what Walter Ong ("Newman's Essay on Development," in Houppert, ed., *John Henry Newman*, pp. 36–7) said of the *Essay:* "Newman had set out to argue against Evangelical Protestants and Anglicans, both of whom theoretically based their religious views on revelation, but we do not find him joining issue with them primarily on the ground of the content of revelation. We do not find one side

maintaining that it says this and the other side maintaining that it says that, after the fashion to most parties to disputes over revealed doctrine. It is not a question of what God says, but of what His deposited doctrine does. . . ." Here, of course, it is less a question of what doctrine does as what the interpreters of doctrine do.

37. See *On Consulting the Faithful in Matters of Doctrine*, edited with an introduction by John Coulson (Kansas City: Sheed and Ward, 1961).

38. Church, *Oxford Movement*, p. 13.

39. Church, *Oxford Movement*, p. 19.

40. Church, *Oxford Movement*, p. 18.

41. Church, *Oxford Movement*, p. 20.

42. Church, *Oxford Movement*, p. 21. See also Thomas Mozley, *Reminiscences* (Boston: Houghton Mifflin and Company, 1882), pp. 408–18; and Faber, *Oxford Apostles, passim.*

43. *Oxford Movement*, p. 133; cf. also *Apo.*, p. 70.

44. Dessain, "Cardinal Newman on the Theory and Practice of Knowledge," p. 23. On the question of whether or not Newman was successful in his own pastoral ministry, see Rev. James Tolhurst, "The Idea of the Church as a Community in the Anglican Sermons of John Henry Newman," *The Downside Review*, 101 (April 1983), p. 147.

45. Cf. Samuel Ijsseling, *Rhetoric and Philosophy in Conflict: An Historical Survey* (The Hague: Martinus Nijhof, 1976), p. 77.

46. Cf. *V.M.*, I, p. 129. "But the middle path adopted by the English Church cannot be so easily mastered by the mind, first because it is a mean, and has in consequence a complex nature, involving a combination of principles, and depending on multiplied conditions; next, because it partakes of that indeterminateness which, as has been already observed, is to a certain extent characteristic of English theology. . . ."

47. See, for example, *G.A.*, pp. 321, 349. For a similar analysis, see Harvey, *The Historian and the Believer*.

48. See "Monophysitism" in *New Catholic Encyclopedia*, IX (New York: McGraw–Hill Book Company, 1967), p. 1064: "The schismatic and eventually heretical movement that sprang from the exaggerated insistence on one nature . . . in Jesus Christ. The actual heretical concept of the absorption of the divine nature in the human nature or vice versa is called Eutychianism after the fifth–century Constantinopolitan archimandrite, Eutyches." Cf. *Apo.*, pp. 108–9:

> 'It was difficult to make out how the Eutychians or Monophysites were heretics, unless Protestants and Anglicans were heretics also; difficult to find arguments against the Tridentine Fathers, which did not tell against the Fathers of Chalcedon. . . . The principles and proceedings of the Church now, were those of the Church then; the principles and proceedings of heretics then, were those of Protestants now. . . . The shadow of the fifth century was on the sixteenth. . . . What was the use of continuing the controversy, or defending my position, if, after all, I was forging arguments for Arius or Eutyches, and turning devil's advocate against the much-enduring Athanasius and the majestic Leo?'

49. "The whole world judges with assurance." See "Donatism" in *New Catholic Encylopedia*, IV (Washington, D. C.: The Catholic University of America, 1967), p. 1001: "A schismatic movement that affected the Church in North Africa during the 4th and 5th centuries, Donatism was primarily religious in origin and stemmed from an exaggerated insistence on the holiness of the minister in the confection of the sacramental rites. . . ."

50. Cf. Biemer, *Newman on Tradition*, pp. 48ff., on how the idea of development had

been foreshadowed in Newman's thought, not only in the Oxford sermon of 1843, but in many other works, including the *Via Media*.

51. Cf. *Apo.*, p. 138:

> As soon as I saw the hitch in the Anglican argument, during my course of reading in the summer of 1839, I began to look about, as I have said, for some ground which might supply a controversial basis for my need. The difficulty in question had affected my view both of Antiquity and Catholicity; for, while the history of St. Leo showed me that the deliberate and eventual consent of the great body of the Church ratified a doctrinal decision as a part of revealed truth, it also showed that the rule of Antiquity was not infringed, though a doctrine had not been publicly recognized as so revealed, till centuries after the time of the apostles.

52. This pronouncement is itself an obviously rhetorical one, pointing to the genuine *audience* for (though not to the means of attaining) religious truth, and replacing the *"quod semper"* etc. of Vincent Lérins.

53. Cf. *Dev.*, pp. 52–3, where Newman indicates that ideas often begin as "an impression on the Imagination" and only later become "a system or creed in the Reason"; also John Coulson, *Religion and Imagination,* pp. 53–9.

54. *DMC*, 233: "God Deals with us very differently; conviction comes slowly to some men, quickly to others; in some it is the result of much thought and many reasonings, in others of a sudden illumination."

55. Chadwick, *From Bossuet to Newman,* p. 157.

56. Perhaps I can better make this point by locating the stages on Newman's way towards Rome by indicating the kinds of "facts" with which he was primarily concerned: (1) 1839: I have already indicated how the Monophysite and Donastist heresies, and the re-interpretation of Augustine, imposed on Newman a new position; thus, historical and doctrinal argument provides the major source of change; (2) Reaction: Newman's response over the next two years was first "negative," then "positive." As he notes, after encountering Augustine, "I had no longer a distinctive plea for Anglicanism, unless I would be a Monophysite. I had . . . to fall back upon my three original points of belief" (*Apo.*, 101)—dogma, Church, anti–Rome—the first two of which, however, "were better secured in Rome." Newman was thus left with what he terms the "practical principle" and "negative ground" of Anti–Romanism: "Instead then of speaking of errors in doctrine, I was driven . . . to insist upon the political conduct, the controversial bearing, and the social methods . . . of Rome" (*Apo.*, 103). In other words, the "stuff" of Newman's thought and argument had changed: historical interpretation and the study of texts gives way to the practical acts of Rome (past and present). This same material, however, is then used somewhat more positively in *Tract* 90, where Newman more generously distinguishes doctrinal truths held by Rome, from her popular errors; (3) The Three Blows (1841): (a) "In the Arian History I found the very same phenomenon, in a far bolder shape, which I had found in the Monophysite" (*Apo.*, 114); (b) "The Bishops one after another began to charge against me. . . . I recognized it as a condemnation" (*Apo.*, 115); (c) The Jerusalem Bishopric, which united Anglicans with Protestants without respect of theological beliefs, ". . . was the third blow, which finally shattered my faith in the Anglican Church" (*Apo.*, 117). In this third stage, again, *acts* are as important as verbal argument.

57. Cf. *OUS*, p. 219.

58. In their own ways each of Newman's major works tells such a story of transformation, seeks to transform, and offers at least an example (if not a full–blown rhetoric) of the method or art of transformation. Thus the Oxford sermons, like the *Grammar,* focuses on

the religious believer, argues by converging probabilities, and provides an *organum investigandi*. The *Via Media* and the *Essay on the Development of Christian Doctrine* "narrate" the story of the transformation of Scripture to doctrine (or doctrine to doctrine), argue persuasively, and seek to edify and transform, and offer "rhetorics" of such transformations. And *The Idea of a University* describes the transformation of the young scholar, seeks to transform the reader, and offers a rhetoric of liberal education. In the *Apologia* Newman construed Kingsley's interest to be less in *what* Newman meant ("not my words, not my arguments, not my actions") than *how* he meant what he did ("that living intelligence, by which I write, and argue, and act").

59. See DeLaura, "Newman's *Apologia* as Prophecy," in DeLaura, ed., *Apo.*, p. 494.

60. Again, this seems to me a reasonable account of Newman's shift of the *status* of Kingsley's case against him, from a formulaic "what" to a more dynamic "how."

61. Cf. Chadwick, *From Bossuet to Newman*, p. 165; *Dev.*, p. 29.

62. Cf. Ong, "Newman's Essay on Development in its Intellectual Milieu," in Joseph Houppert, ed., *John Henry Newman*, p. 48–9: ". . . the dispute which the *Essay on Development* signalizes is conducted as a philosophical rather than as a theological dispute, as an attack on an error which is not primarily theological, but which runs through any monistic—idealistic or materialistic—explanation of reality. . . ."

63. *From Bossuet to Newman*, p. 157.

64. Chadwick, *From Bossuet to Newman*, p. 155.

65. *Newman on Development*, p. 48.

66. "Newman's Essay on Development," in Houppert, ed., *John Henry Newman*, p. 40.

67. See also *Dev.*, p. 113.

68. Cf. *Dev.*, p. 111: "Physical facts are present; they are submitted to the senses, and the senses may be satisfactorily tested, corrected, and verified. . . . But it is otherwise with history, the facts of which are not present; it is otherwise with ethics, in which phenomena are more subtle, closer, and more personal to individuals than other facts, and not referable to any common standard by which all men can decide upon them."

69. Cf. *ECH*, II, pp. 186–248; *G.A.*, pp. 457ff.; *P.N.* II, p. 151.

70. See Norris, *Method*, Chapter V.

71. *L.D.*, XV, p. 381.

72. Cf. Walgrave, *Newman the Theologian*, p. 241: "Newman's passage from Anglicanism to Catholicism implied a profound change in his conception of apostolic tradition. From a strict application of the rule stated by St. Vincent de Lérins, he went over to the theory of development, sustituting a dynamic for a static conception." It should be noted that my denomination of development above as "mutable doctrine" should not be confused with modernist conceptions of change as "biologistic" or "evolutionary"—as though doctrine were *merely* relative to historical periods and had no integrity as knowledge. On this point see Walgrave, p. 295–96; and Lash, *Change in Focus*.

73. Lash, *Newman on Development* p. 42.

74. Lash, *Newman on Development* p. 43.

75. Lash, *Newman on Development* p. 33.

76. Cf. *Dev.*, pp. 100–1:

If this is, on the whole, a true view of the general shape under which the existing body of developments, commonly called Catholic, present themselves to us, antecedently to our looking into the particular evidence on which they stand, I think we shall be at no loss to determine what both logical truth and duty prescribe to us as to our reception of them. It is very little to say that we should treat them as we are accustomed to treat other alleged facts and truths and the evidence for them, such as come to us with a fair presumption in their favour. Such are of everyday's occurrence; and what is our behaviour towards them? We meet them, not with suspicion and criticism, but with a frank confidence. We do not in the first instance exercise our reason upon opinions which are received, but of our faith.

See also Coulson's discussion on ideas being first "credible to the imagination," *Religion and Imagination,* pp. 46ff.

77. *Newman on Development,* p. 80.

78. Norris, *Method,* p. 71.

79. Norris, *Method,* p. 73; cf. Walgrave, *Newman the Theologian,* p. 265, on the first "note": "It should now be evident that the normative force of a rule like this one can be appreciated only by considering each phenomenon it applies to, not in isolation, but as an element in a wider whole. The life of an idea is only one aspect of a wider life, that of a single living whole, one and many–sided, the life of a whole community." Also Chadwick, *Bossuet to Newman,* p. 155: the "seven 'tests' which Newman half-heartedly alleged for distinguishing true developments from false developments [are] (tests which are rather pegs on which to hang a *historical* thesis than solid supports for doctrinal explanation). . . ."

80. *Newman on Development,* p. 101; *Three Uses of Christian Discourse,* "The Loci of Authority," p. 161.

81. Hans Küng, *Infallible? An Inquiry* (Garden City, N.Y.: Doubleday and Company, Inc., 1983). p. 233.

82. Newman quoted in Jeremy Miller O.P., "Newman's Dialogical Vision of the Church," *Louvain Studies,* 8 (Spring 1981), p. 324. See also *Apo.,* pp. 238–39.

83. Miller, "Newman's Dialogical Vision," p. 326.

CHAPTER FIVE

1. "Literature," in *Idea,* pp. 226–45. Cf. Harrold, *John Henry Newman,* p. 255: "Our principal source for Newman's mature conception of literature is in fact *The Idea of a University.*"

2. Cf. Culler, *Imperial Intellect,* p. 237: "In his essay on 'Literature,' he distinguished the writing which merits that name (and under which he included the whole range of the humanities) from science. . . ."

3. Cf. Campbell, *Philosophy of Rhetoric,* p. 3: "The imagination is addressed by exhibiting to it a lively and beautiful representation of a suitable object. As in this exhibition, the task of the orator may, in some sort, be said, like that of the painter, to consist in imitation. . . ."

4. *Rhetoric,* p. 4: "I propose in the present work to adopt a middle course between these two extreme points [rhetoric defined as "all composition in prose," and as "persuasive speaking"]; and to treat of 'Argumentative Composition,' *generally,* and *exclusively;* considering Rhetoric . . . as an off–shoot from Logic."

5. Newman, "Poetry, with Reference to Aristotle's *Poetics,*' in *ECH,* I, pp. 1–29.

6. See M. H. Abrams, *The Mirror and the Lamp* (New York: Oxford University Press, 1953), pp. 14–21.

7. Alvan S. Ryan, quoted in Harrold, *John Henry Newman,* p. 248. But see also Newman's letter of 1832 to Rogers, quoted in Maisie Ward, *Young Mr. Newman* (New York: Sheed and Ward, 1948), p. 186: "Do not stirring times bring out poets? Do they not give opportunity for the rhetoric of poetry, and the persuasion?"

8. Harrold, *John Henry Newman*, p. 251.

9. Lash, *Newman on Development*, p. 24.

10. For the combination of "reason" and "speech," or "wisdom" and "eloquence," see, for example, Cicero, *De Inventione,* 6. 7–13; *De Oratore,* 1. 35–47; 3. 15–23; Quintilian, *Institutes,* 8. Pref. 20: "Therefore I would have the orator, while careful in his choice of words, be even more concerned about his subject matter. For, as a rule, the best words are essentially suggested by the subject matter. . . ."

11. Vargish, *Contemplation of Mind,* p. 45.

12. Cf. *G.A.,* p. 173: ". . . It follows that, when words are substituted for symbols, it will be its aim to circumscribe and stint their import as much as possible, lest perchance A should not always exactly mean A, and B mean B; and to make them, as much as possible, the *calculi* of notions, which are in our absolute power, as meaning just what we choose them to mean. . . ."

13. See David F. Rea, "John Henry Newman's Concept of Rhetoric," (Master's Thesis, Fordham University, 1956), p. 73.

14. See *OUS,* p. 271.

15. Walter J. Ong, *The Presence of the Word* (New York: Simon and Shuster, 1967), p. 33.

16. *Presence,* pp. 111, 117.

17. Cf. also *OUS,* p. 61; *G.A.,* pp. 278–79; *PPS,* 7, IV, p. 42.

18. "English Catholic Literature," in *Idea,* p. 261.

19. *Contemplation of Mind,* p. 126.

20. Grassi, *Rhetoric as Philosophy,* pp. 96–7.

21. *Contemplation of Mind,* p. 48; but see also pp. 52ff.

22. Powell, *Three Uses of Christian Discourse,* p. 143.

23. *Three Uses of Christian Discourse,* p. 145.

24. Coulson, *Religion and Imagination,* p. 55.

25. Coulson, *Religion and Imagination,* p. 151.

26. See David Tracy, *Blessed Rage for Order* (New York: The Seabury Press, 1975), ch. 9. I ignore here the considerable differences regarding the nature of religious language between (especially) Newman and Arnold.

27. *Religion and Imagination,* p. 23. As theologian Stephen Happel concludes, regarding Coleridge's views on language and its relation to religion, "Thus the only language that can overcome this dissymmetry between knowing and doing, between the primary subjectivity and its articulation is not information, but a persuasive speech. . . . The heart of these recognitions must be the nature of religious language as a kind of rhetoric, since rhetoric articulates the radically inter–subjective, communicative character of language." "Imagination, Method in Theology, and Rhetoric: On Re–Examining Samuel Taylor Coleridge," *Louvain Studies,* 8 (Fall 1980), pp. 166–67.

28. Cf. Coulson, *Religion and Imagination,* pp. 72ff., "The Social Framework of Belief;" and Polanyi, *Personal Knowledge,* especially chaps. 8 and 10.

29. Coulson, *Religion and Imagination,* p. 29.

30. Cf. Paul Ricoeur, *Interpretation Theory: Discourse and the Surplus of Meaning* (Fort Worth: The Texas Christian University Press, 1976), p. 50: ". . . the tension in a metaphorical utterance is really not something that occurs between two terms in the utterance, but rather between two opposed interpretations of the utterance. It is the conflict between these two interpretations that sustains the metaphor. In this regard, we can even say, in a general fashion, that the strategy of discourse by means of which the metaphoric

utterance obtains its result is absurdity. This absurdity is only revealed through the attempt to interpret the utterance literally."

31. See Grassi, *Rhetoric as Philosophy*, p. 33.

32. "Hume's Explanation of Inductive Inference," in Alexander Sesonske and Noel Fleming, eds., *Human Understanding: Studies in the Philosophy of David Hume* (Belmont, CA: Wadsworth Publishing Company, Inc., 1965), p. 72.

33. *Religion and Imagination*, p. 52.

34. Grassi, *Rhetoric as Philosophy*, p. 33.

35. For Ricoeur, literature and metaphor are the "positive and productive use of ambiquity;" *Interpretation Theory*, p. 47.

36. Michael C. Leff, "Topical Invention and Metaphorical Interaction," *The Southern Speech Communication Journal*, XLVIII (Spring 1983), p. 219.

37. Grassi, *Rhetoric as Philosophy*, p. 99.

38. Cf. Stephen Pepper, *World Hypotheses* (Berkeley: University of California Press, 1942).

39. *Religion and Imagination*, p. 10. See also Leff, "Topical Invention," p. 228: ". . . topical arguments do not seem entirely removed from the imaginative inferences that operate in metaphor."

40. Grassi, *Rhetoric as Philosophy*, pp. 45–6: "The difference between critical and topical philosophy, as worked out by Vico, is by no means a dated, but a very current, problem. Today we are proud, for example, of the science of cybernetics and we rely on it for the future of the human community, but we forget that for it, too, the main problem is finding the points of departure, for the cybernetic process can only work on and draw its conclusions from elements already 'found'. The necessary achievements of human *ingenium* cannot be reduced to purely rational, derivative processes. . . ."

41. Grassi, *Rhetoric as Philosophy*, p. 44: "Vico's rejection of the critical method . . . is based on the recognition that the original premises as such are nondeducible and that the *rational process* hence cannot 'find' them; that, moreover, rational knowledge cannot be a determining factor for rhetorical or poetic speech because it cannot comprehend the particular, the individual, i.e., the concrete situation. . . ." Cf. Valesio, *Novantiqua*, p. 22: "[L]inguistics keeps telling us that straightforward, integrated, informative communication is the norm, while devious, metaphoric, ambiguous linguistic communication . . . is something secondary. . . . But doesn't literature, all of literature (and if not literature, history; if not history, our own private life), if we gaze at it not blinking, tell us that the real harmony is the inverse one . . . ?"

42. Cf. Coulson, *Religion and Imagination*, p. 67.

43. Cf. Kenneth Burke, *A Rhetoric of Motives* (Berkeley: University of California Press, 1969), p. 86: "In keeping with the genius of Hazlitt's expression, 'ideas of the imagination,' we began thinking that there should be a term for ideas and images both. Titles (or 'epithets') seemed to meet the requirement. For the rhetorician uses 'titles' (either imaginal or ideological) to identify a person or a cause with whatever kinds of things will, in his judgment, call forth the desired response. He will select such 'titles' in accordance with the bias of his intention and the opinions of his audience. But what are such 'titles' (or 'entitlings,' or 'identifications') but another term for the Aristotelian 'topics' which shift so easily and imperceptibly between ideas and images that you wonder how the two realms could ever come to be at odds?"

44. Cf. Coulson, *Religion and Imagination*, p. 55: ". . . inquiry is 'inconsistent with assent,' since it implies doubt; investigation, on the other hand, is a necessity. 'In the case of

educated minds . . . such a trial of their intellects is a law of their nature, like the growth of childhood into manhood.' "

45. Cf. Coulson, *Religion and Imagination,* on Newman's *theological* method, p. 55: "This is a method with which we are already familiar in T. S. Eliot and, before him, in Lancelot Andrewes—Christianity is a meeting of virtues which appear to be opposed, but 'sever them, and farewell all.' " Kierkegaard, as well as Newman, describes what has been effected as an equilibrium. This is the master principle of Newman's method as a theologian."

46. Cf. Powell, *Three Uses of Christian Discourse,* p. 4, passim.

47. *Religion and Imagination,* p. 54.

48. Cf. *OUS,* p. 317: "Wonderful it is to see with what effort, hesitation, suspense, interruption,—with how many swayings to the right and to the left—with how many reverses, yet with what certainty of advance, with what precision in its march, and with what ultimate completeness, [any Christian dogma] has been evolved."

49. Coulson, *Religion and Imagination,* p. 66.

50. Jeremy Miller, "Newman's Dialogical Vision of the Church," 8 (Spring 1981), p. 329.

51. Coulson, *Religion and Imagination,* p. 68.

52. See Toulmin, *The Uses of Argument,* pp. 36–8, and Chapters Two, Three and Seven in the present work.

53. See also Tracy, *Blessed Rage for Order,* pp. 210–11.

54. Holloway, *The Victorian Sage,* p. 9.

55. Lash, *Newman on Development,* p. 39.

56. *Religion and Imagination,* p. 50.

57. Ong, "Newman's Essay on Development," in Houppert, ed., *John Henry Newman,* p. 40.

58. Cf. *Idea,* p. 53: "These various partial views or abstractions, by means of which the mind looks out upon its object, are called sciences, and embrace respectively larger or smaller portions of the field of knowledge; sometimes extending far and wide, but superficially, sometimes with exactness over particular departments, sometimes occupied together on one and the same portion, sometimes holding one part in common, and then ranging on this side or that in absolute divergence one from another."

59. Cf. Idea, p. 346–47:

I think I am not mistaken in the fact that there exists, both in the educated and half–educated portions of the community, something of a surmise or misgiving, that there really is at bottom a certain contrariety between the declarations of religion and the results of physical inquiry; a suspicion such that, while it encourages those persons who are not over–religious to anticipate a coming day, when at length the difference will break out into open conflict, to the disadvantage of Revelation, it leads religious minds, on the other hand, who have not had the opportunity of considering accurately the state of the case, to be jealous of the researches, and prejudiced against the discoveries, of Science. The consequence is, on the one side, a certain contempt of Theology; on the other, a disposition to undervalue, to deny, to ridicule, to discourage, and almost to denounce, the labours of the physiological, astronomical, or geological investigator.

60. Lash, *Newman on Development,* p. 13: "In 1945 Nédoncelle charged the majority of French Newmanists with overlooking the fact that, as a controversialist, Newman regularly accepted his opponent's choice of weapons . . . (1945, p. 72).' "

61. *Newman on Development*, p. 26.
62. *Newman on Development*, p. 26.
63. Cf. Idea, p. 349:

In Physics is comprised that family of sciences which is concerned with the sensible world, with the phenomena which we see, hear, and handle, or, in other words, with matter. It is the philosophy of matter. Its basis of operations, what it starts from, what it falls back upon, is the phenomena which meet the senses. Those phenomena it ascertains, catalogues, compares, combines, arranges, and then uses for determining something beyond themselves, *viz.*, the order to which they are subservient, or what we commonly call the laws of nature. It never travels beyond the examination of cause and effect.

64. I might note that this personalizing of the ostensibly impersonal is a tendency manifested also in "The Influences of Natural and Revealed Religion Respectively" (1830), where Newman construed a "completion" of natural facts in a revealed *Person,* and observed what he called a "method of Personation" throughout Revelation and Church structures.

CHAPTER SIX

1. For historical and textual background see Fergal McGrath, S. J., *Newman's University: Idea and Reality* (London: Longmans, Green and Co., 1951); I. T. Ker, "Editor's Introduction," in *The Idea of a University*. Edited with introduction and notes by I. T. Ker (Oxford: At the Clarendon Press, 1976), pp. xi–lxxv; Martin J. Svaglic, "Introduction," in *The Idea of a University*. Edited with an introduction by Martin J. Svaglic (Notre Dame: Notre Dame University Press, 1982), pp. viii–xxvii; Culler, *The Imperial Intellect,* chs. 6–8; Richard W. Clancey, "Dublin Discourses: Rhetorical Method in Textual Revisions," *Renascence,* XX (Winter 1968), 59–74; *L. D.,* XIV, *passim;* Ward, I, pp. 305–416.

2. For an overview and background see, for example, W. H. G. Armytage, "The Conflict of Ideas in University Education: 1850–1867," *Educational Thought,* 3 (1953), pp. 327–43; also Crane, "Shifting Definitions and Evaluations of the Humanities," pp. 126ff.; and Bruce A. Kimball, *Orators and Philosophers: A History of the Idea of Liberal Education* (New York: Teachers College, Columbia University, 1986).

3. Clark Kerr, *The Uses of the University* (New York: Harper and Row, 1963). For a brief history of the rise of the modern university, see Charles Wegener, *Liberal Education and the Modern University* (Chicago: The University of Chicago Press, 1978), ch. 1–2, and Kimball, *Orators and Philosophers,* chs. V and VI.

4. "Some Thoughts Concerning Education," in *John Locke on Education*. Edited, with an Introduction and Notes, by Peter Gay (New York: Bureau of Publications, Columbia University, 1964), p. 165.

5. Among those Newman had in mind here is Macaulay, whose essay on Bacon he had before him as he wrote (Culler, *Imperial Intellect,* p. 187). Thus Macaulay writes (*Essays and Poems,* II, p. 229): "An acre in Middlesex is better than a principality in Utopia." See also W. H. Burston, ed., *James Mill on Education* (Cambridge: At the University Press, 1969), p. 41, *passim.*

6. See Kimball, *Orators and Philosophers,* pp. 230–31.
7. Vargish, *Contemplation of Mind,* p. 132.
8. *Imperial Intellect,* p. 223.
9. *Imperial Intellect,* p. 222.

10. Again, this is not a matter merely of showing that Newman was consistent in his thinking, as I. T. Ker has done (*Idea,* pp. 613–14), since Culler's real point is that Newman's pragmatic appeal undermines his defense of learning as good in itself—in sum, that Newman concedes too much to the utilitarians. See Culler, "Newman on the Uses of Knowledge," *General Education* (1953), p. 269–79. Also Fergal McGrath, S. J., *The Consecration of Learning: Lectures on Newman's Idea of a University* (New York: Fordham University Press, 1962), p. 198.

11. Walter Pater, "Style," in *Appreciations* (New York: Macmillan Co., 1910), p. 14.

12. As Crane notes ("Shifting Definitions," pp. 157–58), the whole tenor of the discussion about the humanities from the Romans on was "practical and rhetorical;" and Kimball (*Orators and Philosophers,* p. 230) observes that "until the eighteenth century, the usefulness . . . of knowing classical languages and writings for studying the professions was so self–evident as not to require extended comment." So also Alfred North Whitehead, *The Aims of Education* (New York: Macmillan Company, 1929), p. 3: "Pedants sneer at an education which is useful. But if education is not useful, what is it? Is it a talent, to be hidden away in a napkin? Of course, education should be useful, whatever your aim in life. It was useful to Saint Augustine and it was useful to Napoleon. It is useful, because understanding is useful;" and *Idea,* p. 197: "For why do we educate, except to prepare for the world? . . . If then a University is a direct preparation for this world, let it be what it professes. It is not a Convent, it is not a Seminary; it is a place to fit men of the world for the world."

13. Much of the *Idea* itself I ignore here: Discourses One to Four on the place of theology in the university might have been my focus, or Discourses Eight to Nine on the relation of liberal education to the Church; by the same token, I merely refer the reader below for a (minimal) historical background of Newman's discourses. An "exhaustive" account of the *Idea* would relate Newman's theory to his practice as Rector, situate the discourses within the historical context of the original audience, explain in greater depth the connection between moral and intellectual excellence, and so on. If not exhaustive, however, the present account does seek to be comprehensive, though only from a particular aspect, the intellectual.

The Catholic University of Ireland opened its doors in November, 1854. A decade earlier the British government of Sir Robert Peel, in an attempt to conciliate rising Catholic opposition against the injustice of only one university in Ireland, and that chiefly an Anglican institution, proposed in 1845 three "Queen's Colleges," on the then still somewhat new principle of "mixed education"—that is, Catholics and Protestants would be educated together without either religious entrance requirements or religious instruction.

In point of fact, middle–class Irish Catholics had been made familiar with the principle in the National Education Act of 1831 and had even come to embrace it after a fashion, as an improvement in their lot and a practical vehicle for advancement. As Ker notes, however ("Editor's Introduction," in *Idea,* p. xxi), many had grown dissatisfied with the administration of the act in the schools, and this dissatisfaction led, by the time of Peel's proposal, to a not–quite unified Catholic opposition to the new scheme. In 1850 the Catholic Bishops of Ireland, backed by the Vatican, formally condemned the idea of the Queen's Colleges and unrealistically set out to establish their own university on the model of Louvain in Belgium. In April 1851, Newman received a call from Archbishop Paul Cullen of Dublin to help with the project and to deliver several lectures on mixed education. Several months later Newman wrote on the topic, in *The Present Position of Catholics* (1851): "It has lately been forcibly shown that the point which the Catholic Church is maintaining against the British government in Ireland, as respects the Queen's Colleges for the education of the middle and upper classes, is precisely that which Protestantism maintains, and successfully maintains, against that same Government in England—viz., the secular instruction should not be separated from religious. The Catholics of Ireland are asserting the very same principle as the Protestants of England; however, the Minister does not feel the logical force of that fact; and the same persons who think it so tolerable to indulge Protestantism in the one country, are irritated and incensed at a Catholic people for asking to be similarly indulged in the other" (p. 179).

14. It should be clear that I disagree with P. A. Dale ("Newman's 'The Idea of a University': The Dangers of a University Education," *Victorian Studies,* XVI (September, 1972), pp. 5–36), who argues that at bottom the *Idea* is merely a conservative religious reaction to contemporary educational developments (e.g., the reform of Oxford and Cambridge and the rise of London University); and with Walter Cannon, who also finds Newman "reactionary" ("The Normative Role of Science in Early Victorian Thought," *Journal of the History of Ideas,* XXV (October–December 1964), p. 502.

15. John M. Gill ("Newman's Dialectic in *The Idea of a University*," *Quarterly Journal of Speech,* XLV [December 1959], pp. 415–18) rightly identifies Newman's device of moving his discussion along by asking, and then answering, rhetorical questions. This accounts in a general way for the surface rhetorical dynamic of the text, but fails to discern, at the deeper intellectual level, the *rhetorical* "dialectic" (to use Gill's term) that informs Newman's theory and practice. See also Harrold, *John Henry Newman,* pp. 226–27.

16. Timothy Corcoran, S. J. ("Liberal Studies and Moral Aims: A Critical Survey of Newman's Position," *Thought* [June 1926], pp. 54–71) writes that liberal knowledge in Newman is "strictly static, connoting a finished and completed 'state of mind';" and James L. Kinneavey ("Restoring the Humanities: The Return of Rhetoric from Exile," in James J. Murphy, ed., *The Rhetorical Tradition and Modern Writing* [New York: The Modern Language Association, 1982, p. 23] stresses "the disinterested nature of humanistic education" in Newman, going so far as to speculate that it "probably . . . contributed to the decline of the hegemony of rhetoric in the humanities." For similar views see Ben Knights, *The Idea of the Clerisy in the Nineteenth Century* (Cambridge: Cambridge University Press, 1978), p. 195: "Yet, for Newman, the knowledge that really matters is objectively independent of the march of the mind;" and John Beer, "Newman and the Romantic Sensibility," pp. 198, 204.

17. Cf. J. Dover Wilson's claim about Arnold (Mathew Arnold, *Culture and Anarchy.* Edited by J. Dover Wilson [Cambridge: At the University Press, 1969], p. xi) that "Here, in his passion for education . . . is to be found the centre of all his work. . . ." Also Newman in the *Idea,* p. 20: ". . . though it has been my lot for many years to take a prominent . . . part in theological discussions, yet the natural turn of my mind carries me off to trains of [educational] thought like those which I am about to open. . . ."

18. As Crane has argued ("Shifting Definitions," p. 164), "[I]t is possible that if we ask ourselves how these men [writers on liberal education] have approached the study of what they take to be humanistic subject matters we shall find a more satisfactory basis, in a consideration of both the virtue and limitations of their *methods* . . ." (emphasis added).

19. Cf. Gadamer, *Truth and Method,* p. 264: "It is enough to say that we understand in a different way, if we understand at all." For support for this approach to Newman, and a foreshadowing of the project here, see Ian Gregor, "Newman's The Idea of a University: A Text for Today?" in T. R. Wright, ed., *John Henry Newman: A Man for Our Time?* (Newcastle upon Tyne: Grevatt and Grevatt, 1983), pp. 18–27. In revising the Discourses

Newman clearly sought to transcend narrow topical interests: see Clancey, "Dublin Discourses," p. 71; Culler, *Imperial Intellect*, p. 153; Ker, "Editor's Introduction," in *Idea*, p. xxxix.

20. Newman's position in this regard anticipates the hermeneutical theories of Gadamer and Ricoeur. For a discussion of the sort of rhetorical-hermeneutical reading I pursue here, see Barbara Warnick, "A Ricoeurian Approach to Rhetorical Criticism," *The Western Journal of Speech Communication*, 51 (Summer 1987), pp. 227–44. Pertinent articles by Ricoeur appear in Paul Ricoeur, *Hermeneutics and the Social Sciences*. Edited and translated by John B. Thompson (Cambridge: Cambridge University Press, 1981).

21. See, for example, *Idea*, pp. 12, 24, 50, 52, 96.

22. For a modern endorsement of the *rhetor* as oriented to the whole, see Everett Lee Hunt, "General Specialists," *Quarterly Journal of Speech*, II (July 1916), pp. 253–63, and "General Specialists: Fifty Years Later," *Rhetoric Society Quarterly*, XVII (Spring 1987), pp. 167–76.

23. As Culler observes (*Imperial Intellect*, p. 222): "What it [society] gains in the skilled worker it loses in the judicious citizen, and this is a necessary result of the two principles on which society is organized."

24. See *H. S.*, III, pp. 179–91, 213–27.

25. See Harrold, *John Henry Newman*, p. 92: "[Newman's] educated man would be truly a 'liberal individual,' but closer to the pattern of a Roman gentleman in the days of Cicero than to that of a twentieth-century social and economic leader." Harrold qualifies any claims to democratic tendencies in Newman, but in doing so underestimates the radical implications of Newman's views. Newman himself desired no sweeping social changes, but that is a very different thing from his views—educational or otherwise—not having pluralistic and anti-elitist consequences.

26. See, for example, Ben Knights, P. A. Dale, Dwight B. Heath, Timothy Corcoran, S. J.

27. Cf. *Idea*, p. 54: "Viewed altogether, they [the sciences] approximate to a representation or subjective reflection of the objective truth, as nearly as is possible to the human mind, which advances towards the accurate apprehension of that object, in proportion to the number of sciences which it has mastered; and which, when certain sciences are away, in such a case has but a defective apprehension, in proportion to the value of the sciences which are thus wanting, and the importance of the field on which they are employed."

28. See *Idea*, p. 57: "And further, the comprehension of the bearings of one science on another, and the use of each to each, and the location and limitation and adjustment and due appreciation of them all, one with another, this belongs, I conceive, to a sort of science distinct from all of them, and in some sense a science of sciences, which is my own conception of what is meant by Philosophy, in the true sense of the word, and of a philosophical habit of mind, and which in these Discourses I shall call by that name".

29. Others of Newman's contemporaries also speak in terms of "viewing." See, for example, Mill, "Inaugural Address," in *Works*, XXI, p. 219: "The last stage of general education, destined to give the pupil a comprehensive and connected view of things which he has already learnt separately, includes a philosophic study of the methods of the sciences; the modes in which the human intellect proceeds from the known to the unknown."

30. Cf. *Idea*, p. 120–21: "There is no enlargement, unless there be a comparison of ideas one with another, as they come before the mind, and a systematizing of them. We feel our minds to be growing and expanding *then*, when we not only learn, but refer what we learn to what we know already. It is not the mere addition to our knowledge that is the

illumination; but the locomotion, the movement onwards, of that mental centre, to which both what we know, and what we are learning, the accumulating mass of our acquirements, gravitates."

31. Culler, *Imperial Intellect*, p. 109.

32. Sillem, *P.N.*, I, p. 136. This would seem to clash with the idea of the university as geared to *notional* knowledge, but we are surely correct to hold, as John E. Wise does ("Real Knowledge and the University," in Victor R. Yanitelli, S. J., ed., *A Newman Symposium* [New York: Fordham University Press, 1952], p. 57) that Newman's ultimate orientation is to the real.

33. For further instances of this idea, see *PPS*, 2, VIII, p. 84; *P.N.*, II, pp. 5, 11, 17; *Idea*, p. 57.

34. Cf. Culler, *Imperial Intellect*, pp. 218–19: "The mind invade[s] the anarchy of sense perception like the Creator putting forth his virtue over chaos. . . . And yet the order [is] *in* the facts."

35. Cf. *Dev.*, p. 58: "Principles require a very various application according as persons and circumstances vary, and must be thrown into new shapes according to the form of society which they are to influence."

36. *Victorian Sage*, p. 159.

37. Cf. George Levine, *The Boundaries of Fiction* (Princeton: Princeton University Press, 1968), p. 182; and Walter Houghton, *The Victorian Frame of Mind: 1830–1870* (New Haven: Yale University Press, 1957), p. 14.

38. Cf. The Revd. J. P. Marmion, "Newman and Education," *The Downside Review*, 97 (January 1979), p. 29: "[Newman's] understanding of how people reason combines both a very intellectual approach with an appreciation of the role of feeling. It is not a matter of pure passionless reason, but an involvement of the whole of human nature, so that not just the mind, but the whole person is involved. His ideal university, his school, his Oratory were all based upon this understanding, and were designed to allow for proper human development."

39. *Victorian Sage*, p. 160.

40. Graff makes a similar criticism of Northrop Frye in *Literature Against Itself*, p. 182: "The trouble is that Frye never locates a connection between these two orders—though he comes close to doing so in *The Critical Path*, when he says that 'the vision of things as they could or should be certainly has to depend on the vision of things as they are.'" For a defense of Arnold's epistemological realism, see Nathan A. Scott, Jr. *The Poetics of Belief: Studies in Coleridge, Arnold, Pater, Santayana, Stevens, and Heidegger* (Chapel Hill: The University of North Carolina Press, 1985), and Livingston, *Matthew Arnold and Christianity*.

41. Peter Berger and Hansfried Kellner, *Sociology Reinterpreted: An Essay on Vocation and Method* (Garden City, N. Y.: Doubleday and Co., 1981), pp. 51ff. The rhetoric, politics, and hermeneutics of the social sciences are far enough advanced for us to question to what extent bracketing is possible; still, we can at least admit of *degrees* of fixity and indeterminacy. For an excellent discussion of these issues, see Paul Ricoeur, "Science and Ideology," in *Hermeneutics and the Human Sciences*, pp. 222–46, and Bernstein, *Beyond Objectivism and Relativism, passim*.

42. On this point, see Wise, "Newman and the Liberal Arts," p. 65, and Dale, "Dangers," p. 29.

43. Walter J. Ong, "Newman's Essay on Development," in Houppert, ed., *John Henry Newman*, p. 45.

44. See Corcoran, S. J., "Liberal Studies and Moral Aims," pp. 64–5. We should consider, at least briefly, the objection that the *Idea*, after all, says very little about the "whole man"—the phrase itself is never used—or about the moral dimension of liberal education. One reason commonly forwarded as to why the book is silent about these matters is simply that Newman's ideal, at least in its secular aspect, is opposed to morality and religion. Another reason given is that, opposed as intellect and religion are, Newman can be seen to reserve his discussion of these for the last two discourses, so that it is possible to say that Discourses VIII and IX move from "reason" to the "heart" (Dale, "Dangers," pp. 23ff).

But these explanations are manifestly at odds with Newman's explicit caveats in the *Idea*, not to mention with the structure of the text itself as well as Newman's epistemology as a whole. Specifically, the *Idea* is, as Newman says, an abstraction from the whole of the university, considered in its "integrity" and "essence." Newman speaks, for example, of the "philosopher as we are abstractedly conceiving of him" (*Idea*, 123); indeed, the first sentence of the work announces this separation: "The view taken of a University in these Discourses is the following:—that it is a place of *teaching* universal *knowledge*. This implies that its object is, on the one hand, intellectual, not moral . . ." (*Idea*, 5). The very next paragraph, however, reminds us of that larger whole, the university in its essence *and integrity*, where we are returned to the assistance of the Church—just as elsewhere we are returned to the realm of the moral and ethical. (See H. S., III, "Colleges and Correctives of Universities: Oxford," pp. 213–27. For support see Wise, "Newman and the Liberal Arts," pp. 259–60: "Far from minimizing the place of virtue, the place of faith, the function of the Church, in a university, no one has ever made more of it than Newman." See also Blehl, "Newman, the Fathers, and Education," p. 209; and D. G. Mulcahy, "Personal Influence, Discipline, and Liberal Education in Cardinal Newman's Idea of a University," *Newman–Studien*, XI (Heroldsberg Bei Nurnberg, 1980), pp. 150–58.)

To say, as Newman does, that "Philosophy, however enlightened, however profound, gives no command over the passions. . . . Liberal Education makes not the Christian, not the Catholic, but the gentleman" (*Idea*, p. 110); ". . . what have Philosophers to do with the terror of judgment or the saving of the soul?" (Idea, p. 175)—to say these things is to distinguish actual knowing as distinct from actual conduct; Newman speaks, for instance, of "*command* over the passions." On the other hand, once we recollect that knowing *is* for Newman a function of "practice" and "action," then, while knowing is not habitual conduct, nevertheless it cannot be removed from its ground in "facts," "action," and "experience." Newman does not feature this unity because, rhetorically, his stress (as he says) lies elsewhere. But the underlying unity of morality (or religion) and intellect is as strong as it was earlier in Erasmus or Vives, or as it is later in F. R. Leavis and Robert Hutchins, and Newman can say with perfect consistency that ". . . education is a higher word [than instruction]; it implies an action upon our mental nature, and the formation of a character; it is something individual and permanent, and is commonly spoken of in connection with religion and virtue" (*Idea*, p. 105); "[Liberal education is] founded in man's nature and the necessity of things, exemplified in all great moral works whatever" (*Idea*, p. 423); "Right Reason, that is, Reason rightly exercised leads the mind to the Catholic faith . . ." (*Idea*, p. 157). Whatever we may wish to say reason ultimately leads to, it is clear that for Newman reason in itself is not conduct. Because it is grounded in conduct, however, it implies and takes up into itself a person's character and moral (and ultimately religious) outlook.

45. Samuel Johnson, "Rambler No. 41" in W. J. Bate and Albrecht B. Strauss, eds., *The Yale Edition of the Works of Samuel Johnson* (New Haven: Yale University Press, 1969), III, p. 223: Hobbes, *Leviathan* (Oxford: Oxford University Press, 1946), I, 2; Bacon, *Advance-*

ment, V, in *Works,* IV, pp. 435–37.

46. Cf. *Idea,* p. 125: "I say then, if we would improve the intellect, first of all, we must ascend; we cannot gain real knowledge on a level; we must generalize, we must reduce to method, we must have a grasp of principles, and group and shape our acquisitions by means of them. It matters not whether our field of operation be wide or limited; in every case, to command it, is to mount above it." Thus Vico in *The Autobiography* (Translated by Max Harold Fisch and Thomas Goddard Bergin [Ithaca: Cornell University Press, 1944], p. 124) writes: ". . . if in the age of perception, which is youth, the students would devote themselves to Topics, the art of discovery which is the special privilege of the perceptive, . . . they would then be furnished with matter in order later to form a sound opinion on it. For one can not form a sound judgment of a thing without having complete knowledge of it; and topics is the art of finding in anything all that is in it. Thus nature itself would aid the young to become philosophers and good speakers."

47. Cf. "Elementary Studies: and "Discipline of Mind" in *Idea,* pp. 272–309 and 385–405.

48. Whitehead, *Aims,* p. 42. See also *Idea,* p. 104: "You see, then, here are two methods of Education; the end of the one is to be philosophical, of the other to be mechanical. . . ."

49. Part of the difficulty of explaining Newman on this point is that the *Idea* does not thematize everything we need to know about the generalist, so that we need to listen sensitively to Newman's "drift;" part of the difficulty is that, since Newman himself is working topically ("philosophically"), not as a specialist but as a generalist using midlevel abstractions, we ourselves need to appropriate his concepts and "realize" them through our own horizon of understanding. On generalism, see Kimball, *Orators and Philosophers,* pp. 194 ff.; and Richard McKeon, "The Liberating Arts and the Humanizing Arts in Education," in Arthur A. Cohen, ed., *Humanistic Education and Western Civilization* (New York: Holt, Rinehart and Winston, 1964), p. 171:

> The liberating and humanizing arts are *general* disciplines for the interpretation and control of *particular* processes; they render *parts* of experience intelligible and consequential in the context of *wholes.* From the earliest stage in their evolution as *eukuklios padeia* they have found a bond or union among the arts and sciences as well as differentiations and separations, and four different aspects of generality have emerged relative to four varieties of particularities in the history of the development. They are general in the sense of applying to all subject matters. . . . They are general in the sense of embracing all fundamental skills. . . . They are general in the sense of bearing on the formation of the whole man. . . . The fourth sense, which is implicated in these three senses, has become more explicit in recent times: they are general in the sense of being the arts of all men. . . .

But these arts, and the ends that they serve, are difficult to pin down: see Marrou, *A History of Education in Antiquity* (Madison: University of Wisconsin Press, 1982), p. 177; also pp. 81, 83.

50. But see Jerome Hamilton Buckley, *The Victorian Temper: A Study in Literary Culture* (Cambridge: Cambridge University Press, 1951), p. 199: "[B]y the end of the Victorian era, philosophy, like the new theoretical physics, was no longer the property of the common man."

51. Cf. Ben Knights, *The Idea of the Clerisy in the Nineteenth Century* (Cambridge: Cambridge University Press, 1978), p. 188: "The intention of the advocates of education [in the nineteenth century] was not to send out specialists or professionals. . . . society needed educated men, capable of finding their way among the specialisms . . . to see the whole. . . ."

Also Kenneth Burke, "Biology, Psychology, Words," in *Dramatism and Development* (Barre, Mass.: Clark University Press, 1972), p. 26: ". . . our ultimate statements about human motivation must be either theological or philosophical. They cannot be scientific, in our sense of the sciences as specialized disciplines. And in this sense there can be no science for mediating among the sciences. Nor in this sense can there be a specialized *science* of the *ultimate* ground, or scene." In "Technology and the Study of Man," in W. Roy Niblett, ed., *The Sciences, the Humanities and the Technological Threat* (London: University of London Press Ltd, 1975), pp. 3–20, Leo Marx argues against Clark Kerr's vision of the multiversity, whose ideal is the technician. Marx calls for inter–disciplinary education that would seek comprehensive connections among disciplines as a balance to (not substitute for) specialization. The fragmentation of the disciplines and their moral co–option by an increasingly technical and bureaucratized world–view threatens to destroy the whole by concentrating on the parts: "The [present] model is a machine in the sense that the needs of the human parts which comprise the whole are relatively insignificant: so far as the larger system has a goal it is, in Mumford's words, 'its own ceaseless expansion and inflation.' "

52. Cf. *Idea*, p. 54: Sciences "proceed on the principle of a division of labour, even though that division is an abstraction, not a literal separation into parts. . . ."

53. This is the task of no other subject matter discipline; nor is it the task of a single course, or series of courses. It is the task rather, for Newman, of the university curriculum as a whole. For rhetoricians this is also the special vocation of the department of "rhetorical studies," dedicated *inter alia* to the exploration of, and reflection on, just such connections and the making of such connections. It is not possible here to explore the nature of such a department, although it is not without interest that Everett Lee Hunt ("General Specialists," p. 262), attempting to influence the direction of the emerging speech profession in this country at the beginning of the century, urged precisely such an enlarged conception of rhetoric and rhetoric departments. Rhetoric for Hunt is not a subject matter science but a universal art:

> The Public Speaking department is to serve as a clearing house of ideas. The instructor should inspire in his students a vital interest in the affairs of the world, in politics, sociology, economics, literature, and art. He must realize with Cicero that all the arts which pertain to culture, have, as it were, a common bond; and he should make his students realize it. *Too many students are graduating without the slightest realization of the relationship of the various departments in which they have worked.* They have no vivid sense that we live in a universe instead of a multiverse" (emphasis added).

For similar perspectives, see, for example, Donald Leman Clark, "The Place of Rhetoric in a Liberal Education," *Quarterly Journal of Speech*, 36 (October 1950), pp. 291–95; Kimball, *Orators and Philosophers*, pp. 237–41; Charles W. Kneupper, "Developing Rhetoric as a Modern Discipline: Lessons from the Classical Tradition," in Charles W. Kneupper, ed., *Oldspeak/Newspeak* (Arlington: Rhetoric Society of America, 1985), pp. 108–18: "Rhetoric in the classical system was the *function which integrated the humanities*. It is not the mere knowledge of history, political science, literature, languages, psychology or sociology which enable [sic] the solution of the personal and practical problems of modern life. It is the use of that knowledge in making judgments of future possibilities and persuading others to share that judgment that enables effective problem solving in human life."

54. Cf. Sillem, *P. N.*, p. 134: "Newman's method was designed to show that the life work of a philosopher is a persistent development and deepening of the personal knowledge he has

of the things and people in the world around him. It was designed to bring his whole self into an ever closer touch with *real things* . . ." (emphasis added).

55. See *Idea,* p. 146.

56. Cf. Whitehead, *Aims,* pp. 74, 73: "The antithesis between a technical and a liberal education is fallacious. There can be no adequate technical education which is not liberal, and no liberal education which is not technical: that is, no education which does not impart both technique and intellectual vision. In simpler language, education should turn out the pupil with something he knows well and something he can do well. . . . Essentially culture should be for action . . . the goal . . . is the marriage of action to thought." Cf. Newman in *Idea,* p. 104: "I only say that Knowledge, in proportion as it tends more and more to be particular, ceases to be knowledge. . . . When I speak of Knowledge, I mean something intellectual, something which grasps what it perceives through the senses; something which takes a view of things . . . which reasons upon what it sees. . . ." Thus Newman does not oppose "viewing" and "particulars," the general and the technical, but reconciles them as mutual, if unequal, values of philosophizing. Culler (*Imperial Intellect,* p. 199) summarizes Newman's view this way: "Newman's formal solution to his problem, then, is not that there is a knowledge of particulars which implicitly contains a knowledge of all other things, but rather that there is a mode of knowing which is perfectly satisfactory to one whose purposes are not technical and that this mode of knowing is less exacting in its mastery than technical knowledge is." Whether it is less "exacting" is disputable; perhaps it is more accurate to say that it is equally demanding, but in its own way.

In *The Higher Learning In America* (New Haven: Yale University Press, 1936), Robert M. Hutchins opposes the cultivation of the intellect to vocationalism (pp. 33ff.), and narrow utility to broad utility (p. 62), quite as Newman does, but also like Newman he ultimately seeks to reconcile them in a reconstituted sense of both. In *Identity, Youth and Crisis* (New York: W. W. Norton and Co., 1968), pp. 36ff., Eric Erikson distinguishes those youth who take to the new technologies from those whom he dubs "new–humanist youth," though he ultimately seeks to unite them; and in *Dimensions of a New Identity* (New York: W. W. Norton and Company, Inc., 1974), p. 105, he writes: "[A] new identity will be very much attached to an intimate mastery of a set of skills dictated by the state of science and technology as well as the arts, and no attempt to 'humanize' life should belittle or bedevil this mastery itself. Competence without conviction, to be sure, is not more than a form of fact–slavery; but conviction without competence is less than liberation." Thus Don S. Browning (*Generative Man: Psycho–Analytic Perspectives* [Philadelphia: Westminster Press, 1973], p. 151) writes: ". . . the thrust of Erikson's work is to set forth still another character type which would be a synthesis of the two: a man who would be at once a technologist and a universalist, accomplished in the dominant disciplines of our culture and yet ethically sensitive to their humanistic control and employment." According to Browning (pp. 156–57), Erikson (in contrast, for example, to Philip Rieff) sees the function of the ego not only as reality–management but as wholeness: "It forever seeks to correlate the various fragments of one's experience into a meaningful *whole.*"

57. Cf. *Idea,* p. 123: "To have even a portion of this illuminative reason and true philosophy is the highest state to which nature can aspire, in the way of intellect. . . ." On Newman's acceptance of the idea of a "major," see McGrath, *Consecration,* p. 208: "The first two years were to be devoted to Arts and Science ending in what was to be called the degree of Scholar. There were then to be two more years devoted to a more specialised course in Arts or Science or Law, leading to the B.A." See also Ker, "Editor's Introduction," in *Idea,* p. 575, on Newman's commitment to research in the university, and *Ward,* II, p. 498.

58. Newman's celebrated portraits of the gentleman in Discourses Seven and Eight include "social" graces which some may consider quaint—"The true gentleman in like manner carefully avoids whatever may cause a jar or a jolt in the minds of those with whom he is cast;" "He has his eyes on all his company; he is tender towards the bashful, gentle towards the distant, and merciful towards the absurd;" "He respects piety and devotion," (*Idea*, 179–80) and so on. But these are themselves neither as Victorian, nor as exclusively "social" (since intellectual work is ineluctably social also), as some would have it; and in any case a great deal of what Newman says about the gentleman is intellectual and not dated at all. See also *Idea*, p. 10: "This is real cultivation of mind; and I do not deny that the characteristic excellences of a gentleman are included in it. Nor need we be ashamed that they should be. . . . Certainly a liberal education does manifest itself in a courtesy, propriety, and polish of word and action, which is beautiful in itself, and acceptable to others; but it does much more. It brings the mind into form. . . ."

59. See also *Idea*, pp. 154–55: "It shows him how to accomodate himself to others, how to throw himself into their state of mind, how to bring before them his own, how to influence them, how to come to an understanding with them, how to bear with them. He is at home in any society, he has common ground with every class; he knows when to speak and when to be silent; he is able to converse, he is able to listen. . . ."

60. *Imperial Intellect*, p. 39.

61. Cf. *Idea*, p. 12: "Some one . . . will perhaps object that I am but advocating that spurious philosophism, which . . . I may call 'viewiness' . . . [which] would teach youths nothing soundly or thoroughly, and would dismiss them with nothing better than brilliant general views about all things whatever. This indeed, if well founded, would be a most serious objection to what I have advanced in this Volume. . . ."

62. *Clerisy*, p. 195.

63. Dale, "Dangers," p. 25.

64. Kerr, *The Uses of the University*, p. 41; Corcoran, "Liberal Studies and Moral Aims," p. 62.

65. Dwight B. Heath, "Liberal Education: John Henry Newman's Conception," *Educational Theory*, IX (July 1959), pp. 152–55.

66. See John Coulson, "Newman's Idea of an Open University and Its Consequences Today," in James D. Bastable, ed., *Newman and Gladstone: Centennial Essays* (Dublin: Veritas Publications, 1978), p. 234: "Furthermore, Newman does not see his *idea* as confining a university education either to England and Oxford or to the gentry. It is open to all who are prepared to undertake a liberal and liberalising discipline, as his lectures to the Evening Classes in 1858 make quite clear: 'We will give lectures in the evening, we will fill our classes with the young men of Dublin'."

67. See Werner Jaeger, *Paideia: The Ideals of Greek Culture*, 3 vols. (New York: Oxford University Press, 1945), I, p. xxiv: "But it would be a most dangerous misconception of what we have described as the Greek will to shape individual character on an ideal standard, if we imagined that the standard was ever fixed and final."

68. Cf. David J. Delaura's argument ("Pater and Newman: The Road to the 'Nineties," *Victorian Studies*, X [September 1966], pp. 45, 58) that both Arnold and Pater wrenched away Newman's religious uses of "the chosen few" to apply to education specifically and culture generally.

69. See Vargish, *Contemplation of Mind*, p. 147: "Liberal knowledge heightens the student's ability not so much to reason but to perceive."

70. Levine, *Boundaries*, p. 176, has rightly said of Newman that he is "a polar opposite

of one who is inflexibly narrowminded." See also *Prepos.*, pp. 6, 178, 295–96.

71. *Imperial Intellect,* p. 191: "[It] . . . adds up to doing the impossible. . . ." This way of putting it betrays an anti–rhetorical concern with subject matters and data to be mastered, over methods and disciplines as capacities to be cultivated.

72. See *Idea,* p. 134: "We know, not by a direct and simple vision, not at a glance, but, as it were, by piecemeal and accumulation, by a mental process, by going round an object, by the comparison, the combination, the mutual correction, the continual adaptation, of many partial notions. . . ."

73. Pedagogically, it would seem to follow that it is not the student *per se,* but the faculty and curriculum that require to be informed by this posture and direction. As a way of attempting to "realize" Newman's own view concretely, we can consider at least four levels or ranges of totality within which one can operate "philosophically."

One can try to get a view, first of all, of *any* particular problem, in any subject matter field, no matter how "fixed" or "scientific" the discipline, so long as (1) the view is a product of personal discrimination of indeterminate relations among concrete particulars; (2) the view is sought for its own sake; and (3) the orientation is *outward,* back toward more encompassing wholes. No doubt it is possible (and necessary) to quarrel over what is and is not a "field," hence when one is and is not pointed "outward," but the moral here is that the investigation of problems within particular fields is "liberal" to *the degree that* it seeks connections, directly or indirectly, beyond its area of specialization. Thus the first "level" or "range" of liberal education is *within a field,* where the thinker implicitly or explicitly connects it to his larger world, seeking a "judicious admixture" of the determinate and indeterminate, the technical and the general. As Allan Bloom (*The Closing of the American Mind* [New York: Simon and Schuster, 1987], p. 343) has recently put it, "For this, a very small, detailed problem can be the best way, if it is framed so as to open out on the whole." From this perspective it is not difficult to see that Newman's view rejects any notion of "the two cultures," the sciences versus the humanities: within his conception of the liberal, the humanities (or more broadly, the human sciences) are intrinsically more indeterminate and value–laden, hence better able to offer opportunities for the sort of "viewing" he has in mind, but the natural sciences are nevertheless plausible, indeed indispensable resources for liberal education. (For an excellent discussion of how such "viewing" might be taught, see Joseph J. Schwab, *College Curriculum and Student Protest* [Chicago: The University of Chicago Press, 1969].)

Second, we can try to get a view of relations *between and among fields,* what is commonly called "inter–disciplinary studies." In fact, such studies are preeminently liberal (and rhetorical) so long as the three conditions mentioned above hold. The problem, of course, is that, given the way interdisciplinary education has been pursued over the last two decades, they have not held. What we have usually had instead was an Irish stew of subject matters, superficially mixed together and dignified with the title interdisciplinary (the parallel to the smorgasbord of course offerings that makes up the undergraduate curriculum)—what Newman called "a smattering of a hundred things." In contrast, Newman's own view of liberal education is resolutely antisuperficial and even (presumably) antielective. That is, the mere yoking together of disparate subject matters, or the mere fact of a broad range of "offerings," does not necessarily propitate the god of liberal education and cultivate the ability to view wholes in a principled way; on the contrary, it is likely to bring about just that "viewiness," that *random* connectedness, Newman condemns. What is required instead is a careful planning of integrated series of courses, held together by a central program or "core" that changes as significant circumstances (of many different sorts) change. In such a program, "interdisciplinary studies" would play a leading, even paradigmatic role.

Third, one can seek a view outside fields as such, within the greater and more indeterminate spheres of our private, social, political and cultural lives. Here is the indefinitely large area where we share many diverse sets of commonplaces with many diverse groups, and where we are "liberal" to the extent that we seek knowledge of the shifting, overlapping, changing, and maximally ambiguous realities that constitute our various "worlds." For that reason, this is the most dangerous sphere, because it is potentially the most utilitarian in the narrow sense. All knowledge, in the three areas mentioned, is always already "practical" because it is directed to the whole of man's nature and world. In this third area, this practical dimension is thematized, not for its own sake (e.g., for political purposes), but for its further opportunities for "philosophy." Naturally this is the ground most coveted today by Marxist and other political academics, who see *praxis* as the rationale for the scholar's work. But this is to be at once too moralistic and insufficiently so: it privileges politics, but at the expense of the full range of values and of reality. In *tying down* scholarship to a political position or agenda, or to politics simply, it substitutes part for the whole. In Newman's conception of the liberal, the "practical" will be seen to be an inevitable, even a privileged dimension of philosophy; this implies that all scholarship is political and must be so. But philosophy extends beyond politics because it extends beyond such a narrow sense of the "practical." For the fourth "level," see the brief remarks on the "science of sciences" on p. 194 in the text of the present volume.

74. Here, as in several other things, I follow Culler, whose interpretation has most of the elements of the truth, but who has pieced them together to construct a very one–sided Newman.

75. Kimball, *Orators and Philosophers*. The conflict between these two camps is seen to provide most of the impetus for, and the changing and ambiguous terms and distinctions of, the discussion about liberal education. A full account of the two sides would include the oppositions between science and the humanities, ancients and moderns, liberal and useful, generalist and specialist, invention and proof, thought and word, word and thing, knowing and doing, theory and practice, method and content. The historical alternation of perspectives is manifest from antiquity on, including the shift from scholasticism to the rhetoricized dialectic of Ramus and the rhetorical humanisms of Erasmus, Luther and Vives; from the rhetoricized organon of scientific method in Bacon to the empiricism of Locke, back to the neo-Ciceronianism of certain English rhetorical theorists such as John Wilson or the *espirit de finesse* of Pascal, and forward to the experimental method of Hume, Mill, and Comte. For accounts, see Crane, "Shifting Definitions," pp. 16–170; Richard McKeon, "Rhetoric in the Middle Ages," and "Philosophy in the Twelfth Century: The Renaissance of Rhetoric," in *Rhetoric: Essays in Invention and Discovery*, pp. 121–66 and 167–93; Hannah H. Gray, "Renaissance Humanism: The Pursuit of Eloquence," *Journal of the History of Ideas*, XXIV (October–December 1963), pp. 497–514; Walter J. Ong, *Ramus, Method, and the Decay of Dialogue* (Cambridge: Harvard University Press, 1958; Rpr. New York: Octagon Books, 1979), esp. chs. VIII–XII; Barbara Shapiro, *Probability and Certainty in Seventeenth Century England* (Princeton: Princeton University Press, 1983); Wilbur Samuel Howell, *Eighteenth Century British Logic and Rhetoric* (Princeton: Princeton University Press, 1970), and *Logic and Rhetoric in England, 1500–1700* (New York: Russell and Russell, 1956).

76. *Clerisy*, pp. 188ff.; *Newman in His Times*, pp. 137–74.

77. *Imperial Intellect*, p. 185; and Svaglic, "Introduction" in Martin J. Svaglic, ed., *The Idea of a University* (Notre Dame: University of Notre Dame Press, 1960), p. xv. It should be noted that Culler, notwithstanding his bow to Aristotle's first philosophy, also writes that "the idea of a science which has as its subject matter the very sciences themselves is less

closely associated with metaphysics than with certain traditional conceptions of logic, and Newman, who had studied the history of logic with Whately, was probably hearkening back to these conceptions in developing his idea of the Science of Sciences" (p. 185).

78. Cf. Artz, "Newman as a Philosopher," p. 268: ". . . Newman's new *organum* contains also a conscious parallel to an Aristotelian idea, however not of his *Organon*, but of his *Nicomachean Ethics*. . . . the number of quotations [in the *Grammar of Assent*] is characteristic: I know of 17 quotations from the *Nicomachean Ethics*, 3 from the *Rhetoric*, 2 from the *Poetics*, and none from other Aristotelian writings." As Sillem has put it, "Newman liked to define Philosophy, not 'objectively' as a knowledge of things considered as beings [essences], but 'phenomenologically' as 'reason exercized upon knowledge,' or reason exercized on the certitudes we have acquired in a well-sifted experience." (*P. N.*, I, pp. 136, 158). Sillem calls this a "personal" (I call it a rhetorical) metaphysics. For a similar emphasis, see Gray ("Renaissance Humanism," p. 506): "For the majority of [Renaissance] humanists, philosophy signified ethics or practical philosophy as opposed to pure logic or metaphysics." Cf. Michael Novak, *Belief and Unbelief* (New York: Macmillan Company, 1965), p. 55; and as quoted in Sallie McFague, *Speaking in Parables* (Philadelphia: Fortress Press, 1975), p. 3 note: "In between imaginative literature and academic theology there is a form of intelligence which is precise, discursive, and analytical, but also in touch with concrete experience and with the imagination. That is the model for academic intelligence."

79. Walgrave, *Newman the Theologian*, pp. 113–14. True universality cannot by definition exclude any legitimate sense of first principles, so that the first principles of being qua being, as of the "lesser" sciences, require to be discriminated as to their nature, function and scope by a mind sensitive to the concrete. This discrimination is not in the first instance a technical study, but a disciplined art, somewhat less technical than what Robert Hutchins seems to have intended when he spoke of "metaphysics"—the study of first principles—as the basis of liberal education, in *The Higher Learning*, esp. pp. 98ff. Hutchins' perspective is less rhetorical than Newman's. On Hutchins' use of the term "metaphysics," see Richard McKeon, "Education and the Disciplines," pp. 372ff. On the art of discrimination see Culler, *Imperial Intellect*, p. 187: ". . . Newman devised a 'vertical' discipline which would enable the *nonspecialist* to reduce . . . abstractions into a true and balanced picture of reality" (emphasis added).

80. William Whewell, *On the Principles of English University Education* (London: John W. Parker, 1938), p. 15. Spencer and Huxley, through disagreeing with Whewell on many points, agreed that mathematics, logic and science best trained the mind. See, for example, Herbert Spencer, *Essays on Education* (London: J. M. Dent and Sons, 1963); and Thomas H. Huxley, *Science and Education* (New York: D. Appleton, 1898); also Mark Pattison, *Suggestions on Academical Organisation* (Edinburgh: Edmonston and Douglas, 1868; Rpr. New York: Arno Press, 1977), p. 265: "The higher education must be thorough; it must take hold of the highest mental faculty, and form and develop it. This faculty is the scientific reason in its highest form."

81. *English University Education*, p. 45.

82. Juan Luis Vives, *Vives: on Education, A Translation of the De Tradendis Disciplinis of Juan Luis Vives* Together with an Introduction by Foster Watson (Cambridge: At the University Press, 1913). See also Edward Gibbon, *An Essay on the Study of Literature* (London: T. Becket and P. A. De Hondt, 1744). Gray, "Renaissance Humanism," p. 501, writes: The [Renaissance] humanists had a horror of abstract speculation carried on for its own sake, of specialization which led to absorption in purely 'theoretical' questions or in the

elaboration of exclusively 'technical' concerns. Their orientation was toward rhetoric rather than logic, ethics than metaphysics. . . . The central point of this contrast was formulated in terms of the 'merely intellectual' on the one side, the 'actively persuasive' on the other."

83. *De Tradendis,* p. 180. Cf. Marrou, *A History of Education in Antiquity,* p. 169: "In theory, the crowning-point of all this learning was 'judgment', literary criticism—'the finest flower of the grammarian's art.' But this did not mean that its primary purpose was aesthetic; it was the rhetor rather than the grammarian who studied the classics, in the hope of discovering the secrets of their style—so that he might borrow them for himself."

84. See Manwaring, *Institutes of Learning,* p. 2: "The principal Point, in good Education, is to form the manners;" Gibbon, *An Essay on the Study of Literature;* David Hume, "Of Eloquence," in *Of the Standard of Taste and Other Essays* (Indianapolis: Bobbs–Merrill, 1965), pp. 60–71.

85. "Shifting Definitions," p. 96.

86. Nancy S. Struever, "The Conversable World: Eighteenth Century Transformations of the Relation of Rhetoric and Truth," in Struever and Vickers, eds., *Rhetoric and the Pursuit of Truth.* In similar ways, Gadamer and Rorty continue to expand and transform the metaphor of conversation.

87. *Imperial Intellect,* p. 200: "So too with the orator. He must be able to speak about things which he could not do, and therefore Aristotle in the *Rhetoric* treats the various subjects which the orator must understand in merely a loose and popular way, and he refers the reader for a more technical handling to the various specialized treatises. That something of this rhetorical tradition was present in Newman's mind is evident from the emphasis which he places upon the polite accomplishment of conversation." Thus has rhetoric ever been trivialized, made to appear a failure at what it never attempted to be, a subject matter specialization.

88. Cf. T. P., p. 24; P. N., II, p. 163.

89. Cf.. Cicero, *De Oratore,* 2. 35; Quintilian, *Institutes,* 12.2. 15ff. Cf. Gray, "Renaissance Humanism," p. 505, who notes that the assumptions of the Renaissance humanists about the orator ". . . grew out of the conviction that knowledge should serve practical ends, that human learning ought to have utility for human life, that education should instruct both will and intellect, and that in persuasion and eloquent discussion lie the effective means of conveying truth."

90. Newman is quoting Oxonian John Davison (see *ECH,* II, pp. 375–420) who, with Copleston, defended Oxford against the "Edinburgh Reviewers."

91. J. M. Cameron, *On the Idea of a University* (Toronto: University of Toronto Press, 1978), pp. 21, 22: "[Newman's] argument is that European civilization and culture are normative, that they set standards that are final and definitive of what is human in the highest possible degree. I think we have to say that for us such a view is quite out of the question. This scarcely needs to be argued." To the contrary,. . . .

92. For support for the claim here, see Blehl, "Newman, the Fathers, and Education," p. 209: "The concrete situation . . . determined the emphasis Newman places on one or the other aspect of his educational views"; and Tierney, "Newman's Doctrine of University Education," p. 126: "Himself a classical scholar, mathematician and musician, philsopher and theologian, he was bound rigidly neither to the old scheme of the Seven Arts nor to the too exclusive classical and literary curriculum which had largely taken its place."

93. See *H. S.,* III, pp. 103–4: "All this suggests to us, what of course must ever be borne in mind, that while the necessities of human society and the nature of the case are guarantees

to us that such Schools of general education will ever be in requisition, still they will be modified in detail by the circumstances, and marked by the peculiarities, of the age to which they severally belong."

94. *Imperial Intellect*, p. 182; "Editor's Introduction," p. lvii, n. 6.

95. Levine, *Boundaries of Fiction*, pp. 245, 218; and yet Levine also seems to see this as a shortcoming (p. 221).

96. See Bastable, "The Germination of Belief," p. 107: "Newman's philosophy lies in his fruitful appreciation of first principles rather than in the conceptual elaboration of their consequences: but it *is* 'something to have started a problem and mapped in part a [sic] country';" *V. M.,* I, "Preface," p. xx–xxiii; and Lash, "Was Newman a Theologian?" p. 323.

97. *Imperial Intellect,* p. 256: "What was needed was a collective mind, some organ which would be judicious because it was not a mere individual and yet receptive to new truth. . . . Such an organ was the university."

98. *Liberal Education and the Modern University,* p. 111, emphasis added.

99. This facility with a wide range of open–ended *topoi* Wayne C. Booth calls (facetiously?) "polytopicality," and its study "rhetorology" ("The Idea of a University as Seen by a Rhetorician," Ryerson Lecture, The University of Chicago, 1987, p. 30).

100. Zyskind, "Philosophic Strands," in Kiefer and Munitz, eds., *Perspectives in Education, Religion, and the Arts,* p. 378.

101. Thus *The Idea of a University* functions in just the way Eugene Garver (*Machiavelli and the History of Prudence,* p. 50) shows that the text of *The Prince* functions for its audience:

> *The Prince* teaches prudence by presenting its own argument as an example of prudent action which forces the reader to engage in a prudential activity: the argument of *The Prince* is itself an articulate and accessible example of what it would mean to combine flexibility and continuity, to make practical intelligence responsive to circumstances. . . . Instead of having either rules or cases to live up to or imitate, Machiavelli offers only the *relation* between rule and case, the prudential relations found in acts such as reading the past and applying knowledge to action, and in terms such as *judgment, tact, decorum, and taste* [emphasis added].

See also Kahn (*Rhetoric, Prudence, and Skepticism in the Renaissance,* p. 92) who predicates much the same prudential instancing of prudence in Erasmus's *Adages:* "As his comments on the form of the *Adages* testify, Erasmus is less concerned with the product of interpretation than with the process—less concerned, that is, with presenting a kernel of doctrinal truth than with educating his readers to an activity of judgment and to the exercise of that judgment in their own lives."

CHAPTER SEVEN

1. Representative work on what rhetoricians these days are calling epistemic rhetoric includes the following: Alan Brinton, "William James and the Epistemic View of Rhetoric," *Quarterly Journal of Speech,* 68 (1982), pp. 158–69; Barry Brummett, "Some Implications of 'Process' or 'Inter–Subjectivity': Post-Modern Rhetoric," *Philosophy and Rhetoric,* 4 (1971, pp. 21–51; Richard A. Cherwitz and James W. Hikins, *Communication and Knowledge: An Investigation in Rhetorical Epistemology* (Columbia: University of South Carolina Press, 1986); Richard E. Crable, "Knowledge–as–Status: On Argument and Epistemology," *Communication Monographs,* 49 (1982), pp. 249–62; Walter R. Fisher, *Human Communication as Narration: Toward a Philosophy of Reason, Value, and Action* (Columbia:

University of South Carolina Press, 1987); C. Jack Orr, "How Shall We Say: 'Reality Is Socially Constructed through Communication?' " *Central States Speech Journal,* 29 (Winter 1978), pp. 263–74; Celeste Condit Railsback, "Beyond Rhetorical Relativism: A Structural Material Model of Truth and Objective Reality," *Quarterly Journal of Speech,* 69 (November 1983), pp. 170–86; Robert L. Scott, "On Viewing Rhetoric as Epistemic," *Central States Speech Journal,* 18 (February 1967),pp. 9–17; Robert L. Scott, "On Viewing Rhetoric as Epistemic: Ten Years Later," *Central States Speech Journal,* 27 (Winter 1976), pp. 258–66; Harold Zyskind, "A Case Study in Philosophic Rhetoric: Theodore Roosevelt," *Philosophy and Rhetoric,* 2 (Fall 1968), pp. 228–54; Walter B. Weimar, "Why All Knowing is Rhetorical," *Journal of the American Forensic Association,* 20 (Fall 1984), pp. 63–71. But see also the works of Chaim Perelman, Stephen Toulmin, Wayne Booth, and Kenneth Burke. For a review of much of this literature, see Michael C. Leff, "In Search of Ariadne's Thread: A Review of the Recent Literature on Rhetorical Theory," *Central States Speech Journal,* 29 (Summer 1978), pp. 73–91. For work outside of "rhetoric" proper, see, for example, Basil Mitchell, *The Justification of Religious Belief* (New York: Oxford University Press, 1981); Renford Bambrough, *Reason, Truth and God* (London: Methuen and Co., 1969); Peter L. Berger, *A Rumor of Angels,* and with Thomas Luckman, *The Social Construction of Reality* (Garden City, N.Y.: Anchor Books, 1967); Richard J. Bernstein, *Beyond Objectivism and Relativism;* Thomas S. Kuhn, *The Structure of Scientific Revolutions* (Chicago: University of Chicago Press, 1962); Thomas Szasz, *The Myth of Psychotherapy: Mental Healing as Religion, Rhetoric, and Repression* (Garden City, N.Y.: Anchor Press, 1978).

2. Alan Brinton, "William James and the Epistemic View of Rhetoric," p. 165.

3. *Three Uses of Christian Discourse,* Chs. III and IV.

4. On induction, see Whately, *Logic,* pp. 252–61. For Campbell the enthymeme (the major premise usually suppressed) was not useless, but played a legitimate though secondary role in rhetoric, "justifying a passion," for example, once it was raised through non-deductive appeals (*Philosophy of Rhetoric,* p. 92). See McKerrow, "Campbell and Whately on the Utility of Syllogistic Logic," *Western Speech Communication,* 40 (Winter 1976), pp. 3–13.

5. Newman accepts the association of ideas, writing in 1863: "Such association is the first element of order" (*T.P.,* p. 112).

6. Cf. Ong, *Rhetoric, Romance and Technology,* p. 8:

With the advent of the age which from one point of view we call the technological age and from the other point of view the romantic age, rhetoric was not wiped out or supplanted, but rather disrupted, displaced, and rearranged. It became a bad word— as did many of the formally good words associated with it, such as art, artificial, commonplace, and so on. Rhetoric was a bad word for those given to technology because it represented 'soft' thinking, thinking attuned to unpredictable human actuality and decisions, whereas technology, based on science, was devoted to 'hard' thinking, that is, formally logical thinking, attunable to unvarying physical laws (which, however, are no more real than variable human free acts). . . . Rhetoric was a bad word also for those given to romanticism because it seemed to hint that the controlling element in life was a contrivance rather than freedom in the sense of purely 'spontaneous' or unmotivated action, sprung up unsolicited from the interior wells of being.

See also Bate, *From Classic to Romantic,* esp. ch. IV; Sillem, *P.N.,* I, pp. 203–20; and Gerard A. Hauser, "Empiricism, Description, and the New Rhetoric, *"Philosophy and Rhetoric,* 5 (Winter 1972), pp. 24–44.

7. It will be recalled from Chapter Two above that what is "real" is grasped in whole or in part in terms of its own particular characteristics and circumstances, its "associations" (*G.A.*, 22), or the "things" which make it up; whereas the "notional" is an abstraction from the concrete, or a common term or category applicable only to that aspect of concrete things from which it was originally drawn (*G.A.*, 30ff.). Price (*Belief*, pp. 314–48) is correct to point out that this real-notional distinction is one of degree only, a point to remember when trying to account for Newman's seeing the "real" (and thus the rhetorical) in *all* knowing.

8. Or we may say that it is *both* inference and assent, inasmuch as assent may be taken as the fulfillment of the act of inferring. In this way, "action" in Newman again takes on a dual aspect, that of "reasoning" and "committing," "knowing" and acting."

9. See *Dev.*, pp. 11–12; *G.A.*, pp. 223ff.

10. In his Introduction to the *Grammar of Assent* (New York: Doubleday and Co., 1955), Etienne Gilson rightly pinpoints *religious* assent as Newman's focus; but this should not be taken as meaning that the *Grammar* presupposes religious affiliation or that it does not apply beyond religious belief or dogmas.

11. Cf. McDermott, ed., *The Writings of William James* p. 456.

12. *Newman the Theologian*, pp. 336–37. Cf. *P.N.*, II, p. 96.

13. I am grateful for several points of this analysis to Professor David Smigelskis of the University of Chicago.

14. In particular I argue against the position of Karlyn Kohrs Campbell in "The Ontological Foundations of Rhetorical Theory," *Philosophy and Rhetoric*, III (Spring 1970), 97–108, which holds that "symbolic action" is a sufficiently broad philosophical base for rhetoric.

15. Kenneth Burke, *A Grammar of Motives*, p. xv. Hereafter cited in the text as GM.

16. Kenneth Burke, *Permanence and Change* (Indianapolis: The Bobbs–Merrill Company, 1965), p. 218. Hereafter cited in the text as PC. The terms "motive," "cause" and "reason" are philosophically so vexed, for example in disputes over the "scientific" ("causal") and hermeneutical nature of psychoanalysis, that, absent a long digression here to clarify things more, my discussion of Burke is bound to raise questions over his meaning. My own view is that Burke is unaware of positing a false dichotomy between motion and action, cause and choice. In point of fact his own discourse is, as Ricoeur has said of Freud's, a "mixed discourse," one that asserts both causal explanations and hermeneutical or rhetorical "reasons" in accounting for men's symbolic actions. Ironically, Burke's lack of insight in this regard leads him to disguise the fact that his own psychological analyses of motives are heavily causal by highlighting "choice" when it suits his purposes, as in his refusal to follow Freud's own psychological analyses of motives in "Freud and the Analysis of Poetry" (in *The Philosophy of Literary Form*) and to highlight motive–as–cause when he wants to press his own imperialistic causal claims, as in *The Rhetoric of Religion*. For the discussion of "mixed discourse" see Paul Ricoeur, *Freud and Philosophy: An Essay on Interpretation*. Translated by Denis Savage (New Haven: Yale University Press, 1970). For a critique of Burke's resistance to Freud, see Louis Fraiberg, *Psycho-Analysis and American Literary Criticism* (Detroit: Wayne State University Press, 1960), pp. 183–201. For differing accounts of the "cause"/"reason" distinction, see, for example, the essays by Stephen Toulmin, Antony Flew, and Richard Peters, in Margaret MacDonald, ed., *Philosophy and Analysis* (Oxford: Basil Blackwell, 1954), pp. 132–56; A. C. MacIntyre, *The Unconscious* (London: Routledge and Kegan Paul, 1958); and Adolf Grünbaum, "Are Hidden Motives in Psychoanalysis Reasons but not Causes of Human Conduct?" in Stanley B. Messer, Louis A. Sass, and Robert L. Woolfolk, eds., *Hermeneutics and Psychological Theory* (New Brunswick: Rutgers University Press, 1988), pp. 168–74.

17. Kenneth Burke, *The Philosophy of Literary Form* (New York: Vintage Books, 1941), p. 9. Hereafter cited in the text as PLF.

18. Kenneth Burke, *Language as Symbolic Action* (Berkeley: The University of California Press, 1966), p. 3. Hereafter cited in the text as LSA.

19. William H. Rueckert, *Kenneth Burke and the Drama of Human Relations,* Second Edition (Berkeley: University of California Press, 1982), p. 139.

20. Kenneth Burke, *The Rhetoric of Religion* (Berkeley: The University of California Press, 1970), pp. 14–15. Hereafter cited in the text as RR.

21. See also Rueckert, *Kenneth Burke,* p. 155: "Invariably, Burke takes an idea or person or particular kind of act and analytically breaks it down into its perfect cluster; the cluster is logologically complete when its range of possibilities or meanings has been logically exhausted. Burke's works are full of such perfect clusters: he has worked them out for hierarchy, deaths and dyings, the range of mountings, catharsis, 'possession,' persuasion, the negative, dialectic, and all the terms of the pentad."

22. See *Grammar of Motives,* p. 65.

23. Cf. *G.A.,* 159ff. An opposing view, of Burke as radical relativist, is provided by Frank Lentricchia in *Criticism and Social Change* (Chicago: The University of Chicago Press, 1983). In my view Lentricchia simply fails to see how Burke's relativism exists in tension with his search for an analytical or structuralist calculus of motivational fixities (as well as how such a calculus provides the moralizing foundation for such relativism).

24. For support for this claim, see Charles W. Kneupper, "Dramatism and Argument," in George Ziegelmueller and Jack Rhodes, eds., *Dimensions of Argument: Proceedings of the Second Summer Conference on Argumentation* (Annandale, Va.: Speech Communication Association, 1981), p. 394.

25. In this regard I see Burke and Rorty on the same plane, as moralists of the human condition, and consider Burke open to the same objections that Richard Bernstein has levelled against Rorty in *Philosophical Profiles* (Philadelphia: University of Pennsylvania Press, 1986), p. 55: "If we accept Rorty's claim that all justification, whether of knowledge or moral choices, cannot hope to escape from history and only makes sense with respect to social practices, we are still faced with the critical task of determining which social practices are relevant, which ones ought to prevail, be modified, or abandoned. 'Hammering this out' is not a matter of 'mere' rhetoric or 'arbitrary' decision, but requires argumentation."

26. See *Justification,* chs. 5 and 6.

27. See *Rhetoric of Religion,* p. 300:

Above all, logology fails to offer grounds for the *perfection* of promises and threats that theology allows for. And there are incentives [i.e., motives] in both animality and symbolicity that will keep men always asking about *ultimate principles* of reward and punishment, in their attempts to scare the devil out of one another. Being creatures that necessarily think in terms of time, they will incline to conceive of such a culminative logical design in terms of sheerly *temporal* firsts and lasts. Hence, there is the goad towards theological translation into terms of a final destiny in an afterlife. A sheerly logological explanation must leave such doctrinally stimulated hunger unappeased.

28. See *G.A.,* pp. 105ff.

29. Quoted in Gordon Huntington Harper, ed., *Cardinal Newman and William Froude, FRS: A Correspondence* (Baltimore: Johns Hopkins Press, 1933), pp. 119–20.

30. Locke, *Essay,* II, p. 364.

31. Locke, *Essay,* II, p. 429; cf. *G.A.,* p. 300.

32. Cf. *G.A.,* p. 160: "There are many truths in concrete matter, which no one can

demonstrate, yet everyone unconditionally accepts; and though of course there are innumerable propositions to which it would be absurd to give an absolute assent, still the absurdity lies in the circumstances of each particular case. . . ."

33. See *G.A.*, pp. 191-192.

34. James C. Livingston, *The Ethics of Belief: An Essay on the Victorian Religious Conscience*, AAR Studies in Religion (Tallahassee, Fla.: American Academy of Religion and Scholars' Press, 1974), p. 21; cf. *G.A.*, p. 163; also M. Jamie Ferreira, *Doubt and Religious Commitment* (Oxford: Clarendon Press, 1980), pp. 24–8, and "Newman on Belief— Confidence, Proportionality, and Probability," *Heythrop Journal*, XXVI (1985), pp. 164–76.

35. Stephen Toulmin, *The Uses of Argument* (Cambridge: Cambridge University Press, 1958), p. 98. Hereafter cited in the text as UA.

36. Cf. Richard Whately, *Logic*, p. 257; also McKerrow, "Campbell and Whately," p. 7, where McKerrow quotes Whately on the conclusions of syllogisms being necessary but only materially probable.

37. Cf. Peter T. Manicas, "On Toulmin's Contribution to Logic and Argumentation," in Richard L. Johannesen, ed., *Contemporary Theories of Rhetoric: Selected Readings* (New York: Harper and Row, 1971), pp. 256–70.

38. Cf. Stephen Toulmin, "Logic and the Criticism of Arguments," in *The Rhetoric of Western Thought*, 3d ed., James W. Golden, Goodwin F. Berquist, and William E. Coleman, eds. (Dubuque, Iowa: Kendall/Hunt Publishing Company, 1976), pp. 391–401.

39. *A Rumor of Angels*, pp. 52, 57. We find similar moves in David Tracy, Sallie McFague, Paul Tillich, William James, Friedrich Schleiermacher, and Soren Kierkegaard, among others.

40. Michael Novak, *Belief and Unbelief: A Philosophy of Self-Knowledge* (New York: The New American Library, 1965), p. 64. See also James, *Writings*, p. 740: "There is no inconsistency anywhere in this, and no 'vicious circle' unless a circle of poles holding themselves upright by leaning on one another, or a circle of dancers revolving by holding each other's hands, be 'vicious;' " and Polanyi, *Personal Knowledge*, p. 299:

> An enquiry into our ultimate beliefs can be consistent only if it presupposes its own conclusions. It must be intentionally circular.
> The last statement is itself an instance of the kind of act which it licenses. For it stakes out the grounds of my discourse by relying essentially on the very grounds thus staked out; my confident admission of circularity being justified only by my conviction, that in so far as I express my utmost understanding of my intellectual responsibilities as my personal belief, I may rest assured of having fulfilled the ultimate requirements of self–criticism; that indeed I am obliged to form such personal beliefs and can hold them in a responsible manner, even though I recognize that such a claim can have no other justification than such as it derives from being declared in the very terms which it endorses. Logically, the whole of my argument is but an elaboration of this circle. . . .

41. The phrase is from Wayne Booth, *Modern Dogma* (p. xvi), who seems to have borrowed it from Newman and Polanyi.

42. Polanyi, *Personal Knowledge*, p. 266. Cf. *Dev.*, pp. 100–1; *G.A.*, pp. 248–49.

43. See Michael Polanyi, "Authority and Conscience" in *Science, Faith and Society* (Chicago: University of Chicago Press, 1964).

44. See Hans Küng, *Freud and the Problem of God* (New Haven: Yale University Press, 1979), p. 77: "It is the same with lovers: every lover necessarily projects his own image of her

on to the beloved. But does this mean that the beloved does not exist. . .? With the aid of his projections can he not even understand her more profoundly than someone who tries as a neutral observer to judge her from outside?" See also Berger, *A Rumor of Angels*, p. 57.

45. See Ray McKerrow, "The Ethical Implications of a Whatelian Rhetoric," *Rhetoric Society Quarterly*, XVII (Summer 1987), pp. 321–27. See also Livingston, *The Ethics of Belief*, ch. II.

SELECTED BIBLIOGRAPHY

WORKS BY NEWMAN

(Citations refer to editions by Longmans, Green and Company unless otherwise noted.)

Apologia Pro Vita Sua. Edited, with an Introduction and Notes, by Martin J. Svaglic. Oxford: Clarendon Press, 1967.

The Arians of the Fourth Century, 1891.

Autobiographical Writings. Edited with Introductions by Henry Tristram. New York: Sheed and Ward, 1957.

Cardinal Newman and William Froude, FRS: A Correspondence. Edited by Gordon Huntington Harper. Baltimore: Johns Hopkins Press, 1933.

Discussions and Arguments, 1891.

An Essay on the Development of Christian Doctrine, (1878). Reprint. Westminster, Md.: Christian Classics, Inc., 1968.

Difficulties of Anglicans, 2 vols., 1918.

Discourses to Mixed Congregations, 1921.

Essays Critical and Historical, 2 vols., 1919.

An Essay in Aid of a Grammar of Assent. Edited with Introduction and Notes by I. T. Ker. Oxford: Clarendon Press, 1985.

Historical Sketches, 3 vols., 1908.

The Idea of a University. Edited with Introduction and Notes by I. T. Ker. Oxford: Clarendon Press, 1976.

The Letters and Correspondence of John Henry Newman. Edited by Anne Mozley. 2 vols., 1890.

The Letters and Diaries of John Henry Newman, 31 vols. Edited at the Birmingham Oratory by Charles Stephen Dessain and Vincent Ferrer Blehl, S. J. London: Thomas Nelson and Sons, 1961–present.

Newman's University Sermons: Fifteen Sermons Preached before the University of Oxford, 1826–1843. With Introductory Essays by D. M. Mackinnon and J. D. Holmes. London: S.P.C.K., 1970.

Newman and Gladstone: The Vatican Decrees. With an Introduction by Alvan S. Ryan. Notre Dame: University of Notre Dame Press, 1962.

296

On Consulting the Faithful in Matters of Doctrine. Edited with an introduction by John Coulson. London: G. Chapman, 1961.

The Philosophical Notebook of John Henry Newman. Edited by Edward J. Sillem. 2 vols. Louvain: Nauwelaerts, 1969.

Plain and Parochial Sermons, 8 vols., 1891.

Present Position of Catholics in England, 1893.

Sermons Bearing on Subjects of the Day, 1918.

Sermons Preached on Various Occasions, 1919.

The Theological Papers of John Henry Newman on Faith and Certainty. Partly prepared for publication by Hugo M. de Acheval, selected and edited by J. Derek Holmes, with a note of introduction by Charles Stephen Dessain. Oxford: Clarendon Press, 1976.

Sermons Preached on Various Occasions, 1921.

Two Essays on Eccleiastical and Biblical Miracles, 1924.

The Via Media of the Anglican Church, 2 vols., 1885.

SECONDARY SOURCES ON NEWMAN

Artz, Johannes. "Newman as Philosopher." *International Philosophical Quarterly,* XVI, 3 (September 1976), 263–89.

Bastable, J. D. "Cardinal Newman's Philosophy of Belief." *Philosophical Studies,* 5 (December 1955), 44–70.

———. "Truth and Goodness in Higher Education." *Philosophical Studies* (Irl.), XXVII (1980), 221–28.

———. "The Germination of Belief Within Probability According to Newman." *Philosophical Studies,* XI (1961–62), 81–111.

———, ed., *Newman and Gladstone: Centennial Essays.* Dublin: Veritas Publications, 1978.

Beer, John. "Newman and the Romantic Sensibility," in Hugh Sykes Davies and George Watson, eds., *The English Mind: Studies in the English Moralists* Presented to Basil Willey. Cambridge: Cambridge University Press, 1964, pp. 193–218.

Biemer, Gunter. *Newman on Tradition.* London: Herder and Herder, 1967.

Benard, Rev. Edmund Darvil. *A Preface to Newman's Theology.* St. Louis: B. Herder, 1946.

Bibliography

Blehl, Vincent F. "Newman, the Fathers, and Education." *Thought* (Summer 1970), 196–212.

Blehl, Vincent, and Connolly, Francis X., eds., *Newman's Apologia: A Classic Reconsidered.* New York: Harcourt, Brace and World, Inc., 1964.

Boekraad, Adrian J. *The Personal Conquest of Truth According to John Henry Newman.* Louvain: Editions Nauwelaerts, 1955.

Boekraad, Adrian J. and Henry Tristram. *The Argument from Conscience to the Existence of God According to John Henry Newman.* Louvain: Editions Nauwelaerts, 1961.

Cameron, J. M. *The Night Battle: Essays.* Baltimore: Helicon Press, 1962.

———. "Newman and Locke: A Note on Some Themes in *An Essay in Aid of a Grammar of Assent.*" In *Newman-Studien,* IX, Nurnberg: Glock and Lutz, 1974.

———. *John Henry Newman.* London: Longmans, Green and Company, 1956.

———. *On the Idea of a University.* Toronto: University of Toronto Press, 1978.

Casey, Gerard. *Natural Reason: A Study of the Notions of Inference, Assent, Intuition, and First Principles in the Philosophy of John Henry Cardinal Newman.* New York: Peter Lang, 1984.

Chadwick, Owen. *From Bossuet to Newman.* Cambridge: Cambridge University Press, 1957.

Church, R. W. *The Oxford Movement: Twelve Years: 1833–1845.* Edited with an Introduction by Geoffrey Best. Chicago: University of Chicago Press, 1970.

Clancey, Richard W. "Dublin Discourses: Rhetorical Method in Textual Revisions." *Renascence,* XX (Winter 1968), 59–74.

Colby, Robert A. "The Structure of Newman's *Apologia Pro Vita Sua* in Relation to His Theory of Assent." *The Dublin Review,* 460 (Summer 1953), 140–56.

Connolly, Francis X., ed. *A Newman Reader: An Anthology of the Writings of John Henry Newman.* Garden City, N.Y.: Doubleday and Company, 1964.

Corbett, E. P. J. "Some Rhetorical Lessons from John Henry Newman." *College Composition and Communication,* 31 (December 1980), 402–11.

Corcoran, Timothy, S. J. "Liberal Studies and Moral Aims: A Critical Study of Newman's Position." *Thought* (June 1926), 54–71.

Coulson, John. *Newman and the Common Tradition.* Oxford: Clarendon Press, 1970.

————. "Newman's Idea of an Open University and Its Consequences Today," in J. D. Bastable, ed., *Newman and Gladstone: Centennial Essays*. Dublin: Veritas Publications, 1978, pp. 221–37.

Coulson,, John, and Allchin, A. M., eds., *The Rediscovery of Newman: An Oxford Symposium*. London: Sheed and Ward, 1967.

Culler, A. Dwight. *The Imperial Intellect*. New Haven: Yale University Press, 1955.

Dale, P. A. "Newman's 'The Idea of a University': The Dangers of a University Education." *Victorian Studies*, XVI (September 1972), 5–36.

D'Arcy, S. J., Martin Cyril. *The Nature of Belief*. London: Sheed and Ward, 1931.

DeLaura, David J., ed., *Apologia Pro Vita Sua*. New York: W. W. Norton and Company, 1968.

————. *Hebrew and Hellene in Victorian England: Newman, Arnold, and Pater*. Austin: University of Texas Press, 1969.

Dessain, Charles Stephen. *John Henry Newman*. London: Thomas Nelson and Sons, 1966.

————. "Cardinal Newman on the Theory and Practice of Knowledge. The Purpose of the *Grammar of Assent*." *The Downside Review*, 75 (January 1957), 1–23.

Dulles, Avery. "Faith, Reason, and the Logic of Discovery." *Thought*, XLV (Winter 1970), 485–502.

Evans, Gillian R. " 'An Organon More Delicate, Versatile and Elastic': John Henry Newman and Whately's *Logic*." *The Downside Review*, 99 (July 1979), 175–91.

Faber, Geoffrey. *Oxford Apostles: A Character Study of the Oxford Movement*. London: Faber and Faber, 1974.

Ferreira, M. Jamie. *Doubt and Religious Commitment*. Oxford: Clarendon Press, 1980.

Fey, William R., O.F.M., Cap. *Faith and Doubt: The Unfolding of Newman's Thought on Certainty*. Shepherdstown, W.Va.: Patmos Press, 1976.

————. "Philosophy and Theology in Cardinal Newman." *Laurentianum*, 1 (1976), 60–81.

Gable, O. S. B., Sister Mariella. "The Rhetoric of John Henry Newman's *Parochial and Plain Sermons* with Special Reference to His Dependence on Aristotle's *Rhetoric*." Ph.D. Dissertation, Cornell, 1934.

Gates, Lewis. "Newman as a Prose Writer," in *Three Studies in Literature*. New York: Macmillan Company, 1899.

Bibliography

Gill, John M. "Newman's Dialectic in *The Idea of a University.*" *Quarterly Journal of Speech*, XLV (December 1959), 415–18.

Griffen, John R. *Newman: A Bibliography of Secondary Sources.* Front Royal, Va: Christendom College Press, 1980.

Happel, Stephen. "Imagination, Method in Theology, and Rhetoric: On Re-Examining Samuel Taylor Coleridge." *Louvain Studies,* 8 (Fall 1980), 143–69.

Harper, Gordon Huntington, ed., *Cardinal Newman and William Froude, FRS: A Correspondence.* Baltimore: Johns Hopkins University Press, 1933.

Harrold, Charles Frederick. *John Henry Newman: An Expository and Critical Study of His Mind, Thought and Art.* New York: Longmans, Green and Co., 1945.

Heath, Dwight B. "Liberal Education: John Henry Newman's Conception." *Education Theory,* IX (July 1959), 152–55.

Holloway, John. *The Victorian Sage: Studies in Argument.* New York: W. W. Norton and Company, 1965.

Holmes, Jan Derek. "Personal Influence and Religious Conviction—Newman and Controversy," *Newman-Studien,* X. Heroldsberg bei Nürnberg: Glock und Lutz, 1978, 26–46.

———. "Cardinal Newman's Apologetic Use of History." *Louvain Studies,* 55 (Fall 1983), 338–49.

Horgan, John D. "Newman on Faith and Reason." *Studies: Irish Quarterly Review* (1953), 132–50.

Houghton, Walter E. *The Art of Newman's Apologia.* New Haven: Yale University Press, 1945.

Houppert, Joseph W., ed., *John Henry Newman.* St. Louis: B. Herder, [n.d.]

Juergens, Sylvester P. *Newman on the Psychology of Faith in the Individual.* New York: Macmillan Company, 1928.

Kaiser, F.S.C., Brother F. James. *The Concept of Conscience According to John Henry Newman.* Washington, D. C.: Catholic University of America Press, 1958.

Ker, I. T. "Recent Critics of Newman's *A Grammar of Assent.*" *Religious Studies,* 13 (March 1977), 63–71.

———. "Editor's Introduction" in *The Idea of a University.* Edited by I. T. Ker. Oxford: Clarendon Press, 1976.

Lash, Nicholas. *Newman on Development.* Shepherdstown, W. Va.: Patmos Press, 1975.

————. "The Notions of 'Implicit' and 'Explicit' Reason in Newman's University Sermons: A Difficulty." *The Heythrop Journal* (1970), 48–54.

————. "Was Newman a Theologian?" *The Heythrop Journal,* XXVII (July 1976), 321–25.

————. "Did Newman Have a 'Theory' of Development?" in James D. Bastable, ed., *Newman and Gladstone: Centennial Essays.* Dublin: Veritas Publications, 1978, pp. 161–75.

Levine, George. *The Boundaries of Fiction: Carlyle, Macaulay, Newman.* Princeton, N.J.: Princeton University Press, 1968.

Loughery, Rev. James G. "The Rhetorical Theory of John Henry Newman." Ph.D. Dissertation, University of Michigan, 1951.

Lyons, James W. *Newman's Dialogues on Certitude.* Rome: Catholic Book Agency, 1978.

Marmion, The Revd J. P. "Newman and Education." *The Downside Review,* 97 (January 1979), 10–29.

McGrath, S. J., Fergal. *The Consecration of Learning.* New York: Fordham University Press, 1962.

————. *Newman's University: Idea and Reality.* London: Longmans, Green and Company, 1951.

Miller, O. P., Jeremy. "Newman's Dialogical Vision of the Church." *Louvain Studies,* 8 (Spring 1981), 318–31.

Mulcahy, D. G. "Personal Influence, Discipline and Liberal Education in Cardinal Newman's Idea of a University." *Newman-Studien,* 11. Heroldsberg bei Nurnberg, 1980, 151–58.

Newman, Jay. *The Mental Philosophy of John Henry Newman.* Waterloo, Ontario, Canada: Wilfrid Laurier University Press, 1986.

Norris, Thomas J. *Newman and His Theological Method.* Leiden: E. J. Brill, 1977.

O'Donoghue, N.D. "Newman and the Problem of Privileged Access to Truth." *Irish Theological Quarterly,* 42 (1975), 241–58.

Pailin, David. *The Way to Faith: An Examination of Newman's Grammar of Assent as a Response to the Search for Certainty in Faith.* London: Epworth Press, 1969.

Petitpas, H. M. "Newman's Idea of Literature: A Humanist Spectrum." *Renascence,* 17 (1964), 97–105.

Powell, Jouett Lynn. *Three Uses of Christian Discourse in John Henry Newman: An Example of Non-Reductive Reflection on the Christian Faith.* Diss. Series No. 10. Missoula, Mont.: Scholars Press, 1975.

Price, H. H. *Belief.* London: George Allen and Unwin, 1969.

Rea, David F. "John Henry Newman's Concept of Rhetoric." Master's Dissertation, Fordham University, 1956.

Ryan, John K., and Edmund Darvil Benard, eds. *American Essays for the Newman Centennial.* Washington, D. C.: Catholic University of America Press, 1947.

Selby, Robin C. *The Principle of Reserve in the Writings of John Henry Cardinal Newman.* Oxford: Clarendon Press, 1976.

Siebenschuh, William R. "What is Art and What is Evidence: Newman's *Apologia Pro Vita Sua,*" in *Fictional Techniques and Factual Works.* Athens, Georgia: University of Georgia Press, 1983.

Sillem, Edward J. "Cardinal Newman's *Grammar of Assent* on Conscience as a Way to God." *The Heythrop Journal,* (June 1964), 377–401.

———. *General Introduction to the Study of Newman's Philosophy.* Vol. I of *The Philosophical Notebook of John Henry Newman.* 2 vols. Revised by A. J. Boekraad. Louvain: Nauwelaerts Publishing House, 1970.

Snyder, Phillip. "Newman's Way with the Reader in *A Grammar of Assent.*" *The Victorian Newsletter,* 56 (Fall 1979), 1–6.

Strong, L. A. G. "Was Newman a Failure?" *The Nineteenth Century,* (May 1933), 620–28.

Tardivel, Ferdinande. *La Personalité Litteraire de Newman.* Paris: Gabriel Beauchesne et Ses Fils, 1937.

Tierney, Dr. Michael. "Newman's Doctrine of University Education." *Studies* (Summer 1953), 121–31.

———, ed., *A Tribute to Newman: Essays on Aspects of His Life and Thought.* Dublin: Browne and Nolan, 1945.

Tolhurst, D. D., Revd. James. "The Idea of the Church as a Community in the Anglican Sermons of John Henry Newman." *The Downside Review,* 101 (April 1983), 140–64.

Townsend, Francis G. "Newman and the Problem of Critical Prose." *Victorian Newsletter,* 11 (Spring 1957), 22–5.

Trevor, Meriol. *The Pillar of the Cloud.* Garden City, N.Y.: Doubleday and Co., 1962.

Vargish, Thomas. *Newman: The Contemplation of Mind*. Oxford: Clarendon Press, 1970.

Verdeke, Gerard. "Aristotelian Roots of Newman's Illative Sense," in J. D. Bastable, ed., *Newman and Gladstone: Centennial Essays*. Dublin: Veritas Publications, 1978, pp. 177–95.

Walgrave, O. P., J.–H. *Newman the Theologian*. Translated by A. V. Littledale. New York: Sheed and Ward, 1960.

Ward, Wilfrid. *Last Lectures*. London: Longmans, Green and Co., 1918. Reprint. Freeport, N.Y.: Books for Libraries Press, 1967.

———. *The Life of John Henry Cardinal Newman*, 2 vols. London: Longmans, Green and Company, 1913.

Weatherby, Harold L. *Cardinal Newman in His Age: His Place in English Theology and Literature*. Nashville: Vanderbilt University Press, 1973.

Wicker, Brian. "Newman and Logic." *Newman-Studien*, V. Nurnberg: Glock and Lutz, 1972, 251–68.

Wieland, James. "John Henry Newman, *The Tamworth Reading Room:* Towards The Idea of a University." *The Downside Review*, 103 (April 1985), 127–36.

Wilberforce, Samuel. "Review of Dr. Newman's *Apologia Pro Vita Sua*." *Quarterly Review*, 116 (October 1864), 528–73.

Willam, Franz Michel. *Die Erkenntnislehre Kardinal Newmans: Systematische Darlegung und Dokumentation*. Frankfurt: Verlag Gerhard Kaffke, 1969.

Wise, John E. "Newman and the Liberal Arts." *Thought*, XX (June 1945), 253–70.

Wright, T. R., ed., *John Henry Newman: A Man for Our Time?* Newcastle Upon Tyne: Grevatt and Grevatt, 1983.

Yanitelli, S. J., Victor R., ed. *A Newman Symposium*. New York: Fordham University Press, 1952.

Yearley, Lee. *The Ideas of Newman: Christianity and Human Religiosity*. University Park: Pennsylvania State University Press, 1978.

Zeno, O.F.M., Cap., Fr. P. *Our Way to Certitude: An Introduction to Newman's Psychological Discovery: The Illative Sense, and His Grammar of Assent*. Leiden: E. J. Brill, 1957.

OTHER WORKS: BOOKS

Abrams, M. H. *The Mirror and the Lamp: Romantic Theory and the Critical Tradition*. Oxford: Oxford University Press, 1953.

Bibliography

Aldrich, Henry. *Artis Logicae Rudimenta*. Oxford: Henry Hammans, 1862.

Altick, Richard D. *Victorian People and Ideas*. New York: W. W. Norton and Company, 1973.

Angell, Richard B. *Reasoning and Logic*. New York: Meredith Publishing Company, 1964.

Aristotle. *"Art" of Rhetoric*. Translated by J. H. Freese. Cambridge: Harvard University Press, 1926; repr. 1975.

———. *Nicomachean Ethics*. Translated, with Introduction and Notes, by Martin Ostwald. Indianapolis: Bobbs–Merrill, 1962.

———. *The Organon, or Logical Treatises of Aristotle*. Translated by Octavius Freire Owen. 2 vols. London: Henry G. Bohn, 1858.

Arnhart, Larry. *Aristotle on Political Reasoning: A Commentary on the Rhetoric*. Dekalb: Northern Illinois University Press, 1981.

Arnold, Matthew. *The Complete Prose Works of Matthew Arnold*. 11 vols. Edited by R. H. Super. Ann Arbor: University of Michigan Press, 1961–77.

Augustine, St. *On Christian Doctrine*. Translated, with an Introduction, by D. W. Robertson, Jr. Indianapolis: Bobbs–Merrill, 1958.

Bacon, Francis. *The Works of Francis Bacon*. 7 vols. Edited by James Spedding, Robert Leslie Ellis, and Douglas Denon Heath. London: Longman and Company, 1858.

Bate, Walter Jackson. *From Classic to Romantic*. New York: Harper and Row, 1946.

Berger, Peter L. *A Rumor of Angels*. Garden City, N.Y.: Doubleday and Company, 1970.

———. *The Heretical Imperative: Contemporary Possibilities of Religious Affirmation*. Garden City, N.Y.: Doubleday and Company, 1980.

Bernstein, Richard J. *Beyond Objectivism and Relativism: Science, Hermeneutics, and Praxis*. Philadelphia: University of Pennsylvania Press, 1983.

———. *Philosophical Profiles*. Philadelphia: University of Pennsylvania Press, 1986.

Blair, Hugh. *Lectures on Rhetoric and Belles Lettres*, 2 vols. Edited by Harold F. Harding. Carbondale: Southern Illinois University Press, 1965.

Booth, Wayne C. *Modern Dogma and the Rhetoric of Assent*. Chicago: University of Chicago Press, 1974.

———. *Critical Understanding: The Powers and Limits of Pluralism*. Chicago: University of Chicago Press, 1979.

————. *The Idea of a University as Seen by a Rhetorician.* Ryerson Lecture, University of Chicago, 1987.

————. *The Company We Keep: An Ethics of Fiction.* Berkeley: University of California Press, 1988.

Brown, Frank Burch. *Transfiguration: Poetic Metaphor and the Language of Religious Belief.* Chapel Hill: University of North Carolina Press, 1983.

Buckley, Jerome Hamilton. *The Victorian Temper: A Study in Literary Culture.* Cambridge: Cambridge University Press, 1951.

Burke, Kenneth. *A Grammar of Motives.* Berkeley: University of California Press, 1969.

————. *A Rhetoric of Motives.* Berkeley: University of California Press, 1969.

————. *Attitudes Toward History.* Los Altos, California: Hermes Publications, 1959.

————. *Language as Symbolic Action: Essays on Life, Literature and Method.* Berkeley: University of California Press, 1966.

————. *Permanence and Change.* Indianapolis: Bobbs–Merrill, 1965.

————. *The Philosophy of Literary Form.* New York: Vintage Books, 1941.

————. *The Rhetoric of Religion: Studies in Logology.* Berkeley: University of California Press, 1970.

————. "Dramatism," in the *International Encyclopedia of the Social Sciences,* ed. David L. Sills. New York: Macmillan Company, 1968, VII, 445–51.

————. "Biology, Psychology, and Words," in *Dramatism and Development.* Barre, Mass.: Clark University Press, 1971, pp. 11–55.

Butler, Joseph. *The Analogy of Religion, Natural and Revealed, to the Constitution and Course of Nature.* London: J. M. Dent and Company, [n.d.].

Campbell, George. *The Philosophy of Rhetoric.* Edited by Lloyd F. Bitzer. Carbondale: Southern Illinois University Press, 1963.

Carlyle, Thomas, *Collected Works.* 30 vols. London: Chapman and Hall, [n.d.].

Channing, Edward T. *Lectures Read to the Seniors in Harvard College.* Edited by Dorothy I. Anderson and Waldo W. Braden. Foreword by David Potter. Carbondale: Southern Illinois University Press, 1968.

Cherwitz, Richard A. and James W. Hikins, *Communication and Knowledge: An Investigation in Rhetorical Epistemology.* Columbia: University of South Carolina Press, 1986.

Bibliography

Cicero. *De Inventione, De Optimo Genere Oratorum, Topica*. With an English Translation by H. M. Hubbell. Cambridge: Harvard University Press, 1949; repr. 1976.

———. *De Oratore*. 2 vols. With an English Translation by E. W. Sutton. Cambridge: Harvard University Press, 1942; repr. 1979.

———. *De Officiis*. With an English Translation by Walter Miller. Cambridge: Harvard University Press, 1913; repr. 1975.

Clifford, William Kingdon. *Lectures and Essays*. 2 vols. Edited by Leslie Stephen and Frederick Pollock. London: Macmillan and Company, 1879.

Cohen, Morris R. and Ernest Nagel. *An Introduction to Logic and Scientific Method*. London: Routledge and Kegan Paul, 1961.

Coleridge, Samuel Taylor. *Treatise on Method*. Edited, with Introduction and Notes, by Alice D. Snyder. London: Constable and Company, Ltd., 1934.

Copleston, Edward. *A Reply to the Calumnies of the Edinburgh Reviewers Against Oxford*. London: J. Cooke, J. Parker, and J. MacKinley, 1810.

Coulson, John. *Religion and Imagination*. Oxford: Clarendon Press, 1981.

Crane, R. S. *The Idea of the Humanities and Other Essays*. 2 vols. Chicago: University of Chicago Press, 1967.

Davies, Hugh Sykes and George Watson, eds. *The English Mind: Studies in the English Moralists Presented to Basil Willey*. Cambridge: Cambridge University Press, 1964.

Davis, Walter. *The Act of Interpretation*. Chicago: University of Chicago Press, 1978.

DeLaura, David J., ed. *Victorian Prose: A Guide to Research*. New York: Modern Language Association of America, 1973.

Descartes, René. *Philosophical Essays*. Translated, with an Introduction and Notes, by Laurence J. LaFleur. Indianapolis: Bobbs–Merrill, 1977.

De Quincey, Thomas. *The Collected Writings of Thomas De Quincey*. Edited by David Masson. Edinburgh, 1889–1890. Reprint. New York: AMS Press, 1968.

Dewey, John. *The Public and Its Problems*. Athens, Ohio: Swallow Press, 1954.

———. *Essays in Experimental Logic*. Chicago: University of Chicago Press, 1916. Reprint. New York: Dover Publications, [n.d.]

Evans, J. D. G. *Aristotle's Concept of Dialectic*. Cambridge: Cambridge University Press, 1977.

Ferreira, M. Jamie. *Scepticism and Reasonable Doubt*. Oxford: Clarendon Press, 1986.

Fish, Stanley. *Is There a Text in This Class? The Authority of Interpretive Communities.* Cambridge: Harvard University Press, 1980.

Fisher, Walter R. *Human Communication as Narration: Toward a Philosophy of Reason, Value, and Action.* Columbia: University of South Carolina Press, 1987.

Fortenbaugh, William W. *Aristotle on Emotion.* New York: Barnes and Noble, 1975.

Gadamer, Hans-Georg. *Truth and Method.* New York: Crossroad Publishing, 1986.

Garver, Eugene. *Machiavelli and the History of Prudence.* Madison: University of Wisconsin Press, 1987.

Gibbon, Edward. *An Essay on the Study of Literature.* London: T. Becket and P. A. DeHondt, 1764. Reprint. New York: Garland Publishing, Inc., 1970.

Graff, Gerald. *Literature Against Itself: Literary Ideas in Modern Society.* Chicago: University of Chicago Press, 1979.

Grassi, Ernesto. *Rhetoric as Philosophy: The Humanist Tradition.* University Park: Pennsylvania State University Press, 1980.

Gregg, Richard B. *Symbolic Inducement and Knowing: A Study in the Foundations of Knowing.* Columbia: University of South Carolina Press, 1984.

Grimaldi, S. J., William M. A. *Studies in the Philosophy of Aristotle's Rhetoric.* Wiesbaden: Franz Steiner Verlag, 1972.

Harrold, Charles Frederick. *Carlyle and German Thought: 1819–1834.* New Haven: Yale University Press, 1934.

Harvey, Van A. *The Historian and the Believer.* Philadelphia: The Westminster Press, 1966.

Horner, Winifred Bryan. *The Present State of Scholarship in Historical and Contemporary Rhetoric.* Columbia: University of Missouri Press, 1983.

Houghton, Walter. *The Victorian Frame of Mind: 1830–1870.* New Haven: Yale University Press, 1957.

Howell, Wilbur Samuel. *Eighteenth–Century British Logic and Rhetoric.* Princeton: Princeton University Press, 1971.

———. *Logic and Rhetoric in England, 1500–1700.* New York: Russel and Russel, 1956.

Hume, David. *Dialogue Concerning Natural Religion.* New York: Hafner Publishing Co., 1959.

307

Bibliography

————. *An Inquiry Concerning Human Understanding*. Indianapolis: Bobbs–Merrill, 1955.

————. *A Treatise of Human Nature*. Edited, with an Analytical Index, by L. A. Selby-Bigge. Oxford: Clarendon Press, 1980.

————. *An Inquiry Concerning the Principles of Morals*. Indianapolis: Bobbs–Merrill, 1957.

————. *Of the Standard of Taste and Other Essays*. Edited by John W. Lenz. Indianapolis: Bobbs–Merrill, 1965.

Hutchins, Robert M. *The Higher Learning in America*. New Haven: Yale University Press, 1936.

Huxley, Thomas H. *Science and Education*. New York: D. Appleton, 1898.

Ijsseling, Samuel. *Rhetoric and Philosophy in Conflict. An Historical Survey*. The Hague: Martinus Nijhoff, 1976.

James, William. *The Writings of William James*. Edited, with an Introduction and New Preface by John J. McDermott. Chicago: University of Chicago Press, 1977.

Kahn, Victoria. *Rhetoric, Prudence and Skepticism in the Renaissance*. Ithaca: Cornell University Press, 1985.

Kaufman, Gordon. *An Essay on Theological Method*. Missoula, Montana: Scholars Press, 1975.

Kerr, Clark. *The Uses of the University*. New York: Harper and Row, 1963.

Kiefer, Howard E. and Milton K. Munitz, eds., *Perspectives in Education, Religion, and the Arts*. Albany: State University of New York Press, 1970.

Kimball, Bruce. *Orators and Philosophers: A History of the Idea of Liberal Education*. New York: Teachers College, Columbia University, 1986.

Knights, Ben. *The Idea of the Clerisy in the Nineteenth Century*. Cambridge: Cambridge University Press, 1978.

Küng, Hans. *Infallible? An Inquiry*. Translated by Edward Quinn. Garden City, N.Y.: Doubleday and Company, 1983.

Lanham, Richard A. *The Motives of Eloquence*. New Haven: Yale University Press, 1976.

Lash, Nicholas. *Change in Focus*. London: Sheed and Ward, 1973.

Leavis, F. R. *Education and the University*. New York: George W. Stewart, 1948.

Lechner, O.S.U., Sr. Joan Marie. *Renaissance Concepts of the Commonplace*. New York: Pageant Press, 1962.

Lentricchia, Frank. *Criticism and Social Change*. Chicago: University of Chicago Press, 1983.

Levine, George and William Madden, eds. *The Art of Victorian Prose*. New York: Oxford University Press, 1968.

Levine, Richard A. *The Victorian Experience: The Prose Writers*. Athens, Ohio: Ohio University Press, 1982.

Livingston, James. C. *The Ethics of Belief: An Essay on the Victorian Religious Conscience*. AAR Studies in Religion. Tallahassee, Fla.: American Academy of Religion and Scholars Press, 1974.

————. *Matthew Arnold and Christianity: His Religious Prose Writings*. Columbia: University of South Carolina Press, 1986.

Locke, John. *An Essay Concerning Human Understanding*. Edited by Alexander Campbell Fraser, 2 vols. New York: Dover Publications, Inc., 1959.

————. *The Reasonableness of Christianity*. Edited by I. T. Ramsey. Stanford: Stanford University Press, 1958.

Macaulay, Thomas Babington. *Critical, Historical, and Miscellaneous Essays and Poems,* 3 vols. New York: Lovell, Coryell, and Company, [n.d.].

MacDonald, Margaret, ed., *Philosophy and Analysis*. Oxford: Basil Blackwell, 1954.

Macquarrie, John. *God–Talk*. New York: Harper and Row, 1967.

Mallet, Charles Edward. *A History of the University of Oxford*. 3 vols. New York: Longmans, Green and Company, 1928.

Manwaring, Edward. *Institutes of Learning*. London: W. Innys and R. Manby, 1737. Reprint. Menston, England: Scholar Press Limited, 1968.

Marrou, H. I. *A History of Education in Antiquity*. Madison: University of Wisconsin Press, 1982.

McFague, Sallie. *Speaking in Parables: A Study in Metaphor and Theology*. Philadelphia: Fortress Press, 1975.

————. *Metaphorical Theology: Models of God in Religious Language*. Philadelphia: Fortress Press, 1982.

Bibliography

McKeon, Richard. *Introduction to the Philosophy of Cicero*. Chicago: University of Chicago Press, 1950.

————. *Rhetoric: Essays in Invention and Discovery*. Edited with an Introduction by Mark Backman. Woodbridge, CT.: Ox Bow Press, 1987.

Mill, John Stuart. *A System of Logic, Ratiocinative and Inductive*, in *Collected Works of John Stuart Mill*. Edited by John Robson. Vols. VII–VIII. Toronto: University of Toronto Press, 1963.

Millgate, Jane. *Macaulay*. London: Routledge and Kegan Paul, 1973.

Mitchell, Basil. *The Justification of Religious Belief*. New York: Oxford University Press, 1981.

Murphy, James J. *Rhetoric in the Middle Ages: A History of Rhetorical Theory from St. Augustine to the Renaissance*. Berkeley: University of California Press, 1974.

————, ed., *The Rhetorical Tradition and Modern Writing*. New York: The Modern Language Association of America, 1982.

Nelson, John S., Allan Megill, and Donald N. McCloskey, eds. *The Rhetoric of the Human Sciences: Language and Argument in Scholarship and Public Affairs*. Madison: University of Wisconsin Press, 1987.

Ong, Walter J. *American Catholic Crossroads*. New York: Collier Books, 1962.

————. *The Presence of the Word*. New York: Simon and Shuster, 1967.

————. *Ramus, Method, and the Decay of Dialogue*. New York: Octagon Books, 1979.

————. *Rhetoric, Romance and Technology*. Ithaca, N.Y.: Cornell University Press, 1971.

Ortega y Gasset, José. *Mission of the University*. New York: W. W. Norton and Company, 1944.

Owen, G. E. L., ed. *Aristotle on Dialectic: The Topics*. Oxford: Clarendon Press, 1968.

Paley, William. *A View of the Evidences of Christianity*. Annotations by Richard Whately. New York: James Miller, 1865.

Perelman, Chaim, and Olbrechts-Tyteca, L. *The New Rhetoric: A Treatise in Argumentation*. Notre Dame: University of Notre Dame Press, 1969.

Perelman, Chaim, *The New Rhetoric and the Humanities: Essays on Rhetoric and Its Applications*. Dordrecht: D. Reidel Publishing Co., 1979.

------. *The Realm of Rhetoric*. Notre Dame: University of Notre Dame Press, 1982.

Polanyi, Michael. *Personal Knowledge*. Chicago: University of Chicago Press, 1958.

------. *Science, Faith and Society*. Chicago: University of Chicago Press, 1946.

------. *The Tacit Dimension*. Garden City, N.Y.: Doubleday and Company, 1966.

Prickett, Stephen. *Romanticism and Religion*. Cambridge: Cambridge University Press, 1976.

Price, H. H. *Belief*. London: George Allen and Unwin, 1969.

Quintilian. *The Institutio Oratoria of Quintilian*. Translated by H. E. Butler. 4 vols. Cambridge: Harvard University Press, 1920; repr. 1980.

Ricoeur, Paul. *The Conflict of Interpretations*. Evanston: Northwestern University Press, 1974.

------. *Freud and Philosophy: A Study in Interpretation*. Translated by Denis Savage. New Haven: Yale University Press, 1970.

------. *Interpretation Theory: Discourse and the Surplus of Meaning* Fort Worth: Texas Christian University Press, 1976.

------. *Heremeneutics and the Human Sciences*. Edited and translated by John B. Thompson. Cambridge: Cambridge University Press, 1981.

Rorty, Richard. *Philosophy and the Mirror of Nature*. Princeton: Princeton University Press, 1979.

Rueckert, William H. *Kenneth Burke and the Drama of Human Relations*. 2nd Edition. Berkeley: University of California Press, 1982.

Schoof, O. P., Mark. *A Survey of Catholic Theology: 1800–1970*. Translated by N. D. Smith, with an Introduction by E. Schillebeecks, O. P. Glen Rock, N.J.: Paulist Newman Press, 1970.

Scott, Nathan A. *The Poetics of Belief: Studies in Coleridge, Arnold, Pater, Santayana, Stevens, and Heidegger*. Chapel Hill: University of North Carolina Press, 1985.

Sesonske, Alexander, and Fleming, Noel, eds. *Human Understanding: Studies in the Philosophy of David Hume*. Belmont, Calif.: Wadsworth Publishing Company, 1965.

Shapiro, Barbara. *Probability and Certainty in Seventeenth-Century England*. Princeton: Princeton University Press, 1983.

Solomon, Robert C. *The Passions: The Myth and Nature of Human Emotion*. Notre Dame: University of Notre Dame Press, 1983.

Bibliography

Spencer, Herbert. *Essays on Education*. London: J. M. Dent and Sons, 1963.

Stone, Julius. *Legal Systems and Lawyers' Reasonings*. Stanford: Stanford University Press, 1964.

Struever, Nancy S. and Brian Vickers, eds. *Rhetoric and the Pursuit of Truth: Language and Change in the Seventeenth and Eighteenth Century*. Los Angeles: University of California, 1985.

Toulmin, Stephen. *The Uses of Argument*. Cambridge: Cambridge University Press, 1958.

Tracy, David. *Blessed Rage for Order: The New Pluralism in Theology*. New York: Seabury Press, 1978.

———. *The Analogical Imagination: Christian Theology and the Culture of Pluralism*. New York: Crossroad Publishing, 1981.

———. *Plurality and Ambiguity: Hermeneutics, Religion, Hope*. San Francisco: Harper and Row, 1987.

Valesio, Paolo. *Novantiqua: Rhetorics as a Contemporary Theory*. Bloomington: Indiana University Press, 1980.

Various Authors (*Vari Autori*). *John Henry Newman, Theologian and Cardinal*. Atti del Simposio Internazionale (7–12 Ottobre 1979). Rome: Urbaniana University Press, 1981.

Vico, Giambattista. *The Autobiography of Giambattista Vico*. Translated by Max Harold Fisch and Thomas Goddard Bergin. Ithaca: Cornell University Press, 1944.

———. *On the Study Methods of Our Time*. Translated, with an Introduction and Notes, by Elio Gianturco. Indianapolis: Bobbs–Merrill, 1965.

Vidler, Alec R. *The Church in an Age of Revolution*. New York: Penguin Books, 1971.

Vives, Juan Luis. *Vives: On Education, A Translation of the De Tradendis Disciplinis of Juan Luis Vives*. With an Introduction by Foster Watson. Cambridge: Cambridge University Press, 1913.

Wallace, Karl R. *Francis Bacon on Communication and Rhetoric*. Chapel Hill: University of North Carolina Press, 1943.

Ward, Wilfrid. *Problems and Persons* (1903). Reprint., Freeport, N.Y.: Books for Libraries Press, 1968.

Wegener, Charles. *Liberal Education and the Modern University*. Chicago: University of Chicago Press, 1979.

Whately, E. Jane. *Life and Correspondence of Richard Whately, D. D.* 2 vols. London: Longmans, Green and Company, 1866.

Whately, Richard. *Elements of Logic.* Delmar, N.Y.: Scholars' Facsimiles and Reprints, 1975.

———. *Elements of Rhetoric.* Edited, with an Introduction by Douglas Ehninger. Carbondale: Southern Illinois University Press, 1963.

———. *Essays [Second Series] on Some of the Difficulties in the Writings of the Apostle Paul, and in Other Parts of the New Testament.* London: John W. Palmer and Son, 1854.

———. *Historic Doubts Relative to Napolean Buonaparte.* Andover: Warren F. Draper, 1874.

———. *The Use and Abuse of Party–Feeling in Matters of Religion; Being the Course of the Bampton Lectures for the Year 1822.* London: John W. Palmer and Son, 1859.

———. *Introductory Lessons on Christian Evidences.* Philadelphia: H. Hooker, 1856.

Wheelwright, Philip. *Metaphor and Reality.* Bloomington: Indiana University Press, 1962.

———. *The Burning Fountain: A Study in the Language of Symbolism.* Bloomington: Indiana University Press, 1954.

Whewell, William. *On the Principles of English University Education.* London: John W. Parker, 1938.

White, Hayden and Margaret Brose, eds., *Representing Kenneth Burke: Selected Papers from the English Institute,* New Series, No. 6. Baltimore: Johns Hopkins University Press, 1982.

White, James Boyd. *When Words Lose Their Meaning: Constitutions and Reconstitutions of Language, Character, and Community.* Chicago: University of Chicago Press, 1984.

———. *Heracles' Bow: Essays on the Rhetoric and Poetics of the Law.* Madison: University of Wisconsin Press, 1985.

Whitehead, Alfred North. *The Aims of Education.* New York: Macmillan Co., 1924.

Willey, Basil. *Nineteenth Century Studies.* Cambridge: Cambridge University Press, 1980.

Williams, Raymond. *Culture and Society: 1780–1950.* New York: Columbia University Press, 1983.

———. *Marxism and Literature.* Oxford: Oxford University Press, 1977.

Wisdom, John. *Paradox and Discovery.* Berkeley: University of California Press, 1970.

Wittgenstein, Ludwig. *On Certainty.* Edited by G. E. M. Anscombe and G. H. von Wright. New York: Harper and Row, 1969.

Zyskind, Harold. "The Rhetorical Principles of Theodore Roosevelt." Ph.D. Dissertation, University of Chicago, 1965.

OTHER WORKS: ARTICLES

Abrams, M. H. "How to Do Things with Texts." *Partisan Review,* XLVI (1979), 566–88.

Alston, William P. "Emotion and Feeling" in *The Encyclopedia of Philosophy,* vols. 1–2. (New York: Macmillan and Company, 1967), 479–86.

Berlin, James A. "Matthew Arnold's Rhetoric: The Method of an Elegant Jeremiah." *Rhetoric Society Quarterly,* XLII (Winter 1983), 29–40.

Bitzer, Lloyd. "The Rhetorical Situation." *Philosophy and Rhetoric,* 1 (1968), 1–14.

Brinton, Alan. "William James and the Epistemic View of Rhetoric." *Quarterly Journal of Speech,* 68 (1982), 158–69.

Brockriede, Wayne. "Where is Argument?" *Journal of the American Forensic Association,* IX (Spring 1975), 179–82.

Brown, Frank Burch. "Transfiguration: Poetic Metaphor and Theological Reflection." *The Journal of Religion,* 62 (January 1982), 39–56.

Brummet, Barry. "Some Implications of 'Process' or "Intersubjectivity': Post-Modern Rhetoric." *Philosophy and Rhetoric,* 4 (1972), 21–51.

Clark, Donald Leman. "The Place of Rhetoric in a Liberal Education." *Quarterly Journal of Speech,* XXXVI (October 1950), 291–95.

Conley, Thomas. "The Enthymeme in Perspective." *Quarterly Journal of Speech,* 70 (May 1984), 168–87.

Consigny, Scott. "Rhetoric and Its Situations." *Philosophy and Rhetoric,* 7 (1974), 175–86.

Crable, Richard E. "Knowledge-as-Status: On Argument and Epistemology." *Communication Monographs,* 49 (1982), 240–62.

Demos, Raphael. "On Persuasion." *The Journal of Philosophy,* XXIX (April 1932), 225–32.

Einhorn, Lois. "Richard Whately's Public Persuasion: The Relationship Between His Rhetorical Theory and His Rhetorical Practice." *Rhetorica,* IV (Winter 1986), 47–65.

Fisher, Walter and Wayne Brockreide, "Kenneth Burke's Realism." *Central States Speech Journal,* 35 (Spring 1984), 35–42.

Gabin, Rosalind J. "Aristotle and the New Rhetoric: Grimaldi and Valesio. A Review Essay." *Philosophy and Rhetoric,* 20 (1987), 171–82.

Galati, Michael. "A Rhetoric for the Subjectivist in a World of Untruth: The Tasks and Strategies of Soren Kierkegaard." *Quarterly Journal of Speech,* 55 (1969), 372–80.

Garver, Eugene. "Rhetoric and Essentially Contested Arguments." *Philosophy and Rhetoric,* 11 (Summer 1978), 157–72.

Grimaldi, S. J., W. M. A. "The Aristotelian Topics." *Traditio,* 14 (1958), 1–16.

Grassi, Ernesto. "Critical Philosophy or Topical Philosophy? Meditations on the *De nostri temporis studiorum ratione.*" In *Giambattista Vico: An International Symposium,* ed. by Giorgio Tagliacozzo and Hayden V. White. Baltimore: Johns Hopkins Press, 1969, 39–50.

Gray, Hanna H. "Renaissance Humanism: The Pursuit of Eloquence." *Journal of the History of Ideas,* XXIV (October–December, 1963), 497–514.

Harvey, Van A. "The Ethics of Belief Re-Considered." *The Journal of Religion,* 59 (October 1979), 406–20.

Hauser, Gerard A. and Donald P. Cushman. "McKeon's Philosophy of Communication: The Architectoric and Interdisciplinary Arts." *Philosophy and Rhetoric,* 6 (Fall 1973), 211–34.

Hempel, Carl. "The Function of General Laws in History." *The Journal of Philosophy,* 39 (January 1942), 35–7.

Hipple, Jr., Walter J. "Matthew Arnold, Dialectician." *University of Toronto Quarterly,* XXXII (October 1962), 1–26.

Houghton, Walter E. "The Rhetoric of T. H. Huxley." *University of Toronto Quarterly,* XVIII (1949), 159–75.

Hunt, Everett Lee. "Matthew Arnold, The Critic as Rhetorician." *Quarterly Journal of Speech,* IV (November 1934), 483–507.

———. "General Specialists." *Quarterly Journal of Speech,* II (July 1916), 253–63.

———. "General Specialists: Fifty Years Later." *Rhetoric Society Quarterly,* XVII (Spring 1987), 167–76.

315

Bibliography

Johnstone, Christopher Lyle. "An Aristotelian Trilogy: Ethics, Rhetoric, Politics, and the Search for Moral Truth." *Philosophy and Rhetoric,* 13 (Winter 1980), 1–24.

Lanham, Richard. "The Rhetorical Padeia: The Curriculum as a Work of Art." *College English,* 48 (February 1986), 132–141.

Leff, Michael C. "Modern Sophistic and the Unity of Rhetoric," in John S. Nelson et. al., eds., *The Rhetoric of the Human Sciences.* Madison: University of Wisconsin Press, 1987, pp. 19–37.

———. "The Topics of Argumentative Invention in Latin Rhetorical Theory from Cicero to Boethius," *Rhetorica,* I (Spring 1983), 23–44.

———. "In Search of Ariadne's Thread: A Review of the Recent Literature on Rhetorical Theory." *Central States Speech Journal,* 29 (Summer 1978), 73–91.

———. "Topical Invention and Metaphorical Interaction." *The Southern Speech Communication Journal,* XLVII (Spring 1983), 214–29.

Manicas, Peter T. "On Toulmin's Contribution to Logic and Argumentation." In *Contemporary Theories of Rhetoric: Selected Readings.* Edited by Richard L. Johannesen. New York: Harper and Row, 1971, pp. 256–70.

McCarthy, Patrick J. "Reading Victorian Prose: Arnold's 'Culture and Its Enemies.'" *University of Toronto Quarterly,* XL (Winter 1971), 119–35.

McKeon, Richard. "Arts of Invention and Arts of Memory: Creation and Criticism." *Critical Inquiry,* I (June 1975), 723–39.

———. "Creativity and the Commonplace." *Philosophy and Rhetoric,* 6 (1973), 199–210.

———. "Education and the Disciplines." *International Journal of Ethics,* 47 (1936–37), 370–81.

———. "The Liberating Arts and the Humanizing Arts in Education," in Arthur Cohen, ed., *Humanistic Education and Western Civilization.* New York: Holt, Rinehart and Winston, 1964, pp. 159–81.

———. "Philosophy of Communications and the Arts," in Howard E. Kiefer and Milton K. Munitz, eds., *Perspectives in Education, Religion, and the Arts.* Albany: State University of New York Press, 1970, pp. 329–50.

———. "Philosophy and Action." *Ethics,* 62 (1952), 79–100.

———. "Philosophy and Method." *The Journal of Philosophy,* XLVIII (October 1951), 653–82.

————. "The Uses of Rhetoric in a Technological Age: Architectonic Productive Arts," in Richard McKeon, *Rhetoric: Essays in Invention and Discovery*. Edited with an Introduction by Mark Backman. Woodbridge, Conn.: Ox Bow Press, 1987, pp. 1–24.

McKerrow, Ray E. "Campbell and Whately on the Utility of Syllogistic Logic,' *Western Speech Communication,* 40 (Winter 1976), 3–13.

————. "Richard Whately's Theory of Rhetoric." Ray E. McKerrow, ed., *Explorations in Rhetoric: Studies in Honor of Douglas Ehninger*. Glenview, IL: Scott, Foresman and Co., 1982, pp. 137–56.

————. "Richard Whately on the Nature of Human Knowledge in Relation to Ideas of His Contemporaries." *Journal of the History of Ideas,* XLII (1981), 439–55.

————. "Probable Argument in Whately's Theory of Rhetoric." *Central States Speech Journal,* 26 (Winter 1975), pp. 259–66.

————. "Richard Whately: Religious Controversialist of the Nineteenth Century." *Prose Studies: 1800–1900,* 2 (1979), 160–87.

————. " 'Method of Composition': Whately's Earliest Rhetoric." *Philosophy and Rhetoric,* 11 (Winter 1978), 43–58.

————. "The Ethical Implications of a Whateian Rhetoric." *Rhetoric Society Quarterly,* XVII (Summer 1987), 321–27.

Miller, Perry. "The Rhetoric of Sensation." In Harry T. Levin, ed., *Perspectives in Criticism*. Cambridge: Harvard University Press, 1950, pp. 103–22.

Ochs, Donovan J. "Aristotle's Concept of Formal Topics," *Speech Monographs,* 46 (Winter 1969), 419–25.

O'Keefe, Daniel. "Two Concepts of Argument." *The Journal of the American Forensic Association,* XIII (Winter 1977), 121–28.

Orr, C. Jack. "How Shall We Say: 'Reality Is Socially Constructed through Communication?' " *Central States Speech Journal,* 29 (Winter 1978), 263–74.

Railsback, Celeste Condit. "Beyond Rhetorical Relativism: A Structural-Material Model of Truth and Objective Reality." *Quarterly Journal of Speech,* 69 (November 1983), 152–67.

Rosner, Mary. "Reflections on Cicero in Nineteenth Century England and America." *Rhetorica,* IV (Spring 1986), 153–82.

Schaeffer, John D. "Vico's Rhetorical Model of the Mind: Sensus Communis in the *De Nostri temporis studiorum ratione.*" *Philosophy and Rhetoric,* 14 (Summer 1981), 152–67.

317

Bibliography

Scott, Robert L. "On Viewing Rhetoric as Epistemic." *Central States Speech Journal*, 18 (February 1967), 9–17.

———. "On Viewing Rhetoric as Epistemic: Ten Years Later." *Central States Speech Journal*, 27 (1976), 258–66.

Self, Lois S. "Rhetoric and Phronesis: The Aristotelian Ideal." *Philosophy and Rhetoric*, 12 (Spring 1979), 130–45.

Semmel, Bernard. "T. B. Macaulay: The Active and Contemplative Lives." In Richard A. Levine, ed., *The Victorian Experience: The Prose Writers*. Athens, Ohio: Ohio University Press, 1982, pp. 22–46.

Struever, Nancy S. "Topics in History." *History and Theory*, 19 (1980), 66–79.

———. "The Conversable World: Eighteenth-Century Transformations of the Relation of Rhetoric and Truth." In Nancy S. Struever and Brian Vickers, eds., *Rhetoric and the Pursuit of Truth*. Los Angeles: University of California, 1985, pp. 77–119.

Warnick, Barbara. "A Ricoeurian Approach to Rhetorical Criticism." *The Western Journal of Speech Communication*, 51 (Summer 1987), 227–44.

Wisdom, John. "Gods," in *Philosophy and Psycho-Analysis*. New York: Philosophical Library, 1953, 149–68.

Zyskind, Harold. "Some Philosophic Strands in Popular Rhetoric." In Howard E. Kiefer and Milton R. Munitz, eds., *Perspectives in Education, Religion, and the Arts*. Albany: State University of New York Press, 1970, pp. 373–95.

———. "A Case Study in Philosophic Rhetoric: Theodore Roosevelt." *Philosophy and Rhetoric*, 1 (1968), 228–54.

INDEX

A priori proofs, 4

Action, 3, 54, 225; as a principle of rhetoric, 212–14; 237n.11

Adler, Alfred, 234

Ambiguity: in language, 145–46, 152; in Scripture, 115

Analogy: of development, 161; of growth, 136–37

Analytic paradigm, 88, 230–31

Analyticity, 229–32; and substantial arguments, 261n.71

Anglicans, 113ff.

Antagonism, principle of, 158–61

Antecedent considerations, 37, 40, 41–46, 50, 55, 70, 180, 249n.29, 266n.9

Antecedent probability, 36, 38, 40, 41–46, 50, 55, 59, 64, 81, 100–1, 106, 110, 161, 261n.41

Antiphon, 42

Anti-Romanism, 112, 125; and the *Via Media,* 112

Antiquity, 112ff.

Apologetics, Christian, 3

Apprehension, 63–71, 256–57n.18; as conceptual, 69–70; defined, 65; notional, 65–66, 255n.7; real, 4, 21, 64–71, 89ff., 201, 213–14, 255n.7, 266n.9, 292n.7

Aquinas, St. Thomas, 152

Aristotle, x, 6, 7, 10, 22–24, 79–82, 88, 97, 101, 103, 141, 147, 171, 195, 198, 209–10, 221

Argument, Newman's fascination with, 32

Arnold, Matthew, xi, 6, 30–31, 154, 182–83, 191

Artz, Johannes, 237n.9, 288n.78

"Aspects," 52, 119, 121, 140, 145, 181

Association of ideas, 74–76

"Attitudinizing," Kenneth Burke's concept of, 219, 221

Augustine, St., 10, 126–27, 240n.35

Bacon, Francis, 17, 29, 72, 103, 130, 183

"Backing" for warrants, 228–32

Backman, Mark, 25–26

Beer, John, 14

Belief, 63; in Hume's *Treatise on Human Nature,* 73–76; and vivacity, 74–75

Bentham, Jeremy, 6, 79, 170, 187

Berger, Peter L., 233–34

Bernstein, Richard J., 106–7, 264n.110, 265n.114, 293n.25

Bible, the, 57, 112–13

Blair, Hugh, 11

Blehl, Vincent F., 289n.92

"Blik," 223

Bloom, Allan, 286n.73

Bloughram, Bishop, 149, 150

Boekraad, Adrian J., 250n.40

Booth, Wayne C., 26, 221, 235, 265n.114

"Bracketing," 182

Browning, Don S., 284n.56

Buber, Martin, 235

Buckley, Jerome H., 282n.50

Burke, Edmund, 8, 29, 252n.45

Burke, Kenneth, xi, 24–26, 41, 89, 98, 172, 209, 212–13, 217–24, 234, 265n.111, 274n.43, 283n.51, 293n.27

Butler, Bishop Joseph, 8, 34, 161, 225, 232

Cameron, J. M., 5, 7, 130, 289n.91

Campbell, George, 6, 11, 62, 72, 74–76, 81, 210–11, 213, 235, 272n.3

Carlyle, Thomas, 6, 12, 15, 22, 29, 30, 54, 63, 93, 199

Casey, Gerard, 262n.76

Catholic Church, the, 115, 122, 137–38. *See also* Romanism

Catholic University of Ireland, ix, 227n.12

Certainty, 226–37

Chadwick, Owen, 129, 267n.16

Channing, Edward T., 250n.38

Christian doctrine. *See* Dogma

Church, R. W., 123, 268n.22

Cicero, Marcus Tullius, 6–10, 15–17, 28, 42, 78, 146, 192, 195, 210, 243n.65

Clerisy, the, 177, 200

Clifford, James, 12, 55, 232

Clusters, of terms, 223

Cogito, the, 254n.75

Index

Coleridge, Samuel Taylor, 9, 29, 31, 152, 156, 195

Combination, the principle of. *See* Compromise

Communication, 139ff.

Compromise, the principle of, 180

Comte, Auguste, 12, 55

Concrete, the, 66, 255–56n.10

Conscience, 36ff., 103–4, 234–35

Consigny, Scott, 244n.74

Conspiratio, of hierarchy and laity, 133, 138

Consulting the faithful, 133, 138

Constitution, as representative anecdote for action in Burke, 221–22; British, 19

Controversy, 81–84, 123. *See also* Inquirers and controversialists

Copi, Irving M., 94

Copia, in rhetoric, 266nn. 4, 7

Copleston, Edward, 8, 10, 34, 72

Corbett, E. P. J., 237n.13

Corcoran, S.J., Timothy, 237n.13

Core curriculum, 200–3. *See also* Curriculum

Coulson, John, xiii, 15, 142, 153–55, 158–60, 274–75nn. 44, 45, 285n.66

Crane, R. S., 197, 237n.11, 278n.18

Credences, 51, 184

Crimean War, 19

criteria of adequacy, 58–61, 102–7, 158–62, 238n.16, 264–65nn. 106–8, 110–11, 293n.25

Culler, A. Dwight, ix, 14, 62, 116, 118, 171, 190, 195, 197, 202, 204, 206, 272n.2, 279n.23, 284n.56, 286n.71, 287nn. 77, 79, 289n.87, 290n.97

Curriculum, qualities of a liberal, 199–202

Dale, P. A., 191

Daly, Gabrielle, 250n.40

Darwin, Charles, 6

Davis, Walter, 246n.95

Davison, John, 203

Data, in the *Essay on Development,* 132

DeLaura, David J., 13, 15

Demos, Raphael, 89, 98

De Quincey, Thomas, 10, 11, 251n.44, 252n.58

Descartes, René, 95, 253n.75

Development of Christian doctrine. *See* Dogma

Dewey, John, 18, 95, 255n.5

Dialectic, 2, 15, 19

Dissoi logoi, 44

Doctrine. *See* Dogma

Dogma: principle of, 33, 111, 115ff., 121; development of, 51–52, 67, 125–37, 140; corruption of, 113ff., 125–29

Donatist controversy, 269n.49

Dramatism, 220, 224

Economy, principle of, 9–10, 158, 235

Edinburgh Reviewers, 170ff.

Education, liberal: and Aristotle, 171; and elitism, 177, 189–92, 200; and generalism, 171, 186–92; and rhetoric, 277n.12; and specialism, 187–89; and Vives, 195, 197; interdisciplinary, 286n.73

Eikos, 41–42, 44

Emerson, Ralph Waldo, 199

Epistemic rhetoric. *See* Rhetoric

"Energy": in Whately, 73; in Campbell, 74–75

Entelechy, principle of, 220–21

Erikson, Erik, 234, 284n.56

Ethics of Aristotle [*Nichomachean Ethics*], 78–80

Ethics of belief, 63, 226, 235; and rhetoric, 234–35

Ethos, 78, 83

Eutychians. *See* Monophysites.

Evangelicals, 33, 61, 123

Evidentialists, the, 33, 39, 55–56

"Factory-girl argument," 99–102

Faith, religious, 34–39, 57, 114, 149, 248n.19, 249n.33, 250n.37; deposit of, 52

Fathers of the Church, 9–10, 112–14, 135

Ferreira, M. Jamie, 48–49, 68, 96

Fey, William R., 5

Field-dependency, of arguments, 89

First principles, 22, 34, 46–54, 70, 195, 225; determinate and indeterminate, 50–51; grounded and ungrounded, 49; in *The Idea of a University,* 179; particular, 51–

Index

53; true and false, 53–54; universal, 51–53

Fisher, Walter, 98, 221, 237n.13

Fortenbaugh, William W., 258nn. 50, 53

Froude, William, 63, 130, 225–26

Gadamer, Hans-Georg, 88, 106, 234–35, 264n.106, 278n.19

Garver, Eugene, 290n.101

Gaskell, Mrs., 99

Gates, Lewis E., xi, 13

Generalist, the, 172, 177, 186. *See also* Education, liberal

Gentleman, the, 176–77, 189–92, 285nn. 58, 59

Gibbon, Edward, 8, 195

Gorgias, Plato's, 9

Graff, Gerald, 105, 265n.111, 280n.40

Grassi, Ernesto, 150, 274nn. 40, 41

Gray, Hanna H., 288n.78, 289n.89

Habermas, Jurgen, 106

Happel, Stephen, 273n.27

Hare, R. M., 223

Harrold, Charles Frederick, 14–15, 108–9, 141, 242n.54, 272n.1, 279n.25

Harvey, Van A., 104–5

Heath, Dwight B., 191

Hegel, G. H. F., 129

Hermeneutics, 1

History, as a discipline, 108–9, 266nn. 2–3

Hobbes, Thomas, 183

Holloway, John, xi–xii, 13, 14, 47, 102, 120, 161–62, 179, 181

Horney, Karen, 234

Houghton, Walter E., xi, 14, 31, 248n.13

Hume, David, 5, 6, 45, 62, 67, 71–76, 130, 155, 211, 213, 230, 232

Hunt, Everett Lee, 283n.53

Huxley, T. H., 6, 12, 31, 182

Ideas, 72–76; as developing, 201; as living, 67, 133, 154

Illative sense, 102, 198, 228

Images, 67, 73–76, 98–99, 151–54

Imagination, and literature, 150–58

"Imaginative reason," 182

Impressions, in literature, 150–51

Induction, 96, 99–100, 130

Infallibility, 159–60

Inference: and syllogism, 85ff.; and logic, 84–89, 92–102; formal, 84–89, 91; informal, 21–23, 26, 89–99, 127, 184, 201, 213–17; natural, 84–85, 91

Inquirers and controversialists, 83–84

Invention, 16–20, 157

Isocrates, 16, 143

Jack-of-all-trades, 177, 190

Jaeger, Werner, 285n.67

James, William, 104, 259n.53

Jerusalem bishopric, 127

Judgment, xii, 33, 37, 39, 78, 103, 122, 134, 172–74, 195, 197–208, 225; private, 4, 33, 267n.13

Jung, C. G., 234

Justice, Divine, 55, 58–60

Kahn, Victoria, 290n.101

Keble, John, 12, 236n.4

Ker, I. T., 202

Kerr, Clark, 191

Kimball, Bruce A., 277n.12

Kneupper, Charles W., 283n.53

Knights, Ben, 191, 195, 282n.51

Knowledge, 149–50, 180; secular and sacred, 179

Kuhn, Thomas, 41

Kung, Hans, 137, 234, 294–95n.44

Language, 261n.75; and attitudinizing, 219; and informal inference, 90–92; and literature, 139–50; and logic, 92–94; and real apprehension, 96ff., 151; and symbolic action, 217–24; and things, 142–43; and thought, 86–87; rational, 151; Scriptural, 158–59; Vico's conception of, 150–51

Lash, Nicholas, ix, xiii, 5, 68, 69, 109–10, 119, 136, 141, 166, 237n.12, 275n.60

Legal reasoning. *See* Reason

Leff, Michael C., 26

Lentricchia, Frank, xi. 293n.23

Levine, George, x, 14, 202

Liberal education. *See* Education, liberal

Liberalism, religious, 4, 33–34, 72, 211

Index

Literature, 139–50; and imagination, 150–58; and society, 146–47; defined, 139–40
"Living," ideas as. *See* Ideas
Locke, John, 5, 45, 72, 170, 225–27, 232
Logic, 127, 147, 157; and formal inference, 84–89; and informal reference, 88–89; and psychology, 72–76
Logos, two-fold, 139–40
Logology, xi, 220, 224

Macaulay, Thomas Babington, 6, 29–30
Machiavelli, Niccolo, 29
Marmion, Rev. J. P., 280n.38
Marx, Karl, 67
Marx, Leo, 283n.51
Marrou, H. I., 289n.83
Maurice, F. D., 6
McGrath, S.J., Fergal, 284n.57
McKeon, Richard, 23–26, 282n.49
McKerrow, Ray E., 44
Metaphor, 155–58
Metaphysics, 49, 195, 201
Mill, John Stuart, x, 6, 28, 31, 55
Mitchell, Basil, 223
Mixed Education, 200, 277n.13
Monophysites, 125, 269n.48

Newman, Jay, xi, 7, 14, 68, 99, 102
Newman, John Henry
  Apologia Pro Vita Sua, 125–29, 270n.56
  Arians of the Fourth Century, 9
  and Aristotle, 23, 44–45, 78–81, 97, 195, 209–10, 259n.55
  and antecedent probabilities/considerations, 35–38, 41–46
  art of discrimination, 204
  and Burke, Kenneth, 212–24, 292n.16. *See also* Burke, Kenneth
  and Campbell, George, 74–76, 210–11
  and conscience, 36, 157–58, 264n.105. *See also* Conscience
  and criteria of truth, 58–61, 102–7, 158–62, 264–65nn. 106–8, 110–11, 293n.25
  critics of, 1, 4–5, 6–7, 12–15, 171–72, 191, 202
  Development of Christian Doctrine, Essay on the, 51–52, 125–37
  Discourses on the Scope and Nature of University Education, 170
  and division of labor. *See* Education, and specialism
  and *Edinburgh Reviewers,* 170–72
  and faith. *See* Religion
  and fellow Victorians, 29–31, 180
  and first principles, 46–54. *See also* First principles
  and generalism, 186–92, 281n.44, 282nn. 46, 49, 283n.56, 286n.73. *See also* Education, and generalism
  and the gentleman, 189–92. *See also* Education, and the gentleman
  Grammar of Assent, An Essay in Aid of, 48–53, 63–107
  and hermeneutics, 1, 279n.29
  and history, 108–11, 131–32, 266nn. 2–3
  and Hume, David, 73–76, 130, 210
  Idea of a University, The, 142–49, 170–207
  and imagination, 150–58
  and implicit/explicit reasoning, 37, 39–40, 55–57
  and informal inference, 21–23, 84–102, 134. *See also* Inference, informal
  and judgment, 202–8. *See also* Education; Judgment
  and language, 7, 34, 90–92, 100–2, 139–58, 261n.75, 273n.27
  and legal reasoning, 94–96, 262n.83
  and liberal education. *See* Education
  and literature, 139–58, 272nn. 1–2, 7, 273n.10, 274n.41
  and Locke, John, 226–27
  and logic, 85–89, 92–98, 100–2, 127, 260n.68, 262n.80
  and method, 4, 5–7, 19–20, 21–23, 28–33, 54–62, 99–107, 108–37, 179–83, 194–207, 239n.19, 275n.45, 290n.101. *See also* "Views"; Rhetoric; Inference, informal
  On Consulting the Faithful in Matters of Doctrine, 103
  as opportunist, 28–29
  Oxford Movement, 123, 268nn. 22, 23
  Oxford University Sermons, 32–47, 54–62, 82
  Parochial and Plain Sermons, 147–48

"practice" and the concrete, attitudes towards, 2ff., 21–24, 29–33, 54–62, 65–69, 114–16, 134, 277n.12

Present Position of Catholics in England, 47–49

principle of antagonism, 158–61

qualities of the curriculum, 199–203, 205. *See also* Education

and religion, 32–40, 108–39, 165–66

and rhetoric, x–xv, 6, 7–12, 14, 15–27, 28, 39, 41–45, 54–62, 63–107, 140ff., 161–69, 170–208, 209–35, 237n.13, 241n.42, 243n.64, 246n.97, 277n.15, 283n.53, 289n.87, 290n.1. *See also* Rhetoric

and science, 142–43, 162–69, 275n.58, 276n.63, 279nn. 27–28

and specialism. *See* Education, and specialism; Newman, John Henry, and division of labor

"Tamworth Reading Room, The," 148–50

and theology. *See* Theology

theory, attitudes towards, 2–4, 7, 29, 54–55, 69–71, 84ff., 180–83, 267n.16, 284n. 56

and topics. *See* Topics

and Toulmin, Stephen, 225–32, 261n.71

and transcendence, 233–34

and utility, principle of, 170ff.

Via Media, The, 111–25

and "views," "viewing," ix–x, xiv, 19, 44, 110–11, 116–21, 173, 183, 193, 267n.21, 282n.46, 286–87n.73. *See also* "Views"

and Whately, Richard, 72–73, 75–76, 190, 210–11. *See also* Whately, Richard

Nichomachean Ethics. *See* Ethics of Aristotle

Nicolina, F., 256n.15

Norris, Thomas J., 23, 109–10

Novak, Michael, 233–34, 288n.78

Notions, 65–66, 70, 201

Notional apprehension. *See* Apprehension

O'Donoghue, N. D., xi, 102

"Offices": of the Church, 160; of rhetoric. *See* Rhetoric

Ong, S.J., Walter J., 130, 145, 263n.92, 268–69n.36, 291n.6

Opportunistic thinking, Newman's, 28–29

"Orientation," Burke's concept of, 41

Orator, the ideal, 16, 78, 176, 192, 279n.22, 283n.53, 289n.89

Oxford, University of, 8–10, 84

Oxford Movement, the, 122–23, 268n.22

Paley, William, 33–34, 55

Paradigm, Kuhn's concept of, 41, 102–5

Paradox of substance, Kenneth Burke's concept of, 218–19

Pater, Walter, 6, 172

Peel, Robert, 148, 150

Pentad, the, Kenneth Burke's concept of, 219

Perelman, Chaim, 26, 89, 98, 221, 251n.44, 257n.23

Perspectivism, 52, 62, 66, 104–5, 111, 116, 184–85. *See also* Views

Persuasion, 80, 98; "all available means of," 38, 101, 120, 216, 228

Philosophia prima, 173

Philosophy, 109, 237n.9; in education, 172–208

Phronesis, 46, 79–80, 103, 106, 124, 198

Plato, 10, 18, 178, 195

Pluralism, 216

Poetry, 141, 145

Polanyi, Michael, 89, 233–34, 294n.40

Popper, Karl, 155

Powell, Jouett Lynn, 3, 153, 210

Practical, the. *See* Newman, John Henry, "practice"; theory

Presumption, 47–48, 60, 110

Prejudice, 47ff., 251n.45

Price, H. H., 68–71, 225

Prickett, Stephen, 15

Principles, first. *See* First principles

Probability, 8, 21, 88–99, 231–32, 251n.44, 252n.51; converging or cumulative, 21, 89, 96, 227

Protagoras, 44

Protestantism, in the *Via Media,* 112ff.

Quintilian, 16, 17, 78, 176, 195, 273n.10

Real apprehension. *See* Apprehension

"Realization," 98, 157–58

Index

Reason (*see also* Inference): and the jurisprudential analogy, 94; as mystical, 54,
61, 68, 70; as secular, 33; explicit and
implicit, 39ff., 250n.39; informal (*see* Inference, informal); legal, 94–95, 262–
63nn. 83, 85
Reid, Thomas, 72, 74, 96
Religion: Newman's sense of, 32–40; and
action, 33; and faith, 33ff.; as a form of
knowledge, 32–33; natural and revealed,
36; in education, 172; proofs of, 35
Rhetoric (*see also* Topics): and topics, 17–
20; as architectonic, 21–24, 210ff.; as
epistemic, xii, 45, 209–35, 245n.81; as
philosophic, 24–26, 197; as style, 9–10;
classical, 8, 10, 15–16, 78–80, 82; defined, 241n.42, 246n.97; ends of, 161–
62; in Aristotle, 8, 15ff., 79–81; in Burke,
Kenneth, 24–26; in Cicero and Quintilian, 8, 16–17, 78; in Hume, Campbell
and Whately, 72–76, 211–12; in
McKeon, Richard, 25–26; offices of, 16–
17; ontological basis and scope of, 212–
24; range of, 7–12; "resolutive," 123,
128, 209; "transformative," 123, 128,
209
Republic, of Plato, 18
Richards, I. A., 45
Ricoeur, Paul, 273n.30
Rogers, Carl, 234
Rorty, Richard, 26, 235
Rueckert, William, 293n.21
Romanists, the, 113ff.
Rome. *See* Romanists

Sacramental Principle, the, 9–10, 111
Schaeffer, John D., 266n.7
Schleiermacher, Frederick, 128
Scholae, of the Church, 137, 159
Schoof, T. M., 250n.40
Science, 162–69; and language, 142–43;
and rhetoric, 141ff., 162–69; and the-
ology, 163–66; experimental, 168
Sciences, the science of, 194, 202
Semeia, 41
Sensus communis, 264n.106
Shelley, Percy Bysshe, 141
Sillem, Edward, 252n.41, 288n.78

Smigelskis, David, 292n.13
Sola scriptura, principle of, 115
Sophists, the, 143
Soundness, in arguments, 230–31
Spencer, Herbert, 6, 12, 55
Stewart, Dugald, 187
Stone, Julius, 94
Substance, Kenneth Burke's concept of,
217–24; paradox of. *See* Paradox of sub-
stance
Svaglic, Martin, 6, 15, 195, 252n.52
Syllogism, 72, 78, 87, 90–102, 140, 206,
211, 228, 262n.78
Symbolic action, Kenneth Burke's concept
of, 217–24

Teleology, 234
Theory, 58–59, 70, 195. *See also* Newman,
John Henry, "practice"; theory
tive science, 39; as rhetorical, 39–40, 123;
in education, 173–77
Thucydides, 209
Toland, John, 45
Topics, 17–20, 22, 43, 45, 69–70, 96,
109–10, 117ff., 156–59, 180, 184–85,
202ff., 234, 244nn. 70, 74; common, 17,
43; "root-topics," in *The Idea of a Univer-
sity*, 174, 206; special, 17, 19, 42, 117,
179
Toulmin, Stephen, 26, 98, 209, 221, 225–
37
Type-jump, Toulmin's concept of, 229
Theory, 58–9, 70, 195. *See also* Newman,
John Henry, "practice"; theory
Tracy, David, 26, 237n.13
Tristram, Henry, 3

Unity, Newman's principle of: of knower
and known, 180–81; of knowing, 179–
80; of reality, 179
Universality in philosophy, 194–97, 288n.79
Universals, in education, 191–92
University: and liberal education, 170–208;
and research, 188–89; for all classes of
society, 191; in essence and integrity, 176
Utility, principle of, in education, 170ff.

Valesio, Paolo, 15, 20

Validity, 84–102, 229–31
Vargish, Thomas, 152–53, 242n.55
Verdeke, Gerard, 259n.54
Vico, Giambattista, 52, 150, 157, 195, 282n.46
Victorian Age, 58
"Views," ix, 2, 105, 109–10, 116ff., 173, 177ff., 185, 267n.21, 286–87n.73
"Viewiness," 117, 136, 190, 285n.61
Vincentian canon, 122, 124–25, 132
"Vivacity," 73–76, 98
Vives, Juan Luis, 80, 195, 197

Walgrave, J. H., 13, 216, 272n.79
Ward, W. G., 6, 227
Ward, W. R., 239n.23
Ward, Wilfrid, 14, 236n.6, 242n.49, 259n.57, 261n.70
Warrants, 228–32
Weatherby, Harold, xi, 14, 102, 195, 242n.53
Wegener, Charles, 204
Whately, Richard, 3, 6, 8, 9, 10, 11, 28, 34–35, 44–45, 62, 71–73, 75, 81, 84, 190, 210–11, 213, 232, 235, 253n.70, 272n.4
Wheelwright, Philip, 52, 66
Whewell, William, 31
White, Blanco, 78
Whitehead, Alfred North, 170, 277n.12, 284n.56
Wicker, Brian, 87, 260nn. 63, 68
Wilberforce, Henry, 29
Wilberforce, Samuel, 28
William, Franz, 240n.32
Willey, Basil, 31
Williams, Isaac, 28
Wilson, J. Dover, 278n.17
Wisdom, John, 96
Wise, John E., 281n.44
"Whole Man," the, 64, 76–84, 119–20, 161, 182, 192–94, 207–8, 215, 255–56n.10, 281n.44
Woodfield, Malcolm, 236n.8
Wordsworth, William, 184

Zyskind, Harold, 204